Entrepreneurship, Technological Innovation,
and Economic Growth

Entrepreneurship, Technological Innovation, and Economic Growth

Studies in the Schumpeterian Tradition

Edited by
Frederic M. Scherer and Mark Perlman

Ann Arbor
THE UNIVERSITY OF MICHIGAN PRESS

Library of Congress Cataloging-in-Publication Data

Entrepreneurship, technological innovation, and economic growth :
  studies in the Schumpeterian tradition / edited by Frederic M.
  Scherer and Mark Perlman.
      p.   cm.
    Includes bibliographical references and index.
    ISBN 0-472-10336-9 (alk. paper)
    1. Entrepreneurship.   2. Technological innovations—Economic
aspects.   3. Economic development.   4. Schumpeter, Joseph Alois,
1883–1950.   I. Scherer, F. M. (Frederic M.)   II. Perlman, Mark.
HB615.E6347   1992
338′.064—dc20   92-7679
                                                   CIP

Contents

Introduction

Frederic M. Scherer and Mark Perlman

This volume brings together papers presented at the third biennial meeting of the International J. A. Schumpeter Society, held at Airlie House, Virginia, in June, 1990. The society was founded in 1986 at a meeting in Augsburg, Germany. The second biennial meeting was held in Siena, Italy, during 1988. The fourth meeting is scheduled for Kyoto, Japan, in 1992.

The Schumpeter Society is decidedly international, with 515 members in 1991 representing thirty-one of the world's nations. Airlie House was chosen as a conference site because it combines the scenic beauty of rural Virginia with proximity to Washington, D.C., which is a place of special interest to the many Schumpeter Society members attending the meeting from overseas. The meeting was supplemented by a trip to Charlottesville, Virginia, and to Monticello, the home of Thomas Jefferson, author of, among other things, the U.S. Declaration of Independence. Visiting Jefferson's home and holding the biennial Schumpeter Prize award dinner at the University of Virginia in Charlottesville seemed particularly appropriate at a time when individuals throughout the world are striving to achieve more democratic institutions.

The International Schumpeter Society's members are mainly economists, but there are also representatives of numerous other disciplines. People join the society for a variety of reasons. Some members were former colleagues or students of Joseph Schumpeter during his period at Harvard University in the 1930s and 1940s. What brings most members of the society together, however, is interest in what might be broadly characterized as the Schumpeterian tradition of economic analysis. This tradition embodies several themes. For one, Schumpeter emphasized the crucial role that technological innovation and technological change play in generating economic growth. Second, for Schumpeter, entrepreneurship was a fundamental driving force in the achievement of technological innovation. Third, Schumpeter triggered a lively debate over the type of economic structure that most fruitfully fosters technological innovation. Finally, many scholars are fascinated with what Schumpeter called "the process of creative destruction"—that is, a process through which innovation constantly reshapes the very market structures out of which it arises in an evolutionary way.

This set of scholarly interests seemed ideally suited to exploring the conference's main theme, stated formally as "Entrepreneurship, Technological Innovation, and Economic Growth: International Perspectives." Since the early 1970s, most of the world's major industrial economies have experienced a significant decline in average rates of productivity growth—that is, in the growth of output per unit of labor input. Thus, for a cross-section of twelve representative OECD nations, the annual rate of growth of output per person employed fell from an average of 4.16 percent in the 1961–68 period to an average of 1.45 percent in 1979–85. In the early stages of this productivity growth slump, it was widely believed that the principal stimulating event might have been the crude oil shocks that occurred in 1973–74 and 1979–80. However, the productivity growth shortfall has persisted in times of low oil prices as well as with high prices. Something more fundamental, possibly in the linkages between economic growth, innovation, and entrepreneurship, may well underlie at least a part of the observed productivity growth slowdown. Since the slump has been worldwide, the society's international membership seemed a particularly well-suited cast of characters to address the question of what has been happening and why. This volume offers a selection of the conference essays addressing various facets of that critical issue.

A formal dinner in the Rotunda of the University of Virginia provided an important side benefit of the conference—the award of the biennial Schumpeter Prize for the best work in a prespecified field of endeavor. The 1990 Schumpeter Prize was shared by three individuals: W. Brian Arthur for his work on path-dependent economic systems; Joel Mokyr for his book, *The Lever of Riches;* and Manuel Trajtenberg, for his book on product innovation in the CT scanner field.

Much credit for the conference's success must go to the members of its scientific committee, who participated actively in the choice of papers. The scientific committee members consisted of Gunnar Eliasson, Chris Freeman, Henry Grabowski, Arnold Heertje, Ken-ichi Imai, and Erhard Kantzenbach, with F. M. Scherer serving as chairperson. Financial support for the conference was provided by the Toni Stolper Estate, the Earhart Foundation, the Public Policy Research Center of the Graduate School of Business Administration of the University of Florida, Merck and Company, Archer Daniels Midland Company, Eli Lilly and Company, Thermo Electron Corporation, Exxon Corporation, and *Forbes* Magazine. The Schumpeter Prize was donated by the German economic weekly magazine *Wirtschaftswoche*. To these and many others who contributed organizational talent to the Airlie House conference, a great debt is owed.

As already noted, the meetings were held in Virginia, and the society's Schumpeter Award dinner was held in the Rotunda of the University of

Virginia. That university itself, as well as its Rotunda, were projects explicitly designed by Thomas Jefferson (1743–1826), known to most people as the third President of the United States (1801–9). However, in the United States generally and in Charlottesville (site of the University of Virginia), specifically, there has long been a "Jefferson cult," as well there should be. Professor Kenneth G. Elzinga of the Department of Economics, accordingly, was asked to give an address about Mr. Jefferson and the dynamics of change. He made many interesting and even startling comparisons between Jefferson's and Joseph A. Schumpeter's lives and frustrations. Both were interested in economics and politics, both enjoyed and exploited their university connections, and both had their libraries burned by the British (or their allies). While both were men of considerable achievement, Jefferson's in the political sphere was clearly far greater. Indeed, by comparison with almost anyone else in modern Western history, Jefferson's record is of the first magnitude. On his tombstone Jefferson chose to have engraved only the following deeds—author of the Declaration of Independence, author of the Virginia Statute offering Religious Freedom, and father of the University of Virginia. Yet in truth, these were only *some* of his major deeds; there were many others—political, technological (he was a significant inventor), philosophical, and even economic (Jefferson explicitly favored Jean Baptiste Say over Schumpeter's "wooden Scottish philosopher," and Jefferson authorized the first national program for internal infrastructure improvements and unilaterally authorized the purchase of the Louisiana territory, extending U.S. territory from the Atlantic to the Pacific Oceans). When John F. Kennedy invited the then living American Nobel Laureates to dinner at the White House, he was only half-joking when he said to them that he had intentionally collected at his table the most distinguished minds that the White House had ever hosted since the time of Thomas Jefferson—and when he was there, Jefferson often had eaten alone. We include Elzinga's essay because it places the 1990 conference in a historic place (Virginia) and at a time when the political principles of Thomas Jefferson were approaching worldwide (particularly Central European) acceptance.

Richard R. Nelson's essay, "U.S. Technological Leadership: Where Did It Come From and Where Did It Go?" focuses on two things in particular—leadership in mass production industries and leadership in high-technology innovation. The former was historic; the latter mostly apparent in the decades during and immediately after World War II. Why each occurred was largely institutional, and Nelson lists what he considers to have been the human capital and other resource input factors. During the last two decades, U.S. predominance in these two areas has clearly diminished, Nelson argues, for four reasons: (1) the free flow of world trade eroded the market size advantages U.S. firms previously held; (2) the flow of technological knowledge became more universal, and those with requisite skills and capital anywhere in the world could easily pick up whatever became available; (3) other nations accelerated the development of their scientifically and technically skilled labor forces; and (4) a sharp decline in the spillover from U.S. R&D projects into the civilian economy. Bo Carlsson's commentary serves more to clarify than to challenge some of Nelson's points.

In his essay, "*Capitalism, Socialism, and Democracy* and Large-Scale Firms," Paolo Sylos-Labini undertakes a review and assessment of the arguments and conclusions of Schumpeter's 1942 classic. Overall, he is struck by the inadequacy of many of Schumpeter's judgments in that work. Schumpeter clearly misjudged the ability of centrally planned economies to innovate. And when arguing that small firms enjoyed innovative flexibility, Schumpeter did not perceive how large firms' institutionalized R&D operations could keep them on the innovation frontier. But most of all, he did not appreciate the synergistic influence of small, research-based firms on large corporations. In short, part of Schumpeter's error of judgment was to underplay the role of small firms in capitalist economies, and it is the absence of their performance of this function ("the competition which counts") that helps explain why centrally planned economies are so ossified.

In their essay, "Specialization and Size of Technological Activities in Industrial Countries," Daniele Archibugi and Mario Pianta document a strong tendency for national technological advancement efforts to be more narrowly specialized if a nation's over-all effort is small. They also show a weaker tendency over time toward increased specialization of activity by all nations. This analysis was accomplished using both patent and citation data from the U.S. and European patent offices. Alfred Kleinknecht, while praising the paper for the huge amount of data processed and the results found by the two authors, wonders whether part of the recent changes, particularly in the case of the Europe Patent Office output, is a time-threshold effect—the Europe Patent Office being relatively new. He also identifies the assumptions that the authors must make about the relevance of patent data to questions relating to innovation.

No small part of the Schumpeterian legacy has been the emphasis on innovation, but just what induces innovation is the topic fascinating Rudi Kurz. His focus is on recent West German experiences, where he discovers that, in its earlier years, the Federal German Republic offered open individual economic opportunity including "extraordinary profits based on a temporary monopoly" as well as "high levels of education and widespread R&D activity of firms . . . to enable them to perceive and to react to fundamental changes." In the early 1980s, the governmental role became more conservative fiscally, and in embracing deregulation, the government may have encouraged "encrusted institutions that hamper dynamic forces." Much of the remainder of the essay is a careful survey of more recent developments (of course, all prior to the reunification), but they have not served to recapture the advantages of the earliest years. "In sum, a large gap still exists between rhetoric and reality, and there is urgent need for 'modernization.'"

While Richard Nelson argued that part of the historic economic advantage the United States once had, and is now losing, was the size of its internal market, what has interested Cornelis W. A. M. van Paridon has been the success of Dutch firms in what has been quite a small domestic market. His essay, "Technology in a Small and Open Economy: The Case of the Netherlands," begins by noting that it is the interplay of technological progress and increasing economies of production scale, as well as market scale, that contain the basic answers to his question. Of course, he acknowledges from the beginning that, if the Dutch economy's unusual openness is properly seen, it is hardly as small as the country might seem to "deserve"; over 50 percent of the Dutch GNP was in the value of its exports. And many Dutch firms (e.g., Phillips, Shell, Unilever, and AKZO) are anything but small. Yet, when it comes to technological progress (R&D), the Dutch firms have been laggard, and part of his concern is whether the Dutch government can intervene and successfully stimulate desirable growth—growth that would help domestic employment and similar needs even more than international trade. Another part of his concern is whether the Dutch government itself can give private industrial firms lessons in efficiency. On the whole doubtful, he nevertheless concludes, "I struggle and emerge victorious (the motto of the province of Zeeland) remains hopefully an appropriate motto for the Netherlands."

In his "Privatization, M&As, and Interfirm Cooperation in the EC: Improved Prospects for Innovation?" Paul J. J. Welfens asks whether the current trend toward privatization and scheduled 1992 factor and product market changes will serve to encourage European total factor productivity growth. The growth of Japanese competition, often relying on cooperation with its U.S. affiliates, only serves to heighten the tensions. Part of Welfens's analysis involves a discussion of the role of telecommunications, including fax and electronic data transmission, in the internationalization of competition and the integration of markets. Another part touches on the interactive roles of the EC civil bureaucracy and the traditional individual national interests as they relate to innovation policies. Much of the answer to his question also emphasizes the tie between the EC and the former CMEA countries.

The history of the international marketing of one major innovation, or the "Systematic Innovation and Cross-Border Networks: The Case of the Evolution of the VCR Systems," by Yasunori Baba and Ken-ichi Imai, offers the authors a fine opportunity to dispel some myths about Japanese entrepreneurial and innovative resourcefulness and the reasons for their success. They show how Japanese interfirm cooperation serves as a heuristic rather than simply as a basis for stagnant conspiracy. Discussion of how that heuristic operates and integration of that point into the Schumpeterian intellectual legacy is one of their major contributions, particularly since it is tied to a concrete example. The authors are well aware that if the Japanese have all but cornered the hardware aspect of this industry, U.S. firms retain an advantage in the lucrative software aspects (i.e., the video films).

No recent U.S. problem has created a more stirring literature than the question of "for whom does the U.S. corporation operate," a topic raised to the dominant consciousness of many of us half a century ago by Adolph A. Berle and Gardner Means in their *The Modern Corporation and Private Property,* and even longer ago by Louis D. Brandeis in his *Other People's Money.* William Lazonick's "Controlling the Market for Corporate Control: The Historical Significance of Managerial Capitalism," is a rigorous discussion of why he has concluded that the recent U.S. movement toward mergers and acquisitions, financed by leveraged buyouts, is counterproductive from the standpoint of the national welfare, as well as from that of productive efficiency. He focuses on "'financial commitment' as distinct from financial mobility, in the rise of U.S. managerial capitalism and on how, in recent decades, the weakening of financial commitment has contributed to U.S. industrial decline." His analysis, although largely confined to the U.S. scene, tries to put the recent shifts in U.S. managerial purpose into a broader international framework. No small part of his thinking involves the peculiar institutionalism of the U.S. scene, specifically (pointing to) the alternative uses of corporate profits. Quite apart from his normative assessments of what has happened to the U.S. economy, Lazonick's principal conclusion is that U.S. professional economists have failed in their work as analysts because they seem to have forgotten (or never learned) the significance of the Berle and Means or the Brandeis legacies. He provides considerable documentation for this view.

Anne P. Carter's essay, "Appropriation and Profit Incentives in a Leaky System," adds a significant contribution to the Schumpeterian literature about innovation. Her point is that there are obvious externalities to most innovation processes, and it becomes interesting to see whether these externalities can be captured as rents by enterprising individuals or whether they remain in true "Pigovian" form. Her essay, presented in a formal mode, also offers some simulation testing results.

Experimentally examining the structural dynamics of the Federal German economy by analyzing "frontier-production functions," Horst Hanusch and Markus Hierl also offer some estimates of R&D expenditures by individual German firms and compare them with some estimates of optimal technical efficiency (somewhat comparable to a measure of profitability). Presumably, the "frontier-production function" optimizes in some critical senses that optimum. Their observational period of about a quarter of a century is handled from a static standpoint. They promise future reports on the material handled from a dynamic standpoint.

In his essay, "Business Competence, Organizational Learning, and Economic Growth: Establishing the Smith-Schumpeter-Wicksell (SSW) Connection," Gunnar Eliasson has sought to make dynamic learning as distinct an objective for the management of any firm as is its profitability (Eliasson's phrase is: "top level organizational competence, *the main agent behind economic growth*"). In short, unlike such predecessors as J. S. Mill and J. Westerman (a Swedish writer of the eighteenth century), many recent economists have come to think that it is only profits, not knowledge, that really matter in the life of a firm. Eliasson's aim is to fit experimental organizational learning into the dynamic economics tradition associated with the three giants mentioned in his subtitle. In contrast to that SSW tradition, there now stands the mighty Walras-Arrow-Debreu (WAD) tradition. After a lengthy but necessary introduction, Eliasson offers a historical and then partially formal comparison and evaluation of the two contending schools. William S. Comanor's commentary on the Eliasson essay serves initially to highlight the differences between the two traditions. His criticism is that Eliasson's work, adjudged by him as imaginative and excellent, is only just begun. Much remains to be answered.

Improved quality and lower prices are identified by Burton H. Klein as the usual measurements of economic growth. The price element relates in good part to wage rates and productivity increases. As he finds that the wage rates among the leading industrial countries are within a range of 5 percent, the big factor is the rate of productivity increase. Klein examines the dynamic economic performance of nine major industrialized economies and notes that, among the leaders, the wage-cost component has been falling not only relatively but absolutely. As the road to economic success for all nations and any firm is to seek product improvement and cost-cutting production process measures, Klein proposes a system (really a tax system) that, in effect, encourages such success. Turning to Schumpeter's *Theory of Economic Development,* Klein attempts to use his set of observations to round out the definition of Schumpeter's "dynamic equilibrium." Semantically, we know the process as "positive-sum games." Klein notes that progress is achieved when new products appear as a result of interfirm competition, when production processes are made economically more efficient (usually through capital substitution induced by competition), and through increased worker productivity (by which he seems to mean the application of greater worker intelligence and adaptability). In brief, the first two elements are induced by competition. The third element Klein sees as neglected by most economic analysts, who, because they cannot find a name for the author (or source) of the increased output, tend to ignore it. Klein draws examples from various modern firms, many of them Japanese. His fascination with the "imposition" of a negative tax (really a reward to the winner and penalties to the losers) on the most competitive firms reemerges at the end of his essay. His view is that governmental policy can thus "lead the horse to water, and that the horse, thus led, will drink of his own will."

Joseph A. Weissmahr, commenting on Klein's essay, stresses that Klein's model system is one that is feasible "only in an economy operating far from equilibrium." Schumpeter's contributions were ignored because he wanted them to be grafted onto the equilibrium tree, where such a graft would not take. Weissmahr's differences with Klein relate to the latter's assumption that human decision is the source of competitive victory. Weissmahr draws attention to von Neumann and Morgenstern's fictitious $(n + 1)^{th}$ player, necessary to explain why, in certain situations, the end product of a game could only sum to zero. In Weissmahr's thinking, something like the sun is, in effect, the $(n + 1)^{th}$ player; it contributes its energy to production and asks (and gets) nothing in return. Others might prefer "serendipitous human ingenuity" or the physiocratic "gift of nature" as the $(n + 1)^{th}$ factor. But whatever it is called, its existence is historically evident, and economists must reincorporate it into their theory if they wish to move from statics to dynamics. Klein, he concludes, puts too much faith in the competitive process. He thinks that competition may be an important direct part of the story, but it operates best indirectly when it stimulates "the selection mechanism of evolution in nature and in the economy."

Could it be that Veblen was wrong when he urged the effective social superiority, measured by survivability, of the engineer's mentality over the businessman's mendacity? David B. Audretsch and Zoltan J. Acs seem to suggest that often it is the salesman, not the designer, who holds the key to economic success. They discuss what is involved in firm entry and firm survival in their essay, "Technological Regimes, Learning, and Industry Turbulence." Using U.S. data, they begin by observing that while the net number of firms does not seem to vary much year by year, figures involving gross entries and departures yield a very different picture. Their reasoning leads to the question of whether industrial success is the result of brilliant newcomers' entries or whether it is a matter of "easy-in, quickly-out." They offer a general model into which they fit three others', namely Gort and Klepper, Winter, and Helmstädter. Their data come from the U.S. Small Business Data Base, and their measurement techniques closely resemble measures used by Beesley and Hamilton. One of their startling empirically derived conclusions is that it is not capital shortage, but marketing inadequacy (poor advertising), that seems to emerge as the greatest source of firm turbulence.

Written seemingly in the Mengerian Austrian tradition, Paul L.

Robertson's and Richard N. Langlois's "Modularity, Innovations, and the Firm: The Case of Audio Components," sees innovative success stemming from the consumers' as much as, or more than, from the producers' side. They incorporate Coase's work on transaction costs in explaining what goes on in successful vertical integration, and they see most economists interpreting the problem as minimizing net transaction costs. But as one radio commentator likes to put it, "there is another side to the story." Just how consumers minimize their transaction costs may contain a great deal of insight. Generally, producers offer preset packages, and there is little that consumers can do to cope with, much less minimize, their own transaction costs, other than to accept the least bad of what is offered. But in some industries, the consumer can select the various items for his or her own plate, and then the take-it-or-leave-it producer is at a disadvantage. One such development has been the introduction of component modules with consumers being able to select such modules as are compatible with their tastes. Such a system may increase the speed of technological innovation—particularly because it may offer extra advantages of specialization to the producers of modules as well as speed of substitutions by consumers. Their exemplar case involves the development of high-fidelity and stereo sound systems, the history of which they trace with care. Ultimately, they conclude, the range of modular choice may become so great that the typically informed consumer cannot observe qualitative improvements, and then the process stops.

"Taking Schumpeter's Methodology Seriously" serves both as the title of Yuichi Shionoya's essay and as the reason for Schumpeter's apparent lack of success in influencing the economics profession. After explaining just what is meant by methodology and identifying the intellectual-institutional time and place constraints of the young Schumpeter, influenced in particular by the seminal work of Ernst Mach, the author goes on to reveal that the most provocative element in Schumpeter's portrayal of his own methodology (found only in the original, 1912 German version of his *Theory of Economic Development,* where it took about one sixth of the total pages) was intentionally omitted thereafter because he thought that economists would classify him as a sociologist and therefore choose to ignore his views. Shionoya has laid out rather comprehensively the breadth of Schumpeter's methodological views, and although he concludes that one can integrate them (and he believes he has), difficulty in others' doing so has made Schumpeter's contributions seem to many to be more intuitive than scientific. This is an excellent survey as well as a provocative essay.

Hyman P. Minsky's discussion of the Shionoya essay begins with praise for the comprehensiveness of, and the scholarly understanding explicit in, Shionoya's work. But he differs on the current significance of Machian instrumentalism, which, he avers, Shionoya believes served as the core of Schumpeter's methodology. Rather, Minsky thinks that, from a methodological standpoint, Schumpeter really divided the field of informed scholarly knowledge between those who had vision and those who had technique. Minsky thought that, unlike Schumpeter, who had less than the necessary math or the confidence that goes with mathematical knowledge, Keynes possessed the techniques necessary to convey his vision. Minsky also concludes that Schumpeter's unadulterated admiration for Walras's work led Schumpeter to overlook the fact that the Walrasian system, which was based on Adam Smith's innovative vision of an interdependent equilibrium, was not totally compatible with his own vision. Indeed, of the three great competitors of their age (Schumpeter, Keynes, and Mitchell), only Mitchell understood that each of their visions was incompatible with formal economic theory as it had developed. On that score, only Mitchell's work, albeit not part of the theory corpus, emerges intact.

Jefferson and Schumpeter: Contrasts and Compatibilities

Kenneth G. Elzinga

In sports, politics, academic life, and marriage, interpersonal comparisons are continuously being made. Usually the comparisons involve assessments of who is better and who is worse, or who is right and who is wrong. The comparisons are sometimes quantitative, especially among athletes; sometimes qualitative, especially among politicians; and sometimes intensely personal, especially between spouses and even among professors.

We convene as a society named after a professor, Joseph A. Schumpeter, and we gather in a building designed by a politician, Thomas Jefferson. Just as Schumpeter has been compared to such economists as Keynes and Marx, Jefferson has been compared to other political figures, such as Hamilton and Franklin. Comparing Schumpeter and Jefferson is my peculiar assignment.

Contradictions

In appearance, Schumpeter and Jefferson would never be confused for each other. Schumpeter, in his mature years, was bald with an angular nose, a proud round jaw, and a smooth complexion. Jefferson's complexion was ruddy and he kept a full head of hair, which turned from red to gray as he aged. Jefferson remained lean and angular all his life; Schumpeter more contoured and soft featured.

Both Schumpeter and Jefferson had the reputation of being horsemen. Graduate students in economics, entering a profession with few dashing personalities, often hear of Schumpeter's alleged aspiration to be the greatest economist in the world, the greatest lover in Vienna, and the greatest horseman in Europe; he claimed to have succeeded in two of these. Schumpeter's love for horses, however, was more the stuff of legend than of actuality. At the Schumpeters' country home in Connecticut, his animal companion was

The author is indebted to Merrill D. Peterson and F. M. Scherer for their comments on an earlier draft of this essay.

canine, not equine. Jefferson, on the other hand, was an accomplished rider and had a lifetime interest in owning horses, a practice of many landowners in central Virginia even to this day.

Jefferson and Schumpeter lived at different times. Jefferson was born April 13, 1743, and died July 4, 1826. Schumpeter was born almost sixty years later, on February 8, 1883, and died January 8, 1950. Jefferson outdistanced the actuarial tables of his day, living to be eighty-three; Schumpeter died short of the allotted three score and ten. Jefferson obviously could not have been influenced by Schumpeter; in Schumpeter's published works there are, to my knowledge, only two references to Jefferson.[1]

Jefferson and Schumpeter not only lived at different times, they lived in them very differently. Schumpeter's politics were, shall we say, adaptable. He lived under the Hapsburg monarchy the first thirty-five years of his life, served briefly as Minister of Finance for the Marxist Social Democratic party in Austria, was a friend of Otto Bauer, the leader of the left wing of that party, and then lived comfortably under democratic capitalism in the United States. One can find academic references to Schumpeter as a socialist; some defenders of capitalism claim him for their camp. Schumpeter was not a political chameleon; rather, he was too universal, too eclectic, to fit a single mold.

There was no doubt about the colors Jefferson flew. He was a political revolutionary. By word and deed, Jefferson chose irrevocably to separate himself from the monarchy and the military establishment of his day. He also distanced himself from the religious establishment.

Jefferson does not fit Hollywood's image of a revolutionary. He was not a fiery orator, he was not even a particularly good public speaker. Indeed, he disliked speech making, preferring that people be persuaded by reading or dialogue. Schumpeter far outpaced Jefferson in locution. Lionel Robbins said of Schumpeter: ". . . in our profession, with the single exception of Keynes, he was probably the best talker of his generation."[2]

The personalities of Schumpeter and Jefferson also were very different. With Jefferson, what you saw is what you got.[3] With Schumpeter, you could not be sure what you got by what you saw—or heard—and sometimes read.

---

1. In his *Business Cycles* (New York: McGraw-Hill, 1939, 1:301), Schumpeter makes reference to the "strongly depressive effect" of Jefferson's embargo of the British in 1807–9. In his *History of Economic Analysis* (London: Allen and Unwin, 1954, 515), Jefferson receives no mention in the index, but a footnote in the text gives Jefferson credit for introducing to the United States *A Treatise on Political Economy* by French economist Destutt de Tracy.

2. Lionel Robbins, "Schumpeter's *History of Economic Analysis*," *Quarterly Journal of Economics* 69 (1955): 1.

3. With the exception of indebtedness. All his life, Jefferson preached against debt, both private and public. But he, himself, went deeply into debt.

Even Schumpeter's friends found him perplexing. Haberler described Schumpeter as "exceedingly complex" and Morgenstern characterized him as "almost inscrutable in spite of his writings."[4] Schumpeter was a verbal provocateur. He enjoyed verbal jousting for the sake of the joust.[5] Jefferson, in contrast, avoided arguments if he could and stayed clear of personal disputes. His personality was not complex.

Schumpeter's circle was largely confined to the academy. Here, too, he differed from Jefferson, who was at home with tradesmen, laborers, artisans, scientists, slaves, and farmers, as well as diplomats and statesmen. Because he wore so many hats, Jefferson was in contact with a wide range of people. Jefferson's ease with people of many stripes was connected to his political philosophy: he genuinely believed that ordinary people could govern themselves. This is a remarkable proposition, even today. It was thoroughly radical in the eighteenth century, and it was not shared by all of Jefferson's fellow revolutionaries. Jefferson believed that his celebrated differences with Alexander Hamilton about self-government could be described this way: "Hamilton feared most the ignorance of the people; while he feared more the selfishness of rulers independent of the people."

Schumpeter would have pinned his colors to Hamilton's mast. In his review of Hayek's *The Road to Serfdom,* Schumpeter wrote:

> The principles of independent initiative and self reliance are the principles of a very limited class. They mean nothing to the mass of people who—no matter for what reason—are not up to the standard they imply. It is this majority that the economic achievement and the liberal policy of the capitalist age have invested with dominant power. . . . And in this situation there is no point in appealing to Cicero or Pericles, whose

---

4. Gottfried Haberler, "Joseph Alois Schumpeter, 1883–1950," *Quarterly Journal of Economics* 64 (1950): 333, 334; O. Morgenstern, "Obituary: Joseph Alois Schumpeter, 1883–1950," *Economic Journal* 61 (1951): 197, 202. Morgenstern added that Schumpeter ". . . was pleased to make quixotic and paradoxical statements, to shock even his friends with his extravagant views." See also Robert L. Heilbroner with Paul Streeten, *The Great Economists* (London: Eyre and Spottiswodde, 1955), 256–59.

5. Christian Seidl argues that Schumpeter's positions and postures often were affected to make verbal waves. See Seidl, "Joseph Alois Schumpeter: Character, Life, and Particulars of his Graz Period," in *Lectures on Schumpeterian Economics,* ed. Christian Seidl (Berlin: Springer-Verlag, 1984), 187–89. Schumpeter's verbal jousting did not carry over to his classroom. He has been acclaimed as an outstanding teacher. Parenthetically, his teaching career did not begin with satisfied customers: Schumpeter's first batch of students at the University of Graz revolted at the material he assigned, boycotted his classes, and called for his resignation. But in his years at Harvard University, Schumpeter was considered unusually attentive to inquiring students—a professor who spent many hours preparing both the content and delivery of his lectures.

individualism blossomed in societies whose very basis was slavery, or to Benjamin Franklin, who spoke for a small body of hardy pioneers every one of whom cheerfully faced the alternative of getting on or perishing.[6]

As a professor, Schumpeter took steps to conceal how hard he actually worked. He enjoyed the image of the hare and not the tortoise and relished the reputation of the genius who never broke a sweat.[7] This is not to say Schumpeter's long hours were a substitute for brilliance, for he was both tortoise and hare. As Spiethoff wrote: "Josef Schumpeter war nie Anfanger."[8] Jefferson never hid the fact that he was a hard worker. As a student, he was almost robotic, studying generally for fifteen hours per day; his one bow to leisure while a student was to run a mile before dark.[9]

Both Schumpeter and Jefferson were connected to universities, but in totally different ways. Schumpeter was a faculty member at four different universities and enhanced each faculty he joined. Jefferson was the founder of a university. On his tombstone, at his request, he is remembered for only three things: the author of the Declaration of Independence, the author of the Virginia Statute for Religious Freedom, and the father of the University of Virginia. Very few founders of universities select the school's location, design the facility, oversee its construction, promote the funding, secure the charter, involve themselves in hiring the first faculty, design the curriculum, and then do not want the institution named after them.

The investments Schumpeter and Jefferson made in human capital differed markedly. Schumpeter eventually put all his eggs in one basket: academic economics. The rate of return on this single-minded investment was enormous: president of the American Economic Association; president of the Econometric Society; president-elect of the International Economics Association; professor of economics at the University of Bonn and Harvard University; namesake of an academic society; and a distinguished classroom teacher.

Thomas Jefferson was elected to only two presidencies: the United States of America and the American Philosophical Society. But he put his vocational eggs in more baskets than Schumpeter. In addition to being an elected politi-

6. Joseph A. Schumpeter, "Review of Friedrich Hayek, *The Road to Serfdom,*" *Journal of Political Economy* 54 (1946): 269, 270.

7. Samuelson refers to this as Schumpeter's "pose." See Paul A. Samuelson, "Schumpeter's *Capitalism, Socialism, and Democracy,*" in *Schumpeter's Vision,* ed. A. Heertje (New York: Praeger, 1981), 1.

8. A. Spiethoff, "Josef Schumpeter In Memoriam," *Kyklos* 3 (1949–50): 289, 290.

9. Jefferson recommended a reading agenda of over twelve hours per day for law students, only a third of it devoted to law. See George H. Nash, *Books and the Founding Fathers* (Washington, D.C.: Library of Congress, 1989), 12.

cian, Jefferson was a diplomat, a farmer, an inventor, an educator, and an architect.

Both men were published writers. Jefferson, in the Declaration of Independence, authored some of the most famous words ever written. His only full-length book, *Notes on the State of Virginia,* attained international recognition as a literary and scientific contribution of the U.S. enlightenment.[10] But Jefferson had less interest than Schumpeter in writing "for publication." The bulk of his output was in the form of letters, addresses, and state papers.[11] Schumpeter had a passion for writing books and articles and his output was impressive in both quality and quantity. His *History of Economic Analysis* stands as one of the most amazing works of scholarship in all of economics.

With all of their differences, the major distinction between Joseph Schumpeter and Thomas Jefferson, of course, is their vocations—their respective professional callings. Schumpeter had political aspirations at one time, perhaps seeing public service as an exit from the University of Graz. But even as a young man he worried about whether a professor should be involved in the political arena, and he later avoided all public policy involvement, an academic purity not shared by his Keynesian colleagues at Harvard.[12] Schumpeter is remembered above all as a scholar and the founder of a perspective on economics.[13] Jefferson is remembered above all as a statesman and one of the founders of a nation. One cannot imagine either man doing the work of the other.

So we have two very different characters, alike, it could be argued, only in that each man was extraordinary. If one strains a bit, some personal similarities between Jefferson and Schumpeter can be found.

Compatibilities

Both Jefferson and Schumpeter formally studied law, but neither man became lawyers by profession—for which society is the winner. Jefferson and Schumpeter also shared a note-taking obsession. Both had a pack rat's mentality for

---

10. See Adrienne Koch and William Peden, eds., *Selected Writings of Thomas Jefferson* (New York: Modern Library, 1944), 187–292.

11. Boorstein attributes the lack of writing, indeed the relative lack of books, in revolutionary America to the great scarcity of both type and paper. Jefferson was an exception among plantation owners in having a large library. See Daniel J. Boorstein, *The Americans: The Colonial Experience* (New York: Pelican Books, 1965), 1:351–52.

12. See Seidl's discussion of this in "Schumpeter," 201–5.

13. I choose the word *perspective* because there is no Schumpeter school of economics. Schumpeter claimed, in his departure address from Bonn, that he did want a school founded upon his work. The breadth of his work and its lack of focus on policy has made his wish come true. Karl Acham has translated part of Schumpeter's June 20, 1932, address to the Bonn faculty in "Schumpeter—The Sociologist," in Seidl, ed., *Lectures,* 171–72.

their thoughts and observations. For future reference, if not for posterity, both took notes with a passion.[14]

But Schumpeter's notes were intellectual in character: he wanted to be able to recall the ideas of others so he could link and distinguish and appraise their content. Jefferson's notes were more quantitative in character: by recording such facts as prices, temperatures, wind directions, and the mortar yields of limestone deposits, Jefferson hoped to make scientific sense of the world about him.

Schumpeter sought to understand what caused broad changes in economic activity. His two volume *Business Cycles* is the fruit of his labor to understand the changes in aggregate economic activity. Jefferson, in contrast, measured changes in economic activity at the hyper-microeconomic level. For example, Jefferson gathered eight years of data on when thirty different fruits and vegetables first appeared in fresh produce markets and when they were no longer available. It takes effort, genuine effort, even to imagine comparable interests in a national leader today. It would be as if Margaret Thatcher or Helmut Kohl or George Bush gathered monthly production statistics on DRAM and EPROM semiconductor output.

Schumpeter and Jefferson shared three bonds of tragedy. Each saw—not literally—their personal libraries destroyed. Schumpeter's library was lost to the Allied bombing of Julich, Germany, where his books had been stored for shipment to the United States. Jefferson's first library was consumed by fire in his ancestral home; his second library of some six thousand volumes became the nucleus of the Library of Congress, but was destroyed by the British when they sacked Washington, D.C., in 1814.

Both men became widowers after short marriages. Schumpeter eventually remarried, but tradition has it that Jefferson honored his wife's dying request of never remarrying.

The third misfortune Schumpeter and Jefferson shared is they each went broke. Schumpeter fell heavily into debt due to financial speculations during his stint as president of the Biedermann Bank in Vienna. Seidl places the shortfall at about a quarter million dollars in 1983 dollars.[15] Although Schum-

---

14. Ragnar Frisch described Schumpeter in the following way.
Schumpeter's system of classifying notes was something I have never been able to understand. In the course of a conversation he would constantly jot down remarks on small bits of paper which he stuck into his pocket in no apparent order. I have always wondered in what sort of receptacles he finally stored them, possibly barrels. I imagine the essential thing for him was to memorize the ideas by *writing* them. ("Some Personal Reminiscences on a Great Man," in *Schumpeter: Social Scientist,* ed. S. E. Harris [Freeport: Books for Libraries Press, 1969], 9)
15. Seidl, "Schumpeter," 192.

peter fell into debt, Jefferson slid into financial ruin—owing $100,000 at the close of his life, a staggering sum in 1826. The debt required him to sell off many of his assets; a lottery was designed to allow Jefferson to repay his liabilities and permit him to remain at Monticello until his death. The lottery failed, and Monticello passed from Jefferson's family.

Economists might puzzle over how two men, so gifted in intelligence, could be so bad at personal economics. In his biography of Jefferson, McLaughlin writes:

> [Jefferson's] personal flaw was perhaps an aristocrat's mentality about money; deep down, he believed it would somehow always be there. He preached to others throughout his life the necessity of keeping out of debt, but he was seldom willing to forgo anything he wanted for himself, his family, or friends, no matter how little he could afford it. Austerity was simply not part of Jefferson's personal life. It became, however, a part of the life of Monticello.[16]

Schumpeter had taken a risk that did not pay off. He learned from his bankruptcy and remained solvent the rest of his days. Jefferson's problem was more fundamental: he did not grasp the distinction between a stock and a flow. Jefferson maintained extensive records on individual receipts and expenditures at Monticello, for Monticello was his business as well as his home. But he did not measure the revenues and costs as flows. It is as if Jefferson kept a checking account, faithfully recording each check written and each deposit made, but never calculated a running balance. He knew all the top lines, but he did not know the bottom line.

Given the dissimilarities and the stylized similarities between Professor Schumpeter and Thomas Jefferson, it is legitimate to ask: is there any substantive nexus between the two men? The answer is yes, there are two.

Jefferson and Schumpeter: A Nexus

The first nexus I shall claim for Schumpeter and Jefferson involves the phenomenon of innovation. Schumpeter is the economist most identified with this phenomenon. He showed that innovation was a powerful force behind the business cycle; he argued that innovation was more important for an economist to understand than Marshallian equilibrium; and he distinguished inven-

---

16. Jack McLaughlin, *Jefferson and Monticello: The Biography of a Builder* (New York: Henry Holt, 1988), 379.

tion from innovation and underscored the role of the entrepreneur who transforms invention into innovation.

Thomas Jefferson did what Schumpeter taught: he was an innovator, but in the political realm. His innovation was democracy. He was not the inventor, but he was an innovator. Among political systems, no innovation has been more important in the past two hundred years than Jeffersonian democracy.

Years ago a history text published in England described Thomas Jefferson as "a young Virginian, who was perhaps more than any other of the popular leaders [in the colonies] under the dominion of abstract beliefs in the rights of man."[17] This assessment of Jefferson misses the mark. Jefferson did not invent the idea of the sovereignty of the people. One could argue that the most famous words Mr. Jefferson penned, the Declaration of Independence, were derived from John Locke. Jefferson's genius was to implement "abstract beliefs in the rights of man" into a functioning democratic system.

This is the Schumpeterian equivalent in statecraft of being an innovator. Just as the business entrepreneur must determine how the aisles of a supermarket are going to be laid out if retailing is to move from clerk service to self-service, as a political entrepreneur, Jefferson had to implement individual rights into a functioning political system if democracy was to move from an idea to an organism.

As Merrill Peterson said, "Political philosophers, although they had written of 'the sovereignty of the people,' had not considered the mundane means and contrivances necessary to realize it."[18] Jefferson and his colleagues worried about the mundane means and contrivances. In this political sense, the Founding Fathers of the United States were laying out the aisles of the first supermarket or planning production of the first fork-lift truck or developing the first commercial railroad between two regions or designing the first just-in-time inventory flow.

One does not generally associate statesmen with the entrepreneurial process.[19] But Jeffersonian democracy was an innovation in political organization. It also provided a favorable habitat for wealth-creating activity that, until recently, was unmatched anywhere in the world. Democracy by Jefferson provided the limited government and the protection of property rights that enabled the business entrepreneur to innovate. Schumpeter was a beneficiary

---

17. *The Cambridge Modern History: The United States* (Cambridge: Cambridge University Press, 1907), 7:166.

18. "Thomas Jefferson," *Encyclopedia of the Social Sciences* (New York: Macmillan, 1968), 8:250.

19. When the biographical literature defines Jefferson in entrepreneurial terms, it refers to his nail-making factory at Monticello or his farming endeavors. But in these profit-making endeavors, he was neither singularly nor relatively successful.

of Jefferson's political innovations. The environment that Schumpeter enjoyed as a professor in the United States enabled him to be more productive than had he remained in (and survived) Europe during the war years and thereafter.

Jefferson would have benefitted from knowing the Schumpeterian distinction between invention and innovation in the world of commerce. Jefferson understood and appreciated inventions. He was an inventor himself, he was in contact with inventors, and he had a keen interest in developments in applied science and agronomy. Jefferson revealed his conviction that invention was important to the growth of a new nation by calling for the introduction of a patent system.[20]

But Jefferson did not anticipate the impact of innovation upon a nation's economy, particularly in manufacturing. Jefferson thought the farmer was the most valued member of society and land the most valuable asset. It was not until later, as Jefferson watched the economy suffer from the consequences of the U.S. embargo of Britain, that he ascribed importance to manufacturing. Jefferson wrote Benjamin Austin in 1816: "We must now place the manufacturer by the side of the agriculturist. . . . Experience has taught me that manufactures are now as necessary to our independence as to our comfort."[21] But even here Jefferson's rationale for a larger U.S. manufacturing sector was to avoid international entanglements.[22]

In his *Theory of Economic Development,* Schumpeter put the economic spotlight on the entrepreneur—those individuals engaged in what Schumpeter described as "the carrying out of new combinations."[23] Jefferson would have appreciated Schumpeter's concept of carrying out new combinations, because Jefferson had a love for new ideas: he valued the inventor, the tinkerer. But Jefferson never envisioned the Schumpeterian gale of creative destruction. He never anticipated the impact of some innovations. Jefferson was an agrarian. He did not understand, as Schumpeter later was to explain, the changes that

---

20. In 1790, Congress passed a general patent law that was inspired by Jefferson. As secretary of state, Jefferson personally examined each early patent application.

21. M. White and L. White, *The Intellectual versus the City* (Cambridge, Mass.: Harvard and MIT Press, 1902), 18.

22. Jefferson's affection remained with agriculture. He also wrote William Crawford in 1816, "The agricultural capacities of our country constitute its distinguishing feature, and the adapting our policy and pursuits to that, is more likely to make us a numerous and happy people, than the mimicry of an Amersterdam, a Hamburgh, or a city of London" (quoted in Dumas Malone, *The Sage of Monticello,* vol. 6, *Jefferson and His Time* [Boston: Little, Brown, 1982], 148).

23. Joseph A. Schumpeter, *Theory of Economic Development* (Cambridge, Mass.: Harvard University Press, 1955), 132.

entrepreneurs in manufacturing and distribution and finance would bring to a young nation's income and its social fabric.[24]

A second nexus between Schumpeter and Jefferson is that Jefferson had a keen interest in the subject that Schumpeter studied with such devotion. Jefferson's interest in the subject of economics is not appreciated widely because Jefferson's contributions in other areas swamp the attention he gave to economics. But Jefferson had the keenest interest in the science of economics among all U.S. presidents. Three pieces of evidence support this statement.

Jefferson read economics. He had studied Adam Smith's *The Wealth of Nations,* and, like Schumpeter, he was not effusive in his praise of Smith. Jefferson preferred Say's *Traite d'Economique Politique,* which he described as "shorter, clearer, and sounder" than *The Wealth of Nations.*[25]

In addition to reading economics, Jefferson wanted economics read. To this end, in 1812, Jefferson took receipt of Destutt de Tracy's *A Treatise on Political Economy,* assisted in its translation from French to English, negotiated with publishers, and even read galley proofs for the volume. Tracy, who receives several mentions in Schumpeter's *History of Economic Analysis,* received a letter from Jefferson about economics in which Jefferson wrote: "There is no branch of science in which information is more wanted here, and, under the want of which, we are suffering more."[26]

Finally, Jefferson placed the subject of political economy into the original curriculum of the University of Virginia and took a personal interest in staffing the position. Parenthetically, the current practice of U.S. universities raiding faculties in Europe is not new. It began with Jefferson, who sent Dr. George Gilmer on a mission, principally to Oxford, Cambridge, and Edin-

---

24. Another nexus between Schumpeter and Jefferson (not explored in this essay) pertains to Schumpeter's sociology of democracy, in which Schumpeter argued, contrary to the classical theory of Rousseau, that the rules governing the contest for votes in a democracy constitute the essence of democracy. Frey considers this insight to be the essence of modern public choice economics (see Bruno Frey, "Schumpeter, Political Economist," in *Schumpeterian Economics,* ed. H. Frisch [New York: Praeger, 1981], 126–42). Schumpeter's theory of democracy has connections to Jefferson's colleague and friend James Madison and, beyond that, to Hobbes. Acham has argued that Schumpeter's focus on democracy as political method, and not as a set of goals or results, is Schumpeter's major contribution to sociology (see Acham, "Schumpeter," 160–63). In an essay that draws some comparisons of Schumpeter and Jefferson, Wright contends that Schumpeter never understood America's Founding Fathers, asserting that it is "hard to believe, indeed, that Schumpeter ever read the American constitutionalists" (see David McCord Wright, "Schumpeter's Political Philosophy," in Harris, ed., *Schumpeter,* 130).

25. See Malone, *Sage,* 6:141. Schumpeter would have applauded Jefferson's ranking of Say over Smith for, Schumpeter wrote, "Say's work is the most important in the links in the chain that leads from Cantillon and Turgot to Walras" (*Economic Analysis,* 492). Walras was at the top in Schumpeter's ranking of Economics.

26. Schumpeter, *Economic Analysis,* 305–8.

burgh, to recruit six of the University of Virginia's eight member faculty. Gilmer was not fully successful. The proposed salary at the University of Virginia was generous by U.S. standards, but it did not measure up to faculty incomes at Oxbridge. From New England, there came cries of indignation at Jefferson's implied insult to the quality of U.S. colleges and universities.[27]

Jefferson wanted only the professorships of law and moral philosophy (i.e., economics) to be filled by citizens of the United States. His choice for the economics post, Dr. Thomas Cooper, proved too controversial, so George Tucker became the first economist at Mr. Jefferson's university. Tucker received faint praise from Schumpeter as a "not insignificant" early U.S. economist.[28]

Because of Jefferson's admiration for Cooper, Cooper's text offers insight into Jefferson's views. His *Lectures on the Elements of Political Economy* is a book much influenced by Smith, Ricardo, McCulloch, and Mill—a textbook that is antimercantilist through and through and that preaches the benefits of free trade and laissez-faire.[29] One can imagine Schumpeter applauding these policy principles.

Conclusion

Joseph Schumpeter claimed that an economist who was not also a mathematician, a statistician, and a historian was not qualified to do economics—a sobering statement for many of us who draw paychecks as economists. Jefferson would have appreciated these high standards, for he believed that a statesman who did not know science, history, and the classics was not qualified to do politics—a sobering statement for many elected officials today. Jefferson and Schumpeter would have appreciated the breadth of learning and study each had achieved.

When Joseph Schumpeter crafted his two volume *Business Cycles,* he

27. See Malone, *Sage,* 6:397–401; Dabney Virginius, *Mr. Jefferson's University: A History* (Charlottesville: University Press of Virginia, 1981), 1–8.

28. Schumpeter, *Economic Analysis,* 519–22, esp. 519. De Tracy's treatise, which Jefferson brought to the United States, was not Tucker's textbook choice. Smith's *Wealth of Nations* and Say's *Treatise* were the textbooks assigned. See Tipton R. Snavely, *George Tucker as Political Economist* (Charlottesville: University Press of Virginia, 1964), 13.

29. Cooper became president of South Carolina College, where he was also professor of chemistry and political economy, having been relieved of his duties of also teaching rhetoric, criticism, and belles lettres. Cooper, and Cooper's text, receive no mention in Schumpeter's *History of Economic Analysis.* Cooper was in the grain of Schumpeter's assessment of U.S. economics in the nineteenth century: "Teaching fed mainly on McCulloch and Say, and where home-grown texts were used, it was McCulloch and Say again . . ." (*Economic Analysis,* 515). This describes the Cooper text quite well.

informed the reader that the subtitle, not the title, described the work. The subtitle is: *A Theoretical, Historical, and Statistical Analysis of the Capitalist Process*. Schumpeter did his economics on a grand scale.

An early edition of the *Encyclopedia Britannica* describes Jefferson as "the most conspicuous apostle of democracy in America." This "conspicuous apostle" penned these words:

> We hold these truths to be self-evident, that all men are created equal, that they are endowed by their Creator with certain unalienable Rights, that among these are Life, Liberty, and the pursuit of Happiness.

Jefferson did his politics on a grand scale.

BIBLIOGRAPHY

Acham, Karl. [1932] 1984. "Schumpeter—The Sociologist." In *Lectures on Schumpeterian Economics,* ed. Christian Seidl. Berlin: Springer-Verlag.

Boorstein, Daniel J. 1958. *The Americans: The Colonial Experience.* New York: Pelican Books.

The Cambridge Modern History: The United States. 1907. Cambridge: Cambridge University Press.

Dabney, Virginius. 1981. *Mr. Jefferson's University: A History.* Charlottesville: University Press of Virginia.

Frey, Bruno. 1981. "Schumpeter, Political Economist." In *Schumpeterian Economics,* ed. Ragnar Frisch. New York: Praeger.

Frisch, Ragnar. 1969. "Some Personal Reminiscences on a Great Man." In *Schumpeter: Social Scientist,* ed. S. E. Harris. Freeport: Books for Libraries Press.

Frisch, Ragnar, ed. 1981. *Schumpeterian Economics.* New York: Praeger.

Haberler, Gottfried. 1950. "Joseph Alois Schumpeter 1883–1950." *Quarterly Journal of Economics* 64:333–34.

Heilbroner, Robert L. (with Paul Streeten) 1955. *The Great Economist.* London: Eyre and Spottiswodde.

Hession, Charles, and Hyman Sandy. 1969. *Ascent to Affluence.* Boston: Allyn and Bacon.

Koch, Adrienne, and William Peden, eds. 1944. *Selected Writings of Thomas Jefferson.* New York: Modern Library.

Malone, Dumas. 1982. *Jefferson and his Time: The Sage of Monticello.* Boston: Little Brown.

McLaughlin, Jack. 1988. *Jefferson and Monticello: The Biography of a Builder.* New York: Henry Holt.

Morgenstern, Oscar. 1951. "Obituary: Joseph Alois Schumpeter 1883–1950." *Economic Journal* 61:197, 202.

Nash, George H. 1989. "Books of the Founding Fathers." Library of Congress.

Robbins, Lyonel. 1955. "Schumpeter's History of Economic Analysis." *Quarterly Journal of Economics* 69:1.

Samuelson, Paul A. 1981. "Schumpeter's Capitalism, Socialism and Democracy." In *Schumpeter's Vision,* ed. Arnold Heertje. New York: Praeger.

Schumpeter, Joseph A. 1939. *Business Cycles.* New York: McGraw-Hill.

Schumpeter, Joseph A. 1946. "Review of Friedrich Hayek, *The Road to Serfdom.*" *Journal of Political Economy* 54:269–70.

Schumpeter, Joseph A. 1954. *History of Economic Analysis.* London: Allen and Unwin.

Schumpeter, Joseph A. 1955. *Theory of Economic Development.* Cambridge, Mass.: Harvard University Press.

Seidl, Christian, ed. 1984. "Joseph Alois Schumpeter: Character, Life and Particulars of his Graz Period." In *Lectures on Schumpeterian Economics,* ed. Christian Seidl. Berlin: Springer-Verlag.

Sills, David. 1968, ed. "Thomas Jefferson." *International Encyclopedia of the Social Sciences.* New York: Macmillan and the Free Press.

Snavely, Tipton R. 1964. *George Tucker as Political Economist.* Charlottesville: University Press of Virginia.

Spiethoff, A. 1949/50. "Josef Schumpeter in Memoriam." *Kyklos* 3:289–90.

White, Morton, and Lucia White. 1902. *The Intellectual Versus the City, from Thomas Jefferson to Frank Lloyd Wright.* Cambridge, Mass.: Harvard and MIT Press.

Wright, David McCord. 1969. "Schumpeter's Political Philosophy." In *Schumpeter: Social Scientist,* ed. S. E. Harris. Freeport: Books for Libraries Press.

U.S. Technological Leadership: Where Did it Come From and Where Did it Go?

Richard R. Nelson

Introduction

During the quarter-century following World War II, the United States was the world's most productive economy by virtually all measures. U.S. output per worker was higher than anyone else's by a considerable amount; so, too, was total factor productivity. These differences held not just in the aggregate but in almost all industries. Many factors lay behind the U.S. edge in total factor productivity, but it seems clear that more advanced technology was prominent among these.[1] Firms in the United States were in the forefront of developing the leading edge technologies, their exports in these accounted for the lion's share of world markets, and their overseas branches often were dominant firms in their host countries. The U.S. R&D and educational systems were the object of envy and emulation by other nations.[2]

No longer. The U.S. technological lead has badly eroded in many industries, and, in some, the United States now is a lagger. How did these developments come about and what do they forbode? This essay will illuminate these questions. I begin by describing when and how the U.S. technological leadership of the 1950s and 1960s came into being. I then turn to the factors behind its obvious erosion in the 1970s and 1980s. Finally, a reprise.

I am indebted to many scholars whose writings have helped me to sort out the two quite different sources of U.S. postwar dominance that I distinguish. Nathan Rosenberg, Christopher Freeman, Harvey Brooks, and Robert Ayres have written things that have strongly pointed to the arguments I develop here, even if they do not themselves develop them. And I am indebted to Freeman and Ayres, and to Nathaniel Leff, Lewis Branscomb, Rolf Piekarz, and Keith Pavitt, for explicit, helpful, and encouraging comments on an earlier draft of this essay.

1. Denison 1967 gives a long listing of possible sources and concludes in the end that "differences in knowledge" must have been quite important.

2. Probably J. J. Servan Schreiber 1968 is the best known of books by Europeans citing these and other U.S. advantages, but there were many others.

Long-standing U.S. Strengths

I will argue that there were two distinguishable components of the postwar U.S. technological dominance. One was a lead in mass production industries, and this was of long standing. The other was in high tech and this was new. Each stemmed from different sources. And they eroded for conceptually separate, if institutionally connected, reasons.

This section will be concerned with documenting the fact that many of the U.S. strengths that marked the 1950s and 1960s has been there for a long time. While Great Britain was the pioneer and dominant technological power of the first industrial revolution, in a number of areas, the United States caught on quickly. As early as 1835 de Tocqueville noted: "It is difficult to say for what reason the Americans can navigate at a lower rate than other nations" ([1835] 1954, 441). But apparently they could. And U.S. prowess was not just in shipping. "The United States of America has only been emancipated for half a century from the state of colonial dependence in which it stood to Great Britain; the number of large fortunes there is small and capital is still scarce. Yet no people in the world have made such rapid progress in trade and manufactures as the Americans . . ." (de Tocqueville [1835] 1954, 165, 166).

Habakkuk opens his *American and British Technology in the Nineteenth Century* (1962) by confirming and reinforcing de Tocqueville's judgment. "There is a substantial body of comment, by English visitors to America in the first half of the nineteenth century, which suggests that, in a number of industries, American equipment was, in some sense, superior to the English even at this period" (4–5). As early as 1835, Cobden had noted, in the machine shop of a woolen mill at Lowell, "a number of machines and contrivances for abridging labour greater than at Sharp and Roberts" (de Tocqueville [1835] 1954, 441). He thought agricultural implements in New England exhibited "remarkable evidences of ingenuity . . . for aiding and abridging human as well as brute labour." And two groups of English technicians who visited the United States in the 1850s reported that U.S. workers produced "by more highly mechanized and more standardized methods a wide range of products including doors, furniture, and woodwork; boots and shoes; ploughs and mowing machines, wood screws, files, and nails; biscuits, locks, small arms, nuts and bolts" (de Tocqueville [1835] 1954, 165–66).

Gun manufacturing in the United States almost certainly was more mechanized and advanced than the British. Thus, in 1854, Parliament established a select committee "to consider the Cheapest, most Expeditious, and most Efficient Mode of producing small arms for Her Majesty's Service" that endorsed a proposal to adopt the procedures and kinds of machinery employed in the U.S. Springfield and Harper's Ferry armories (see Hounshell 1984, 17).

Note that while the examples are varied, virtually all of them are associated with technologies especially important on the U.S. scene, of long sea coasts and rivers, ample, rich agricultural land and natural resources, and much wilderness separating relatively isolated communities. They also reflect that the United States was short of experienced skilled labor.[3]

The last half of the nineteenth century was the well-known great age of U.S. invention and innovation in consumer and producer goods. It also was an era where the system of interchangeable parts was rapidly coming into play in a number of manufacturing industries.[4] A rapidly growing mass market of relatively well-to-do households and an expanding rail and communications network that broke down distance barriers led, in a number of industries, to the rise of large companies engaged in mass production and nationwide marketing. In many of these industries, U.S. firms developed a clear lead in process technology or product design or both over British and continental firms. Firms in the United States dominated world production and trade in such diverse products as sewing machines, typewriters, matches, and refrigerated meat, for example (Chandler 1977, chaps. 9–11).

By the 1890s, the United States led the world in steel production and its firms were widely recognized as the most efficient. While most of the key discoveries and inventions bearing on steel production were made in Europe, the United States clearly excelled in their effective implementation. As in other industries, the large U.S. market for steel stimulated firms to build plants of large size, and large scale facilitated low-cost production. In turn, low-cost steel stimulated the invention and deployment of innovative uses of steel: the United States pioneered steel skeleton building construction, for example.

While many observers took the post–World War II wave of direct investment by U.S. manufacturing companies in Europe as a new phenomenon, it is not. During the late nineteenth and early twentieth centuries, the dominant U.S. firms in many of the industries I have mentioned placed plants in Europe, and controlled the European market in that way rather than through exports (Chandler 1977, 368).

It is hard to pinpoint exactly when U.S. productivity and per capita income surged above that in Britain; it was probably before the turn of the century. Maddison's data show the United States close to England by 1890. By 1913, productivity and per capita income in the United States was significantly higher than in England, and higher still than on the continent (Maddison 1982, table C10, 212). Partly this was due to the high productivity of U.S. agriculture, but it is apparent that by then labor productivity in U.S. manufacturing also was higher in most industries than in Europe. Industrial

---

3. Rosenberg 1972 provides a good general discussion of these points.

4. Or "nearly" interchangeable parts. Hounshell (1984) argues that the production of interchangeable parts by machine alone (i.e., not requiring hand finishing) was achieved only late in the century.

productivity was higher for at least two reasons. Maddison's data (Maddison 1982, table 3.5, 54) show that by that time U.S. industry was operating with significantly higher capital-labor ratios than in Britain. This both was caused by and supported the higher wage rates in U.S. industry, and was made possible by the high U.S. savings and investment rates that significantly exceeded those in England. But total factor productivity undoubtedly was higher too. If it were simply greater capital intensity, but the same total factor productivity, the rate of return on capital should have been significantly lower in the United States than in Europe. The evidence suggests that, if anything, it was higher.[5]

The point of view I am implicitly espousing here is that it is conceptually inadequate to say, simply, that the situation in the United States encouraged firms to adopt more scale- and capital-intensive production than was the norm in Europe, but that this did not represent any technological edge, in the sense that U.S. firms were doing things that European firms could not have if they chose. In fact, U.S. firms were exploring and getting under control technologies the Europeans had little grip on, and would bring into play only by learning from the United States, and with a lag.

By the start of World War I, the United States clearly had seized leadership in the mass production industries, marked by high capital intensity and economies of scale. In addition, the United States had established the private organization and public infrastructure needed to operate effectively in the new science-based industries that were coming into prominence.

By 1860, the science of chemistry had developed to a point where trained chemists could understand aspects of various manufacturing processes that untrained people could not fathom. Chemists began to play a central role in technological innovation in iron and steel making, in the making of traditional inorganic chemicals such as soda, in the creation of new organic chemical substances such as dyes and (later) plastics, and in a variety of other fields (see Rosenberg 1985). Later in the nineteenth century, the understanding of electricity and magnetism reached a similar stage. In both the new chemical and electrical industries, technological advance became dependent upon the availability of scientifically trained people and, thus, on the university systems providing this training. Increasingly, technological advance in these fields began to take place in industrial R&D laboratories dedicated to invention and staffed by university-trained scientists.[6]

---

5. Over the second half of the nineteenth century, the yield on British consuls never got above 3.5 percent; the yield on the best American railway bonds (to be sure somewhat more risky) never sunk that low and tended to be over 5.0 percent. Relatedly, this was a period when capital was flowing from the United Kingdom to the United States, not the other way around.

6. Landis (1970) provides a good general discussion, particularly of European developments. Beer (1959) is good on the chemical industry in Germany, England, and France. Thackray (1982) discusses the rise of chemistry in the United States. Reich's focus (1985) is on the

Germany, rather than the United States or Great Britain, took the forefront in the new chemical technologies. Her university system was the first to incorporate teaching and research in chemistry and chemical engineering, and German universities became the locus of training not only for German chemists, but also of British and Americans. The German chemical companies were significantly in the lead in setting up organized R&D facilities.

Although it lagged behind the Germans, the U.S. university system also geared itself up to train applied chemists and chemical engineers, with schools such as MIT and the Case Institute in the forefront. By 1910 or so, U.S. companies such as Du Pont, Dow, and Kodak had established R&D laboratories, and had developed the capability to produce the full range of industrial chemicals and a wide range of fine chemicals. The German lead in synthetic organic chemistry, however, remained wide and was not made up until well after World War I.

In contrast with chemistry, U.S. universities were about as quick as the Germans to establish programs in electrical engineering. From the beginning, U.S. companies in the new electrical industry had available to them U.S.-trained personnel. In addition, the U.S. electrical industry benefited enormously from educated European emigrees such as Thomson, Tesla, Steinmetz, and Alexanderson. General Electric and AT&T were among the first in the electrical industries to establish R&D laboratories. In many fields, U.S. companies shared the lead with German ones and were ahead in a number of areas. Thus, AEG extensively used technology defined by Edison's patents.[7] Companies in the United States tended to be the leaders in lighting systems technologies. British and German firms tended to be ahead in certain other fields, such as radio.

Thus, by World War I, the U.S. university system had geared itself up to provide the trained scientists and engineers needed by U.S. companies in the new science-based industries. While even after World War II some of the most creative scientists in U.S. industrial labs were still European trained, since the 1920s the vast bulk have been U.S. trained.

By World War I, U.S. firms in the chemical and electronic industries had established first class industrial laboratories that were insulated from pressures to solve immediate shop-floor problems and were able to dedicate their efforts to invention. Chandler (1977) and Lazonick (1988) have documented how this adaptation was facilitated by more general changes in corporate management and structure. During the last half of the nineteenth century, U.S. firms tended

---

electrical equipment industry. See also Noble 1977 for a general discussion of the rise of science-based industry in the United States.

7. See Fox in Kranzberg 1986. Fox's and other chapters in Kranzberg present pictures of how engineering education grew up in the United States, Germany, Britain, and France. Freeman 1982 is good on how the chemical and electrical industries fared in these countries.

to become not simply bigger, but more consciously managed from the top through a hierarchical structure that permitted the establishment of suborganizations specialized by region, product, or function, in the present case R&D. Lazonick has argued that British industry, if not the German, was far slower in adopting these new structures (1988).

The Interwar Period: Consolidation of the U.S. Lead in Mass Production Industries

During the interwar period, U.S. firms consolidated and perhaps even extended their lead in the mass production industries. The large U.S. market continued to play a role. During this era, technological advance in many industries continued to involve the progressive exploitation of latent scale economies, particularly the further development of mass production methods. There was also a proliferation of new consumer goods, such as automobiles and electrical appliances, drawn by the large and affluent U.S. market.

The restraints on international trade that marked this era surely hindered the ability of companies in the other, smaller manufacturing powers to exploit these possibilities. They also undoubtedly damped intercompany rivalry and fostered cartelization in Europe. The greater extent of competition, as well as the larger market, tended to spur invention and innovation in the United States relative to Europe in industries where scale was important.

The rapidly advancing industries of the interwar period tended to be ones resting on technologies or products where the United States already had established great strength. As noted, the United States had pioneered in mass production techniques. The new mass produced goods of the interwar period depended upon steel, a product the United States had learned to produce more cheaply than other nations before the turn of the century. Electrical engineering, another area of established U.S. strength, also was important in the new package of technologies employed in the mass production industries of the 1920s and 1930s.

A new factor probably was U.S. schooling. The interwar period saw a dramatic increase in the proportion of U.S. youth who went beyond primary school to secondary school, with many going on to college. Nothing like this occurred in Europe.[8] It is unclear whether or not this lent any advantage to

---

8. Quantitative comparisons for the era prior to World War II are scarce. However, Denison (1967, table 8.1, 80) shows a dramatic difference between the United States and France, the United Kingdom and Italy, in the proportion of the male labor force that had completed twelve years of schooling or more in the 1950s. For the most part, that labor force consisted of men who had joined the labor force prior to the war and, thus, the data reflect educational attainments in the 1920s and 1930s.

U.S. shop-floor workers relative to Europeans.[9] However, as Lazonick argues (1988), it did provide U.S. firms with a supply of people with schooling in the liberal arts and, often on top of that, some technical skills. This greatly facilitated the growing professionalization of management in U.S. industry.

But while the dominance of U.S. firms in mass production industries was well recognized, until World War II many Europeans continued to look down on the United States in technologies where scientific and engineering sophistication were important. In fields such as synthetic organic chemical products, chemical process equipment, fine machinery, and electronics, arguably the high technologies of the era, the United States was competent but by no means dominant.

The early U.S. lag behind Germany in the chemical industries has been noted. By the late 1930s, the United States had largely caught up, but German companies were still patenting more extensively in many areas than those in the United States and U.S. companies were dependent on German ones for certain kinds of process equipment. The major U.S. electrical equipment companies were world class, and were doing well in the rapidly growing fields connected with radio and electronics more generally. But there were companies of comparable technological competence in Germany and Britain. At that time, U.S. university training and research in the leading edge sciences and technologies was more than respectable and the large proportion of U.S. youth completing high school clearly established the potential for a rapid increase in the U.S. supply of university-trained scientists and engineers. But that surge had yet to begin. And many U.S. students who did seek advanced training in the sciences went to Europe because, in many fields, German university training and research, and in some sciences British, were widely regarded as superior to U.S. training.[10]

The Postwar Era: The U.S. Breakaway at the Technological Frontiers

Just as after World War I, the United States came out of World War II buoyant, her technological capabilities stretched by the wartime production experience, while Europe came out prostrate. And unlike World War I, after World War II Japan, too, was a demolished economy and nation.

---

9. Keith Pavitt has suggested to me (personal communication) that the data on formal schooling may overstate the U.S. advantage in structured teaching of work skills because they probably do not count vocational training and apprenticeship, which were (and are) strong in Germany and Scandinavia.

10. For a good discussion of both the chemical and electrical industries in Europe and the United States both up to and beyond World War II, see Freeman 1982. Cohen (1976) discusses the lag of U.S. university research, at least until the 1930s.

By the mid 1950s, most of the war-devastated countries had regained and surpassed prewar productivity and income levels, but, as table 1 shows, the U.S. productivity and income edge remained enormous. While some Europeans seemed surprised at the U.S. income and productivity lead even after European recovery, they should not have been. The preceding section has documented that the U.S. productivity lead in general, and leadership in mass production industries in particular, had been in place since the turn of the century.

What was new was U.S. dominance in the high-technology industries of the postwar era. What lay behind this? I believe there were several intertwined but distinguishable developments.

At the roots of all was the enormous sense of confidence and pride in America's strength that victory in the war had engendered and a new, strongly burning belief in the role of science and technology in winning the war and opening horizons for the future. Books about wartime science clearly were designed to kindle this appreciation on the part of the public (see, e.g., Baxter 1946). Vannevar Bush's *Science, The Endless Frontier* (1945) gave the trumpet call, and the United States was off to levels of investment in science and technology that were historically unprecedented.

One manifestation was the dramatic increase in the proportion of U.S.

TABLE 1.   Real Gross Domestic Product per Person Employed

Year	United States	Japan	West Germany	France	United Kingdom
1950	$8,794	$1,536	$3,485	$3,858	$4,716
1955	10,028	2,113	4,784	4,713	5,234
1960	10,733	2,883	6,463	5,974	5,802
1965	12,503	4,365	8,002	7,755	6,526
1970	13,184	6,852	9,884	9,687	7,510
1971	13,563	7,120	10,129	10,165	7,839
1972	13,911	7,731	10,581	10,709	7,932
1973	14,203	8,198	10,988	11,144	8,422
1974	13,827	8,144	11,193	11,416	8,256
1975	13,856	8,364	11,329	11,549	8,207
1976	14,133	8,725	12,049	10,065	8,475
1977	14,391	9,063	12,438	12,335	8,640
1978	14,475	9,403	12,741	12,762	8,912
1979	14,423	9,764	13,104	13,188	9,018
1980	14,315	10,142	13,208	13,342	8,894
1981	14,537	10,483	13,262	13,482	9,065
1982 (preliminary)	14,400	10,691	13,345	13,742	9,409
1983 (estimated)	14,712	10,836	13,805	13,875	9,715

Source: National Science Board, *Science Indicators* 1985 (Washington: GPO).

high school graduates who went to college. Earlier I noted the U.S. lead over the rest of the world in the proportion of youth going through secondary school that occurred during the 1920s and 1930s and the beginnings of middle class college education. After World War II, as other industrial countries began to catch up to the United States in secondary education, the United States pulled ahead of the pack in college training.[11] In part, this was simply a matter of the relative U.S. affluence and confidence in the future. However, government policies strongly encouraged it. The G.I. Bill of Rights, which guaranteed educational funding to all qualified veterans, was both emblematic and an important factor in its own right. College fellowships were made available through a number of other public programs. And the state-supported part of the U.S. higher education system provided significant public funding and student subsidies.

Only a relatively small portion of the new wave of university students went into natural science and engineering. But the sheer numbers meant that there was a very large increase in the U.S. supply of trained scientists and engineers. This both met and was pulled by a major increase in demand that came from several sources.

A small but important proportion was employed by the rapidly expanding U.S. university research system. The scientists and engineers who had engaged in the wartime efforts were strikingly successful in their arguments that university science warranted public support, and, during the half-decade after World War II, the United States put into place government machinery to provide that support. The new university research support programs of the National Science Foundation and the National Institutes of Health provided public funding of university basic research across a wide spectrum of fields. However, the bulk of government support of university research came not from these agencies but from agencies pursuing particular missions and using university research as an instrument in that endeavor. Thus, the Department of Defense and the Atomic Energy Commission provided large-scale funding for university research in fields of particular interest to them. And the support was not just for basic research, these agencies also provided funding that involved university applied science and engineering departments in work at the forefront of materials, electronics, and technologies. By the middle 1950s, U.S. research universities clearly were ahead of those of the rest of the world in most fields. Just as young U.S. scholars flocked to German universities to learn science during the last part of the nineteenth century, so young Europeans, Japanese, and other students from all over the world came to the United States for their training.

However, the lion's share of the increased demand for engineers and

---

11. See the data presented in Denison 1967, chap. 8.

TABLE 2.   Scientists and Engineers Engaged in R&D (per 10,000 workers)

	France	West Germany	Japan	United Kingdom	United States
1965	21.0	22.7	24.6	19.6	64.7
1966	29.2	22.4	26.4	NA	66.9
1967	25.3	24.9	27.8	NA	67.2
1968	26.4	26.2	31.1	20.8	68.0
1969	27.1	28.4	30.8	NA	66.7
1970	27.3	30.8	33.4	NA	64.1
1971	27.9	33.4	37.5	NA	60.7
1972	28.2	35.6	38.1	30.4	58.0
1973	28.5	37.1	42.5	NA	56.4
1974	28.9	37.8	44.9	NA	55.6
1975	29.4	38.6	47.9	31.1	55.3
1976	29.9	39.2	48.4	NA	54.8
1977	30.0	41.8	49.9	NA	55.7
1978	31.0	NA	49.4	33.3	56.5
1979	31.6	45.3	50.4	NA	57.7
1980	32.4	NA	53.6	NA	60.0
1981	36.3	46.5	55.6	35.8	62.0
1982	37.9	47.0	57.1	NA	62.8
1983	39.1	48.4	58.1	35.1	63.8
1984	41.2	49.1	62.4	34.2	65.1
1985	NA	NA	63.2	32.8	67.4
1986	NA	NA	NA	NA	69.0

Source: National Science Board, *Science and Technology Indicators* 1987 (Washington: GPO).
Note: NA = not available.

scientists came from a vast expansion in the number of U.S. companies carrying out R&D and in the size of their R&D programs.[12] Table 2 shows the proportion of scientists and engineers engaged in R&D (including corporate, university, and other R&D organizations) as a fraction of the work force. The U.S. lead in the early 1960s is striking. Table 3 shows the same phenomenon in terms of R&D as a fraction of GNP.

The rise of corporate R&D in the United States had two sources. Partly it was the result of major increases in private corporate R&D funding, based on optimistic beliefs in the profitability of such investments that, by and large, turned out to be well founded. Partly it was due to massive DOD, and later NASA, investments in new systems. In the mid 1960s, private funds accounted for about half of corporate R&D, government funds the other half. In some industries, for example pharmaceuticals and the other chemical industries, corporate funds provided almost all the support. In some, electronics in

---

12. For an analytic history of U.S. industrial R&D, see Mowery 1983.

TABLE 3. National Expenditures for R&D (as a percentage of GNP)

	France	West Germany	Japan	United Kingdom	United States
			Total R&D		
1970	1.91	2.06	1.85	2.07	2.57
1971	1.90	2.19	1.85	NA	2.42
1972	1.90	2.20	1.86	2.11	2.35
1973	1.76	2.09	1.90	NA	2.26
1974	1.79	2.13	1.97	NA	2.23
1975	1.80	2.22	1.96	2.19	2.20
1976	1.77	2.15	1.95	NA	2.19
1977	1.76	2.14	1.93	NA	2.15
1978	1.76	2.24	2.00	2.24	2.14
1979	1.81	2.40	2.09	NA	2.19
1980	1.84	2.42	2.22	NA	2.29
1981	2.01	2.44	2.38	2.41	2.35
1982	2.10	2.59	2.47	NA	2.51
1983	2.15	2.54	2.61	2.25	2.56
1984	2.25	2.52	2.61	NA	2.59
1985	2.31	2.67	2.77	2.42	2.69
1986	2.41	2.74	NA	NA	2.72
1987	NA	NA	NA	NA	2.77
			Nondefense R&D		
1971	NA	2.03	1.84	NA	1.65
1972	1.58	2.08	1.84	1.56	1.60
1973	1.38	1.94	1.89	NA	1.58
1974	1.43	1.98	1.96	NA	1.63
1975	1.46	2.08	1.95	1.55	1.63
1976	1.44	2.01	1.94	NA	1.62
1977	1.44	2.01	1.92	NA	1.61
1978	1.41	2.10	1.98	1.61	1.63
1979	1.42	2.27	2.08	NA	1.69
1980	1.43	2.30	2.21	NA	1.79
1981	1.50	2.34	2.37	1.72	1.81
1982	1.63	2.48	2.46	NA	1.88
1983	1.69	2.43	2.60	1.60	1.87
1984	1.76	2.41	2.59	NA	1.86
1985	1.85	2.53	2.75	1.71	1.86
1986	1.94	2.60	NA	NA	1.85
1987	NA	NA	NA	NA	1.88

Source: National Science Board, *Science and Technology Indicators* 1987 (Washington: GPO).
Note: NA = not available.

particular, there was both strong private R&D effort in such firms as AT&T and IBM, and large scale DOD funding of work in these and other companies. In industries such as jet engines and space systems, almost all the funding was DOD or NASA.

It was U.S. dominance in computer and semiconductor technologies that most struck, and concerned, European analysts during the 1950s and 1960s. These were considered to be the leading edge technologies of the post–World War II era, and many foreign observers attributed the U.S. advantage here to DOD support. Military (and to a lesser extent space) R&D support certainly was an important part of the reason for the U.S. lead. But military demands and money were going into an R&D system that was well endowed with trained scientists and engineers, had a very strong university research base, and was populated with companies that were technically capable in their own right.

During the 1930s, those concerned with the capabilities of the armed forces, both in Europe and the United States, were sharply aware of the advantages that could be gained by an enhanced ability to solve complex equation systems rapidly. Ballistics calculations were perhaps the dominant concern, but there were others as well.[13] Prior to and during World War II, the German and British as well as the U.S. government funded research aimed at developing a rapid computer. However, it is clear enough that, during and shortly after World War II, by which time the feasibility of electronic computers had been established, the United States vastly outspent other governments in bringing this embryonic technology into a form that was operational in terms of military needs. Several of the major research universities were involved in the effort, notably MIT, and IBM and AT&T participated actively. It is interesting that early assessments were that the nonmilitary demand for computers would be very small. However, by 1960, it was apparent that the nonmilitary demand would be very large, and it also turned out that the design experience that the major U.S. companies had had in working on military systems was directly relevant to civilian systems.

The story regarding semiconductors is somewhat different.[14] In this case, while military funds had gone into research on semiconductor devices during World War II, it was the Bell Laboratories that made the critical discoveries and inventions, using their own money and motivated by the perceived technological needs of the telephone system, not military demands. However, once the potentials of semiconductor technology were demonstrated, the armed services, and later NASA, quickly recognized the relevance of this

---

13. For a good history, see Flamm 1987, Katz and Phillips 1982.

14. See Levin in Nelson 1982. Malerba (1985) discusses the reasons for Europe's lag in semiconductors.

technology to their needs. Significant government R&D funds went into supporting technical advances in semiconductors and, perhaps more important as it turned out, the DOD and NASA signaled themselves as large potential purchasers of transistors. The evidence is clear that large amounts of private R&D money went into trying to advance semiconductor technology in anticipation of a large government market if the efforts were successful. And, in the field of semiconductor technology as well as computer technology, it turned out that, in the early stages at least, design experience with transistors (and the later integrated circuits) that were of high value to the military set companies up to produce items for civilian products.

By the mid 1960s, the new U.S. lead in high-tech industries, as the old lead in mass production industries, was widely taken as a fact of life, a source of pride for U.S. citizens and concern for Europeans, but presumably a fact not easy to change. Ironically, by that time, U.S. dominance was fast eroding. It was shrinking both in the areas of long-standing U.S. preeminence—mass production industries—and in the new high-technology fields that the United States seized after World War II.

The Closing Gaps

The period since the middle 1960s has seen a dramatic closing of the economic and technological gaps among the major industrial powers. Tables 1–7 show the moving picture, in a variety of dimensions.

The closing of the productivity and income gap is at once the broadest and the most fundamental manifestation of convergence. As Table 1 shows, in the 1950s, U.S. GNP per person employed was roughly double that in the major European countries and nearly five times that in Japan. While U.S. productivity grew at a respectable rate during the 1950s and 1960s, European productivity grew at historically unprecedented rates and Japan's rate of productivity growth was even higher than the European rate. The beginnings of the 1970s marked a slowdown in productivity growth in all countries. But the discrepancies in the rates of growth persisted. By the early 1980s, GNP per person employed in West Germany and France were very close to U.S. levels and Japan was nearly at the same level. The exact rankings since that time have been very sensitive to the price deflators used, suggesting that, for all practical purposes, the lead countries now are very close in overall productivity and income levels.

The general productivity edge the United States had over the other major industrial nations had existed since well before World War I. Thus, convergence after 1965 closed a nearly century old gap. The specific U.S. lead in high-technology industries was a more recent phenomenon. Interestingly, it appears to have held up better than the general U.S. economic lead.

Table 4 shows the share of the major industrial nations in exports of high-technology products over the period since 1965. Contrary to popular belief, the U.S. share has held up well during this time. The dramatic change regarding exportation is in the position of Japan relative to Europe. Japan's share has risen significantly, and those of the European countries have tended to decline. Table 5 shows U.S. exports and imports of high-technology products since 1970. It is the growth of U.S. imports, particularly since 1983, not a decline of export performance, that is the principal source of the erosion of the U.S. high-technology trade balance.

The data on patents of high-technology products, shown in tables 6 and 7, display the same pattern as export shares. From the middle 1960s to the middle 1980s, the share of patents given to U.S. investors has been relatively constant. Japan's share has risen dramatically, mainly at the expense of Europe. Many analysts have noted that U.S. patenting has shown an absolute decline since the late 1960s. That is so, but so has the level of patenting of the major European nations. Of the major industrial nations, only Japan has experienced an increase in patenting.

Within the group of industries in question, more detailed analysis displays a more variegated picture regarding U.S. performance. Between the

TABLE 4.   Export Shares of High-Technology Products

	France	West Germany	Japan	United Kingdom	United States	Other
1965	7.49	16.47	7.24	12.22	28.40	28.18
1966	7.69	16.35	8.61	12.78	27.49	27.09
1967	7.60	16.22	8.90	11.32	28.86	27.10
1968	6.89	15.78	10.03	10.55	29.74	27.00
1969	7.00	16.02	11.42	10.17	28.91	26.48
1970	6.94	16.18	11.78	9.90	28.81	26.40
1971	7.49	9.32	13.61	11.17	29.80	28.61
1972	7.33	16.71	13.74	10.19	24.59	27.44
1973	7.59	18.07	13.22	9.57	24.74	26.81
1974	7.36	17.86	12.77	9.37	25.91	26.72
1975	8.16	16.49	12.10	10.03	26.26	26.97
1976	8.35	17.11	14.84	9.00	25.26	25.44
1977	8.35	17.25	15.41	9.45	23.67	25.87
1978	8.26	16.85	15.99	9.91	23.70	25.29
1979	9.04	16.83	14.34	10.05	24.22	25.51
1980	8.18	15.77	15.16	10.97	25.46	24.46
1981	7.57	14.39	18.35	9.29	27.53	22.87
1982	8.19	10.60	18.33	10.09	28.67	24.12
1983	7.48	14.24	19.67	8.71	26.92	22.98
1984	7.32	13.57	22.24	8.41	26.38	22.08

Source: National Science Board, *Science and Technology Indicators* 1987 (Washington: GPO).

TABLE 5.   U.S. Trade in High-Technology Products

	Exports	Imports	Balance
1970	24.5	10.0	14.5
1971	25.7	11.0	14.6
1972	25.6	13.6	12.0
1973	32.1	15.9	16.1
1974	39.8	18.2	21.7
1975	38.6	16.0	22.6
1976	40.6	20.9	19.7
1977	40.6	22.7	17.8
1978	48.2	28.1	20.1
1979	55.4	29.0	26.4
1980	63.8	32.7	31.1
1981	64.3	36.0	28.3
1982	58.1	34.5	23.6
1983	57.9	39.9	18.1
1984	60.7	55.1	5.6
1985	61.4	58.1	3.3
1986	63.3	65.5	−2.3

Source: National Science Board, *Science and Technology Indicators* 1987 (Washington: GPO).

middle 1960s and the middle 1980s, the U.S. export share held up well in aircraft, aircraft engines and turbines, computing and other office machinery, and in several classes of chemical products. The U.S. export share declined significantly in professional and scientific instruments and in telecommunications, and U.S. firms were routed in consumer electronics. The data on trends in national patenting show a pattern very similar to that of export shares in the different industries. By and large, U.S. export shares have held up in industries where U.S. patenting has held up and declined where patents by other countries have risen sharply relative to U.S. patenting.[15]

The definition of high-technology industries is somewhat arbitrary, being tied to R&D intensity. A number of industries whose product and process technologies are complex and sophisticated, and where technical advance has been significant, are excluded from the definition. Automobiles, machine tools, and other kinds of mechanical machinery are examples. By and large, U.S. export share and patenting have fallen significantly in these industries while Europe has done rather well. In contrast, the United States continues to

---

15. Soete (1981) has done extensive work exploring the relationship between national patterns of patenting and national patterns of exports. Patel and Pavitt (1987) have an analysis similar to the one here, and their conclusions are similar. Patel and Pavitt also stress the point that the customary definition of high technology industries is somewhat arbitrary.

be the export and patenting leader in many industries connected with agricultural products and others based on natural resources.

Thus, beneath the surface picture of a general convergence of productivity levels, there is a much more variegated picture. The United States continues to have an advantage in several of the most R&D-intensive industries and those connected to its natural resource advantage. It has declined in the industries—such as automobiles, consumer electronics, and steel making—where it had built an advantage since the late nineteenth century. The interesting question, of course, is how did this broad convergence come about? What are the factors behind it?

I would feature four different developments. First, the free flow of world trade eroded the market size advantages U.S.-based firms used to have. Second, technology became much more generally accessible to those willing to make the required investments and with the requisite skills; hence, technology became much less respecting of firm and national boundaries than had been the case earlier. Third, the other major industrial powers significantly increased the proportion of their work forces trained in science and engineering, and the proportion of their GNPs allocated to research and development, thus establishing strong indigenous competence both to exploit the now easier access to technology as well as to create new technology. Indeed, if one considers nonmilitary R&D as a fraction of GNP, a number of the other nations were spending more than the United States by 1980. This is important, because the fourth major factor behind the convergence was, in my view

TABLE 6.   External Patent Applications by Investors

	United States	Japan	West Germany	France	United Kingdom
1969	131,287	23,815	72,028	26,807	37,275
1970	123,724	26,568	70,137	24,422	33,463
1971	116,052	28,142	70,798	25,586	31,700
1972	119,984	25,760	70,636	27,887	33,324
1973	116,581	31,945	74,073	27,793	33,075
1974	102,711	33,463	67,335	22,821	28,968
1975	93,042	27,666	60,810	23,433	24,402
1976	93,356	29,340	58,310	23,356	24,185
1977	95,749	29,047	59,517	22,967	23,202
1978	85,352	30,182	53,657	22,073	21,286
1979	80,744	33,766	49,539	19,276	18,701
1980	79,078	35,945	48,650	18,839	17,400
1981	73,895	34,903	42,323	15,533	16,890
1982	65,335	36,901	36,985	15,498	16,144

Source: National Science Board, *Science Indicators* 1985 (Washington: GPO).

at least, a sharp decline in the importance of the spillover from military R&D into civilian technology.

The percentage of manufactured products exported and imported has grown rapidly since 1955 in all major industrial countries. Since that time, efficient companies producing attractive products increasingly have faced a world, rather than a national, market. Earlier I suggested that U.S. business was at a significant advantage during the late nineteenth century and the first half of the twentieth by being in the world's largest common market. By 1970, the world was, largely, a common market.

At the same time, business has become increasingly international. Earlier I observed that technologically progressive U.S. companies established branches in Europe even during the late nineteenth century. During the 1950s and 1960s, U.S. overseas direct investment surged dramatically. In *The American Challenge*, J. J. Servan Schreiber expressed concern that U.S. companies were taking over the European economy at least as much by investing there as by exporting. By the late 1960s, Europe was beginning to return the favor by establishing branches or buying plants in the United States. Recently, Japanese companies have become increasingly international.

The internationalization of business has greatly complicated the interpretation of international trade statistics. For example, a nontrivial share of the rising U.S. imports in high-technology industries represents imports from foreign subsidiaries of U.S.-owned companies (see Langlois 1987, chap. 4). It is interesting that, while the U.S. share of world manufacturing exports (low and middle tech as well as high tech) fell somewhat from the middle 1960s to the middle 1980s, the export share of U.S.-owned firms held up, with gains in exports from foreign branches matching declines in exports from U.S.-owned, U.S.-based plants (Lipsey and Kravis 1987).

The internationalization of trade and business has been part and parcel of the second postwar development that I want to highlight—the erosion of firm and national borders as factors obstructing or channeling access to technology.

Modern science has, from its beginnings, been an international activity. British and French scientists continued to communicate during the Napoleonic

TABLE 7. Proportion of Patent Grants by Country (in percentages)

	1965	1970	1975	1980	1982
United States	20.2	19.8	24.2	22.9	21.8
Japan	8.7	9.5	15.8	17.1	19.0
Germany	5.4	4.0	6.2	7.5	6.1
France	13.5	8.1	4.8	10.4	9.0
United Kingdom	10.9	12.6	13.8	8.8	11.1

Source: National Science Board, *Science Indicators* 1985 (Washington: GPO).

wars. The ethos of science always has stressed the public and international nature of scientific knowledge. Attempts by national governments to define and keep separate a particular national science have been condemned by the scientific community as antisocial and counterproductive, except in wartime. Even in wartime science has resisted nationalization.

In contrast, the notion that individuals and firms have proprietary rights in the inventions they develop has been accepted as appropriate for many centuries, and so, too, the idea that it is appropriate for a nation to try to gain advantage from the inventive work of its citizens. Nations have tried zealously to keep national technology within their borders and to prevent it from leaking away to foreigners. In many cases these efforts have proven futile, but they have always been accepted as legitimate. While, traditionally, technologists from different countries have communicated with each other and formed something of a worldwide community, until recently the notion that best-practice technology was approachable by any nation with requisite resources probably was not correct. While some analysts would stress that a company's technology was protected by patents, much more important, I would argue, were know-how and experience, which were kept largely privy. They were, to a considerable extent, hands-on capabilities not imparted in schools and books. The networks of technologists that exchanged information were, I believe, largely national.

The post–World War II era has seen increasing communication among technologists in different countries. One important reason I believe is that, in this postwar era, technologies have become much more like sciences than they used to be.[16] In contrast with an earlier era, a much larger portion of the generic knowledge relevant to a technology now is written down, published in journals, discussed at national and international meetings, and taught in schools of engineering and applied science.

And, of course, the internationalization of business is an important part of this story. It is not just that Europeans can learn what U.S. engineers learn by going to U.S. universities. Europeans can observe U.S. technology in operation in their home countries and can purchase operating U.S. firms. Companies such as IBM have industrial research laboratories in a number of different countries, each employing a mix of nationals. In turn, scientists from IBM and scientists from Phillips and Fujitsu meet at conferences and exchange papers.

I stress the presence of these international networks, involving highly

---

16. This impression is shared by many knowledgeable people. For example, Rosenberg (1982) presents a discussion similar to mine, as does Brooks (1985). Quantitative evidence for it is provided by the fact that in recent years patents cite scientific articles more than they used to, and more recent articles. See Narin (1988).

trained scientists and engineers employed in universities and in industry undertaking significant R&D efforts, to correct a widely held misconception—that aside from matters shielded by patents or secrecy, technology is basically a public good. Generic technological knowledge, of the sort taught in graduate school and written down in books and articles and exchanged among high-level professionals, indeed does have strong public good attributes. But even here, access is limited to those with the requisite training and, in many cases, only someone who is actually doing research in a particular field can understand the significance of publications in that field. And to take industrial advantage of generic knowledge or technology that is licensed from another company or, more generally, of understanding what another company has done and how generally requires significant inputs of trained scientists and engineers, often involving research and development aimed at tailoring what has been learned to specific relevant uses.[17]

By and large, the other major industrial nations have, with a lag, followed the United States in making those big investments in education and training and R&D. The convergence in scientists and engineers in R&D as a proportion of the work force and in R&D as a proportion of GNP (shown in tables 2 and 3) is an essential part of, and a complement to, the internationalization of technology. It is important to recognize that, while there has been a convergence among those nations with modern educational systems, strong internal scientific and engineering communities, and sophisticated industrial enterprises, nations without these attributes have tended to fall farther and farther behind the frontiers. While there are now few important technological secrets, it takes major investments to command a technology.

Military technology is something of an exception to what I have been describing. The major military powers, prominently the United States, continue to bend strong efforts to prevent military technology from leaking away to other, potentially hostile, nations or to nations who might serve as a conduit to the latter for military technology.

I would like to argue here that, while U.S. dominance of the frontiers of military technology gave us significant civilian technology advantages during the 1950s and 1960s, it buys us very little outside the military sphere today. Thus, in terms of access to technology that affects productivity in the manufacturing industry (broadly defined) and cutting edge competitiveness of most products sold on international markets, it does not hurt the Europeans or the Japanese that U.S. companies are engaged in military R&D to a much greater extent than they are, and that access to that technology is difficult if not closed.

---

17. Keith Pavitt has argued this point strongly, most sharply in his inaugural lecture (1987). So have I, in Nelson 1988 and Nelson and Winter 1982.

There are several reasons, I believe, why military R&D has had only a small spillover into civilian technology since the late 1960s.[18] Partly this is because the nature of military demands seems to have shifted away from areas that have both strong civil as well as military applications. At the same time, the percentage of military R&D going into generic research and experimental development has diminished significantly. Secondly, companies and governments have learned to invest in large-scale projects without a military crutch. Thus, since the late 1960s, the cutting edge of semiconductor and computer technology has been concerned with civilian applications, with funding provided primarily by companies or civil government agencies, and with the spillover occurring largely from civilian to military.

Let me summarize my argument. The U.S. economic and technological dominance in the quarter-century after World War II stemmed from two quite different sources and each eroded for different if related reasons. The general economic lead was one of long standing and had to do with many factors, the U.S. resource endowments and great size prominent among them, but also near universal secondary education, and a free-wheeling, competitive economic environment. The opening of world trade in the postwar era and enhanced schooling in other industrial nations took away that U.S. advantage, enabling companies in far smaller countries to operate at large scale if they were aggressive about exporting. The more recent lead in new, high-technology industries reflected unprecedented investments, both private and public, in R&D and higher education, investments that paid off handsomely. Yet the professionalization of technology that was entailed made it accessible to others if they made similar investments. The European nations and Japan did.[19]

---

18. My argument that the civil importance of military R&D has diminished greatly is shared by many observers, but not all. The division is reflected in the dispute a few years back about whether SDI would have a positive or negative effect. There is no convincing quantitative evidence that I know of to back my position. Most regression studies that distinguish between private and government funding of industrial R&D in equations fitted to industry growth of total factor productivity find little or no impact of government (it is mostly defense) funding. But both the data on productivity and the methodology used in these studies is suspect, and, in any case, my argument is that the spillover has fallen over the years, not that it was never high. I base my judgment largely on how I read technology histories in a number of industries, where the importance of government programs to civil technical progress was obvious a couple of decades ago, but very limited recently. See, e.g., the chapters on aircraft, semiconductors, and computers, in Nelson 1982.

19. Baumol (1986) proposes that convergence has been occurring since the turn of the century. I see the data as showing only modest, if any, convergence prior to 1950, in contrast with sharp convergence since then. Abramowitz (1986) also sees a sharp difference between the pre- and post-1950 periods in this respect.

Reprise

In the preceding section I concentrated on what I believe to be the most important feature of the economic performances of the major industrial powers since 1970—convergence. However, much of the public attention has been focused on two other phenomena—the striking performance of Japan and the sluggish economic growth of the United States since 1970.

A number of commentators have predicted that Japan will dominate the next quarter-century technologically and economically, as the United States did after World War II. They point to features of the Japanese political economy that are absent or present to a much weaker degree in the United States and Western Europe—for example, collaborative planning and networking mechanisms and a social and industrial culture that lead to an extraordinarily skilled, flexible, and dedicated work force—and propose that these are especially well suited to advancing and effectively using modern technologies, claiming that it will be very difficult for other societies to emulate them.[20] The term *new technoeconomic paradigm* has been coined by Carlotta Perez (1985 and 1987) to refer to the broad and deep economic and social changes that she argues must be made by nations in order to effectively exploit the new technologies coming into place.

Predictions that the United States will not only fall behind Japan but also below some of the more progressive Western European countries also have become fashionable. Some of these focus on old strengths turning into weaknesses, for example, the drag now exerted by our high level of military R&D, the fact that the U.S. rate of investment in new plant and equipment now is lower than that of our major competitors, and the failure of our primary and secondary education systems to equip our youngsters with the skills needed by the modern economy.[21] Some argue more generally that, precisely because the United States was so successful for so long, it will be difficult to change our institutions and adopt the new structures needed for success in a new era.

That may be. But I would like to argue that, in the present and foreseeable future, it is unlikely that any of the advanced industrial nations will forge and sustain the kind of lead that the United States had after World War II or fall back behind the pack any great distance. The great national differences that used to matter no longer are national. Relatively open markets will

---

20. See Freeman 1987 for an argument that the Japanese system works in fundamentally different, and more powerful, ways than the contemporary U.S. and European ones. Ergas (1987) also entertains this proposition.

21. For example, Kennedy suggests that U.S. military commitments will drag us down (1987). For more multidimensional positions, see, for example, Patel and Pavitt 1987; Pavitt and Patel 1988; Reich 1987.

continue to nullify most advantages that used to be associated with large home markets. Generic technological knowledge will be accessible to nations and to companies that make the needed investments in science and engineering capabilities.

This is not to argue that companies headquartered in certain nations will not have durable advantages in certain technologies and product fields over companies based in others. But well-trained engineers and scientists of whatever nationality will know roughly the same things and will communicate with each other. And a combination of overseas production operations and joint ventures will tend to blur the meaning of "national" technological capabilities. Nor is this to deny that there will not be noticeable and noticed differences across nations in their average levels of productivity and standard of living. But gaps like that between the United States and the rest of the advanced industrial nations that marked the early 1960s, I suspect, will never appear again, absent the aftereffects of war or other catastrophes.

I also believe it will not be so much organizational differences that will determine who is ahead and who behind in general levels of technology and living standards. Contrary to many other scholars, I am impressed by the ability of nations and firms to imitate each other in this regard. Rather, it will be investments in R&D and in physical and human capital, perhaps particularly the latter, that will be significant. I propose that it is differences in these that largely explain why Japan has recently done so well and the United States relatively poorly (for analysis, see Lipsey and Kravis 1987).

I do not want to downplay the importance of making adequate investments in R&D in enabling a firm or a nation to stay in the forefront of technological developments. I earlier stressed the argument that technology is only a public good for those who have made the investments to be able to tap in. But this is well known among the governments of the advanced industrial nations and by large firms, and I believe it a good bet that these will not let their rivals get far ahead in this regard.

On the other hand, the forces keeping national investments in new plant and equipment and worker skills in line with each other seem to me to be much weaker. And with broad technological competence roughly the same, it is these latter investments that will largely determine who is in the best position to develop and exploit technological developments and to improve relative national living standards. While technology no longer respects national boundaries, physical and human capital are relatively tightly bound to particular places. Workers do move across national borders, so does money and credit, and companies set up operations abroad as well as at home, but to a considerable extent physical investment within a nation and the worker skills at hand are determined by its own investments.

This essay has been about the factors behind the postwar U.S. dominance and the sources of convergence, not about the recent slow growth of the United States or about what needs to be done to improve the U.S. growth rate. But if the foregoing is right, a necessary condition, and possibly a sufficient one, is to pick up our old-fashioned investments in new equipment and plant and in people, where recently we have let other nations surpass us. But also, if I am right, this may be far easier to say, or even to get everyone saying, than actually to do.

REFERENCES

Abramovitz, M. 1986. "Catching Up, Forging Ahead, and Falling Behind." *Journal of Economic History* 46:385–400.

Baumol, W. 1986. "Productivity Growth, Convergence, and Welfare." *American Economic Review* 76:1072–85.

Baxter, J. 1946. *Scientists Against Time.* Boston: Little, Brown.

Beer, J. 1959. *The Emergence of the German Dye Industry.* Urbana: University of Illinois Press.

Binswanger, H., and V. Ruttan. 1978. *Induced Innovation: Technology, Institutions and Development.* Baltimore: Johns Hopkins University Press.

Brooks, H. 1985. "Technology as a Factor in U.S. Competitiveness." In *U.S. Competitiveness in the World Economy,* ed. G. Lodge and B. Scott. Boston: Harvard Business School Press.

Bush, V. 1945. *Science, the Endless Frontier.* Washington, D.C.: U.S. Government Printing Office.

Chandler, A. D. 1977. *The Visible Hand: The Managerial Revolution in American Business.* Cambridge, Mass.: Harvard University Press.

Cohen, I. B. 1976. "Science and the Growth of the American Republic." *Review of Politics* 38:359–98.

Denison, E., with J. Poullier. 1967. *Why Growth Rates Differ.* Washington, D.C.: Brookings Institution.

Ergas, H. 1987. "Does Technology Policy Matter." In *Technology and Global Industry: Companies and Nations in the World,* ed. B. Guile and H. Brooks. Washington, D.C.: National Academy Press.

Flamm, K. 1987. *Targeting the Computer.* Washington, D.C.: Brookings Institution.

Freeman, C. 1982. *The Economics of Industrial Innovation.* London: Penguin.

Freeman, C. 1987. *Technology Policy and Economic Performance: Lessons from Japan.* London: Pinter.

Habakkuk, H. J. 1962. *American and British Technology in the Nineteenth Century.* Cambridge: Cambridge University Press.

Hounshell, D. 1984. *From the American System to Mass Production, 1800–1932.* Baltimore: Johns Hopkins University Press.

Kennedy, P. 1987. *The Rise and Fall of Great Powers.* New York: Random House.

Kranzberg, M., ed. 1986. *Technological Education—Technological Style.* San Francisco: San Francisco Press.

Langlois, R. 1987. *Microelectronics: An Industry in Transition*. New York: Center for Science and Technology Policy.

Lazonick, W. 1986. "Strategy, Structure, and Management Development in the United States and Britain." In *Development of Managerial Enterprise*, ed. K. Kobyashi and H. Morikawa. Tokyo: University of Tokyo Press.

Lazonick, W. 1988. "Business Organization and Competitive Advantage: Capitalist Transformations in the Twentieth Century." Columbia University. Mimeo.

Lipsey, R., and J. Kravis. 1986. *The Competitiveness and Comparative Advantage of U.S. Multinationals*. NBER Working Paper no. 2051. Cambridge, Mass.: National Bureau of Economics Research.

Lipsey, R. and J. Kravis. 1987. *Is the U.S. a Spendthrift Nation?* NBER Working Paper no. 2274. Cambridge, Mass.: National Bureau of Economic Research.

Maddison, A. 1982. *Phases of Capitalist Development*. Oxford: Oxford University Press.

Malerba, F. 1985. *The Semiconductor Business: The Economics of Rapid Growth and Decline*. Madison: University of Wisconsin Press.

Mowery, D. 1983. "The Relationship Between Intrafirm and Contractual Forms of Industrial Research in American Manufacturing: 1900–1940." *Explorations in Economic History* 20:351–74.

Narin, F. 1988. "Memo re: Technology/Science Linkages." Computer Horizons, Inc.

Nelson, R., ed. 1982. *Government and Technical Progress, A Cross-Industry Analysis*. New York: Pergamon Press.

Nelson, R. 1988. "Institutions Supporting Technical Advance in U.S. Industry." In *Technical Change and Economic Theory*, ed. G. Dosi, C. Freeman, R. Nelson, G. Silverberg, and L. Soete. London: Pinter.

Nelson, R., and S. Winter. 1982. *An Evolutionary Theory of Economic Change*. Cambridge, Mass.: Harvard University Press.

Noble, D. 1977. *America by Design*. Oxford: Oxford University Press.

Patel, P., and K. Pavitt. 1987. "Is Western Europe Losing the Technological Race?" *Research Policy* 16:59–85.

Pavitt, K. 1987. "On the Nature of Technology." Inaugural lecture. University of Sussex. Typescript.

Pavitt, K., and P. Patel. 1988. *The International Distribution and Determinants of Technological Activities*. DRC Discussion Paper no. 59. Sussex: SPRU.

Perez, C. 1985. "Microelectronics, Long Waves, and World Structural Change." *World Development* 13:441–63.

Perez, C. 1987. "The New Technologies: An Integrated View." SPRU Discussion Paper. University of Sussex. Typescript.

Reich, L. 1985. *The Making of American Industrial Research*. Cambridge: Cambridge University Press.

Reich, R. 1987. *Tales of A New America*. New York: Times Books.

Rosenberg, N. 1972. *Technology and American Economic Growth*. New York: Harper Torchbooks.

Rosenberg, N. 1982. "How Exogenous is Science?" In *Inside the Black Box*. Cambridge: Cambridge University Press.

Rosenberg, N. 1985. "The Commercial Exploitation of Science by American Industry." In *The Uneasy Alliance: Managing the Productivity-Technology Dilemma*, ed. K. Clark, R. Hayes, and C. Lorenz. Boston: Harvard Business School Press.

Servan Schreiber, J. J. 1968. *The American Challenge*. New York: Atheneum Press.

Soete, L. 1981. "A General Test of Technological Gap Trade Theory." *Weltwirtschaft Archive* 117:638–60.

Thackray, A. 1982. *University-Industry Connections and Chemical Research: A Historical Perspective on University-Industry Research Relationships*. Washington, D.C.: National Science Board.

Tocqueville, A. de [1835] 1954. *Democracy in America*. New York: Vintage Books.

Wolff, E. 1987. "Capital Formation and Long-Term Productivity Growth: A Comparison of Seven Countries." C. V. Starr Center Paper, Department of Economics, New York University. Typescript.

Commentary

Bo Carlsson

It is a distinct honor to be asked to comment on the interesting and stimulating essay by Richard Nelson. The main thrust of Nelson's argument is the following: (1) the U.S. technological dominance in the 1950s and 1960s was due to a long-standing lead in mass production and a newly acquired lead (through industrial R&D and university training of scientists and engineers) in high technology; (2) for different but related reasons, the U.S. dominance in each of these areas disappeared during the 1970s and 1980s, in a process of international convergence; and (3) because of the very nature of the forces leading to technological convergence, it is unlikely that any nation in the future will acquire the kind of dominance the United States achieved after World War II.

My comments deal with three issues, namely (1) whether the evidence presented really supports the convergence hypothesis; (2) the problem of using R&D spending as a performance indicator; and (3) the claim that the spillover effects of military R&D have diminished in the 1980s relative to earlier periods.

Nelson uses eight indicators to support his convergence argument. Of these, three do indeed indicate convergence: GDP per person employed, scientists and engineers engaged in R&D per 10,000 workers, and national expenditures for R&D as a percentage of GNP. In each of these, the U.S. lead is shown to be continually diminishing. However, other indicators suggest a different development, namely maintained U.S. performance at a high level with Japan catching up but European countries showing little improvement (export shares of high technology products, country shares of patents granted, and proportion of each generation entering higher education). One indicator shows Japan increasing the number of external patent applications by investors while the number was halved in the United States and European countries.

These observations raise the question of what it is we are in fact observing—a process of convergence or something else? The evidence presented by Nelson suggests that an alternative interpretation may be equally plausible, namely that what is happening is that Japan is catching up with the

United States while Europe lags behind, leaving the United States and Japan in a dual leadership position.

Second, Nelson stresses the importance of R&D and makes a strong case for it. Nevertheless, it is important to keep in mind that R&D expenditures represent *inputs,* not output. It is important to consider not only the level of R&D spending but also its effectiveness. Apparently, the Japanese have made effective use of R&D, even though their own R&D spending levels have not been particularly high until quite recently: they have taken advantage of the public good aspect (spillover) of R&D conducted (and paid for) elsewhere.

This points to an important issue that, until recently, has been almost totally ignored in economics, namely the role and nature of *economic competence,* the ability to generate and take advantage of economic opportunities. Pavel Pelikan (1988 and 1989) has pointed out that economic competence is a scarce and unevenly distributed resource; the theoretical implications of this are only now beginning to be explored. The scarcity (bounded rationality) aspect has been well understood for a long time (not least by Nelson and Winter [1982]), but the unevenness of the distribution, how it is determined, and how it might be influenced, is still largely unexplored. The fact that economic competence is partly tacit and inherently difficult to transfer suggests one reason that R&D spending and economic performance are not always closely correlated. Simply put, the United States appears good at generating economic opportunities via R&D, while Japan is good at taking advantage of such opportunities (and getting better and better at generating them as well).

Third, Nelson argues that the spillover from military R&D has been much smaller in the last two decades than earlier. The implicit argument is that, since the United States has spent less on nondefense R&D than Germany and Japan since at least the early 1970s (while it has spent at least as much as these countries on total R&D), the diminishing spillover is partly to blame for the disappearance of the U.S. technological lead. I find this argument plausible—certainly Nelson is not alone in making the claim—although not well supported or documented by evidence. While Nelson's argument would be strengthened by the presentation of such evidence, I would like to conclude by providing an example that not only supports Nelson's claim but actually goes beyond it: the role of the U.S. military in the development of machine tools.

As I have shown elsewhere (Carlsson 1984 and 1989; Carlsson and Jacobsson 1990), U.S. military needs during World War II led to the buildup of a huge capacity for the mass production of military vehicles (tanks, trucks, airplanes, and ships) that could later be converted to civilian production. After the war, the shift of military needs from mass produced items to highly sophisticated and specialized products (aircraft and space equipment) with few, if any, civilian applications, led the U.S. machine tool industry to specialize in numerically controlled machines that were too expensive and specialized for civilian use. When, in the mid-1970s, Japanese firms introduced cheap, versatile numerically controlled machine tools geared to broad industrial use, U.S. machine tool firms were unable to respond. Thus, defense needs led the U.S. machine tool industry to a position of technological leadership that served portions of the U.S. manufacturing industry well for a couple of decades but that also, unfortunately, led to subsequent economic failure, with grave consequences for the large majority of civilian users of machine tools in the United States.

REFERENCES

Carlsson, Bo. 1984. "The Development and Use of Machine Tools in Historical Perspective." *Journal of Economic Behavior and Organization* 5:91–114.

Carlsson, Bo. 1989. "Small-Scale Industry at a Crossroads: U.S. Machine Tools in Global Perspective." *Small Business Economics* 1:245–61.

Carlsson, Bo, and Staffan Jacobsson. 1990. "What Makes the Automation Industry Strategic?" Working paper. Case Western Reserve University and Chalmers University of Technology. Typescript.

Nelson, Richard R., and Sidney G. Winter. 1982. *An Evolutionary Theory of Economic Change.* Cambridge, Mass.: Harvard University Press.

Pelikan, Pavel. 1988. "Can the Imperfect Innovation Systems of Capitalism Be Outperformed?" In *Technical Change and Economic Theory,* ed. G. Dosi, et al. London: Pinter.

Pelikan, Pavel. 1989. "Evolution, Economic Competence, and the Market for Corporate Control." *Journal of Economic Behavior and Organization* 12:279–303.

Capitalism, Socialism, and Democracy and Large-Scale Firms

Paolo Sylos-Labini

The Economies of Scale and the Process of Concentration

"Can capitalism survive? No. I do not think it can." "Can socialism work? Of course it can." The unifying argument worked out by Schumpeter to justify the drastic answers to both questions that we find as the opening words of parts 2 and 3 of *Capitalism, Socialism, and Democracy* is that modern capitalism is characterized by a process of concentration that is related to the increasing relevance of static and dynamic economies of scale in the most important activities—most important from the point of view of economic development. If we consider the trends prevailing between the last decades of the past century and the first half of this century, Schumpeter was not wrong; in more recent times, however, those trends have changed. On the other hand, Schumpeter, as well as several other economists, neglected the essential connections between small and large firms.

The Capacity for Innovating in Centrally Planned Economies

For some time I have been wondering why the major theorist of innovation did not consider what today clearly appears to be the fatal weakness of centrally planned economies, that is, their limited capacity for innovation. The answer can be found, I think, in the following statements, which justify the above argument concerning the process of concentration.

> Innovation itself is being reduced to routine. Technological progress is increasingly becoming the business of teams of trained specialists who turn out what is required and make it work in predictable ways. (Schumpeter 1942, 132)

Since capitalist enterprise, by its very achievements, tends to automatize progress, we conclude that it tends to make itself superfluous—to break to pieces under the pressure of its own success. The perfectly bureaucratic giant industrial unit not only ousts the small- or medium-sized firm and "expropriates" its owners, but in the end it also ousts the entrepreneur and expropriates the bourgeoisie as a class which in the process stands to lose not only its income but also, what is infinitely more important, its function. (134)

This thesis is strictly connected with—and to a large extent forms the basis of—the well-known Schumpeterian view of the emergence and the spread of the atmosphere of hostility to capitalism, originating from its very achievements. Indeed, capitalism is supposed to become more and more vulnerable owing to the declining relevance, in a world increasingly dominated by big concerns, of individual entrepreneurship.

The whole of our arguments might be put in a nutshell by saying that socialization means a stride beyond big business on the way that has been chalked out by it or, what amounts to the same thing, the socialist management may conceivably prove superior to big-business capitalism as big-business capitalism has proved to be to the kind of competitive capitalism of which the English industry of a hundred years ago was the prototype. (195–96)

The last quotation shows that the intellectual glamour of "cette damnée dialectique hégelienne"—as a French philosopher put it—has had its share of responsibility in leading Schumpeter into a logical trap.

It is fitting to compare the last of the quotations from Schumpeter with the following statement to be found in Marshall's *Industry and Trade* (1923, 176–77).

Marx and his followers resolved to be practical, and argued that history showed a steadily hastening growth of large business and of mechanical administration by vast joint-stock companies, and they deduced the fatalistic conclusion that this tendency is irresistible; and must fulfill its destiny by making the whole state into one large joint-stock company in which everyone would be a shareholder.

Clearly, Marshall considered that trend unlikely; it should be pointed out that Marshall was much nearer to the truth than Schumpeter. I must say that years ago I was nearer to Schumpeter's than to Marshall's position; when I realized that I was wrong, I made public self-criticism on several occasions (Sylos-Labini 1980; 1983, 178–80; 1984, chap. 2; 1986, 91).

A good number of economists have maintained that collectivist economic planning cannot work, or can only work at very high costs, because without the market of the means of production a rational calculation is not possible (e.g., Hayek 1935), since the planners in their boardroom have to solve millions of equations, a practically impossible task. Such an objection is not insuperable, however, both because with modern computers those calculations are no more impossible and because, if the methods of production remain unchanged, the central planning board would be able, by degrees, to solve, with acceptable approximation, all the unknowns. The crucial objection to central planning is the very scarce capacity for innovation in such a system; it is the extremely limited space that it can offer, not so much to the occasions for scientists and technicians as such, as to the possibilities of devising and applying new methods or of devising and launching new products. Even if the planning board were endowed with the most sophisticated computers and staffed by geniuses, it could not predetermine all the great and small process and product innovations that can be introduced—at a risk but with the possibility of pecuniary and nonpecuniary gains—when all subjects—capitalists, managers, and workers—are free to experiment and take initiative. A considerable literature has been developed on the possibility of solving the millions of equations in a centrally planned economy by working out precise managerial rules capable of imitating the functioning of the market and of giving rise to a rational system of prices—with the idea that such a set of rules could produce the results of a perfectly competitive system that nowadays cannot be reached spontaneously even in capitalist economies, since perfect competition has largely disappeared. But the essential point is not the optimal allocation of resources through rational prices; it is, on the contrary, that of getting a system capable of introducing all sorts of innovations and of growing at a rapid rate.

The evidence that centrally planned economies have a very limited capacity for innovation is scant and indirect but unambiguous. In fact, patents exported by the Soviet Union and by Eastern European countries are very few, whereas the hunger in those countries for Western patents and innovations is well known to everyone. The composition of the exports of those countries is evidence of their very low technological development—the bulk of those exports to Western countries and to Japan is composed of raw materials and sources of energy. As for the literature, very little is known to me concerning the issue of innovations in centrally planned economies. One of the few authors I know is Winiecki, who discusses the reasons quality of goods and innovations are very serious problems in centrally planned. economies

(Winiecki 1986). It is important to point out that not only Russia, which was a very backward country at the beginning of its socialist experience, but also countries such as Czechoslovakia and Eastern Germany, which were relatively advanced, have all shown the same very limited capacity for innovation.

If we conceive of innovation in a broad sense and include all those anonymous improvements introduced in agriculture by the farmers themselves when they own their land, then we come to realize how important private ownership of the means of production is, especially for agricultural development. Such improvements are of no scientific importance and are of infinitesimal practical value when taken in isolation, but become very relevant when considered together and in the long run. It is true, however, that the most important innovations are the result of scientific inventions and take place, with few exceptions, in industry; the other sectors—agriculture and private services—as a rule can increase their productivity or produce new products thanks to machinery and appliances supplied by industry.

The Competition that Counts

According to Schumpeter, under conditions of competitive capitalism, inventions as a rule are the products of individual inventors and innovations are carried out by small firms; under conditions of big business—or "trustified"—capitalism, inventions are more and more often the product of research bureaus of large-scale firms and innovations, as a rule, are carried out by the same firms. This does not mean that competition fades away: what tends to disappear, outside agriculture, is atomistic competition. Instead, the competition that counts becomes even more powerful than in the past; it is "the competition from the new commodity, the new source of supply, the new type of organization (the largest scale unit of control for instance)" (Schumpeter 1942, 84). According to Schumpeter, the innovating firm can be large or small, but, given the superiority of the former with respect to financial means and to the possibility of organizing research bureaus, the competition that counts is more and more brought about by large concerns—small firms are more and more pushed to the margin.

Does the Schumpeterian concept correspond to reality? The answer is yes, but only in part, since it seriously underrates the role of small firms. After the work by Schumpeter, a large literature has developed that tends to show the importance of small firms in the process of innovation. Probably the most important point has remained submerged throughout a series of considerations in which small firms are contrasted in their merits and disadvantages with large concerns as if they were located in two different precincts; the most important point is concerned with the function that small firms can perform in the preparation of innovations that are developed and fully exploited by large concerns. "The sequential character of modern research and development also makes it possible for small enterprises to play a creative role in major technological achievements" (Scherer 1980, 416).

If we succeed in getting rid of the "statical bias" permeating most contemporary economic theory and try to conceive of economic activities from the standpoint of a dynamic vertical integration, we realize that the sequential character of technical and organizational change conditions the whole process of growth, in which small and large firms play a complementary role. To put it in different terms: sometimes small firms feed certain processes of innovation subsequently taken up and developed by large firms, as the small firms of Silicon Valley and the giants of the electronic industry clearly illustrate. I became aware of such sequences on the occasion of a field study of the North American petroleum industry that I carried out with a jurist (G. Guarino) on behalf of the Italian prime minister of the time (1955), after oil and gas deposits were discovered in Italy and the government had to prepare an oil law. In the report based on that study (Sylos Labini and Guarino 1956, 32), we wrote: "Lucky individual prospectors can become regular small oil producers—the number of such producers is relatively great; more often, however, owing to the difficulties in finding commercial outlets, difficulties that are particularly serious for small firms, they prefer to hand their oil concessions over to bigger firms either against bonuses or in exchange for overriding royalties."

Innovations also include the discovery of mineral deposits, so that this sequence correctly describes a case of a dynamic vertical integration between small and large units. If we recognize the importance and the ubiquity of this phenomenon, we have to conclude that high and even increasing concentration ratios do not express a tendency toward "a world of monopolies" but acquire a completely different meaning, since small firms can intensify the competition that counts in ways that are largely independent of size.

To be sure, there is a great variety of small firms. There are those that are research oriented; at the opposite pole we find more traditional small firms, those that do not grow and often decline or even disappear owing to the competition of more dynamic firms. Others are simply satellites of large firms; in certain cases, the former play a collateral role in innovations carried out by the latter. On the other hand, we find small firms that compete successfully with large firms, though this often occurs in differentiated markets, small firms being more able than large ones to meet specific needs of consumers and of producers. Thus, when we examine the relationships between small and large firms we find vertical (sequential) and horizontal cooperation as well as competition; we also find areas of the economy where there is neither cooperation nor competition, at least directly. In fact, many small firms succeed by growing in niches created by the increasing differentiation of tastes that, in their turn, are the consequence of increasing per capita incomes. On the other hand, differentiated oligopoly is often the result of product innovations carried out by large and small firms. In general, the development of electronic appliances has opened up new economic space to small firms, both as producers and as users. At the same time, the growth of small firms in certain countries, such as Italy, has been fostered by those laws and guarantees that have sharply reduced flexibility in the administration of the labor force in relatively large firms, where the influence of trade unions is stronger; the growth of small firms of this type, however, has little to do with innovation.

All considered, the weight of small firms in the economy, as measured by total employment, is now increasing (Sylos-Labini 1986, 221, 234), whereas until about two decades ago it was declining in all industrialized countries, at least in relative terms. It seems clear, in any case, that small firms that are research oriented (occasionally in the United States founded and managed by university professors) play a more important role in the process of innovation than in the past. It is not simply a curiosity that a tiny firm in Piedmont produces highly sophisticated robots and sells them to Fiat and to certain large Japanese firms—the pygmy supplying the giants.

From an analytical standpoint, in industry and services, small firms do not operate in conditions of pure competition as a rule, since all sorts of imperfections characterize their markets. In fact, if we exclude agriculture, small firms and competition normally do not go together today. Market imperfections, however, play different roles in the process of growth, depending on the capacity of managers, on the types of industries, and on kinds of innovations. In certain cases they simply serve to protect above-normal profits—or sheer inefficiency and laziness. In other cases they serve, indeed, to protect above-normal profits, not as an end in itself but as a means to innovate more efficiently and to grow more rapidly. The latter cases can apply to small firms that are research oriented. In fact, when a small firm produces a new product—which can be an intermediate product to be used in a much longer production process—clearly, at least for a period, it operates in a monopolistic position—as Schumpeter not only recognized but emphasized in both *Capitalism, Socialism, and Democracy* and in *Business Cycles*. And if, as is often the case, the new product directly competes with a relatively small number of other products that are similar but not identical, we can say that the firm operates in conditions of differentiated oligopoly—the other two kinds of oligopoly being characterized by high concentration and homogeneous products (concentrated oligopoly) and by concentration and product differentiation (mixed oligopoly).

When referring to "trustified" capitalism, Schumpeter neglects the role of small firms operating in conditions of differentiated oligopoly. In fact, both large and small firms play an essential role in the process of innovation today; large firms will be all the more dynamic when they have to compete with dynamic small firms or, vice versa, when they can rely on the cooperation of a good number of small firms, whose development is strictly related to the diffusion of advanced education. If this is so, what is to be recommended is not a policy favoring large size per se (e.g., through mergers; see Adams and Brock 1988), but a policy encouraging basic research inside and outside universities and applied research in all firms, independent of size, as well as a policy favoring the entry of new firms in expanding markets and the cooperation between large and small firms in innovating activities.

It is true that, in several cases, certain innovations have been completely developed by small firms; it is also true that large firms sometimes buy the patents of inventions produced by independent inventors or small firms not to develop them but to sterilize them, at least for a period. Large firms usually adopt this tactic when the innovations made possible by those inventions endanger the market for goods that they already produce. On the other hand, large firms that buy up and incorporate small firms can acquire new dynamism when such firms have successfully carried out profitable innovations but are unable to develop them beyond a certain point. Such small firms disappear and large firms become even larger and more dynamic. At the opposite side, some innovating small firms are born from large ones through the initiative of technicians or researchers who were working in large firms and decided to leave them to become self-employed "when the large firms in which they were working had denied the validity, or the immediate practical utility, of their inventions" (Berardi 1967).

The relationships between large and small firms, then, give rise to a variety of consequences, some positive, others negative. From what I have been able to see, however, the algebraic sum seems to be decidedly positive, especially after the appearance of electronic industry, in which intelligence is the most important raw material and in which the economies of scale are not as relevant as in most mature industries. In my view, the interaction between the two categories of firms is so important that, in contemporary "trustified" capitalism, without it the bureaucratization of big concerns would have spread and the process of growth would have progressively slowed down. In fact, the perfectly bureaucratic giant industrial unit, taken by itself, tends not toward innovation, but toward routine activities and, thus, toward stagnation.

No doubt Schumpeter overrated the role of large firms and their research institutes and ignored the great contributions made by university research institutes. More seriously, Schumpeter underrated the function of small firms and did not see the dynamic role that they can play in connection with large firms. Yet his concept of the process of concentration is not to be completely discarded, first, because, although it is true that the relative importance of large-scale firms is decreasing, their absolute importance is still great and, in certain sectors, still increasing, and, second, because I believe that Schumpeter's concept of the competition that counts can profitably be generalized and extended to small, dynamic firms that operate in conditions of differentiated oligopoly. Such an extension is by no means a secondary question, since, by working it out systematically, we can, on the one hand, improve and enlarge the interpretative power of the Schumpeterian analysis of contemporary capitalism and, on the other hand, we can correct the judgment that Schumpeter gave on the functioning of a centrally planned economy, a judgment that appears to be far too favorable in spite of his warning that his remarks "refer exclusively to the logic of blueprints."

Economies of Scale, Small Firms, and Innovations in a Centrally Planned Economy

The question of small firms and that of the capacity for innovation in a centrally planned economy are strictly connected. A distinction, however, is to be made with reference to the Russian experience.

The indices of industrial output of the Soviet Union in a first stage, say, until the 1950s and 1960s and apart from the tragic intermezzo of World War II, were showing rapid growth. This seemed to give support to the view that socialist economies not only could work but could work well—putting aside the vital questions of freedom and democracy. In my interpretation, the Gosplan had to face two main problems during that period: to build certain fundamental public works and to develop a number of basic industries such as electricity, steel, coal, and petroleum—all industries in which the economies of scale had already been achieved and that were important not only for economic growth but also for rearmament. In addition, Barone's minister of production was in a position to purchase in ready-made production units for such industries from Western countries. (This possibility rendered superfluous the long evolution that had allowed the development of large-scale units in Western countries.)

In the Soviet Union, the difficulties became increasingly serious as soon as the industrial basis was created and it was necessary to take care of a variety of mechanical and light industries. Whereas in heavy industry the economies of scale predominate and the centrally planned economy can also have some advantages over the market economy from the point of view of innovation (which to a good extent can be imported and easily applied in the large units), this is not the case with light industry, where great size is not predominant and where the role of dynamic, small firms appears to be essential, especially in that group of industries that has taken the lead in many processes of innovation, that is, electronics. In the last two or three decades, after a number of attempts that failed at decentralizing many activities and of giving more discretionary power to managers, the difficulties rose very rapidly and the Soviet economy entered a period of general crisis. (Concentrating economic, organizational, and scientific efforts on military production, the Soviet Union has succeeded, at least for a period, in not losing ground in this sector with respect to the United States and other Western countries. But even this sector—after the latest developments in electronics, which, especially in the United States, owe much to the contribution of small firms—has shown increasing signs of weakness.)

General Remarks

Schumpeter was a notorious conservative and could not be suspected of advocating Communism or socialism—although, so it seems, such an indictment was made by one of his critics. In spite of his conservatism, however, the fact remained that his love for paradoxes and his passion "d'épater les épateurs des bourgeois" led him to express a great admiration for Marx—with whom he shared, all qualifications notwithstanding, the thesis of the concentration process—and to present a very favorable judgment of the potentialities of a centrally planned economy, a judgment that, in the light of relatively recent events (well before Gorbachev), appears to have been radically wrong.

Paul Sweezy, who was a pupil of Schumpeter, became a Marxist; Richard Goodwin from one side and Shigeto Tsuru from the other were strongly influenced by Marx *via* Schumpeter. The fact that the economist who maintained that socialism could work economically even better than capitalism was a conservative made his thesis particularly persuasive. All this created, I think, a rather widespread mistrust toward Schumpeter that led several economists to refuse to accept not only his views on centrally planned economies but also some of his very fertile theses, such as the one of the competition that counts. More generally, I think that, in spite of the recent revival of interest in Schumpeter's theoretical constructions, the influence of such constructs is still limited with respect to its relevance. I think that one of the reasons of this state of affairs is Schumpeter's judgment on the functioning of a centrally planned economy, a judgment that is related to his thesis of the concentration process, considered as an overall and irresistible process. If we get rid of this thesis on the analytical plane, then we can remove an important obstacle to a much more vigorous revival of the Schumpeterian construct, thus contributing gradually to the modification of the incredible situation of the economic theory, where the static approach is still the prevailing one, just in an epoch in which all sorts of technological and organizational innovations change and even upset economic life almost without interruption.

REFERENCES

Adams, W., and James W. Brock. 1988. "The Bigness Mystique and the Merger Policy Debate: An International Perspective." *Northwestern Journal of International Law and Business* 2:1–48.

Berardi, Gianfranco. 1967. "Concentrazione 'conglomerate business' e fusioni nell'industria nord-americana." *Rivista di politica economica.*

Hayek, Frederik A. von, ed. 1935. *Collectivist Economic Planning.* London: Routledge and Sons.

Marshall, Alfred. 1923. *Industry and Trade.* London: Macmillan.

Scherer, Frederic M. 1980. *Industrial Market Structure and Economic Performance.* Chicago: Rand McNally.

Schumpeter, Joseph A. 1939. *Business Cycles.* New York: McGraw-Hill.

Schumpeter, Joseph A. 1942. *Capitalism, Socialism, and Democracy.* New York: Harper.

Sylos-Labini, Paolo. 1980. *Preface* to the Brazilian edition of *Oligopoly and Technical Progress,* by Joseph A. Schumpeter. Sao Paulo: Forense Universitaria.

Sylos-Labini, Paolo. 1983. *Il sottosviluppo e l'economia contemporanea.* Roma-Bari: Laterza.

Sylos-Labini, Paolo. 1984. *The Forces of Economic Growth and Decline.* Cambridge, Mass.: MIT Press.

Sylos-Labini, Paolo. 1986. *The classi sociali negli anni '80.* Roma-Bari: Laterza.

Sylos-Labini, Paolo, and Giuseppe Guarino. 1956. *L'industria petrolifera negli Stati Uniti, nel Canada e nel Messico.* Milan: Giuffre.

Winiecki, Jan. 1986. "Distorted macroeconomics of Central Planning." *Banca Nazionale del Lavoro Quarterly Review* 157 (June): 197–224.

Specialization and Size of Technological Activities in Industrial Countries: The Analysis of Patent Data

Daniele Archibugi and Mario Pianta

1. Introduction

In recent years, several studies have addressed the patterns of specialization of industrial countries. For variables such as productivity, production, trade, and patents,[1] the international sectoral distribution across industries or technologies has been analyzed, in an attempt to identify the areas of strength and weakness of each country. Analyses over time have reported for many countries and sectors some evidence of a growing specialization, but conclusive evidence is lacking on the direction taken by this process; a key question is whether industrial countries are expanding their productive and technological activities in the same fields or in different areas, and what impact this has on their overall specialization patterns.

At the same time, a growing convergence among industrial countries has been documented at the aggregate level in terms of production, productivity, and resources devoted to technology (OECD 1988 and 1989). Reconciling the evidence of convergence at the aggregate level with the signs of specialization at the sectoral level is an additional issue to be addressed.

The implications of these processes are important for national technology policy. As technological knowledge becomes more diversified and highly

This paper is part of a research project on the scientific and technological specialization of advanced countries jointly financed by the Commission of European Communities, D.G. XII: Science, Research and Development, Service Evaluation, and the Italian National Research Council. We are grateful to Patrizia Principessa and Roberto Simonetti for research assistance and to Giorgio Sirilli for valuable comments.

This essay is based on an article that appeared in *Research Policy* 20 (1991).

1. See, among others, a study of productivity by Dollar and Wolff 1988; trade data are examined in Dollar and Wolff 1989; for patenting, see Soete 1987; and Patel and Pavitt 1987. See also Gerstenberger 1989.

specific to firms, industries, and countries,[2] to what extent can a country try to cover all fields, or should it concentrate its efforts in few areas where it is more specialized? In more specific terms, what is the trade-off between the extent of a country's presence in all sectors of technological activity and its ability to be internationally competitive in each of them?

In such a context, this essay focuses on the sectoral specialization of technological activities in advanced countries as described by patent indicators. Using a variety of data bases, we will focus on two issues.

1. The profiles of sectoral specialization in the technological activity of advanced countries.
2. The regularities in the patterns of specialization across countries in relation to the size of their technological activities.

In section 2, the trends of the resources devoted to science and technology (S&T) will be documented. While R&D expenditure has increased substantially, patents in external markets are growing at a faster rate, suggesting a globalization in firms' strategies of appropriating the results of their technological efforts.

Our research also has some implications for assessing the value of patenting as an internationally comparable technology indicator. Patenting in the United States is widely used as a base for international comparisons, but we will show that considerable differences exist among the specialization profiles resulting from domestic and foreign patenting. In section 3, patent data in the United States, at the European Patent Office, and in other countries will be considered, broken down according to two different sectoral classifications (IPC and SIC).

In section 4 we will examine the degree of specialization of advanced countries, testing how different the country profiles of technological specialization measured by patents are from the world sectoral distribution of technological activities. The relationship between the degree of specialization and the size of national technological activities will then be explored in section 5.

Throughout this essay, countries will be the unit of analysis, and technological specialization will refer to all activities performed by firms located within national borders. The presence of foreign-owned firms and of affiliates in other countries is not considered in our data. Obviously, cross-border technological activities by multinational firms are of great importance in shaping the patterns of specialization, and they will be taken into account in

---

2. Pavitt (1988) and Cantwell (1989) have already examined cross-country differences in technological accumulation.

the interpretation of the results, which also consider the work by other research teams that provide a useful complement to our analysis (see, e.g., Cantwell and Hodson 1990; Patel and Pavitt 1990).

However, the use of national data does have relevance. First, it is widely accepted that "national systems of innovation" have emerged with individual countries characterized by specific patterns of technological accumulation, industrial structure, and innovative resources, and by a unique set of institutions supporting and regulating technological change.[3] The technological strengths of a country represent a key influence for the locational choices by large firms in their R&D strategy; national patterns of sectoral specialization are both the result and a determinant of the technological strategies of multinational firms.

Second, while capital and firms are highly mobile across borders, many factors contributing to innovative activities, including labor, are much more country specific and can be measured by national indicators. Furthermore, it is at the national level that major technology policy decisions are made, thus shaping the conditions for firms' activities.

2. The Appropriability of Innovations in International Markets

Resources devoted to science and technology (S&T) have dramatically increased over the 1980s, although internationally comparable data on the total amount of resources devoted to S&T are not yet available. However, a proxy of the S&T effort is represented by the resources devoted to formal R&D. Column 1 of table 1 shows that R&D resources have considerably increased in almost all OECD member countries over the period.[4]

The greater the resources devoted by each country to S&T, the more we would expect that it would try to appropriate the benefits in several markets, and patents are one of the methods used by firms to protect their innovations. While domestic patent applications (i.e., patent applications of residents in their own country; see col. 2 of table 1) have increased at a very slow rate, and in eight out of twenty countries a decline has occurred, rapid growth can be found in the number of external patents (col. 4 of table 1; the proportion of applications filed by national firms and inventors in other countries). In parallel, as shown in column 3 of table 1, the number of foreign patents (i.e.,

---

3. The analysis of national systems of innovation has been developed by Freeman, Lundval, Nelson, and others. See the essays in Dosi et al. 1988; Freeman and Lundvall 1988.

4. We are indebted to Mario De Marchi and Giovanni Napolitano for their friendly advice on the elaboration of R&D data.

TABLE 1.   Average Annual Rates of Change of R&D and Patenting in OECD Countries (in percentages)

	R&D Expenditures, 1979–88[a] (1)	Domestic Patents, 1979–88[b] (2)	Foreign Patents, 1979–88[c] (3)	External Patents, 1979–86[d] (4)
United States	5.30	2.44	6.30	6.49
Japan	8.15[e]	8.30	3.85	10.12
Germany	3.58	0.54	4.87	5.27
United Kingdom	2.43[f]	0.64	5.49	6.93
France	4.86	1.16	5.95	5.78
Canada	5.60	6.28	2.88	6.29
Italy	9.43	−11.59[g]	10.01[g]	7.17
Netherlands	3.83[e]	2.00	10.17	4.05
Switzerland	4.75[h]	−2.21	9.87	1.61
Sweden	7.71[e]	−2.39	10.12	6.64
Australia	6.08[i]	3.26	5.31	15.87
Belgium	4.40[e]	−1.05	10.15	5.98
Spain	10.11	−0.31	11.77	2.92
Austria	3.95[j]	−0.75	13.51	7.16
Norway	6.50[e]	1.47	10.21	12.86
Finland	9.61	24.41	11.98	11.51
Denmark	7.18[e]	3.28	7.24	10.41
Ireland	6.06	9.34[e]	3.38[e]	9.30
Portugal	6.76[i]	−6.19	5.33	43.29
Greece	10.30[h]	−0.18	27.88	−1.54

Source: Elaboration on OECD data.
[a]R&D data are in real terms.
[b]Patents by residents of the country.
[c]Patents by foreigners in the country.
[d]Patents by residents located in other countries.
[e]Period indicated is 1979–87.
[f]Period indicated is 1978–87.
[g]Period indicated is 1980–88.
[h]Period indicated is 1979–86.
[i]Period indicated is 1978–86.
[j]Period indicated is 1981–88.

patent applications filed by foreign applicants in a given country) has significantly increased in all OECD countries.[5] The search for appropriating the benefits of innovation is a clear factor contributing to the rapid globalization of technology among advanced countries.

The ratio of external to domestic patents for 1986 is reported in column 1

---

5. A single patent application could, therefore, be counted more than once if it is extended in more than one country.

of table 2. This index reflects the propensity to protect innovations in foreign markets, and it shows that all countries have increased the international dimension of their technological activities. For many countries, including Japan, West Germany, France, Sweden, Belgium, and Switzerland, the ratio has more than doubled over a twenty year period. Two different factors have contributed to this: (*a*) an increase in the average number of countries in which each patent extended abroad is registered; and (*b*) an increase in the number of patents that are extended abroad. However, our data do not allow us to separate the importance of these two factors.

While the trend toward the internationalization of patenting is generalized, there are still significant cross-country differences in national levels, shown by the ratio of external patents to domestic ones. In 1986, the ratio is

TABLE 2. Cross-Country Comparisons of Patenting and R&D

	External to Internal Patents[a] (1)	EPO Applications per Cumulative R&D Expenditure[b] (2)	U.S. Patents Granted per Cumulative R&D Expenditure[c] (3)	Average Citations per U.S. Patent[d] (4)
United States	2.50	0.08	0.36	1.79
Japan	0.26	0.14	0.31	1.80
Germany	3.10	0.40	0.33	1.41
United Kingdom	2.11	0.18	0.17	1.61
France	3.31	0.22	0.17	1.40
Canada	3.21	NA	0.25	1.38
Italy	NA	0.17	0.14	1.24
Netherlands	6.86	0.32	0.21	1.58
Switzerland	6.51	0.64	0.52	1.39
Sweden	4.34	0.19	0.30	1.34
Australia	1.55	NA	0.14	NA
Belgium	5.30	0.18	0.15	1.54
Spain	1.29	NA	0.05	0.92
Austria	1.55	NA	NA	NA
Norway	2.82	NA	NA	NA
Finland	2.33	NA	NA	NA
Denmark	5.11	NA	0.21	1.24
Ireland	0.72	NA	0.14	1.07
Portugal	1.61	NA	0.02	1.67
Greece	0.07	NA	0.04	0.98

Source: Data extrapolated from OECD, EPO, and CHI Research.

Note: NA = not available.

[a]Ratio of the average number of patent applications extended abroad for each domestic application in 1986.

[b]Ratio of European Patent Office applications to cumulative R&D expenditures at constant 1985 prices in million U.S. dollars. The period indicated is 1982–87.

[c]Ratio of U.S. patents granted to cumulative R&D expenditures at constant prices. The period indicated is 1979–88.

[d]The period indicated is 1979–88.

particularly high for small- and medium-sized countries, such as the Netherlands (6.86), Switzerland (6.51), Belgium (5.30), and Denmark (5.11). Countries that have a small internal market are somehow forced to appropriate the results of their innovative efforts in foreign markets. Larger countries, on the contrary, have a weaker propensity to extend their patented inventions abroad.

Table 2 also shows some indicators, at the country level, of the relationship between patents and R&D. R&D should not be considered as the only source of patenting (see Archibugi, Cesaratto, and Sirilli 1987); however, it is an internationally powerful comparable indicator of the inputs devoted to innovation, and it surely represents an important source of patenting.

Patenting patterns differ substantially in domestic and foreign markets. Columns 2 and 3 of table 2 show the ratio of patents registered in the two most important patent offices (the U.S. and the European Patent Office) to R&D expenditures. These data supply information on the markets where each country attempts to appropriate the benefits of most of its innovations. The United States has a high ratio of patents per R&D unit in its own patent office, and the lowest ratio at the EPO. Japan has an above average propensity to patent per R&D unit in the United States, and it is below average at the EPO, while European countries show an opposite pattern.

The ranking of European countries in terms of patents registered at the EPO and in the United States per R&D unit is very similar, with the exception of Sweden. Within Europe, Switzerland, Germany, and the Netherlands have the highest ratios, while Italy and the United Kingdom have relatively low ratios.

The technical importance of patents and their economic impact varies widely, and the absolute numbers of patents registered do not provide entirely reliable information on the quality and impact of patented innovations. For this reason, information on the impact of patents, obtained from the number of citations each patent received from new patents, has also been considered. Data on such patent citations are available only for the United States and refer to the list of citations in the front page of the patent prepared by the U.S. Patent Office examiner. This external assessment of the link of a new patent to previous ones assures a fairly standard approach to the use of citations and is much more reliable than the use of the citations listed by each inventor, which may overstate the importance of previous patents registered by the same inventor or firm and ignore other inventors' patents.

Column 4 of table 2 reports the average number of citations per patent. Japanese patents are cited more often than those of any other country, including the United States. All European countries have a ratio of citations per patent lower than average. Within Europe, the United Kingdom and the Netherlands have a higher than average ratio, while Italian and Spanish patents have a rather low impact.

In spite of cross-country differences in the quantity and quality of patenting, a general trend toward a globalization of firms' strategies for appropriability is evident. The aggregate analysis performed in this section, however, does not indicate the direction of the innovative strategies pursued by firms and governments in each country. The increase in the resources devoted to S&T and the higher propensity to appropriate the results in international markets could be related either to growing competition or to a growing division of labor among advanced countries. The next section addresses this question by identifying national patterns of technological specialization.

3. The Profiles of Technological Specialization from Patent Data

In spite of a number of drawbacks identified by the existing literature, patent data offer the most detailed indicator for studying the patterns of technological specialization at the sectoral level.[6]

Two different sets of data have been considered. The first set includes patents granted in the United States, patents applied for and granted in France and West Germany, and patent applications at the European Patent Office. These data refer to eleven countries, cover the 1981–87 or 1982–87 period, and are disaggregated by thirty-two technology-based International Patent Classes (IPC). The number of patents, percentage distribution across sectors, and the index of technological revealed comparative advantage for each country provide a detailed picture of the pattern of specialization resulting from each data base.[7]

Patents registered in the United States have been used as the sole source of data by most patent studies.[8] The comparison across four patent institutions offers a much-needed test of how reliable U.S. patenting is, and how stable the national patterns of specialization are in different data bases.

The second set of data we used includes the number of patents granted and the front page patent citations in the United States. The data refer to sixteen countries, cover the 1975–88 period, and are disaggregated by the forty-three classes of the Standard Industrial Classification.[9] Again, the num-

---

6. For a survey of the use patents as a technology indicator, see Basberg 1987; Pavitt 1988; Schmoch et al. 1988.

7. The technological revealed comparative advantage index (TRCA, or specialization index) is equal to the ratio of patents registered in a given patent office by country i in the class j to the overall ratio of country i. It is above (below) 1 if there is a comparative advantage (disadvantage).

8. See, among others, those performed by CHI Research, by the Science Policy Research Unit of the University of Sussex, and by the Department of Economics of the University of Reading.

9. This database, acquired from CHI Research—Computer Horizons Inc., is described in detail in Narin and Olivastro 1988.

ber of patents and citations, the percentage distribution across sectors, and the index of technological revealed comparative advantage provide a detailed profile of the technological specialization of the countries considered. Citation data are particularly important because they offer an indication of the impact of a country's patents in each sector, providing additional information on the nature of national technological activities.

The profiles of technological specialization for the more advanced countries are presented and discussed in a separate report (Archibugi and Pianta 1988); however, the Appendix to this essay presents two tables with the specialization profiles of the United States resulting from the two sets of data considered. The data for the United States are reported as an example of the data available for all countries, but they are of particular interest as they allow, for the first time, a comparison between the specialization profiles based on patenting in the domestic and in foreign markets.

The Consistency of Countries' Specialization Profiles

A test of the coherence of the specialization profiles and of the representativeness of U.S. patents is shown for all countries in table 3, with the correlation coefficients between the indexes of specialization calculated on U.S. patents and those based on data from the other patenting institutions.

In general, for all countries (except the United States), the specialization profiles based on patents in the United States and at the EPO are closely

TABLE 3.   Correlation Coefficients of Indexes of Technological Specialization, U.S. Patents Granted to Other Patent Activity

	France		West Germany		EPO Applications
	Applications	Granted	Applications	Granted	
United States	.057	−.017	.262	.179	.046
Japan	.796	.760	.962	.950	.924
West Germany	.366	.502	.378	.342	.489
France	.125	.285	.561	.816	.755
United Kingdom	.075	.256	.455	.528	.535
Italy	.815	.835	.763	.778	.753
Netherlands	.671	.661	.487	.789	.858
Belgium	.563	.681	.500	.735	.554
Switzerland	.766	.795	.314	.612	.787
Sweden	.907	.920	.847	.881	.967
Canada	.189	.303	.546	.500	NA

Sources: CNR-ISRDS; extrapolated from WIPO and EPO data.
Note: NA = not available.

correlated; also U.S. and West German patents show a high correlation, with a closer similarity to patents granted rather than applications.

Special attention should be devoted to those countries—the United States, France, and Germany—whose domestic patent data were considered. The U.S. specialization profile measured on patents registered in the United States shows almost no correlation with the profiles emerging from the patenting activity of U.S. inventors abroad. A similar picture emerges for France, whose domestic specialization profile is significantly correlated only to that emerging from EPO patent applications. Germany, on the other hand, shows a consistent specialization profile in its domestic patenting, in patents registered in France, and at the EPO, with a lower correlation (.342) only with U.S. data.

The conclusions that can be drawn from this effort at measuring the specialization profiles in different patenting institutions is that domestic patenting is an unreliable indicator of a country's specialization, as it is distorted by a large number of inventions of smaller significance that are not extended abroad and are intended only to protect the domestic market from foreign competition. Such characteristics of domestic patenting result in a much less clear pattern of sectoral specialization, as the areas of a country's international technological strength can be less easily identified in the large domestic patenting activity. This has a particular relevance for the analysis of U.S. technological specialization. The specialization profile of the United States based on U.S. domestic patenting described by previous studies (see, e.g., Patel and Pavitt 1987; Soete 1987), therefore, does not appear to be an accurate description of the areas of technological strength and weakness of the United States in international markets, as the tables in the Appendix clearly show.

Patents and Patent Citations in the United States

Information on the relative quality of patents can be obtained from the second set of data, on patents and patent citations in the United States for two time periods, 1975–81 and 1982–88. A test of the stability of the specialization profiles emerging from these four variables is provided in table 4, showing the correlation coefficients between patent and citation indexes in each period, and between the indexes for the two periods, for both patents and citations.

For the majority of countries, a close relationship between patents and citations can be found, with a general decrease over time. Only the smallest countries (Ireland, Portugal, and Greece) show a more erratic pattern. A rather high stability over time of the specialization profiles appears for all countries, except the United Kingdom and France, confirming the importance of the cumulative nature of technological knowledge.

Moreover, the very close relation shown by all countries between the specialization profiles emerging from patenting and citation data confirms that, within a national system of innovation, the quality of innovations is closely related to their volume. But such a relationship decreases over time, as shown by the generalized decline (except in the case of France, Belgium, and Denmark) of the correlation coefficients. This suggests that, besides a growing sectoral specialization measured by patent counts, there may be an even faster process of qualitative specialization, measured by patent citations.

4. The Degree of Specialization of Industrial Countries

From the evidence summarized in the previous section, we can now address the more general question of the degree of specialization shown by the countries considered. Chi-square statistics were calculated for each country on the main patent data bases described previously, and a country's percentage distribution of patents across sectors was compared with the sectoral distribution of the world's patents. In this way, we obtained a measure of how different national profiles are from the world sectoral profile on all patents, a simple definition of a country's technological specialization. The results are shown in table 5. Using chi-square values as an index of technological specialization allows us to examine the changes over time in the position of individual

TABLE 4. Correlation Coefficients for Patents Granted and Patent Citations in the United States, 1975–81 and 1982–88

	Patents and Citations, 1975–81	Patents and Citations, 1982–88	Patents 1975–81 and 1982–88	Citations 1975–81 and 1982–88
United States	.94	.91	.87	.87
Japan	.95	.93	.92	.90
West Germany	.93	.88	.84	.73
United Kingdom	.92	.87	.77	.77
France	.84	.88	.78	.48
Canada	.95	.90	.88	.82
Italy	.91	.86	.84	.71
Netherlands	.96	.78	.87	.48
Switzerland	.97	.94	.94	.93
Sweden	.94	.82	.82	.79
Belgium	.91	.93	.72	.80
Spain	.86	.63	.70	.59
Denmark	.88	.91	.75	.75
Ireland	.96	.74	.05	.12
Portugal	.30	.26	.15	.11
Greece	.67	.40	.04	.17

Source: Data extrapolated from CHI Research-Computer Horizons.
Note: Correlation coefficients are across SIC classes.

TABLE 5. Chi-square Values for the Technological Specialization of Advanced Countries

	41 SIC Classes				31 IPC Classes[a]	
	U.S. Patents Granted		U.S. Patent Citations		U.S. Patents Granted, 1981–87 (5)	EPO Patent Applications, 1982–87 (6)
	1975–81 (1)	1982–88 (2)	1975–81 (3)	1982–88 (4)		
United States	0.94	1.31	1.05	2.06	1.61	7.86
Japan	13.46	14.68	12.96	14.96	20.98	18.94
EC	3.84	4.50	5.76	6.90	4.49	3.47
West Germany	8.16	10.05	13.51	15.39	9.39	3.68
France	4.00	3.86	4.01	3.83	8.46	10.89
United Kingdom	5.91	6.85	10.43	17.91	5.97	5.22
Italy	21.85	24.53	25.55	25.21	26.92	34.12
Netherlands	23.06	20.46	27.52	22.48	21.72	23.19
Belgium	30.72	38.84	56.02	110.56	28.89	38.29
Denmark	24.63	31.88	41.06	62.40	NA	NA
Spain	46.88	53.52	88.73	101.09	NA	NA
Ireland	77.99	22.42	84.78	50.58	NA	NA
Portugal	139.81	212.25	289.36	299.57	NA	NA
Greece	96.13	89.96	153.46	290.15	NA	NA
Canada	12.38	14.09	16.56	13.41	18.63	NA
Switzerland	36.16	34.39	39.54	56.12	41.41	24.98
Sweden	24.72	24.74	23.70	23.15	32.80	43.05

Notes: NA = not available. The chi-square values are used as measures of the distance between the sectoral percentage distributions of patents (by SIC or IPC classes) of the world and those of each country.

[a]The EC data by IPC classes include only seven major countries: West Germany, France, Italy, Netherlands, Belgium, Sweden, and the United Kingdom.

countries, and to compare their degree of specialization, as measured by different indicators.

Taking into account the less differentiated nature of domestic patenting activity, it is no surprise that the United States shows the lowest degree of specialization in the data based on U.S. patents and that the EC countries (as an aggregate) have the lowest specialization at the European Patent Office, the patent institution that is the main vehicle of appropriability within the EC internal market.

For the majority of countries, excluding again the three smallest patenting countries, the degree of specialization appears rather consistent in all the data bases considered. For patents in the United States in the 1980s, even comparing two very different sectoral classifications such as the SIC and the IPC (cols. 2 and 5 of table 5) the ranking of countries is very similar, with a rank correlation coefficient of .96.

The comparison of patents in the United States and patents at the EPO shows greater differences, with rank correlation coefficients of .84 between EPO and U.S. patents when based on the same IPC classification (cols. 5 and 6), and .83 when based on different classifications (the IPC for the EPO and the SIC for the United States; cols. 2 and 6). These results show that, as expected, differences in the Patent Office data base used are more important than the differences in the types of sectoral classification employed.

Over time, these indicators of technological specialization show a general increase in the values for both patents and citations; only France and the Netherlands show a decrease in their degree of specialization, while Canada, Sweden, and Italy have an increasing specialization for patents and a (moderately) declining one for citations. The three smallest countries again have less clear patterns, due to the small number of patents registered.

Comparing the results of patent counts and patent citations, the increase in the degree of specialization based on citations is faster, suggesting a significant differentiation of the technological fields with greater impact.

5. The Relationship between Size and Specialization

A key issue in the exploration of the dynamics of technological specialization of advanced countries is the analysis of the relationship between the size of the technology base and the degree of specialization. The existence of regularities in this relationship can highlight the possible "paths of specialization" followed by countries as they expand their S&T activities and search for technology-based competitive advantages in international markets.

The results discussed in the previous sections make possible a cross-country study of this relationship: as indicator of the technology base we will use the cumulative R&D expenditure at constant prices; as an indicator of the

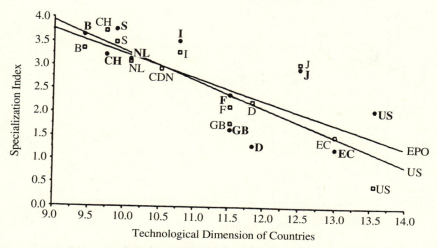

Fig. 1. Technological specialization and R&D resources measured by U.S. and EPO patent counts: □ = U.S. patents granted, 1981–87; ● = EPO patent applications, 1982–87. (B = Belgium, CDN = Canada, CH = Switzerland, D = West Germany, EC = European Community, F = France, GB = United Kingdom, I = Italy, J = Japan, NL = Netherlands, S = Sweden, US = United States.)

level of a country's specialization we will use the chi-square values shown in table 5.

We have plotted (figs. 1, 2, and 3) the position of each country along these two variables in logarithmic scale. The variety of the data bases considered allows us to assess the stability of the distribution (1) across two different classifications, (2) across two different patent institutions, (3) over time, and (4) between indicators of simple count (the number of patents) and impact (citations).

All of the figures show a consistent inverse relationship between the size of the technology base and the degree of specialization. While we discussed cross-country differences in the absolute levels of specialization in section 4, here we can compare the position of individual countries to the overall distribution.

Figure 1 shows, for the period 1981–87, the patterns of specialization emerging from U.S. and EPO patent counts, disaggregated by technology-based IPC classes. A clear inverse relationship emerges. The distribution of the two sets of data is rather similar, with the notable exception of countries where the "domestic market effect" emerges (the United States has a low specialization degree in the domestic market, and the EC and Germany have a similarly low index at the EPO).

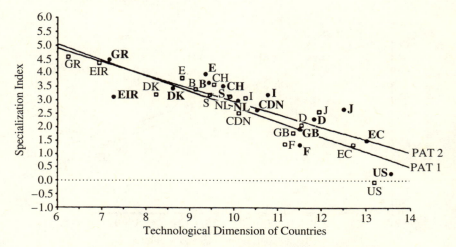

Fig. 2. Technological specialization and R&D resources measured by patents granted: ☐ = patents granted, 1975–81; ● = patents granted, 1982–88. (B = Belgium, CDN = Canada, CH = Switzerland, D = West Germany, DK = Denmark, E = Spain, EC = European Community, EIR = Ireland, F = France, GB = United Kingdom, GR = Greece, I = Italy, J = Japan, NL = Netherlands, S = Sweden, US = United States.)

Japan has a degree of specialization that is considerably higher than what might be expected from the size of its S&T activities. In addition, Italy and, to a lesser extent, Sweden have rather high specialization levels, while Great Britain and France appear to spread their technological specialization across a broader range of sectors.

Figure 2 shows the same relationship for patents granted in the United States according to the SIC classes for two time periods, 1975–81 and 1982–88. Over time, a general shift upward is clearly visible. The countries' relative positions are confirmed, with the United States, Great Britain, and France showing degrees of specialization below the expected ones, while Japan, Italy, Switzerland, and Spain present higher levels of specialization.

Figure 3 presents, for the same periods, data on patent citations in the United States. The upward shift of the regression line from the first to the second period is even more evident than for patent counts (fig. 2). For countries such as the United States, Great Britain, and Belgium the specialization degree has sharply increased, while France, Canada, and the Netherlands are the only countries showing a slight reduction.

A few regularities can be identified from these data. Countries devoting fewer resources to R&D tend to be more specialized, and the degree of specialization is higher in terms of the impact of their technological activities than for the simple count of patent data. The degree of specialization increases

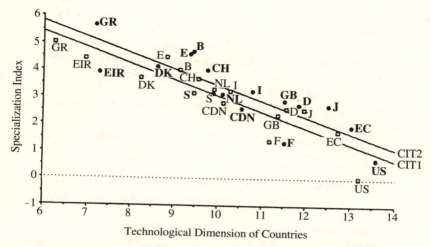

Fig. 3. **Technological specialization and R&D resources measured by patent citations:** □ = patent citations, 1975–81; ● = patent citations, 1982–88. (B = Belgium, CDN = Canada, CH = Switzerland, D = West Germany, DK = Denmark, E = Spain, EC = European Community, EIR = Ireland, F = France, GB = United Kingdom, GR = Greece, I = Italy, J = Japan, NL = Netherlands, S = Sweden, US = United States.)

over time and appears fairly stable when measured in different patent institutions and according to various sectoral classifications.

6. Concluding Remarks

We have presented some fresh evidence on the patterns of technological specialization of the most advanced countries and have discussed some methodological issues in the use of patenting as an internationally comparable technology indicator.

Over the last decade, rapid growth of international patent activity has occurred while domestic patenting has been stagnant. Patenting abroad, as a tool for appropriating returns from innovative activities and for protecting technological advantage, appears to be of increasing importance in the internationalization of economic activity and also for establishing selected, technology-based competitive advantages in the various markets relevant to a country's (and a firm's) operations.

Significant differences have emerged between the specialization profiles measured by patents in the domestic and international markets. While the major sectors of strength of a country's technology do emerge in all data bases, each patenting market has specific characteristics. While the U.S. patent system has often been employed for international comparisons, our findings suggest that U.S. specialization measured on U.S. registered patents is not an adequate description of the country's international strengths.

Countries' profiles of specialization on both patent counts and citations are highly correlated, but the latter shows a higher and faster growing degree of specialization for almost all countries. This suggests that a qualitative indicator of the impact of technological activities is more unevenly distributed across sectors and countries than a quantitative indicator such as patent counts.

These patterns can be viewed as the result of a combination of factors, including:

    i) the heritage of technological knowledge accumulated in the past, which identifies the basic strengths and weaknesses of the national system of innovation;

    ii) increased international competition, which pressures firms and countries to expand their technology-based advantages, building on their existing strengths; and

    iii) the impact of specific government technology policies, which are an essential requirement for international strength in sectors where public procurement plays a crucial role.

We have suggested that the total amount of resources devoted by each country to S&T is related to the degree of specialization across technological fields. Only large countries can afford to distribute their innovations more uniformly across technologies. Small countries, on the contrary, are somehow forced to specialize in selected niches, suggesting that they are more dependent on international technology flows and cooperation than large ones.

In some countries, however, the degree of specialization is substantially higher than what might be expected from this general pattern. The most notable case is Japan, and, to a lesser extent, Italy. At the opposite extreme, Great Britain and France have a comparatively low level of specialization. These differences can be viewed as the outcome of diverging technological strategies followed by firms and governments, due to substantial differences in terms of national technological accumulation, international competitive advantages, and domestic technology policy.

The evidence presented in this essay raises new questions about the possible link between the pattern of technological specialization and the rate of growth of technological activities; countries with higher specialization levels have generally shown a faster growth of the resources devoted to S&T. A parallel link could be explored between the degree of specialization and economic performance; countries with strong technological priorities seem to experience robust economic performance. These issues need to be addressed in future research.

TABLE A1. U.S. Indexes of Technological Specialization Based on International Patent Classes

	U.S. Patents Granted[a]	France		West Germany		EPO Applications[b]
		Applications[a]	Granted[a]	Applications[b]	Granted[b]	
U.S. percentage of external patents	—	24.46	27.81	22.07	28.87	—
U.S. percentage of total patents	56.13	10.79	17.79	6.48	13.71	26.12
Agriculture	1.24	0.45	0.64	0.49	0.68	0.66
Foods	1.07	0.99	0.97	0.88	0.85	1.14
Footw./clothing	1.22	0.64	0.67	0.86	0.78	0.54
Health	1.26	1.24	1.15	1.26	1.14	1.17
Medical	0.89	1.21	1.08	1.14	1.09	1.34
Separ. & mix.	1.05	1.03	1.06	1.10	1.03	1.06
Machin. tools	0.92	0.72	0.71	0.79	0.75	0.67
Hand tools	1.03	0.90	0.91	1.02	1.07	0.85
Printing	0.89	0.74	1.02	0.70	1.35	1.01
Transport	0.94	0.42	0.54	0.76	0.67	0.58
Machinery	1.08	0.97	0.86	0.98	1.10	0.74
Inor. chemic.	0.99	1.22	1.26	1.21	1.10	1.16
Org. chemic.	0.94	0.98	1.02	1.12	1.11	1.03
Org. compounds	1.03	1.53	1.49	1.40	1.41	1.44
Paint, petrol.	1.10	1.67	1.40	1.51	1.28	1.32
Biochemistry	0.95	1.18	1.00	1.15	1.12	1.33
Metallurgy	0.91	1.53	1.32	1.26	1.02	1.08

(continued)

TABLE A1—*Continued*

	U.S. Patents Granted[a]	France		West Germany		EPO Applications[b]
		Applications[a]	Granted[a]	Applications[b]	Granted[b]	
Textiles	0.63	0.52	0.58	0.73	0.62	0.61
Paper	0.89	1.00	0.90	0.89	1.04	1.07
Building	1.13	0.43	0.42	0.56	0.51	0.30
Mining	1.37	1.55	1.26	1.72	1.49	1.58
Engines	0.78	0.82	0.87	0.85	0.81	0.74
Engineering	0.97	0.83	0.91	1.01	0.92	0.87
Light. & heat.	1.09	0.74	0.77	0.79	0.81	0.65
Weapons	1.17	0.58	0.45	1.04	0.79	0.47
Optics photo	0.87	1.18	1.24	0.86	0.97	1.15
Computing	1.03	1.27	1.26	1.07	1.21	1.52
Inform. instr.	0.85	1.06	1.11	0.68	0.90	1.01
Nuclear physics	0.95	1.65	1.27	1.59	1.19	1.19
Electricity	1.02	1.41	1.23	1.33	1.08	1.07
Electron. telec.	0.95	1.61	1.17	1.26	1.05	0.96
Others	1.12	1.13	0.51	0.79	0.00	0.77
Average value	1.00	1.00	1.00	1.00	1.00	1.00

Source: Data from Archibugi and Pianta 1989 and CHI Research.

[a]Data from 1981–87.

[b]Data from 1982–87.

TABLE A2. U.S. Indexes of Technological Specialization Based on Standard Industrial Classes for Patents and Patent Citations in the United States

	Patent Index		Citation Index	
	1975–81	1982–88	1975–81	1982–88
U.S. percentage				
of total patents	62.09	54.89	65.05	57.19
Food	1.07	1.14	1.07	1.19
Textile mill prod.	0.90	0.91	0.93	0.93
Inorg. chem.	0.96	1.06	0.98	1.15
Org. chem.	0.88	0.95	0.85	0.97
Plastic matrls., synth.	0.91	1.02	0.88	1.02
Agric. chem.	0.82	0.86	0.83	0.91
Soaps, detergents	1.02	1.07	1.04	1.03
Paints, allied chem.	1.00	1.06	1.00	1.09
Misc. chem. prod.	1.12	1.10	1.13	1.12
Drugs & medicines	0.82	0.91	0.84	0.97
Petrol., Nat. Gas	1.33	1.45	1.32	1.49
Rubber, misc. plas. prod.	1.02	1.04	1.01	1.04
Stone, Clay, Glass	0.99	1.00	0.98	1.04
Primary ferrous prod.	0.77	0.81	0.77	0.86
Prim./Sec. nonferr. prod.	0.85	0.86	0.91	0.94
Fabricated metal prod.	1.12	1.13	1.12	1.13
Engines & turbines	0.89	0.79	0.84	0.65
Farm, garden mach. & eq.	1.13	1.17	1.13	1.23
Cnstr., mng., metal	1.04	1.09	1.03	1.12
Metal working mach.	0.94	0.95	0.97	0.95
Office comput.	1.01	0.88	1.05	0.92
Spec. ind. mach.	0.86	0.83	0.84	0.83
Genrl. indust. mach.	0.97	0.93	0.96	0.92
Refrig., servc. indust.	1.05	1.09	1.06	1.15
Misc. mach.	0.91	0.89	0.79	0.69
Electr. trans., distr.	1.06	1.02	1.06	1.05
Electr. indust. eq.	0.90	0.88	0.91	0.89
Household appliances	0.99	0.92	1.00	0.95
Electr. lightng., wirng.	1.11	1.14	1.12	1.16
Misc. elec. mach.	0.96	1.01	1.00	1.06
Radio, TV receiving eq.	0.85	0.80	0.86	0.81
Elect. cmp., acc., comm. eq.	1.04	1.00	1.06	1.04
Motor veh.	0.93	0.74	0.85	0.60
Guid. mssls., spce. veh.	1.23	1.24	1.18	1.30
Ship, boat bldng.	1.04	1.06	1.06	1.20
Railroad eq.	0.98	0.97	0.93	0.91
Motorcycles, bicy.	0.87	0.73	0.78	0.56
Misc. transportation	1.10	1.02	1.00	0.81
Ordnance	1.15	1.08	1.13	1.17
Aircraft & parts	0.89	0.79	0.80	0.60

(*continued*)

TABLE A2—*Continued*

	Patent Index		Citation Index	
	1975–81	1982–88	1975–81	1982–88
Prof., scien. instrumen.	0.99	0.98	0.99	0.98
Unclassified patents	1.14	1.02	1.20	1.29
Other industries	1.15	1.20	1.12	1.17
Average	1.00	1.00	1.00	1.00

Sources: Data from Archibugi and Pianta 1989 and CHI Research.
Note: Specialization indexes are based on patent data and patent citations.

REFERENCES

Archibugi, Daniele, Sergio Cesaratto, and Giorgio Sirilli. 1987. "Innovative Activity, R&D, and Patenting: The Evidence of the Survey on Innovation Diffusion in Italy." *Science Technology Industry Review* 1 (2): 135–50.

Archibugi, Daniele, and Mario Pianta. 1988. "The Technological Specialization of Advanced Countries." Commission of European Communities, Brussels. Mimeo.

Basberg, Bjorn. 1987. "Patents and the Measurement of Technological Change: A Survey of the Literature." *Research Policy* 16 (2–4): 131–41.

Cantwell, John. 1989. *Technological Innovation and Multinational Corporations.* Oxford: Basil Blackwell.

Cantwell, John, and Christian Hodson. 1990. "The Internationalization of Technological Activity and British Competitiveness: A Review of Some New Evidence." Department of Economics, University of Reading. Mimeo.

Dollar, David, and Edward N. Wolff. 1988. "Convergence of Industry Labor Productivity among Advanced Economies, 1963–82." *Review of Economics Statistics* 70 (4).

Dollar, David, and Edward N. Wolff. 1989. "Trade Patterns and Productivity Convergence among Industrial Countries, 1970–86." Mimeo.

Dosi, Giovanni, Christopher Freeman, Richard Nelson, Gerald Silverberg, and Luc Soete, eds. 1988. *Technical Change and Economic Theory.* London: Frances Pinter.

Freeman, Christopher, and Bengt-Ake Lundvall, eds. 1988. *Small Countries Facing the Technological Revolution.* London: Frances Pinter.

Gerstenberger, Wolfgang. 1989. *Reshaping Industrial Structures.* Tokio Club Papers no. 2.

Hood, Neil, and Jan Erik Vahlne. 1987. *Strategies in Global Competition.* London: Croom Helm.

Narin, Francis, and Dominic Olivastro. 1988. "Technology Indicators Based on Patents and Patent Citations." In Van Raan 1988.

OECD. 1988. *Main Science and Technology Indicators.* Vol. 1. Paris: OECD.

OECD. 1989. *OECD Science and Technology Indicators.* Vol. 3. Paris: OECD.

Patel, Pari, and Keith Pavitt. 1987. "Is Western Europe Losing the Technological Race?" *Research Policy* 16:59–85.

Patel, Pari, and Keith Pavitt. 1990. "Do Large Firms Control the World's Technology?" SPRU, University of Sussex. Mimeo.

Pavitt, Keith. 1987. "International Patterns of Technological Accumulation." In Hood and Vahlne 1987.

Pavitt, Keith. 1988. "Uses and Abuses of Patent Statistics." In Van Raan 1988.

Schmoch, Ulrich, Hariolf Grupp, Wilhelm Mannsbart, and Beatrix Schwitalla. 1988. *Teknikprognosen mit Patentindikatoren.* Cologne: Verlag TUV Rheinland.

Soete, Luc. 1987. "The Impact of Technological Innovation on International Trade Patterns: The Evidence Reconsidered." *Research Policy* 16 (2–4): 101–30.

Van Raan, Anthony, ed. 1988. *Handbook of Quantitative Studies of Science and Technology.* Amsterdam: Elsevier.

Commentary

Alfred Kleinknecht

Using patent counts and citation analysis, the authors arrive at several interesting findings about the technological specialization of advanced countries. They show that foreign patenting is generally growing faster than domestic patenting (and R&D), indicating a growing globalization of technological competition. The latter is accompanied by increasing specialization. In general, small countries have a stronger pattern of specialization than large ones, and, specialization is greater in foreign patenting as compared to domestic patenting. The specialization patterns in patenting can also be found, even more strongly, in citation scores, and, over time, specialization profiles seem to be quite stable due to the cumulative nature of technical progress.

Looking at individual countries, the following findings appear to be of particular interest: Japan (and less so, Sweden and Italy) has an above-proportional degree of specialization. The Japanese also have a lead on Europe and on the United States in citations that serve as an indicator of importance of patents. As opposed to Japan, Great Britain and France show a relatively weaker specialization, with the Netherlands and France even showing a declining index of specialization.

It seems that little can be criticized in terms of the statistical methods applied in this chapter. The authors have done a decent job on a huge amount of data. Nonetheless, a few remarks are in place. For example, I wonder whether the growing globalization observed in this chapter is not (at least in part) caused artificially because the analysis is based on European patents, and the European Patent System has not been introduced before 1978. There seems to be an iron rule that each new system experiences an incubation period during which users learn how the system works. Such gradual learning-by-using may explain, at least to a certain degree, the rapid increase of European patenting during the 1980s. Independently of this, it would be interesting for policy analysts to have an indication of which patent fields are growing most rapidly, and who is specializing most strongly in which niches.

In general, the relevance of the authors' findings stands or falls on two implicit assumptions: First, patents are an appropriate indicator of innovation;

and, second, innovation has a positive impact on economic performance in terms of economic growth and foreign trade. Much has been written on whether patents can be used as an innovation indicator (see Basberg 1987 for a recent survey). Perhaps the two most important arguments against the use of patents are that many innovations are never patented (or are not even patentable, as, e.g., software), and that a presumably high (but unknown) number of patents seem never to be introduced into a market, i.e., they never become innovations according to Schumpeter's definition. It would be helpful if future research on patents would give us some hints about the true number of "sleeping" patents and about the relationship between patented and nonpatented innovations. In the meanwhile, we have to live with the assumption that there is a reasonably close correlation between patented and nonpatented innovations, patented innovations being the visible part of an iceberg.

The relevance of patent analysis might also be justified in an indirect way, showing that patents are indeed correlated to economic performance. The work by Schmookler (1969) is of course encouraging here, although it somehow exaggerates the strength of the correlation between patenting and demand (Kleinknecht and Verspagen 1990). In the case of the above paper, it would be interesting to examine in a refined analysis by sectors and countries, the correlation of leading positions in patenting and in patent citation with long-run patterns of domestic growth and foreign trade performance. Such an analysis could address a number of intriguing questions. For example, are the niches in which the various countries hold strong patent positions and/or lead in terms of citations indeed the growth sectors in their domestic economies, and do they earn export surpluses in these niches? And if so, what time lags are involved and what is the cause and effect (or is there a simultaneous relationship)? Is the higher degree of specialization of Japan or the Japanese lead in citations indeed a (long-run?) threat to European industry? Or are the Netherlands and France likely to face a difficult future because of their falling index of specialization? Clearly, such questions have been beyond the scope of the above paper. The paper is nonetheless an important step in a potentially rich research area.

REFERENCES

Basberg, B. L. 1987. "Patents and the Measurement of Technological Change: A Survey of the Literature." *Research Policy* 16:77–88.
Kleinknecht, A., and B. Verspagen. 1990. "Demand and Innovation: Schmookler Reexamined." *Research Policy* 19:387–94.
Schmookler, J. 1969. *Invention and Economic Growth.* Cambridge, Mass.: Harvard University Press.

Entrepreneurship, Innovation, and Growth: The Role of Innovation Policy in West Germany

Rudi Kurz

Introduction: The Schumpeterian Perspective as a Guide for Analysis

Schumpeter does not provide us with an elaborate theory of innovation and has little to say about the impact of government policy on innovation. However, his view of economic development as an evolutionary process with innovation (entrepreneurship) at its core may serve as a helpful guide in formulating effective strategies for innovation policy.

In the Schumpeterian perspective, innovation is a social process; it is not just a technological or an economic phenomenon. Our knowledge of the factors that determine the speed and direction of this process is still very insufficient. Yet it is clear that the prime movers are individuals (entrepreneurs) and firms (endowed with "intrapreneurs"). Their activity and success depends crucially on the socioeconomic environment they confront. Innovation policy attempts to create a favorable environment for innovation; it goes far beyond the funding of science, basic research, and (direct or indirect) government subsidies for private R&D. Its subject is the design and redesign of the "national innovation system," adapting it to changing conditions and challenges such as new consumer preferences and values, environmental problems (the greenhouse effect, waste crisis), or an increasing pool of inventions.

As the innovative performance of an economy depends on a variety of factors, innovation policy comprises a wide variety of facets—including traditional R&D policy. Some of the more important facets are the following.[1]

1. Defining wide boundaries for individual freedom, especially freedom of market entry and exit, as a precondition for competition (creative

---

[1]. This selection is based on the consensus in international studies of innovation rather than on hard empirical tests (for a survey see Becher 1989; Kurz, Graf, and Zarth 1989; Piatier 1984. The first comprehensive catalog of innovation determinants was provided by the Charpie Report; see Aubert 1989).

destruction).[2] Free movement of goods, people, and capital facilitates the redirection of resources from existing to new objectives. Schumpeter emphasized the important role of credit and capital.

2. Providing incentives and rewards for innovation, for example, extraordinary profits based on a temporary monopoly. It is the objective of institutional design to get an appropriate balance between incentives to innovate and social costs of restrictions on access (Nelson 1988, 314).

3. Maintaining social acceptance of innovation, that is, coping with the fact that every innovation imposes heavy costs on some individuals and groups.[3] This requires government monitoring and might even require a governmental ban of some innovations.[4] Technological laissez-faire would harm innovation in the long run. However, the design of control mechanisms should ensure that restrictions on individual freedom are minimized.

4. Flexibility of institutions that, at any given time, might be suitable to cope with traditional problems, but may become a barrier for new developments.[5] Hence reshaping property rights, work relations, and so on should be a legitimate subject of social debate and should not be within the realm of taboo or ideology.[6]

5. High levels of education and widespread R&D activity of firms in order to enable them to perceive and to react to fundamental changes. Well-established connections (communication structures, interfirm and firm-university-government networks) to speed up diffusion (see Abramovitz 1986, 405).

Our knowledge of the impact of each of these factors on a nation's innovative performance is still very limited. Given the insufficient state of knowledge, innovation policy necessarily involves a lot of experimentation and is very controversial. This holds true in general and also in the case of West Germany, where—starting in the early 1980s—an attempt has been

---

2. This provides "multiple sources of initiative, and a competition among those who place their bets on different ideas" (Nelson 1988, 313).

3. Schumpeter (1942) discussed this phenomenon using the catchwords "crumbling walls" and "growing hostility." Innovation could happen at too fast a pace, overwhelming our ability to cope with change and thus provoking resistance (see Scheuten 1982, 301).

4. Government has to be active at an early enough stage before vested interests make formulation and enforcement of regulation impossible (see Chesnais 1982, 42).

5. The more successful a given institutional arrangement has proved, the more tempting it is to preserve it.

6. For the significance of institutional innovations see, e.g., Chesnais 1982, 40–43; Langlois 1986.

made to integrate R&D subsidization into a more comprehensive concept of innovation policy.

Principles of Innovation Policy in West Germany

In the early 1970s, the German "Wirtschaftswunder" (economic miracle) ended and Germany shared the fate of other European nations: "Eurosclerosis." The GNP growth rate as well as productivity growth rates declined; traditionally low unemployment and inflation rates vanished—and with them the material foundations of the so-called social-democratic consensus with an elaborated welfare and intervention state at its center. In this crisis of the economy (and of short-run Keynesian economics, too), the concept of supply-oriented economics evolved in the late 1970s with the Council of Economic Experts as its major protagonist.[7] The supply-oriented ideas contributed to the further disintegration of the social-liberal coalition of Chancellor Helmut Schmidt and brought about the political turnaround ("Wende") in 1982 with Helmut Kohl as chancellor of a conservative government.

Today, the nightmare of economic decline is almost forgotten—although we still face unemployment of almost 2 million (7 percent). It is not possible to analyze this change in detail here. However, the supply-oriented concept is relevant in our context because it focuses on Schumpeterian dynamic competition and, hence, innovation and entrepreneurship. In order to set free potential innovations and entrepreneurs, supply-oriented policy recommends relying primarily on the effects of two favorable general conditions for innovation.[8]

1. A reduction of government expenditures (subsidies for industry and the welfare state) and taxes; emphasis is on this order because (large) budget deficits should not be tolerated.
2. A reformation (deregulation, privatization) of encrusted institutions that hamper dynamic forces; overregulation seems particularly burdensome in the labor market and the sectors exempted from antitrust law (*Gesetz gegen Wettbewerbsbeschränkungen*) such as telecommunications, energy, transportation, banking, and insurance.

Reduction of subsidies should include R&D subsidies (basic research exempted), especially direct support for specific projects or industries. But

---

7. The Council's position is quite similar (and interrelated) to the positions of the majority of the large German economic research institutes.

8. A necessary precondition is that monetary policy succeeds in preventing inflation. For more detailed catalogs of policy recommendations, see the Council's reports. In most cases, at least some plausible substantiation is provided there; however, the lack of knowledge about the determinants of innovation is obvious and gives way to voluntary judgments.

there are fields where market mechanisms are assumed to fail and government intervention may continue, for example, space technology and energy technology (see Council 1985, 155); the Airbus is perceived as a necessary market entry subsidy which however tended to become a permanent subsidy (see Council of Economic Experts 1987, 200).

With this background, the *Bundesregierung* (federal government) undertook a reorientation of innovation policy.[9] The basic principle that officially guides federal innovation policy and R&D funding since the reorientation in 1982–83 is to extend basic and preventive research and to keep important long-run options open while reducing R&D subsidies; improved general socioeconomic conditions are expected to do a better job. In more detail the reorientation implies:

—reinforcing basic research,
—increasing funding of preventive research (which includes environmental, health, and climate research),
—continuing to fund market-oriented technologies where private initiative is not sufficient (i.e., Airbus, information technology, biotechnology),
—improving general conditions, especially for innovation in small and medium enterprises (SME),
—supporting R&D in fields with high probable long-term benefits (space, sea research, or nuclear fusion),
—establishing research and fostering discussion on the assessment of technologies, and
—abandoning structural and institutional barriers to R&D (e.g., within the university system) and improving international cooperation.[10]

German Innovation Policy in Practice

R&D Policy

Total R&D spending in West Germany is about DM 66.7 billion, that is, 2.9 percent of GNP (2.6 percent in 1981).[11] Of this amount, 63.5 percent is privately financed (up from 55.4 percent in 1981). The public share is divided

---

9. The intention is documented and reiterated in various official publications: "Die Neuorientierung der Forschungs und Technologiepolitik, deren Grundlinien im Bundesforschungsbericht 1984 und im Jahreswirtschaftsbericht 1984 festgelegt wurden, ist insbesondere auf günstige und verläßliche Rahmenbedingungen und auf die Vermeidung von Wettbewerbsverzerrungen gerichtet" (Bundesminister für Wirtschaft 1986, 24).

10. See Federal Ministry for Research and Technology 1988, 16–22.

11. It is significantly less than in Japan (about 3.1 percent) and about the same as in the United States. However, the dynamics of R&D spending in real terms are the lowest among the

between the federal government (21 percent) and the eleven states (*Bundesländer;* 14 percent).[12] The share of the federal government is not concentrated in one department but is at the disposal of various departments: dominating is the Federal Ministry of Research and Technology (BMFT) with more than half of the federal government R&D spending; it leads the Ministries of Defense (about a fifth), Education, and Commerce with less than 10 percent each. In real terms, the BMFT budget showed no significant increase during the last eight years.[13]

As figure 1 shows, a large part (about 20 percent) of the federal government's R&D spending goes into basic research (e.g., to the Max-Planck-Gesellschaft, Fraunhofer-Gesellschaft, Deutsche Forschungsgemeinschaft). Another 20 percent is dedicated to military research. The rest is widely distributed for a variety of purposes that may be summarized under the labels "preventive research" and "key technologies":[14]

—air and space technologies, 12 percent;
—energy research and technology (primarily nuclear power), 10 percent;
—information technology (including production engineering), 6 percent;
—environmental, climate, and safety research, 5 percent;
—research on materials, physical, and chemical technologies, 4 percent;
—biotechnology, 2 percent;[15]
—subsidies for R&D activity and improved basic conditions (investment in R&D, R&D personnel, technology-oriented new firms, and technical information), 4 percent.

In addition to that, R&D in West Germany is also supported by funds from the EUREKA initiative (a bottom-up approach with no predefined projects or focal points, e.g., JESSI) and various EC programs (to list only a few, BRITE, ESPRIT, RACE, COMMETT, and SPRINT).[16]

---

three competitors: the real increase in the 1980s was 40 percent in West Germany, more than 50 percent in the United States, and more than 100 percent in Japan (see Erber 1989, 444).

12. There is no consistently formulated division of effort between federal and state activity in innovation policy. Therefore, some duplication occurs, as does competition between the states.

13. To illustrate the dimension of the BMFT budget, it is not much larger than the R&D spending of Siemens (DM 7 billion). All federal R&D expenditures are about the same amount as Siemens, Daimler-Benz, and Volkswagen combined.

14. The variety of government R&D funding further increases if the states are included (see Federal Ministry for Research and Technology 1988; Bundesminister für Forschung und Technologie 1990, 31; percentages are for 1988).

15. From 1990 to 1994, DM 1.2 billion of federal funds will be available for biotechnology. For a comprehensive analysis of barriers to innovation in the German biotechnology industry, see Motor Columbus et al. 1989.

16. The Single European Act of 1987 made the support of science and technology an explicit goal of the EC (Art. 130f–q). The second Research and Technology Program for 1987–

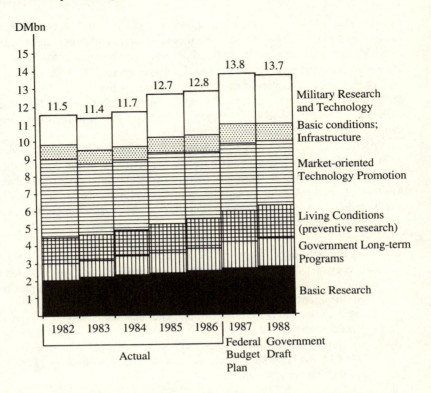

Fig. 1.   Federal R&D expenditures, 1982–88. (Data from Federal Ministry for Research and Technology 1988, 75.)

The major changes in R&D subsidization during the 1980s were:

1. It is less project oriented than eight years ago but it still includes elements of industrial targeting. The majority of funded projects (and there are still about 2,000 of them) in fields such as information technology or biotechnology are cooperative projects including industry, university, and SME.
2. Major indirect programs—such as the Federal Department of Commerce's (BMWi) *F&E-Personalkostenzuschuß* (R&D research per-

---

91 amounted to DM 11 billion. The third program, 1990–94, provides another DM 11.4 billion, primarily for information and communication technologies (40 percent).

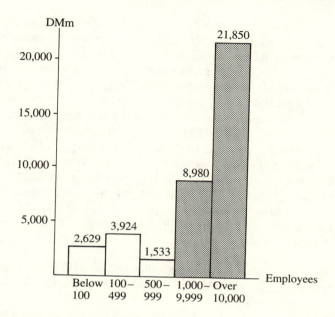

Fig. 2. Total R&D expenditure of R&D-conducting companies by size of company, 1985. (Data from Bundesminister für Forschung und Techno-logie–Bundesminister für Wirtschaft 1989, 12.)

sonnel subsidy) with annually almost DM 400 million—were phased out in the late 1980s. Industry complains that general tax relief does not compensate for that.

In sum, these changes have not been radical. Whether they will contribute to increasing the efficiency of German R&D policy still has to be fully evaluated (see Meyer-Krahmer 1989). Efforts to evaluate the efficiency of R&D programs have been intensified during recent years and parallel or ex-post evaluation research is mandatory for all BMFT programs now.[17]

The Role of Small and Medium Enterprises

SMEs play an important although hard to quantify role in the German innovation system.[18] Data on R&D expenditures (see fig. 2) for instance underesti-

---

17. For a survey, see Hornschild et al. 1990.

18. See Bundesminister für Forschung und Technologie–Bundesminister für Wirtschaft 1989; Bundesminister für Wirtschaft various years.

mate this role. About 25,000 SMEs are active in R&D, that is, every third enterprise in the manufacturing sector. However, empirical evidence makes it clear that most of the successful SMEs in Germany do not comply with Schumpeter's ideal of dynamic innovators: their success is based on close customer contacts and flexible reaction to their changing needs combined with high-quality production and commitment to traditional markets (see Albach 1984). New firms are high tech to a small extent (about 5 percent) and some of them just "crowd out" existing SMEs and do not create new markets.

To support and to stimulate SME innovation activity, the Federal Department of Commerce (BMWi) provided DM 3.3 billion between 1979 and 1987 to subsidize employment of R&D personnel (*Personalkostenzuschuß-Programm*). Based on the recent shift in concept, that program has not been renewed. Instead, the federal government relies primarily on more favorable general conditions for innovation in SMEs. Among these are (besides low interest rates and stability of prices):

—The income tax reform, which in three phases (1986, 1988, and 1990) brought significant tax reductions for nine out of ten SMEs (which are unincorporated).
—Universities and colleges are given more freedom and incentives to cooperate with SMEs.
—SMEs benefit from the reduction of regulations (market entry) and bureaucracy costs.
—In public procurement, there will be more insistence on SME subcontractors (e.g., in the Airbus program or in space projects).[19]
—Consulting assistance and access to technological information for SMEs is improved and subsidized.

Moreover, some funds are available to compensate specific SME problems: the BMFT continues to provide about DM 200 million annually for additional R&D personnel in SMEs. The SMEs also benefit substantially from indirect-specific BMFT programs such as the one on CAD, robotics, and CIM. In 1984, a pilot project for new technology-oriented firms was started and will continue to close the gap in seed capital. The federal government emphasizes that SMEs participate more in public funds (28 percent) than they contribute to total private enterprise R&D expenditures (15–20 percent).[20]

---

19. The public procurement rules (*Verdingungsordnung für Leistungen* [VOL/A]) were reformed in 1984 to make fostering of innovation an explicit criteria in public procurement decisions.

20. See Bundesminister für Forschung und Technologie–Bundesminister für Wirtschaft 1989, 65.

Improvement of General Framework Conditions

Competition Policy
Competition is the driving force of economic development and the foundation of West Germany's economic success.[21] In order not to become an obstacle to innovation, competition policy has been adapted in various forms (e.g., R&D joint ventures will only in rare special cases cause antitrust problems). However, competition policy in Germany is in a crisis caused by the challenge of global competition and European integration. Symptoms of this crisis are:

—the Daimler-Benz/MBB deal that has been strongly opposed by the Bundeskartellamt and nonetheless approved in the political procedure;
—the loss of merger control to the EC Commission, which may replace competition policy by industrial policy to foster European champions; and
—the inability of the Bundeskartellamt to prevent large West German corporations from taking over former state-guaranteed monopolies in East Germany.

Increasing international competition may not bring much release, because takeovers and global partnerships (such as Daimler-Benz/Mitsubishi, IBM/Siemens) emerge faster than barriers to competition (e.g., EC quotas) fall. The traditional symbiosis of large firms and SMEs is rapidly changing. However, it is much too early at the moment to make any definite statements on the consequences for the performance of the German innovation system.

Regulatory Reform
Progress in deregulation or regulatory reform is slow in Germany.[22] This is most visible in the debate on shop-opening hours, which has thus far resulted in no more than the option to keep shops open on Thursdays until 8:30 P.M. (instead of 6:30 P.M.). Much of the deregulation that is and will be enacted is due to the EC 1992 internal market program. In ground transportation, rate setting has been abandoned (in 1989) and replaced by reference rates. But control of market entry (concessions) still exists. As a precondition for deregulation in the trucking industry, the German government requests the harmonization of taxes, safety, and social standards to provide a level playing field for competition with the Netherlands, Italy, and other EC countries. In telecommunications, a major step has been made to open markets for private

---

21. For a general discussion, see Ordover and Baumol 1988.
22. For a more detailed analysis, see Soltwedel 1986. A deregulation commission appointed by the government will come up with proposals in 1991.

innovators. The Deutsche Bundespost has been divided into three public enterprises (telecom, mail services, and banking services) and free market entry has been granted in telecommunication equipment, value-added services (e.g., data transmission) and the networks of satellite and mobile radio transmission. The monopoly is maintained in network transmission and telephone services. Some social regulations have been reduced in the labor market (e.g., dismissal protection). The number and extent of environmental regulations have increased (e.g., on emission control, waste water, chemicals, noise, biotechnology) but little has been done to minimize costs by applying economic instruments that are less harmful to innovation than the command-and-control approach.

Taxation

As Schumpeter (1918) emphasized, people will devote their best energies to innovation and production only if taxes are not too high, because material interest in innovative activities would be destroyed. Only in periods of patriotic excitement can the state demand more without a negative impact. Taxation of profits in Germany is 70 percent of pretax profit and, hence, is higher than in all competing nations.[23] The Council argues that innovation is hampered because of the decrease in profit differential (Barone curve; see Helmstädter 1986). This effect is caused by progressive taxation coupled with limited intertemporal offsetting of losses and profit-independent taxes (e.g., local trade tax on business capital, wealth tax). A major tax reform in three phases from 1986 to 1990 resulted in a net tax relief of DM 48.5 billion. The most important part of this reform was a flattening of the progression in income taxation.[24] Unchanged so far is enterprise taxation. It is doubtful whether the major reform (including a reduction of the corporate income tax rate to 50 percent and the reform of the local trade tax) announced in this field for the next legislature period (1991–95) will actually take place considering the high cost of curing the economic and environmental disaster in East Germany and Eastern Europe.[25]

---

23. This popular figure is however misleading because the calculation starts with taxable profits only and does not account for tax allowances that enable firms in Germany to reduce their economic (pretax) profit significantly. For a survey of studies on the tax burden with results varying from 72 percent to 17 percent, see Fuest and Kroker 1989. Moreover, the level of subsidies and infrastructures provided by government would have to be included.

24. The top marginal rate has been reduced from 56 to 53 percent for annual taxable incomes of DM 120,000 (couples, DM 240,000) and more. The corporate income tax rate on retained profits has been lowered from 56 to 50 percent (the rate for distributed profits remains 36 percent). Among the tax expenditures reduced or abolished to compensate, in part, for the cost of the tax reform are provisions for R&D, energy-saving investment, and residential building.

25. Social security outlays, which amount to 18.6 percent of GNP, will remain high and may even increase if they are merged with East German systems.

Other Areas

There are other major determinants of innovative activity that have to be included in a more complete picture of the German innovation system. These include (to mention only two) education that adds to the stock of human capital and mechanisms and institutions for conflict resolution that guarantee the production factor of "social peace."

Education, vocational training, and the science system are still excellent by international standards and Germans have recently begun to receive Nobel prizes again. This should not divert attention from deficiencies, for example, in the transfer and interaction between universities and industry and within the university system (administrative tasks divert resources from research). Conflict resolution includes labor conflicts (where Germany's record shows that only Switzerland has a lower number of labor days lost by strikes) and the acceptance of new technologies. There is debate whether social acceptance of new technologies (such as nuclear power, biotechnology, and information technology) has suffered in Germany and has driven innovators abroad. There are spectacular individual cases in biotechnology, but, in general, empirical evidence is weak. Government has been slow to support social acceptance by providing information and analysis of the consequences of (not) accepting a certain new technology, for example, by creating an institution comparable to the U.S. Office of Technology Assessment (OTA).

Evaluation and Perspectives

Innovation policy has to include more than technology policy, that is, primarily subsidization of private R&D expenditures. However, a more comprehensive innovation policy that addresses the basic conditions of innovation involves a number of serious problems. Because of large time lags,[26] innovation policy should be "farsighted and persistent" (OECD 1971, 138). However, this is not congruent with the time-horizon of the average politician. Institutions are related to interests and income positions. Powerful coalitions may arise to defend the status quo and so block institutional reforms and, finally, innovation (see Olson 1982). Institutional innovation, therefore, requires the evaluation of conflicting goals and mechanisms of conflict resolution. Finally, at the edge of development, we face limits of knowledge. There is no way to reduce uncertainty about the success of a new institutional arrangement (when entering a new trajectory). Because this knowledge is

---

26. "Policies for . . . innovation may often involve problems which are not stark and obvious—thereby provoking an immediate response—but problems which, if not recognized and dealt with in good time, can lead to irremediable situations. Policy measures must often be applied for a long time before their effects are felt, and results achieved" (OECD 1971, 138).

available only ex post, the situation demands experimentation.[27] Different arrangements may produce equivalent results. Success depends not only on the institutional arrangement itself, but also on the efficiency of exploiting its advantages (see Ergas 1987).

Innovation policy in West Germany has changed gradually over the last eight years, but it is not fundamentally different from innovation policy in previous years. Political emphasis has shifted toward improving the socioeconomic environment of innovative business activities. But only a few major steps have been taken toward actually implementing a more general type of innovation policy.

1. R&D policy still is not congruent with the SME strength of the German economy: space activity (conducted by a couple of large firms) is emphasized while the environmental industry, which is extremely suitable for SMEs, is neglected.
2. Little progress has been made in removing regulatory barriers to innovation.
3. Innovation-oriented tax reform and reduction of the subsidization of declining industries has not been very successful.
4. There is a reluctance to address future problems with vigor, problems such as the necessary energy-saving restructuring of the economy, the redefinition of the role of labor (flexibilization, retraining, participation), and of social security (more private initiative) as well as the implementation of a culture of social dialogue about the consequences of new technologies.

The government—especially the BMFT—addresses some of these problems but reveals no positive leadership. The new challenges of the deteriorating natural environment and world climate do not receive due attention. These challenges demand a dramatic increase in energy and resource productivity, which requires a redirection and a broader concept of government innovation policy. The federal governments' innovation policy is still dominated by outdated ambitions (such as air and space or nuclear energy) and is focusing on *technological* innovation, and technology is perceived primarily as a vehicle for economic growth. In this respect, innovation policy in other EC countries such as Denmark or the Netherlands is more "modern" than in West Germany.

The process of German unification will add more problems than stimulating effects to the German innovation system—at least in the short run. In-

---

27. In the view of an OECD expert group (OECD 1988, 22), we are currently in a time of "experimentation with new institutional structures and arrangements." This seems to be the case today, even more so than in 1988.

creasing deficits will increase pressure for budget cuts—and R&D spending as well as the reform of enterprise taxation will be among the victims. Only in the longer run may the stimulating effects dominate, a result of new brains and entrepreneurs and a pool of unexploited inventions (e.g., in optics and electrical and mechanical engineering).

In sum, a large gap still exists between rhetoric and reality, and there is urgent need for "modernization." If it is true, however, that innovation policy in Germany has not changed significantly since the crisis in the early 1980s, this implies that other factors are responsible for the continuous expansion of the German economy and its success in world markets—for example, firm-internal factors (improved performance under pressure of international competition) and/or favorable exogenous conditions (expanding world trade, EC integration, or declining oil prices). Germany's position might then be more vulnerable to change due to exogenous conditions than the currently bright picture suggests.

BIBLIOGRAPHY

Abramovitz, M. 1986. "Catching Up, Forging Ahead, and Falling Behind." *Journal of Economic History* 46:385–406.
Albach, H. 1984. "Die Rolle des Schumpeter-Unternehmers heute." In *Schumpeter oder Keynes?* ed. D. Bös and H.-D. Stolper, 125–45. Berlin and Heidelberg.
Aubert, J. E. 1989. "Evaluation of Scientific and Technological Programs and Policies: A Selection of Current Experiences in OECD Countries." *STI Review*, no. 6: 147–77.
Becher, G., et al. 1989. *Der Einfluß wirtschafts- und gesellschaftspolitischer Rahmenbedingungen auf des Innovationsverhalten von Unternehmen.* Karlsruhe.
Bond, J. S. 1986. *The Science and Technology Resources of West Germany: A Comparison with the United States.* Washington, D.C.: National Science Foundation.
Bundesminister für Forschung und Technologie. 1990. *Faktenbericht 1990 zum Bundesbericht Forschung 1988.* Bonn.
Bundesminister für Forschung und Technologie–Bundesminister für Wirtschaft. 1989. *Forschungs- und technologiepolitisches Gesamtkonzept der Bundesregierung für kleine und mittlere Unternehmen.* Bonn.
Bundesminister für Wirtschaft. Various years. *Jahreswirtschaftsbericht.* Bonn.
Chesnais, F. 1982. "Schumpeterian Recovery and the Schumpeterian Perspective— Some Unsettled Issues and Alternative Interpretations." In *Emerging Technologies: Consequences for Economic Growth, Structural Change, and Employment,* ed. H. Giersch, 33–71. Tübingen.
Council of Economic Experts. Various years. *Annual Report.* Wiesbaden.
Erber, G. 1989. "Die Bundesrepublik Deutschland im internationalen F&E-Wettbewerb." *DIW-Wochenbericht* 37:443–49.
Ergas, H. 1987. "Does Technology Policy Matter?" In *Technology and Global Indus-*

try: Companies and Nations in the World Economy, ed. B. R. Guile and H. Brooks, 191–245. Washington, D.C.

Federal Ministry for Research and Technology. 1988. *Report of the Federal Government on Research 1988.* Bonn.

Freeman, C. 1990. "Schumpeter's *Business Cycles* Revisited." In *Evolving Technology and Market Structure,* ed. A. Heertje and M. Perlman, 17–38. Ann Arbor: University of Michigan Press.

Fuest, W., and R. Kroker. 1989. *Unternehmensteuerlast: 20 oder 70 Prozent?* Cologne.

Giersch, H. 1984. "The Age of Schumpeter." *American Economic Review, Papers and Proceedings* 74:103–9.

Helmstädter, E. 1986. "Dynamischer Wettbewerb, Wachstum und Beschäftigung." In *Technologischer Wandel—Analyse und Fakten,* ed. G. Bombach, B. Gahlen, and A. E. Ott. Tübingen.

Hornschild, K., et al. 1990. "F&E-Personalkostenzuschuß-Programm: Erfahrungen mit einer Fördermaßnahme für kleine und mittlere Unternehmen." *DIW-Wochenbericht* 10:119–22.

Jackson, P. M. 1988. "The Role of Government in Changing Industrial Societies: A Schumpeter Perspective." In *Evolutionary Economics: Applications of Schumpeter's Ideas,* ed. H. Hanusch, 285–308. Cambridge: Cambridge University Press.

Klein, B. 1977. *Dynamic Economics.* Cambridge, Mass.: Harvard University Press.

Klodt, H. 1987. *Wettlauf um die Zukunft: Technologiepolitik im internationalen Vergleich.* Tübingen: Mohr.

Krupp, H. 1985. "Public Promotion of Innovation—Disappointments and Hopes." In *Innovation Policies: An International Perspective,* ed. G. Sweeney, 48–79. New York: St. Martin Press.

Kurz, R. 1987. "The Impact of Regulation on Innovation: Theoretical Foundations." Discussion Paper, Tübingen.

Kurz, R. 1990. "Innovation als Element dynamischen Wettbewerbs." *List Forum für Wirtschafts- und Finanzpolitik* 16:42–54.

Kurz, R., H.-W. Graf, and M. Zarth. 1989. *Der Einfluß wirtschafts- und gesellschaftspolitischer Rahmenbedingungen auf das Innovationsverhalten von Unternehmen.* Tübingen: Mohr.

Langlois, R. N., ed. 1986. *Economics as a Process: Essays in the New Institutional Economics.* Cambridge: Cambridge University Press.

Meyer-Krahmer, F. 1989. *Der Einfluß staatlicher Technologiepolitik auf industrielle Innovationen.* Baden-Baden: Nomos.

Motor Columbus Ingenieurunternehmen AG, Booz Allen & Hamilton, and Ifo-Institut für Wirtschaftsforschung. 1989. *Biotechnologie: Abbau von Innovationshemmnissen im staatlichen Einflußbereich.* Cologne.

Nelson, R. R. 1988. "Institutions Supporting Technical Change in the United States." In *Technical Change and Economic Theory,* ed. G. Dosi et al., 312–29. London.

Nelson, R. R., and L. Soete. 1988. "Policy Conclusions." In *Technical Change and Economic Theory,* ed. G. Dosi et al., 631–35. London.

OECD. 1971. *The Conditions for Success in Technological Innovation.* Paris: OECD.

OECD. 1980. *Technical Change and Economic Policy: Science and Technology in a New Socioeconomic Context.* Paris: OECD.

OECD. 1988. *New Technologies in the 1990s: A Socioeconomic Strategy.* Paris: OECD.

OECD. 1989. *OECD Economic Surveys: Germany.* Paris: OECD.

Olson, M. 1982. *The Rise and Decline of Nations: Economic Growth, Stagflation, and Social Rigidities.* New Haven.

Ordover, J., and W. Baumol. 1988. "Antitrust Policy and High-technology Industries." *Oxford Review of Economic Policy* 4 (4): 13–34.

Piatier, A. 1984. *Barriers to Innovation.* London.

Ratgeber Forschung und Technologie. 1989. *Fördermöglichkeiten und Beratungshilfen.* Cologne.

Scheuten, W. K. 1982. "The Impact of New Electronics." In *Emerging Technologies: Consequences for Economic Growth, Structural Change, and Employment,* ed. H. Giersch. Tübingen.

Schumpeter, J. A. 1911. *Theorie der wirtschaftlichen Entwicklung.* Leipzig: Drucker & Humbolt.

Schumpeter, J. A. 1918. *Die Krise des Steuerstaats.* Leipzig: Drucker & Humbolt.

Schumpeter, J. A. 1942. *Capitalism, Socialism, and Democracy.* New York.

Soltwedel, Rüdiger, 1986. *Deregulierungspotentiale in der Bundesrepublik.* Tübingen: Mohr.

Stoneman, P., and J. Vickers. 1988. "The Assessment: The Economics of Technology Policy." *Oxford Review of Economic Policy* 4 (4): i–xvi.

Werner, J., ed. 1987. *Beiträge zur Innovationspolitik von E. Kantzenbach, P. Oberender, H.-P. Peters, H. S. Seidenfuß.* Berlin: Drucker & Humbolt.

Technology Policy in a Small and Open Economy: The Case of the Netherlands

Cornelis W. A. M. van Paridon

Introduction

The competitive position of firms and national economies are more and more determined by the interplay of three interrelated processes: technological progress, market scale, and increasing scale of production. They seem to mutually reinforce each other. It can be noticed that, in many cases, the costs of fundamental and applied R&D and of pilot projects are rising faster than the income firms derive from their current sales. As technological developments increase the sophistication of products and processes, the scientific, technological, and industrial resources and skills for development and production are becoming more costly and complex (Walsh 1988). Combined with the rapidity of technological developments and the rise of new competitors, firms are confronted with higher risks and more uncertainty about future developments. A possible way out is an increase in market share of existing markets, an expansion of markets, or an alliance with other firms in order to share costs. But these possibilities do not always exist, or they cannot always be fruitfully exploited.

The same technological developments also show a clear trend toward longer production runs, economies of scale, and greater standardization. At first sight, it seems that this contradicts trends such as increased product differentiation, coproduction, and flexible manufacturing. However, it has to be noted that these developments are only possible with a sufficient scale of production.[1] Due to their flexibility, many small- and medium-sized firms can maintain their competitiveness only when they are able to make full use of the potential economies of scale, but they need a large market. In smaller countries, such a market is normally larger than the total domestic market.

Of course, these developments are relevant for firms in both big and

---

1. In this respect, see also Dertouzos et al. 1989.

small countries. It seems, however, that the competitive position of firms in small countries is more at stake. It seems more difficult to remain competitive, to be able to finance sufficient R&D, and to exploit the benefits of new technologies and potential economies of scale. Firms in small countries do have a major initial disadvantage, namely that of a relatively smaller domestic market. That is especially relevant in the initial phase of the product life cycle. Because the process of economic development has entered the fast lane, with more and more products introduced and with shortened life cycles, firms from small countries feel themselves more and more in a disadvantaged position.

The question arises of what kind of technology policy would be advisable in this situation for the government of a small and open economy such as the Netherlands. To answer this question, it is useful to investigate the smallness issue first. Then, several views on the necessity and desirability of government intervention in the area of technological developments will be discussed. A so-called technological dilemma is sketched, in which a government is confronted with increasing difficulties formulating and implementing an adequate technology policy while, at the same time, the social demand for such a policy becomes quite intense, relevant, and increasing. Finally a solution is formulated that could overcome this dilemma.

The Netherlands: A Small and Open Economy?

At first sight, it is not strange to categorize the Dutch economy as small. The country's surface area, with its 41,000 km^2, is one of the smallest in the OECD.[2] With a population of 14.7 million people, it occupies eleventh place among the OECD economies. The Netherlands is, however, not that small. In the OECD ranking according to GDP it occupies tenth place. Ranked by external trade, the Netherlands even reaches seventh place.[3] This last factor is strongly related to the openness of the Dutch economy: in 1987 the value of Dutch exports was about 53.0 percent of the Dutch GNP.[4] In comparison, the same figure for the United States is 7.4 percent, for Japan 10.5 percent, and Germany 29.0 percent. It shows how vulnerable the Dutch economy is to external developments, but also that the Netherlands has gained great experience with competition in foreign markets. That surely is a strong asset. Dutch firms such as Philips, Shell, Unilever, and AKZO are major multinational

---

2. As an indication, forty-two of the fifty U.S. states have a greater surface area than the Netherlands.

3. The Netherlands is too small for the big countries and quite big among the small ones. There is still a slight disappointment in the Netherlands that the G-7 countries were not the G-8.

4. Of these exports, 75 percent are bound for the EC and about 30 percent for the Federal Republic of Germany.

companies, acting as "global players" on the world market. The Netherlands is second in the export of agricultural products, right after the United States. Amsterdam Schiphol is the fourth busiest airport in Europe, after Paris, London, and Frankfurt. The Netherlands has the biggest share of freight traffic by truck inside the EC, and Rotterdam is the biggest harbor of the world, twice as big as New York. The conclusion must be that, in many sectors, the Netherlands is not a small economy, in the sense that Dutch firms operate very competitively in the world market.

Focusing attention on the area of technology policy, it seems at first sight that the Netherlands is doing quite well. In 1987, the Netherlands spent about U.S. $4.2 billion as gross domestic expenditure on R&D (GERD).[5] As a percentage of GDP, the Netherlands showed a strong increase in recent years, from 1.89 percent in 1980 to 2.32 percent in 1987. The bigger OECD countries, such as the United States, Japan, Germany, and Sweden, surpass this value by about 0.50 percent.[6] However, when the R&D budget in absolute amounts is compared with that of the bigger countries, the picture changes drastically. That U.S. $4.2 billion is about 3.4 percent of the U.S. R&D budget, 9.0 percent of that of Japan, or 18.0 percent of the German budget, to mention the biggest three. With regard to total R&D personnel, the Netherlands could count about sixty-four thousand people, 8 percent of that of Japan and 15 percent of Germany.[7] These differences in available resources are indicative of the reduced ability such a small economy has to stay at the technological frontier in all the important sectors.[8]

With regard to the national R&D budget, therefore, the Dutch economy has to be categorized as small. This particular aspect seems crucial in the current debate about the consequences of technological development, market scale, and increasing scale of production for the technology policy of a small and open economy such as the Netherlands.

Technology Policy in a Small and Open Economy: A Technological Dilemma

Government Policy in Retreat?

In the last decade, all Western economies have shown a reorientation regarding government intervention in the economy. Slow growth, high unemployment rates, uncontrolled government expenditures, increasing bureaucracy,

---

5. The data used in this article are mainly from OECD 1989.

6. It has to be recognized that in certain countries, such as the United States and Sweden, this figure includes a significant share of defense-related R&D activities.

7. No figures are available for the United States.

8. For an international comparison, see also Pavitt and Patel 1988.

overregulated markets, and declining tax morale were all seen as indicators that something had gone fundamentally wrong. This reorientation was also favored by the rise of economic theories stressing the negative impact of government intervention. Government intervention should be diminished, preferably limited to its core activities only. Deregulation, privatization, and tax cuts became major political issues in many Western countries.

It is, therefore, quite remarkable that, in the area of technology policy, government intervention has greatly intensified in the same period. Based on the assumption that technology is the key factor for prosperous economic development, all countries put a strong emphasis on this particular policy area. The legitimacy of technology policy was greatly enhanced by the increasing demand from the side of private firms to subsidize (part of) their R&D efforts. There was also an increase in social demands for a technology policy with regard to nuclear energy, recombinant DNA, and higher safety norms for working conditions and for food products.

This increase in the importance of technology policy seems to be accompanied, however, by a loss of effectiveness. Due to the increased complexity, rapidity, and costs of technological developments in combination with the increased internationalization of the economic process, instruments such as standardization, supply creation (infrastructure and public services as well as incentives policy), and demand creation have become less effective.

This development has led to a "technological dilemma": governments seem less able to pursue a deliberate technology policy while, at the same time, they are more and more involved. It is worthwhile to analyze this dilemma in more detail.[9]

Technology Policy: Its Position and Contents

In the most general way, technology policy should be seen as an integral part of a deliberate government strategy aimed at realizing a sufficient level of welfare through realizing an adequate level of economic development. Normally, this is translated into sufficient growth, balanced government budget, stable balance of payments, reasonable income distribution, stable prices, and a healthy environment. But there is also a more structural aspect: economic development means structural change; it means the simultaneous rise and decline of products, firms, even sectors, through changes in demand, in technology (and so in supply), and in international trade through the rise and decline of competitors.[10] Such a broad government strategy should therefore

---

9. Certain arguments will have a Dutch flavor, but they are relevant for Western economies in general.

10. See van Paridon 1987.

be aimed at facilitating these changes, in the right volume, in the right direction, and with the right speed. In combination with the other goals of economic policy, a mixture of policies is needed with regard to factor costs, education, infrastructure, and research and development. It is therefore essential that technology policy is not too narrowly viewed.

Such a technology policy should also deal with the conditions for the creation, acquisition, diffusion, and application of knowledge. These conditions determine the areas in which a society wants to play a prominent role. This concerns answering such questions as:

—Which technological areas or economic sectors must be selected for such a policy?
—Which resources can be used for this policy?
—Is it useful to promote a technology-push or a demand-pull orientation in this policy or some kind of mixture?
—Which links have to be made between public and private efforts and interventions?
—What contribution can be expected from policies aimed at procurement, at standardization, and at R&D activities?

The question remains whether small countries, and at this level the Netherlands is, without any doubt, a small one, can pursue a specific science and technology policy to increase its competitiveness through raising its technological level by providing some kind of support for certain firms or sectors.[11] I have said that the limited available resources mean a big handicap. Whatever technology policy would be selected due to these limited resources, a government of a small country is always confronted with the problem of choosing between firms, sectors, or technologies earlier than that of a bigger economy. Therefore, it seems that the answer tends to be negative.

However, two comments must be made here. First, a dynamic and policy-relevant criterion of technological progress should be chosen, namely what impact science and technology developments have at the competitive position of products, firms, or sectors. If read in this way, it is possible to get a proper knowledge of the relevancy of technology policy. It broadens the scope in the sense that not only high-tech sectors should be selected but also medium- and low-tech sectors. R&D efforts in these sectors could be, however, more valuable for the national economy in the long run than equal efforts in a high-tech area. Second, smaller countries might choose to give special attention to specific medium-tech or even low-tech sectors, because larger countries show a certain preference to be at the technological frontier in so-called

---

11. See Van Tulder 1989 for information on the Dutch experience.

high-tech sectors. Especially when smaller countries have already built up experience in such sectors, it is advisable to stick to these sectors and to move further along the learning curve instead of changing to a new one.

This is in line with observations by Ergas (1986) regarding the difference between mission-oriented and diffusion-oriented technology policies. Mission-oriented policies, aimed more at fundamental research, concern major projects with national priority, in many cases related to the defense sector. Usually, these projects are very expensive. It is, therefore, not surprising that such policies are more common in bigger countries such as the United States and France. Diffusion-oriented policies are directed at increasing the capabilities of firms to absorb new knowledge and new applications and to translate them into new or improved products for which demand exists. For smaller countries, this seems a much more appropriate strategy. Its results depend on a high level of investment in human capital and of knowledge exchange between firms and a strong cooperation between firms and research institutes in applied research. One should expect that Dutch technology policy is diffusion-oriented. It is in this respect quite remarkable that, among the important OECD countries, the Netherlands spends the highest percentage of its R&D budget on fundamental research, quite the opposite of what one should expect.

Why Technology Policy Has Become Less Effective

There are several reasons why governments are less able to pursue a deliberate technology policy. The first reason is that the increased speed, scale of production, complexity, and internationalization of technological developments has reduced the capability of governments to survey technological developments, to know the relevant options, to make the right choices, and, finally, to put these choices into practice. While companies already have trouble following these developments, it has become impossible for any government to know enough to make sound decisions. The result is that most governments cannot do more than copy what other governments do, with the consequence that they all direct their R&D efforts to the same technologies or sectors.[12]

Another complicating factor has been increased sectoral diversity and, therefore, the complexity of any useful policy. Whether a technology policy aimed at a certain product or sector really succeeds depends on a thorough knowledge not only of the technology itself, but also of the homogeneity of the product, the structure of the market, the level of internationalization, and

---

12. The argument governments usually use to find support for their proposal runs as follows: "We have to do this, because country x or y does the same." The result is that each government supports the same key technologies with consequences that can be foreseen.

the presence of market arrangements. Each combination of these elements requires a different mix of policy measures. Research, diffusion, and translation into the desired outcome are strongly influenced by them.

Increased internationalization is another complicating factor. The possibilities for an independent technology policy have been greatly diminished for any country, but certainly for the smaller ones. The increasing scale of production has created a situation in which almost every sector has entered the world market in one way or another. Whether in regard to buying natural resources, semimanufactures, or knowledge; the use of capital and labor from abroad; or the selling of products or foreign direct investments; it has become quite clear that these activities are no longer confined to one country. Production processes have become increasingly footloose and factors of production increasingly mobile, making firms less and less dependent on domestic governments.

Until now, small countries have been able to gain a strong competitive position in specialized niches of medium-tech or even high-tech products. When their position was challenged by new competitors, they could move to other niches that were left open by bigger countries. In recent times, this challenge by new competitors has been intensified through the development of the newly industrializing countries. At the same time it seems that the possibilities for small countries to upgrade their production structure, even in the medium- and low-tech sectors, have diminished. The increased complexity, high costs, and lack of a substantial domestic market have created a more difficult situation, sometimes described as a "small country squeeze."[13]

Science and technological knowledge have also become increasingly international. Of course, scientific knowledge has always had a global character. Here, the problems are of a different kind. It has become quite difficult for small countries with fewer resources for R&D to keep in touch with all relevant developments. Technological knowledge, which also depends on sufficient funds and skilled labor, used to be much more localized. Nowadays the situation has greatly changed through the activities of transnational operating firms, which have the ability to use technological knowledge in a global way. Such strategies can undermine any national science and technology policy. Some governments have tried to prevent this outflow through an increasingly protectionist attitude regarding nationally financed research programs. Mowery and Rosenberg (1989) note that such a potentially detrimental attitude has become observable in the United States.

The internationalization process has yet another dimension. Most countries cannot do much more than internalize the consequences of technological developments that are created elsewhere as best as possible. It has become

---

13. See, e.g., Freeman and Lundvall 1988; Kristensen and Levinson 1983.

quite clear that each successful government intervention is immediately copied elsewhere.[14] In several markets, it seems that competition between firms has been replaced by competition between national governments. Having smaller budgets, it is clear that smaller countries reach the limits of such a policy much more quickly than the bigger ones.

There are still other developments threatening the small countries' positions. Whenever firms participate in international networks, it can be observed that the participating firms differ in their motives, their relative power, and their abilities to get a fair return for such cooperation. It seems that, in general, firms from smaller countries are in a weaker position, with such consequences as brain drain and a relatively low level of spin-off activities. Smaller countries also face the problem of becoming too advanced. As long as standardization in a particular market has not been reached, this is a dangerous position. If a firm from a small country decides on a certain standard, but other countries finally make a different choice, it normally means a loss for the small one.[15] Because smaller countries normally do not have the power to enforce such standardization, it is preferable for them to wait to make such important decisions, even with the danger of losing an initial advantage. Bigger countries also have a stronger position in this area.[16] Finally, the margins for an independent government policy in this area have been diminished in recent decades due to a number of international treaties, such as GATT, or the creation of the Common Market.

Why There Is More Demand for Technology Policies

I have argued that technology policy should be integrated in a coherent government policy aimed at facilitating structural change, but it had become more difficult to pursue, mainly due to the increased complexity, speed, and internationalization of technological developments. I also mentioned that smaller economies were confronted with this situation earlier than the bigger ones because of their limited budgets.

It is remarkable that this decline in effectiveness has been accompanied

---

14. In both technology policy measures and the selection of relevant technology areas, countries increasingly bid against each other. Although it can be expected that not everyone will win, to say the least, it is almost impossible not to participate in this competition.

15. A fine example is the choice of a VCR system. Philips was one of the first firms in this market, and they chose the P2000 system. Most Japanese firms decided on the VHS system. After a few years, it became clear that, due to a variety of reasons, Philips had no other choice than to change to the VHS system. Their initial lead became a liability.

16. For a description of such developments in the international telecommunications market, see Van Tulder 1988.

by an increase in the demand for such policies. The reasons for this are threefold.

First, there is a demand for such a policy because governments must run their own business properly and efficiently (for instance, health care). A second source of demand for technology policy is also articulated through governments, but mainly formulated by firms and sometimes also by the general public, as is the case with education.

These two kinds of demand are not new, but their impact on technological developments are taken into account more and more. Government can perform a stimulating role by stressing its own efficiency as much as possible, using the available technological knowledge and its applications. By providing the private sector with clear examples of how to make use of the existing stock of knowledge, by showing how such information can come available and how it facilitates government organizations fulfilling their tasks in a more efficient way, governments are not only able to save money—by doing these tasks cheaper or better for the same price—but also to provide private firms, especially the small ones, with proper examples of what technological progress can do for them. Of course, this requires major changes in the way the government organizes its tasks, especially in the way civil servants are responsible for their own output. But by stressing responsibility and efficiency—both qualitatively and quantitatively—it can be made a challenging task.

A third demand for technology policy is formulated by firms and made directly to the government. By stressing the element of national competitiveness and the possible loss of production and employment, many governments have been persuaded to support R&D activities by firms. More and more, the "matching" argument has gotten a prominent place in this respect, in the sense that governments should compensate their domestic firms for subsidies given by foreign governments to foreign firms operating in the same market.[17]

It is clear that governments enter a slippery slope once they react positively to such demands. There are two reasons for this statement. The first is that governments are less and less able to choose, as I argued earlier. This regards

---

17. Although the "matching" argument has gotten public attention in the selling of submarines, airplanes, and telephone exchanges, it is well known that it has increased in importance in other sectors as well.

not only the technological aspects, but also the possible contribution of such projects toward its own policy goals. No one knows what the consequences will be for added value or employment, or whether firms will continue to keep their production at home or move abroad, nor is there much clarity about the right amount of the government contribution and its timing. The second reason deals with the number of firms applying for this kind of support. Assuming that the current trends for costs of R&D and scale of production continue, it can be expected that, whereas now just a few firms are asking for help, in a few years many more firms with much costlier requests will show up. Assuming that their pleas about R&D expectations and the added value and employment consequences are equally convincing, the government will have to pay a multiple of the current amount. This is, therefore, certainly the wrong track. The solution should be found in another direction.

Technology Policy and Economic Theory

The importance of technological progress as a major growth determinant and the probability that the volume of knowledge through R&D could be less than socially optimal were both strong incentives to strengthen the government efforts in technology policy. The technology policy of most governments in Western economies has been based on this vision. It has been criticized, however, especially because it does not take into account the fact that technological developments inevitably create situations of disequilibrium, as Schumpeter described.

Recently, economic theory in the field of international trade has added another reason for governments to support firms in this respect. Here, strong emphasis is laid on imperfect competition and strategic behavior.[18] For technologically advanced products, a relationship can be observed among increasing scale of production with higher sales, decreasing R&D costs per unit and increasing productivity, and lower prices and improved market opportunities. Those firms that build up their production capacity quickly can win a decisive lead over their competitors. Governments can play an essential role through their procurement policy by making available adequate financial means for such a project or by other interventionist measures that give domestic firms such—temporary—protection that they can survive.

Recently, an alternate vision of the relationship between technology and economic development and technology policy has been formulated, the so-called evolutionary approach. In this approach, emphasis is laid on nonequilibrium behavior, creativity, and dynamic learning effects, which create technological trajectories but are also responsible for the occurrence of

18. See Krugman 1986; Richardson 1989; Stegemann 1989.

locked-in situations. The policy orientation of the evolutionary approach is aimed at the creation of such conditions that technological developments can be fluently integrated in overall economic development. Sometimes this implies the setting of early standardization norms or the organization of competing projects, through which an effective trial-and-error process can be stimulated. On the whole, a government should stimulate the start of experimental projects, while it also should give more weight to effective evaluating procedures (MERIT 1990).

For an economy such as the Netherlands, MERIT states that generic R&D measures have to be judged less relevant, just as the choice of costly and prestigious projects that lack the necessary support from within the society are less relevant. They are strongly in favor of policies that bring the domestic scientific research and education systems to bear at a much more advanced level. This can function as a major focal point, making a small country much more attractive for investment from domestic as well as foreign firms that want to be in close proximity to this scientific base.

Even though this evolutionary approach stresses differences with the traditional approach, it cannot be said that their policy recommendations are that divergent. They both agree, in general terms, with government intervention in the area of technological development.

Technology Policy in a Small and Open Economy: Abstinence or Intervention?

This essay has dealt with certain aspects of the process of technological progress that have received much attention in recent years, namely the costs of R&D and the increasing scale of production, and the way a government of a small and open economy such as the Netherlands should deal with them. The position, contents, and relevance of a technology policy for such a government has been discussed. A so-called technological dilemma was sketched: while most governments, certainly small ones, do seem less able to pursue a deliberate technology policy, it can be observed that, at the same time, they have become more involved in such policies.

The main question remains: is there anything a government should do to stimulate the technological process in such a way that it will have positive results for the major goals of economic policy, from growth and employment to income distribution and environmental protection? The answer is affirmative, but the contents of such a technology policy would be different from what is currently done.

That difference regards two points. First, however valuable the initial stages of the technological process are, it seems that current technology policies show a tendency to pay too much attention to the creation of knowledge at the neglect of its diffusion and application. Available data on intrasectoral differences in productivity or in the age of capital stock clearly show that most firms lag far behind what is potentially possible. High yields could be reaped once firms make proper use of the existing body of knowledge. Investment in the diffusion of existing knowledge would yield higher results than a similar amount of investment in the creation of new knowledge. This certainly seems relevant for a small economy such as the Netherlands.

But the difference goes beyond this point. So far, the neoclassical view, with its emphasis on market failure, has prevailed. Current developments, however, are more in line with the dynamic view of this process, as presented by Schumpeter. Schumpeter never wrote about a separate technology policy, distinct and recognizable from other policy areas. In his view of the process of economic development, technology policy, indissolubly tied with other relevant government policies, should be aimed at the realization of the main issue of any market-oriented economy: sufficient structural change, sufficient in size, direction, and speed, as the consequence of developments in demand, in technology (and so in supply), and in the rise and decline of competitors.

By developing a more integrated approach, it seems possible to make both firms and individuals, as suppliers of labor, capital, and knowledge, more responsible and more committed to technological progress, while at the same time the nontraditional goals of economic policy, such as low unemployment, reasonable income distribution, and a healthy environment, can be better met. By stressing the importance and impact of structural changes and technological progress, there is also a better chance for public discussions of these issues. This can create a situation in which the society in general becomes more aware of technological developments, not only of its challenges and the costs of change, but also of its possible future rewards. Whatever time (and money) such a discussion may cost, there is a fair chance that this will be more than compensated with the yield that people are aware of these developments and are better able to anticipate and to support them.

Such an integrated policy should strongly stimulate competition. The creation and preservation of a competitive environment is a major condition for the realization of sufficient change. All measures detrimental for competition, from subsidies and protection to market disturbing arrangements (no matter how valuable they seem in the short run), should be refused because of their long-term negative impact on the competitive environment.

Furthermore, the government itself should become more competition oriented. Efficiency in its own activities should be an important theme. This requires not only changes in organization but especially changes in the attitudes of many civil servants. Of course, sufficient attention should also be given in such an integrated policy to education and the infrastructure. Investment in these factors will certainly benefit a competitive economy such as the Netherlands.

In the near future, the EC 1992 process will be very important for the Netherlands. The realization of a truly integrated market with 320 million inhabitants after 1992 is very important for such a small economy as the Netherlands, not only because of its market size but certainly also because of competition conditions. The availability of a bigger market gives Dutch firms better possibilities for economies of scale and for costly investments in R&D. The integration of a small domestic market in a big European market also means the transition from a situation that has markets with more oligopolistic characteristics toward a situation with much more competition.[19]

For the small and open economy of the Netherlands, the future seems promising but its potential rewards depend on the way the economic actors (including the Dutch government) are able to meet new requirements. I hope that "I struggle and emerge victorious" remains an appropriate motto for the Netherlands.[20]

REFERENCES

Dertouzos, M. L., R. K. Lester, R. M. Solow, and the MIT Commission on Industrial Productivity. 1989. *Made in America: Regaining the Productive Edge.* Cambridge, Mass.: MIT Press.

Ergas, H. 1986. *Does Technology Policy Matter?* Brussels: CEPS.

Freeman, C., and B.-A. Lundvall, eds. 1988. *Small Countries Facing the Technological Revolution.* London: Frances Pinter.

Kristensen, P. H., and J. Levinson. 1983. *The Small Country Squeeze.* Roskilde: Förlaget för Safundsekonomi og Planlaegning.

Krugman, P. R. 1986. *Strategic Trade Policy and the New International Economics.* Cambridge, Mass.: MIT Press.

MERIT. 1990. *Technology and Science Policy in a Changing Economic Theory* (in Dutch). Study for the Scientific Council for Government Policy. The Hague.

Mowery, D. C., and N. Rosenberg. 1989. "New Developments in U.S. Technology Policy: Implications for Competitiveness and International Trade Policy." *California Management Review* 31:107–24.

---

19. It seems that the same failures that occur on the national level also occur at the level of the EC. First, technology policy is treated as a separate policy issue. Second, the EC has started a number of major programs in recent years although the EC does not have the appropriate knowledge about technological progress to know what to choose and what not. Third, right at the moment that a more competitive environment is within reach by creating an integrated market, the EC starts to undermine this by proposing cooperation in the area of R&D, especially between the bigger firms.

20. The motto in the official coat of arms of the province of Zeeland is "Luctor et emergo."

OECD. 1989. *Main Science and Technology Indicators*. Paris: OECD.

Pavitt, K., and P. Patel. 1988. "The International Distribution and Determinants of Technological Activities." *Oxford Review of Economic Policy* 4:35–55.

Richardson, J. D. 1989. "Empirical Research on Trade Liberalization with Imperfect Competition." *OECD Economic Studies* 12.

Stegemann, K. 1989. "Policy Rivalry among Industrial States: What Can We Learn from Models of Strategic Trade Policy?" *International Organization* 43:73–100.

van Paridon, C. W. A. M. 1987. *Changing for Growth: A Study on the Process of Long-Term Economic Development for an Open and Industrialized Economy*. Delft: Eburon.

Van Tulder, R. 1988. "Small European Countries in the International Telecommunications Struggle." In Freeman and Lundvall 1988, 156–69.

Van Tulder, R., ed. 1989. *Small Industrial Countries and Economic and Technological Development*. Netherlands Organization for Technology Assessment, Working Document no. 9. The Hague.

Walsh, V. 1988. "Technology and the Competitiveness of Small Countries: Review." In Freeman and Lundvall 1988, 37–66.

Privatization, M&As, and Interfirm Cooperation in the EC: Improved Prospects for Innovation?

Paul J. J. Welfens

Challenges for Innovativeness in Europe

The 1970s and 1980s have been characterized by a decline of factor productivity growth in major western industrial countries, in particular in the United States, whose leading technological position was eroding under the impact of changing domestic policies and the competitive pressure from Japan and Germany. Most EC countries recorded declining productivity growth in the 1970s, too, where the sustained industrial challenge from Japan—maturing from a follower country to a technology frontier state—helped to revitalize EC integration in the 1980s (Englander, Evenson, and Hanazaki 1988). After 1975, the revealed comparative advantage and the net export position of the EC in high-tech areas have decreased while the United States defended and Japan increased its position; in contrast to Japan and the United States, the EC is less specialized in high-tech exports (Koekkoek 1987). Could the spread of supply-side policy approaches, typically including privatization schemes, and the transition to a single EC market with its changing industrial landscape of bigger and more internationalized firms restore the competitive position of the EC and accelerate factor productivity growth? And which role will national and the supranational levels play for the formation of innovation policies in the EC? Finally, given the tendency that international R&D ventures have generally spread in the 1980s (Chesnais 1988; Guile and Brooks 1987; Pearce 1989), will the role of EC firms increase in the context of the single market program?

The slowdown of total factor productivity growth is not necessarily an indication of declining innovativeness if one takes into account the increasing speed of the diffusion of innovations and a potentially growing role of product innovations that increase the heterogeneity of products, improve the opportunities for price discrimination, and trigger demand-creating process innovations as well. Hence, I consider innovativeness to comprise both the initial commercialization of new technologies as well as the initial introduction of innovations in a region.

Multinational companies that are present in various nations and observe diverging regional market trends as well as technological developments can be expected to play a significant role in innovativeness in an integrated EC market—especially in an environment of advanced communication networks that spur the exchange of information and ideas. A sustained drive toward forming Euronationals in the context of the EC 1992 project could lead to a higher rate of diffusion as well as to intensified oligopolistic competition in an enlarged European market; to share R&D costs in globalizing industries with shortened innovation cycles will be a major impulse for new, cooperative joint ventures and for mergers and acquisitions (M&As) in Western Europe. M&As might indirectly encourage risky innovation projects and, hence, contribute to higher innovativeness in the EC, but leveraged buy-outs associated with high financing costs and increasing exposure to short-term-oriented capital markets could also reduce the scope of feasible innovation projects. At the same time, there is the risk of reduced competition as a consequence of increased inter-firm cooperation and less competition as a consequence of weakening competition policies in the EC and an EC industrial policy that encourages cross-border mergers and the formation of bigger firms. This leads to the question of policy efficiency itself, where declining efficiency could reduce potential gains from improved industrial R&D networks in a changing European industrial landscape.

With changing firm sizes and structures on the national and EC level, the Western European market economies will not only exhibit different patterns of innovation (unless a linear relation between firm size and innovativeness would hold) but also changing prospects for productivity increases and economic growth. Moreover, they face new challenges to national and supranational innovation policy—here defined to comprise technology policy and competition policy—that have become extremely relevant at the EC level.

Thus, developments in both fields are important for an assessment of innovativeness in the EC. The EUREKA initiative of 1985 and EC R&D programs, above all a framework program for the 1987–91 period, have encouraged cross-border R&D in Western Europe. With respect to competition policy, the subsidy rules developed by the EC Commission play a role because, except national subsidies for basic science, all EC countries' national R&D subsidies—which might restrain intra-EC trade and competition—are subject to the supervision of the commission. New competencies for merger control have furthermore increased its role for innovation policy. In December, 1989, the EC treaty of Rome that had covered only vertical and horizontal collusion (articles 85 and 86) was complemented by an EC merger control that was designed as a partial, one-stop merger control: If the worldwide turnover of the would-be combined firms exceeds ECU 5 billion and if the combined sales of at least two involved firms exceeds ECU 250 million, the EC—represented by the EC Commission—can exert merger control; below these thresholds, national competition authorities (not existing in all EC countries) can intervene on the basis of national laws and regulations.

After sketching general considerations about current technological and institutional developments, the second section of this essay is devoted to problems of innovativeness in the EC. In the final section, I will take a brief look at the challenges in Eastern Europe. The basic conclusion to be drawn is that privatization and increased interfirm cooperation as well as multinational-ization, largely fueled by EC 1992, are expected to improve innovativeness at the level of firms. But the efficiency of innovation policy is likely to decline.

Changing Directions of Technological Progress and Industrial Competition

Bonsai Products and Networks

Although factor productivity growth was sluggish in many countries after the 1960s, the industrial market economies developed a host of product innovations that qualitatively improved output in the 1980s. Resource-saving product and process innovations (called "bonsai products" to emphasize the Japanese role) were developed after the oil price shocks of the 1970s. Except in the case of the United Kingdom and the Netherlands, which faced problems of the Dutch disease of deindustrialization, firms in the EC countries decisively contributed to energy-saving and resource-substituting (chemical/biotechnical) processes. Building on acquired technological advantages, firms from Europe and the United States successfully pursued traditional fields of innovation (Patel and Pavitt 1988); however, Japanese firms became rivals in many technological fields, especially in electronics, computer hardware, and biotechnology.

With high foreign direct investment in the United States and the EC, firms from Nipon, Inc., tap the technological pool outside Japan and gain improved access to EC markets by shipping Japanese products under the U.S. label, where they have introduced successful transplants; in Europe, the Japanese transplants are present, too, and have contributed not only to changing the industrial landscape but also introducing organizational innovations (e.g., *kanban*). The resource-saving and cost-reducing just in time organization of modern network production requires sophisticated logistics and communication technologies to link suppliers of intermediate goods to the firm that assembles a product for the market; moreover, facing rapidly changing demand conditions and pressure from innovative competitors, a mutual exchange of proprietary and nonproprietary know-how becomes essential within the network. To reveal tacit know-how and to trade or swap technologies in a sustained innovation process is particularly risky if many firms within such a network act under diverging national regulations. From this perspective, the creation of a single EC market with its associated partial convergence of national regulations can be expected to contribute to improved innovativeness within new EC-based industrial networks.

The Strategic Role of Telecommunications

The mode of a capital cost-reducing flexible production network means high requirements for communication and logistics, which spurs complementary technological progress in telecommunications and computer technology. The new directions of technological progress of the past two decades, namely miniaturization—requiring sophisticated quality control, computer-based flexible manufacturing, and high-quality telecommunications, have not only reduced the traditional role of heavy industry in economic growth, but have implied outright stagnation for the socialist economic systems of Eastern Europe (Welfens 1989). Since the adoption of the EC's Esprit program—its current second phase comprises the microelectronics project JESSI—the commission has emphasized the role of information technologies for technological progress and international competitiveness. Information technology and telecommunications will account for 7 percent of the EC GDP, and the world market for the respective products is growing at an annual rate of 17 percent (EC Commission 1990, 165). Moreover, the EC Commission supports the deregulation of the telecommunications industry throughout the EC.

Modern telecommunications technologies have not only contributed to the internationalization of financial markets, but are themselves vital for the international positioning of firms. It is important to note that advanced telecommunications allow a more flexible and widespread international production for which changing headquarters functions imply not only novel organizational patterns in industry but also adjustments to new industrial structures and, hence, innovations. The strategic role of telecommunication and the importance of flexible networks in international industry create an important contradiction in Europe. Traditionally, the telecommunications industry has been a protected, national state monopoly with limited "diagonal" (industrywide) effects on international competitiveness. However, the latter is now strongly tied to creating efficient communication networks both at home and abroad, so that strong pressure for deregulation and privatization has emerged—with the United Kingdom taking a strong lead in the EC in the 1980s (Letwin 1988; Veljanovski 1989; Vickers and Yarrow 1988; Yarrow 1986). The U.S. and the Japanese models of competing long-distance carriers with their important services for modern business and industry (Bar et al. 1989) provide at least some inspiration to continental Europe, which lags in the use of modems and telefax machines not only behind these two countries, but also behind the United Kingdom with its privatized telecommunications duopoly—in fact, more a monopoly as long as regional cable networks and international satellite operators cannot reinforce Mercury's attempts to eliminate the dominance of British Telecom.

The Challenge of Internationalization

The rise of more mobile, skill-oriented technologies in major industries whose location does not follow the old resource site orientation but the preferences of managers and skilled employees implies that, in connection with the improving human capital basis of the NICs and the spread or deepening of regional economic integration schemes in North America and Europe, a greater international variety of locations has become accessible to individual firms. Stronger competition among countries that try to attract mobile capital by a receptive political environment, in particular by lowering tax rates on capital income, as well as subsidies for R&D and technology-intensive, high value-adding production or exports stimulate the innovation process internationally. In globalizing markets, multinational companies play an increasing role in the innovation process, not least because foreign direct investment (FDI) helps to accelerate the diffusion stage. Moreover, as trade in technology predominantly takes place between parent companies and their respective subsidiaries, increased FDI in the EC can, indeed, be expected to foster innovativeness in Western Europe.

Asymmetric Integration of Capital Markets and the Role of Transnationals

The international flows of technology trade are assymetric and largely shaped by assymetric FDI or restrictions in capital markets. Modern telecommunications contribute to globalizing capital markets and, thus, to potentially widening the markets for corporate control on a transnational basis: efficient capital markets can check "management failure" and encourage innovations that have high long-term yields. However, if international financial markets are unstable and volatile, higher interest rates could result and a short-term investment horizon—unreceptive to innovations—might be reinforced. Here lies the importance of financial markets and financial innovations (Bank of International Settlements 1986). Moreover, these markets' roles increase because of the spread of transnational companies that both produce internationally (multinationals) and rely on an international capital basis (Welfens 1990c and 1991b). The internationalization of industrial property rights has been encouraged by the globalization of financial markets that was reinforced by liberalization schemes adopted in Western industrial countries in the 1980s. Japan, however, is an exception. From a U.S., and even more so from a German,

French, or British view, Japanese firms have advanced to become desired partners in sensitive technological fields, but the globally assymetric access to industrial property rights has continued. Japan stands out as a country with high barriers to inward FDI (Okimoto 1987).

Reduced international transaction and communication costs have contributed to the integration of financial markets that, however, still show country-specific traits (regulations, price-asset ratios) that can profitably be exploited by transnational firms. Exemplified by early but rare models such as Unilever and Royal Dutch Shell, transnational companies are on the rise. More recent cases that are partly built on equity swaps include the Swiss-Swedish ABB, GEC-Alstholm, and industrial joint ventures between U.S. and Japanese as well as between automotive producers, banks, and insurance companies from Europe. The growing number of transnationals that are noted in foreign stock markets testifies both to the growing importance of financial markets as well as to the desire and acceptance of an internationally mixed stock capital.

Imperfections of Markets for Know-How
The increasing share of national income devoted to R&D in market economies and in many NICs as well as the apparently rising share of nontangible investments in most OECD countries (OECD 1987, 165) reveal the increased importance of technology in production. Imperfections in the international markets for know-how, hence, seem all the more negative. The extremely high regional concentration of international trade in technologies—90 percent of global license fees are accounted for by 10 OECD countries (Deutsche Bundesbank 1990)—points to impediments to technology trade that stem from the particularities of the market for information on the one hand and, on the other hand, from obvious imperfections in intellectual property rights. Disregarding the role of embodied technological progress, a cautious estimation of the underdevelopment of markets for technology might be made by comparing the share of the residual technology factor in approaches to growth accounting, where most estimates are in the range of one-fourth to one-third (Jorgenson 1988) and the small share of royalties and license fees in world exports, which is less than 1 percent.

Privatization: The Demise of the State as an Entrepreneur in Europe

Since the diffusion of advanced telecommunications is so important for all industries and, more generally, for a modern nation's competitive advantage, the pressure to privatize significant parts of state-run services, telecommunications in particular, increased in Europe in the 1980s. Leading telecommunications suppliers from North America built up political leverage in the G-7 framework to liberalize the European market. Exposing the telecommunications sector more strongly to the forces of market competition is expected to spur innovations and to accelerate the diffusion process as well as to reduce prices of new services for advanced manufacturing industries. Private competition has been introduced in the United Kingdom and, to a limited extent, in Germany, while Italy opted to accept a joint venture with AT&T. The role of the state as an entrepreneur is thus going into eclipse in most fields. EC 1992 implies the liberalization of other service industries and of transportation, where suppliers of railway systems have formed new consortia.

In connection with the privatizations adopted in major EC countries and the EC 1992 project, the question arises whether this decline in the international technological position of the EC will be reversed. Indeed, the drive to privatize state services and state firms in the context of EC 1992 could lead to a higher rate of innovations in high technology. A unifying European health-care market (with a greater role for private health insurance) could improve the prospects for innovations in drugs and medicine in a bigger and more competitive market. The pharmaceuticals market that has been an oligopolistic world market for many decades could undergo major changes as the contradictions between growing health-care demand in a greying population in the EC (plus Japan) and limitations on public expenditures create reform pressures in public health-care systems. Moreover, a single EC health-care market is likely to become a favorite export target for the innovative Japanese pharmaceutical industry, which is just entering the stage of internalization; EC firms would have to defend their positions by counterinnovations. Aerospace could also benefit from the growing sales volumes and dynamic scale effects that can be expected in the context of a deregulated and liberalized—partly privatized—European airline industry. A higher rate of innovations in the field of computers, electrical components and instruments, and electrical machinery can be expected under the pressure of intensifying competition as a consequence of nondiscriminatory public procurements in the EC. Fields of medium R&D intensity, such as motor vehicles, chemicals, and nonferrous metals could witness an acceleration of innovation as the share of state-owned companies in France, Italy, the Netherlands, Spain, the United Kingdom, and Germany declines. Efficient capital markets can be expected to induce the managements of privatized firms to exploit remaining opportunities for diffusion and to encourage further innovations.

The privatization of state-owned firms and banks was high on the political agenda in Europe in the 1980s, where ideological reorientation toward the market economy model, endogenous disequilibria in markets, and new institutional frameworks meant a changing role for government in industry.

Privatization of firms and deregulation of markets were often two sides of the same coin minted by new, laissez-faire minds (Pera 1988). However, the demise of the state as an entrepreneur is less linked to ideological shifts than to the globalization of markets and the rise of multinational industries. In such an environment, nationally bound, state-owned enterprises are at a clear disadvantage.

Historically, government-owned enterprises have played a role for various reasons in Europe (Ambrosius 1984). The state played an important role as an entrepreneur in Germany and Italy in the nineteenth century; after 1945, Italy, France, Spain, and, in part, the United Kingdom emphasized the strategic role of certain public enterprises. Instead of adopting the U.S. system of controlling industries with declining costs by regulation, governments in Europe used public ownership of utility firms, the communication sector, and some manufacturing activities. By public procurement decisions and, in many cases, by preferential allocation of credits and capital, governments had an impact on the innovativeness of upstream and downstream industries.

Principal agent problems in public firms of course could not be checked by the capital market, which became a particular problem after external shocks in the 1970s required creative structural adjustments. Relying on established Olson-type redistributive coalitions with excellent access to the political system, publicly owned industries not only accepted capital yields below market rates but showed slow reactions to new technology trends and particular communication problems (Borcherding et al. 1982; De Jong 1989; Floyd et al. 1985; Picot and Kaulmann 1989). In addition to the problem of forgoing the full set of opportunities of internationalization, state-owned companies are less exposed to the control of private capital markets.

Determinants of Innovativeness

In a rapidly changing global environment with an increasing role of multinationals, technological joint ventures and intrafirm trade as determinants of innovativeness deserve a brief reconsideration. The innovation process is considered to be comprised of five interrelated elements, namely inspiration, invention, innovation, investment, and imitation (fig. 1). Innovativeness grows out of a dynamic disequilibrium in which new, uncharted technological or organizational opportunities become more attractive than established solutions; the positive sanctions in the form of R&D subsidies or tax breaks and higher expected profits and the negative sanctions associated with market competition as well as appropriability risks are important for innovation processes. The efficiency of the innovation process depends on a complex political process of R&D programming and funding and demand conditions as well as on creativity and control within firms.

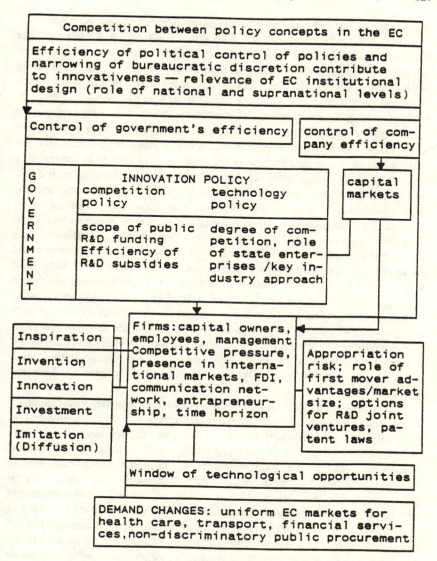

Fig. 1.   Determinants of innovativeness

Larger markets allow R&D costs to be spread across more users; thus, R&D incentives should increase in Europe as a consequence of market integration. Moreover, the increasing role of multinational firms and FDI, respectively, should contribute to intensified technology trade. To the extent that the performance of R&D policies becomes more difficult to assess, innovative-ness in the EC is likely to decline. The same holds true of allowing greater discretionary bureaucratic action, which induces companies to invest in re-distributive coalitions with state R&D agencies. However, with competing approaches to R&D policies within the EC, the efficiency problems of alterna-tive forms of innovation policies become obvious in the long term.

To develop critical innovation momentum, creative tensions between the status quo and an increasing aspiration level are necessary. Mass media com-munication and telecommunications in industry have accelerated and im-proved the international diffusion of information, and greater factor mobility is contributing to rising aspiration levels everywhere, particularly in the EC. The globalization of markets facilitates the spread of R&D costs, and the mutual presence of multinational companies in major regions of the world provides opportunities to swap material and nonmaterial assets as well as to embark upon joint ventures and M&As. The scope of state-owned enterprises means a restriction of the available assets. In principle, state-run firms could adopt the long capitalization horizon necessary to realize innovations with high short-term costs and a high long-term payoff, but at the same time these firms face extreme principal-agent problems and are usually slow in adjusting firm structures to innovations in related industries. Moreover, if management functions become politicized, trade unions might seek redistributive coalitions with a risk-averse management, thus contributing to I-inefficiency. This dy-namic inefficiency can increase if opportunities to cooperate with foreign companies in R&D are not used because of national procurement and cooper-ation strategies.

With respect to EC integration, the question of whether innovativeness as characterized by the chain of inspiration-invention-innovation-investment-imitation will be reinforced in west European industry, with its ongoing changes of business-government relationships on the national and interna-tional level. Under the pressure of more intense global competition, shorter technology cycles, and high capital costs for financing innovations, an in-creasing number of international technology joint ventures have developed both in the EC and worldwide (UNCTC 1988). This is even true in the field of high technology, where cooperative technology joint ventures mean a kind of reciprocal specialization of firms with a mutual sharing of proprietary knowl-edge and tacit know-how; the latter is quite important for a full appropriation of benefits from innovations. Advanced know-how that is subject to erosion in the course of time is shared reciprocally, and the mechanism to ensure cooper-ation is similar to exchanging hostages for achieving peaceful cooperation among principally adversarial countries. Technological complementarities and symmetrical interests in reciprocal technological specialization are the basis for the formation of new alliances between innovation-oriented multi-nationals.

Privatization and the Role of Capital
Markets for Innovation

The privatization of industry and banking is particularly important in the context of capital markets that are supposed to check managerial discretion and to enforce dynamic efficiency: privatization means a widening of the national and international M&A menu as well as a more level playing field in goods markets. If one assumes that public and private R&D expenditures are positively reflected in the valuation of firms, the stock markets play a special role. But capital markets could also favor short-term management actions and hence reduce the feasible scope of innovations where high-grade projects usually require long planning horizons. In Germany, the size of the firm is positively correlated with the length of the planning horizon for R&D projects, and the bigger firms also account for a relatively high proportion of innovations (Penzkofer and Schmalholz 1990).

Large firms are mostly stock companies. This might suggest that the stock market particularly rewards innovative projects or, at least, a good innovation track record. Evidence from the United States suggests not only a question mark for this hypothesis, but also the well-known role of internal capital markets in Germany, France, and Japan, where nonpublic companies and powerful banks on the one hand, and, on the other hand, mutual share-holdings play a significant role. Finally, one may note that "good" relationships between firms and the technology bureaucracy of a country will also be reflected in stock market prices. Thus, there are no unambiguous indicators of innovation efficiency at the firm level.

EC 1992

The realization of the single EC market changes the optimum plant size, implies a greater market with new opportunities for using static and dynamic scale economies, and provides new incentives for restructuring the industrial landscape. Furthermore, government-business relationships are likely to change, and a greater role for supranational EC policy bodies and multinationals is to be expected.

With regard to the EC countries, EC 1992 increases the need for paid-up capital, which will drive many family companies to turn to the stock markets. With higher economic growth expected in the EC in the 1990s, prospects for going public are favorable. Capital needed to finance innovations and investment—with capital-embodied technological progress—can thus be raised. Whether the initiatives of the EC Commission and the likely institutional integration of EC stock markets, currently dominated by London with its huge domestic and international market segments, will bring British "good practice" rules and the acceptance of hostile takeover bids to the whole EC remains to be seen.

Removing impediments to friendly and unfriendly takeovers, buy-outs and buy-ins, as well as spin-offs—within the limits drawn by competition policy—should enhance the dynamic efficiency of industry provided that capital markets are fully developed and not highly volatile. The latter is doubtful; the former is at least questionable in the EC, because fully developed means: (1) nondiscriminatory to foreigners or to the absence of capital controls as well as to state ownership of firms and restrictions of voting rights of stock owners; (2) open access to venture capital; and (3) nondiscriminatory to various forms of ownership. The removal of capital controls by 1992 in the whole EC and the ongoing privatization projects in major EC countries indicate that the first condition is nearly fulfilled. However, at least on the European continent, restrictions of voting rights are commonplace, so that a considerable gap between Germany and France on the one hand and the United Kingdom on the other hand cannot be overlooked. This also holds for the relative importance of stock markets (Franks and Mayer 1990). A venture capital market of the U.S. type is virtually nonexistent on the continent. The third condition of nondiscrimination is not met because of restrictions stemming from regulations in the labor and capital markets.

**EC 1992, Interfirm Cooperation,
and Innovativeness in the EC**

The creation of a single market in the EC will increase competition in Western Europe. Pressure for cost-reducing process innovations will rise in regions that offer comparable location advantages at relatively high costs. Firms in a region with high unit labor costs will face pressures to scale down activities, to more strongly resist wage claims, and—with uniform capital costs in the EC already observable—to realize opportunities to reduce costs in an EC market with a stronger validity of the law of one price and a transitory pressure to reduce the average industry price level in Western Europe.

Merger Intensity and Joint Venture Engagement
in the Context of EC 1992

In a more competitive EC environment it becomes very costly and risky not to exploit available efficiency gains. This constitutes a particular problem for state-owned industries and private firms that are hesitant or incapable of building the new EC firm alliances necessary to profitably serve a big, unified market. A greater market might increase the value of information advantages the management of a firm has. This could contribute to a greater role of management buy-outs, which, however, will not necessarily mean a higher rate of innovation. If buy-outs are financed at high real interest rates, medium-term liquidity considerations could reduce company spending on investment and encourage managements' drives for greater public R&D funding on the national and supranational level. Hence, the privatization of state-owned companies might not improve government budget balances as much as expected, and innovativeness is likely to be impaired if greater state interference becomes common in Europe. Because the 1990s are expected to be a period of high real interest rates in world financial markets, the opportunity costs of public enterprises that do not have considerable external benefits at the national level are high and increasing. Moreover, the discretionary room to allocate subsidies to nationalized firms is narrowed because of stricter competition rules enforced by the EC Commission (e.g., in the case of Renault in 1990).

The EC 1992 project can be expected not only to yield the static benefits mentioned in the report of Cecchini (1988) and some dynamic benefits emphasized by Welfens (1991a), it will also create new opportunities for innovation and growth because established national redistributive coalitions of the Olson type collapse in the face of the innovative projects such as EC 1992. Major suppliers of capital equipment, Germany, the United States, and Japan, are likely to particularly benefit from the modernization of European industry in a new internationalized setting.

Anticipating a larger, unified market, more and more companies in the EC are going European. With major domestic M&A opportunities rapidly being exhausted, many firms turn to intra-EC takeovers and new international joint ventures. New forms of cooperation in R&D-intensive industries played an increasing role in the 1980s (Rath 1988). Table 1 shows that intra-EC M&A activities increased in the late 1980s. In regard to the 1,000 largest European industrial firms, the number of acquisitions made—including majority holdings—doubled in the period from 1983–84 to 1986–87 and increased another 34 percent between 1986–87 and 1987–88. Large firms chased not only small ones, but focused on each other in the capital market. The focus in acquisitions has shifted in the second half of the 1980s toward international operations, where intra-EC operations increased in relative significance—mostly in the sheltered sectors that face increasing international competition after 1992. While the main motives for M&As were improvement of market position, expansion, complementarity, and the desire to restructure and diversify, R&D considerations ranked first when it came to motives for joint ventures (EC Commission 1989); however, one may note that M&As can have considerable positive side effects on R&D at the micro-level (not necessarily at the macrolevel). International and domestic joint venture operations dominated over community operations (table 2). The explanation for this could be that R&D joint ventures are mainly sought with U.S. and Japanese companies, where M&As are, contrary to the intra-EC situation, not a good option for maintaining market position. Figures available for Germany show that European R&D joint ventures dominate in the case of companies with more than 1,000 employees, whereas domestic joint ventures dominate in the case of smaller firms (table 3). The obvious desire in many EC countries to increase the size of plants as a consequence of EC 1992 suggests that the average size of firms will rise in the EC. Interestingly, the intention to produce more specialized products dominates the desire to expand with standardized products in the major EC countries.

This assessment is particularly relevant because it holds not only for the case of Germany with its leading role in the production and export of specialized machinery. A higher rate of product innovations is to be expected from firms that can no longer enforce national price segmentations after 1992, but face the option of segmenting markets more strongly in accordance with incomes and quality preferences. To the extent that a fast diffusion of new technologies is tied to foreign direct investment, higher FDI implies improved prospects for a more intensive technological competition between EC-based firms and U.S. and Japanese subsidiaries in Europe. Moreover, new prospects for interfirm cooperation—for example, in the form of license swaps—might result, so that intensified technological competition and cooperation among fewer companies in the EC is a likely result of the adjustments in the 1990s. It is, however, true that collaborative strategies of firms in high technology meet specific contractual problems that are not really remedied by EC 1992. In view of the imperfections of the market for licensing, the spread of R&D joint ventures in the EC is nevertheless encouraging; know-how cannot easily be

TABLE 1.   Mergers or Takeovers and Acquisitions of Majority Holdings by Type of Operation

	Domestic		Community		International		Total	
	N	Percentage	N	Percentage	N	Percentage	N	Percentage
1983–84	101	65.2	29	18.7	25	16.1	155	100
1984–85	146	70.2	44	21.2	18	8.7	208	100
1985–86	145	63.9	52	22.9	30	13.2	227	100
1986–87	211	69.6	75	24.8	17	5.6	303	100
1987–88	214	55.9	112	29.2	57	14.9	383	100

Sources: Data from EC Commission 1988 and 1989.

codified because it has tacit elements that require demonstration, application, and special contractual relations that are characteristic of modern capitalist firms (Nelson and Winter 1982; Teece 1986; Williamson 1981).

Building EC multinationals is a rather novel tendency that is surprising in view of the expected decreasing market transaction costs in the context of institutional integration of markets. However, if governance costs within the firm plus takeover costs—determined by financial markets—fall faster than market transaction costs, the tendency to establish EC multinationals is not a puzzle. Moreover, with domestic M&A opportunities being rapidly exhausted, firms that face declining opportunities for price discrimination along national boundaries will invest in improved price discrimination options across income groups within the EC so that an EC-wide presence is desirable. Since many firms from EC countries want to go European within a few years, external growth and new forms of interfirm cooperation are the only available option for becoming a European multinational within a short period.

TABLE 2.   New, Jointly Owned Subsidiaries by Type of Operation

	Domestic	Community	International	Total
1983–84	32	11	26	69
1984–85	40	15	27	82
1985–86	34	20	27	81
1986–87	29	16	45	90
1987–88	45	31	35	111

Sources: Data from EC Commission 1988 and 1989.

TABLE 3.   The Influence of EC 1992 on the Strategies of Industrial Firms (net balance between positive and negative impacts)

	Europe	Spain	France	Italy	Netherlands	U.K.	Germany
R&D							
Greater cooperation	42	39	44	47	20	66	30[a]
Greater use of firm resources	44	15	43	43	27	66	46
Production Plant							
Increase size	24	8	17	18	—	17	30
Increase number	7	0	−2	17	—	1	14
Products							
More standardized	24	9	29	33	16	28	21
More specialized	38	38	40	49	31	32	36

Sources: Data from EC Commission 1989, 191; Penzkofer 1989, 17.

[a]For domestic firms, the impact is 32 when there are fewer than 1,000 employees and 19 when there are more than 1,000 employees. For international firms, the impact is 17 when there are fewer than 1,000 employees and 22 when there are more than 1,000 employees.

EC Innovation Policy

Technology policy is one element of innovation policy, and, in the case of the EC, it is an increasingly important one. One major program is the EUREKA project (organized from below and industry, respectively) in which 300 projects are realized by 1,500 participants from 20 Western European countries. Cooperative R&D projects and innovative cross-border networks were systematically encouraged from above by the EC Commission. Various EC R&D programs—the first was COST launched in 1971—have played their own particular role when it came to promoting intra-EC ventures in R&D. ESPRIT, RACE, and BRITE are major, well-known EC programs, where ESPRIT marked a new beginning of EC technology policy in 1980 when the first outline for this information technology program was drafted. EC interference in technology policy is mounting (Klodt et al. 1988).

While former attempts to set up supranational EC programs had met resistance from individual countries, the ESPRIT program enjoyed wide consensus in the EC. An important force in creating this consensus was the "support" of two anticipated pressures, namely the settlement of the dispute between IBM and the U.S. antitrust authorities and the prospective deregulation of AT&T that would be cleared by U.S. antitrust authorities to operate worldwide. Thus, powerful U.S. firms could fully launch their attacks on EC markets in which Japanese competitors were already advancing (Sharp 1989, 208–9). This program, in which costs are generally cofinanced by the EC and industry on a 1:1 basis, is largely believed to have encouraged R&D collaboration in the EC, where large firms usually collaborate in joint R&D within rather stable "clubs" that weaken the incentive to license technologies (Ullrich 1990).

The role of the EC in technology policy is increasing if one takes into account the increasing funds available. While the first EC technology framework program spent ECU 3.7 billion in 1984–87, the second framework program for 1987–91 envisaged ECU 5.4 billion and the third program for 1990–94 will allocate ECU 5.7 billion. Moreover, in 1988, twenty-four seed capital funds were created to support technology-oriented business start-ups, and in 1989 a strategic program for innovation and technology transfer (SPRINT) was adopted by the EC Council (EC Commission 1990).

The other element of innovation policy, competition policy, has also become more important on the level of the EC. However, there are conceptual ambiguities that impair the efficiency of innovation policy from this side. While competition effects are clearly the criterion for merger policies in some EC countries—for example, in Germany and the United Kingdom—other countries and the EC Commission might include aspects of industrial or technological policies in their respective decisions. It is noteworthy that the

EC Commission, with its powerful and complex bureaucracy, is handling problems of merger control rather than a separate EC institution. The EC Commission, which made the first proposal for EC merger control in 1973, has considerably increased its discretionary power because it will lump (similar to the traditional French approach of fostering national champions) competition aspects and implications of technology policy concepts.

Technology Policy: National versus Supranational Approaches

If firms headquartered in different countries cooperate in R&D, this implies that national technology policies increasingly face the problem of positive external (leakage) effects; other countries' current account balances or the governments' budget balances might improve, while positive effects in the domestic economy are uncertain. Hence, from a political point of view, a joint (regional) industrial policy, already visible in the EC, is required. This is more important the smaller a country is. At the same time, the increasing presence of EC multinationals offers an opportunity to build up parallel political leverage in various EC countries. If, for example, both the parent company in Germany and subsidiaries in major EC partner countries press for high-tech subsidies, a parallel steamlining of national technology policies as well as the common orientation of a particular segment of EC industrial policy might be obtained. The problem for a single multinational is, of course, that its demand for high-tech policies creates external benefits for other firms in the same industry. Stricter intraindustry specialization to minimize external intraindustry benefits on the one hand, or, on the other hand, stronger engagement in horizontal M&As plus joint ventures are the basic alternatives for high-tech firms that seek to internalize the benefits of lobbying for government innovation policies.

A New Orientation for EC Innovation Policy

Governments have promoted technological progress for various reasons and with diverging degrees of efficiency. The classical arguments for state promotion of innovation are positive external effects and information market failure (the latter is, of course, also a classical argument for FDI). This problem has long been seen from a national point of view. Governments that seek a politicoeconomic payoff of R&D subsidies were typically promoting high-tech and product innovations that would protect jobs or improve the country's terms of trade and contribute to economic growth and higher tax revenues by way of reducing the price of intermediate goods and factor inputs. However, with an increasing role of multinationals, national technology policies face rising uncertainty as to whether supporting firms in invention and innovation will not mainly benefit other economies and the politicians acting therein. Multilateral or supranational R&D funding thus becomes increasingly appropriate. At the same time, however, political control of supranational policy in general and of technology policy in particular is likely to be weaker than on the national level. In a larger constituency, the incentive for voters to cast well-informed ballots is reduced with a relatively declining weight of individuals' as well as of groups' votes. Moreover, the transparency of technology policy declines in a more complex multinational political and economic environment. The implication is that EC technology policy faces particular efficiency problems. Additionally, in the process of harmonizing national R&D policies, the visible rivalry between alternative concepts of innovation policies in the EC could be lost as a control device.

The Political Economy of Innovation Policy

The fact that international decision making in politics is likely to suffer similar inefficiencies as national politics with its typical mixture of imperfect political competition and budget-maximizing bureaucrats (Frey 1984) is important for assessing the proper role of internationalized competition and technology policy concepts. This is especially true because, on an international level, the efficiency problem of politics naturally seems to increase.

Innovation policy must rely on patent protection if a sustained stream of innovations is to be assured. EC cooperation tends to reinforce effective patent protection. Better patent protection and improvement in the trade of technology can be expected to reduce the incentive for multinationalization. In this field, technology policy could support competition policy.

Competition policymakers tend to view the build up of market power as a continuing threat to allocative efficiency, so that innovation policy faces a latent conflict. The OECD (1989) studied the trade-off between static and dynamic efficiency with ambiguous findings. The view of leading industrial countries, confirmed by some economists (e.g., Ordover and Baumol 1988; Scherer 1985, 13) is that dynamic efficiency criteria are more important for growth and welfare than static ones. This view obviously has also been adopted by the EC Commission (Jacquemin, Buiges, and Ilzkovitz 1990).

Only in the case of the EC does there now exist a supranational competition policy, namely in regard to allowing subsidies, granting R&D group exemptions, and—in the future—controlling part of the mergers in the EC. Block exemptions from the prohibition of collusion have become widespread in the 1980s. In the EC (under article 85, paragraph 3), group exemptions are granted that allow a group of firms not only to cooperate in R&D (in the precompetitive stage) but also to jointly exploit the results of the R&D joint venture, which seems to be an acceptable, pragmatic policy compromise among EC member states (Jacquemin 1988). The current EC joint venture rule, adopted in 1985, gives a five-year exemption; however, in the case of horizontal joint ventures (as opposed to conglomeral or vertical types), this exemption will only be given if the parties' combined market share does not exceed 20 percent.

The EC's policy stance is most liberal and market oriented in the service industry—here it meets the resistance of national governments whose aim is to preserve some degree of bureaucratic monopoly in the continental countries. Removing intra-EC trade barriers and effectively eliminating impediments to factor mobility will strongly stimulate competition in the service industry. However, when there is a close link with high-tech industries—as in the case of telecommunications and computers—then the EC's policy stance leads to distorted international competition because of high and increasing state R&D funding. R&D subsidies are granted by both regional and national governments as well as by the EC. The goal of restricting the benefits of tax-funded R&D subsidies to firms located within the community implies that foreign—in the case of JESSI, mostly U.S. and Japanese—firms in the respective industry have to resort to FDI in Europe if participation in advanced joint research programs is to be ensured (the U.S. Sematech program creates a similar problem).

Prospects for Greater Innovativeness in Europe

After a period of economic stagnation and weakening entrepreneurial spirits, Europe could once again become a global center for innovative activities in the 1990s. The direction of technological progress, the increasing role of private capital markets, and the creation of a single EC market in Western Europe as well as the opening up of Eastern Europe—more generally the marketization drive in the world economy—create new opportunities for Schumpeterian forces in Europe in the medium term. After decades of conglomeral growth, firms in the OECD countries seem to be refocusing their external growth strategies on their core advantages, which could imply increased specialization on R&D at the firm level (Poutrel and Quaisser 1990). If this tendency were supported, the incentive to adopt collaborative R&D projects in Europe could increase because this would become a major avenue to assure access to technological progress in fields that are related to the companies' core R&D and production activities.

While there is some reason to generally anticipate efficiency problems in innovation policy, the disarmament perspectives of the 1990s reduce the role of militarily related R&D policies that have been relatively weak in terms of civilian innovation spin-offs. This should reinforce both the competitive positions of France and the United Kingdom (as well as the United States), which traditionally devoted up to 40 percent of public R&D funds to military projects. This tendency should also contribute to a higher rate of innovation and diffusion in Eastern Europe.

The decline of Council of Mutual Economic Assistance market positions in the 1980s (largely at the expense of rising share of NICs [Inotai 1988]), stagnant productivity growth, and a dismal patent record with visibly slow internal diffusion processes have contributed to the pressure for systemic reforms in Eastern Europe. Inadequate West-East technology transfers and overinvestment in an environment of negative interest rates and bureaucratic rent sharing were other major problems in the Council of Mutual Economic Assistance countries that now offer new prospects for marketization and the realization of static and dynamic efficiency criteria (Welfens and Balcerowicz 1988; Welfens 1990a and 1991a). The greatest challenge for reform-minded Council of Mutual Economic Assistance countries lies in the stimulation of Schumpeterian spirits. In contrast to the older Schumpeter—anticipating (in *Capitalism, Socialism, and Democracy*) innovation-oriented socialist economies after World War II—he was certainly right when he emphasized (Schumpeter 1910, 485) that, without the challenging and inspiring example of successful private entrepreneurs, the economic performance of public enterprises would be much worse than it would be on its own merits. There is a new pool of Schumpeterian talents in a more dynamic Europe.

REFERENCES

Ambrosius, G. 1984. *Der Staat als Unternehmer: Oeffentliche Wirtschaft und Kapitalismus seit dem 19. Jahrhundert.* Göttingen: Vandenhoeck and Ruprecht.
Bank of International Settlements (BIS). 1986. Annual Report 1986. Basel.
Bar, F., et al. 1989. *Information Networks and Comparative Advantage.* Vol. 2, *Comparative Reviews of Telecommunications Policies and Uses in the USA and Japan.* Mimeo. Berkeley: BRIE.
Borcherding, T. E., et al. 1982. "Comparing the Efficiency of Private and Public Production: The Evidence from Five Countries." *Zeitschrift für National-ökonomie,* Suppl. 2: 127–56.
Cecchini, P. 1988. *The Challenge of EC 1992.* London: Gower.
Chesnais, A. 1988. "Technological Cooperation Agreements between Firms." *STI Review,* no. 4: 51–59.
De Jong, H. W. 1989. "The State as Entrepreneur." In *Deregulierung—eine Herausforderung an die Wirtschafts-und Sozialpolitik in der Marktwirtschaft,* ed. H. S. Seidenfus, 173–93. Berlin: Duncker and Humblot.
Deutsche Bundesbank. 1990. "Patent- und Lizenzverkehr mit dem Ausland sowie sonstiger Austausch von technischem Wissen durch Dienstleistungen in den Jahren 1988 und 1989." *Monatsberichte der Deutschen Bundesbank* (May): 28–43.

EC Commission. 1989. *European Economy.* Brussels: EC Commission.

EC Commission. 1990. *General Report—1989.* Brussels: EC Commission.

Englander, A. S., R. Evenson, and M. Hanazaki. 1988. "Innovation and the Total Factor Productivity Slowdown." *OECD Economic Studies* 12: 7–43.

Floyd, R. H. et al. 1984. *Public Enterprise in Mixed Economies.* Washington, D.C.: IMF.

Franks, J., and C. Mayer. 1990. "Capital Markets and Corporate Control: A Study of France, Germany, and the U.K." *Economic Policy,* no. 10: 189–232.

Frey, Bruno, 1984. *International Political Economics.* New York: Basil Blackwell.

Guile, A., and A. Brooks, eds. 1987. *Technology and Global Industry.* Washington, D.C.: National Academy Press.

Hymann, H. 1989. *Privatization: The Facts.* London: Price Waterhouse.

Inotai, A. 1988. "Competition Between European CMEA and Rapidly Industrializing Countries in the OECD Market for Manufactured Goods." *Empirica* 15:189–204.

Jacquemin, A. 1988. "Cooperative Agreements in R&D and European Antitrust Policy." *European Economic Review* 32:551–60.

Jacquemin, A., P. Buiges, and F. Ilzkovitz. 1990. "Horizontal Mergers and Competition Policy in the European Community." *European Economy,* no. 40.

Jorgensen, D. W. 1988. "Productivity and Postwar U.S. Economic Growth." *Journal of Economic Perspectives* 2:23–41.

Klodt, H., et al. 1988. *Forschungspolitik unter EG-Kontrolle.* Tübingen: Mohr.

Koekkoek, A. 1987. "The Competitive Position of the EC in Hi-Tech." *Weltwirtschaftliches Archiv* 123:157–68.

Letwin, O. 1988. *Privatizing the World: A Study of International Privatization in Theory and Practice.* London: Cassel.

Nelson, R. R., and S. G. Winter. 1982. *An Evolutionary Theory of Economic Change.* Cambridge, Mass.: Harvard University Press.

OECD. 1987. *Economic Performance and Structural Change.* Paris: OECD.

OECD. 1988. *The Newly Industrializing Countries.* Paris: OECD.

OECD. 1989. *Competition Policy and Intellectual Property Rights.* Paris: OECD.

Okimoto, D. L. 1987. "Outsider Trading: Coping with Japanese Industrial Organization." In *The Trade Crisis: How Will Japan Respond?* ed. K. B. Pyle, 85–116. Seattle: Society for Japanese Studies.

Ordover, J., and W. Baumol. 1988. "Antitrust Policy and High-Technology Industries." *Oxford Review of Economic Policy* 4:13–34.

Patel, P., and K. Pavitt. 1988. "The International Distribution and Determinants of Technological Activities." *Oxford Review of Economic Policy* 4.

Pearce, R. D. 1989. *The Internationalization of Research and Development by Multinational Enterprises.* London: Macmillan.

Penzkofer, H., and H. Schmalholz. 1990. Unternaehmen als Patentanmelder in der Patentstatistik. *IFO-Schnelldienst,* 43, no. 15:3–8.

Pera, A. 1988. "Deregulation and Privatization in an Economywide Context." *OECD Studies* 11:159–97.

Picot, A., and T. Kaulmann. 1989. "Comparative Performance of Government-owned and Privately Owned Industrial Corporations—Empirical Results from Six Countries." *Journal of Institutional and Theoretical Economics* 145:298–316.

Pirie, M. 1988. *Privatization: Theory, Practice, and Choice.* Aldershot: Wildwood House.

Poutrel, J.-M., and M. Queisser. 1990. "Neue Strategien der Grossen in Europa." *Ifo-Schnelldienst* 12:3–8.

Rath, H. 1988. Neue Formen internationaler Unternehmenskooperation. Entwicklung, Tendenzen und thoeretische Aspekte. In *Innovationsydynamik im Systemvergleich,* ed. P. J. J. Welfens and L. Balcerowicz, 78–95. Heidelberg: Physica.

Scherer, F. M. 1985. "Stand und Perspektiven der Industrieökonomik." In *Industrieoekonomik,* ed. G. Bombach, 3–20. Tuebingen: Mohr.

Schumpeter, J. 1910. "Unternehmer." In *Handwörterbuch der Staatswissenschaften,* 476–87. Jena: Fischer.

Sharp, M. 1989. "The Community and New Technologies." In *The European Community and the Challenge of the Future,* ed. J. Lodge, 202–22. New York: St. Martin's Press.

Teece, D. J. 1986. "Transaction Cost Economics and the Multinational Enterprise." *Journal of Economic Behavior and Organization* 7:21–45.

Ullrich, H. 1990. "Europäische Forschungs- und Technologiepolitik und die Ordnung des Wettbewerbs im Gemeinsamen Markt." In *Jahrbuch für Neue Politische Ökonomie,* ed. K. Schenk. Tübingen: Mohr. Forthcoming.

UNCTC. 1988. *Transnational Corporations in World Development.* New York: UNCTC.

Veljanovski, C., ed. 1989. *Privatization and Competition: A Market Prospectus.* London: Institute of Economic Affairs.

Vickers, J., and G. Yarrow. 1988. *Privatization: An Economic Analysis.* London: MIT Press.

Welfens, P. J. J. 1987. "Growth, Innovation and International Competitiveness." *Intereconomics,* July/August, 168–74.

Welfens, P. J. J., and L. Balcerowicz, eds. 1988. *Innovationsdynamik im Systemvergleich.* Heidelberg: Physica.

Welfens, P. J. J. 1990a. "Economic Reforms in Eastern Europe." Johns Hopkins University. Typescript.

Welfens, P. J. J., ed. 1990b. *European Monetary Integration.* Heidelberg: Springer.

Welfens, P. J. J. 1990c. *Internationalisierung von Wirtschaft und Wirtschaftspolitik* (Internationalization of the Economy and of Economic Policies). Heidelberg: Springer.

Welfens, P. J. J. 1991a. "Internationalization of Production, Foreign Direct Investment and European Integration: Free Trade in Goods, Technology and Assets?" In *Multinationals in the New Europe and Global Trade,* ed. M. Klein and P. J. J. Welfens. 1–49. Heidelberg.

Welfens, P. J. J., ed. 1991b. *Economic Aspects of German Unification.* Forthcoming.

Williamson, H. 1981. *The Economic Institutions of Capitalism.* New York: Wiley.

Yarrow, G. 1986. "Privatization in Theory and Practice." *Economic Policy* 2:323–64, 373–79.

Systemic Innovation and Cross-Border Networks: The Case of the Evolution of the VCR Systems

Yasunori Baba and Ken-ichi Imai

Introduction

The emergence of generic or information technologies (ITs) exerts a strong impact on the entire range of products and services. Eventually, it triggers a "creative gale of destruction" in the existing industrial or market order and brings about a continuous flow of industrial linkages across the borders of specific sectors and scientific disciplines. ITs act as a catalyst, triggering clusters of innovation that branch out in a systemic way. The clusters of innovation surely create an "increasing returns" phenomenon (see Arthur 1985) and "network externalities" in many industries (see David 1987 and Katz and Shapiro 1985). Under these conditions, several technological trajectories and market evolution patterns are highly possible, so that the emergent industrial milieu is conditioned by a heightened degree of uncertainty in the form of unpredictable events. In this essay, we will explain how and where the economic system generates useful information or knowledge to cope with this hyperuncertainty. In the context of current moves toward globalization, we shall examine what type of organizational and managerial arrangements are most suitable for the accumulation of such information or knowledge in global settings.

Emerging network organizations and types of network management—how firms manage flexible process coordination among various business participants and benefit from the interactions—are shown to be important explanatory factors. In the course of our discussion, we shall present the coupled ideas of *systemic innovation* and *cross-border networks*. The insight for our theorizing derives partially from our observation that the video cassette recorder (VCR) industry represents a typical outcome of systemic innovation.

The authors are indebted to Chris Freeman, Eric von Hippel, and Keith Pavitt for their comments.

While battles between systems (e.g., Betamax vs. VHS) entailed great uncertainties in the VCR business, we shall suggest that (1) systems evolve through their interplay with evolving market selection criteria (i.e., which characteristics of a particular technology are the ones that users will eventually come to value most highly) and (2) new types of entrepreneurs, taking shape in spontaneous networks, tend to decide the winning system through rather modest-looking contributions that are often associated with some insignificant "historical event" (Arthur 1985).

A Network View of Technical Change and Entrepreneurship

Throughout the "catching-up" process, the Japanese have imported fresh innovations from abroad and concentrated all their energies on remolding inherited products and production processes, regarding products as archetypes and factories as laboratories (Baba 1986). Firms such as Matsushita and Toyota have taken the lead in deploying managerial and organizational innovations. Clearly, the accumulated knowledge has crystallized into the familiar Japanese production paradigm. Then, what kind of entrepreneurs can be expected to have appeared on the Japanese industrial scene? Given the pattern of technical change, one would assume that firms would all rely on foreign technologies whose dominant design paradigm had already been settled. Competition seems to have started from product development lower down in the design hierarchy, and firms have focused on normal technical progress. In this industrial climate, entrepreneurs of the genuine "Schumpeterian" type seem to have emerged only rarely. However, "Mark II quasi-Schumpeterians" in Japan (i.e., large firms that had been connected with the *zaibatsu* of prewar Japan) seem to have paved the process-*cum*-product innovation path, resulting in a type of continuous innovation in several industries (e.g., consumer electronics and automobiles; see Baba 1989).

Different historical patterns can be shown to have lent different connotations to concepts. Traditionally, the West seems to believe in the strength of knowledge and analytical reasoning as infallible guides to technical change. In addition, Western entrepreneurs tend to be credited with somewhat unusual energy or willpower, enabling them to depart from accepted routines and practices. This combination seems to give rise to an image of "creative destruction" initiated by "heroic" entrepreneurs. In contrast, Japanese technical change has historically been a matter of the progress of techniques. Japan's entrepreneurs also tended to concentrate on reaping benefits from imported technological trajectories, and, with rather mediocre ambitions, they aimed to generate as many marketable product mutations as possible by way of using the market "as a dynamic process of creative discovery" (Heertje 1988, 85).

Put differently, the disproportionate emphasis placed on normal technical progress actually forces firms to take all the business opportunities flowing from interactions of various kinds. As Imai, Nonaka, and Takeuchi point out, hyperinteractions within the boundaries of a firm have a critical effect in linking and coordinating R&D, manufacturing, and marketing to assure profits out of normal technical progress (Imai, Nonaka, and Takeuchi 1985).

Clearly, the Japanese organizational setup lends itself nicely to branching out into new interactions. Japanese industry has traditionally witnessed a variety of cooperative relationships among firms. A long-term, semifixed relationship guarantees its participants a constant flow of opportunities for setting up interactions. Recently, such networks are reported to have taken a step forward from their institution-specific stage (Imai 1988 and 1989); in parallel with the general tendency toward flexible specialization in a firm (Piore and Sabel 1984), the nuclei of specialization have come to be linked across the borders of firms, even beyond the boundaries of affiliates. The formation process turns out to be highly flexible, and interfirm relationships have been cemented by such loose ties as licensing agreements, management contracts, subcontracting, and R&D collaboration. The emerging network organization (Imai 1988 and 1989) should be viewed, first, as a dynamic framework, because the essence of such networks, we believe, inheres in their dynamic properties rather than static ones. From this point of view, it should be stressed that (1) economically valuable information is actually created through some kinds of "on-the-spot" information-exchanging interactions (Hayek 1945), and (2) repeated interactions, and thus the generation of dynamic information, yield a constant flow of business opportunities, however minor. Naturally, a process view assuming the importance of externalities (e.g., learning by using and learning by interaction) should be applied.

Now that contemporary economic environments are characterized by high complexity and fluidity, the emerging network organization seems to endow economies with an adaptation mechanism that is highly flexible in introducing the dynamic factor of the creation of information. While the consideration of transaction costs is known to determine the choice of organizational form, such costs being "the economic equivalent of friction in a physical system" (Williamson 1985), it should also be stressed that the friction actually introduces dynamic properties to inertia, and thus makes possible "dynamic flexibility" (Klein 1984). Since Hayek views the market as a communication system effectively using the knowledge dispersed throughout society (Hayek 1945), it seems not unrealistic to assume that the network gives rise to some sort of knowledge allowing the solution of particular problems. For the moment, we will use the term *context* to refer to the *heuristic information core* that is shared among the network participants. Context does not provide the unique set of solutions whose structure is concretely specified, but it certainly leads the participants' problem-solving activities in the right direction. Put differently, under a given technological trajectory, it is the context that provides the participants with the kind of guidance that indicates the direction their normal technical progress should take and helps them decide which characteristics of a particular technology will eventually come to be valued most highly.

From this stylized heuristic generation process of the network, a fresh view of entrepreneurship can be extracted. One of our basic premises is that the heuristic information core leading to the carrying out of new combinations tends to emerge in the interactive process by itself, so that the generation of new information need not be explicitly planned. In the network view, a group of network participants becomes directly responsible for the management of innovations. As typified by the recent Japanese management practice of forming quasiautonomous workgroups functioning as if they were "internal entrepreneurs," not only the founder or president of a firm, but also the ranks of divisional chiefs may be seen as entrepreneurs. Furthermore, network participants such as equipment suppliers to joint firms or marketers for licensing firms seem to deserve the status of network-type entrepreneurs because of the critical, if inconspicuous, role they play in the coordination process. In our view, when a certain kind of network has triggered the context of a candidate for entrepreneurship, it seems likely that the entrepreneurial function turns out to be executed without excessive reliance on personality-based criteria. This view leads us to the hypothesis that designing an appropriate organizational structure, specifying the environment most favorable for particular types of interaction to take place, is essential if network entrepreneurs are to appear.

Finally, we shall compare networks with markets and hierarchies with the aim of clarifying the concept of network a little further. Our view leads us, first, to the contention that one of the crucial differences between markets, hierarchies, and networks lies in their respective mechanisms and abilities to condense information. In the market, on-the-spot information is condensed to a single signal, that is, the price. While the price mechanism is seen to act as an efficient communication system summarizing diverse information existing in society, it has the admitted limitation that it affords the society "mere pattern prediction," where "all that we shall be able to predict will be some abstract characteristic of the pattern that will appear . . . relations between kinds of elements about which individually we know very little" (Hayek 1989, 7). In hierarchies, on the other hand, information is condensed in organizational "routines" (Nelson and Winter 1982) and expressed later in terms of the internal dialect and "code" of an organization (Arrow 1974). The heuristics are assumed to be embedded mainly in the routines. In the tradition of Schumpeter's hypothesis on "routinized innovation" (Schumpeter 1942), it seems that routines manage what is required and succeed in doing so in a highly *predictable* way. While the combination of the routines and code allows the organization great opportunities to benefit, some of the possibilities it involves can include new combinations outside its organizational focus. Because of the local nature of learning, the possible routes of new interpretation emerge rather narrowly, as does the range of new information.

In contrast, faced with dynamically competitive contemporary economies, the network seems to turn out *organizational arrangements* complementing both markets and hierarchies: (1) in comparison with the market, information condensed through the network is *thicker,* so that the network supplements the "mere pattern prediction" of the market; and (2) in comparison with the hierarchy, information condensed through the network is *freer,* so that the network incorporates some *probabilistic factors* into the rather *deterministic predictions* of the hierarchy. The network, then, may usefully be seen as composed of highly interactive organizations "in which hints for resolving problems can come from a variety of people, [and which] has a great capacity for dealing with uncertainty . . ." (Klein 1977, 135). As is known, the traditional Western view of technical change is largely characterized by its sequential search process down through science, technology, and production. Naturally, this view swings the focus to firms' in-house R&D activities, the coherence aspect of corporate activity, and, hence, the functioning of organizational routines. In sharp contrast, the Japanese equivalent has traditionally tended to concentrate on incremental technical progress. This view sheds light on the emerging Japanese production paradigm, the network aspect of corporate activity, and, hence, the function of context. These views may appear at first glance to conflict, but, as explained above, it seems helpful to view them in complementary terms. In particular, our network view deserves special attention in the analysis of highly complex systems where a good match between core technology and cospecialized or complementary assets becomes indispensable or in the identification of the specific technological requirements of various submarkets that are often located abroad.

The Systemic Aspect of Innovation in the Age of Information

The systemic nature of innovations has recently been highlighted (see David 1987; Langlois 1988; Teece 1988). In particular, information technology (IT) shakes up all existing products and services and acts as a catalyst triggering clusters of innovations that branch out in a systemic way: an original invention often prompts innovations in other activities complementary to it, leading to the generation of a new combination of physical products, software, and human services. We might call an innovation brought about by this broader systemic sequence a *systemic innovation.* Admittedly, this systemic sequence can be seen in traditional industries. However, the IT-triggered systemic sequence should be given prominence because it contributes to a proliferation of innovative linkages between the manufacturing and service sectors, between the household and new services, and between the new services and software industries, accommodating the dawning age of information. Not surprisingly, the systemic sequence currently works reciprocally or, rather, self-enforcingly in that (1) the software—initially as cospecialized assets of the ITs—in turn creates additional demand for the ITs; (2) although service sectors tend to take the initiative in setting the agenda for the application of software, software suppliers sometimes work as boosters for creating new services; and (3) as suggested by the new "information-intensive" technological trajectory (Pavitt, Robson, and Townsend 1989), the ITs may create opportunities for transforming traditional service industries into new service industries. Thus, the frontier of competition is moving away from traditional, stand-alone innovation (i.e., providing novelty in a single product or service), toward the novel mode aimed at systemically supplying an optimal combination of hardware, software, and services.

The traditional "Product Cycle Approach" (Vernon 1966), seen from our systemic viewpoint, can also be advantageously modified (see fig. 1). First, in our view, what should be observed is not the product cycle of a single product, but *systemic* product cycles. Accompanying the cycle of an original product, there appear neighboring cycles of other, complementary products (including software and services). The neighbors follow the original cycle sequentially, but with time lags; also, their cyclical patterns need not be identical. Second, in contrast to the one-way mechanical view assuming product standardization (and hence the decline of the market size), our systemic view suggests the emergence of a cluster of innovations entailing an increasing returns phenomena: although an original product (e.g., the VCR) may follow the traditional course of a product cycle, combining a product with other complementary products (e.g., camcorders) would generate additional technology or market opportunities. Once coupled with a series of new, neighboring products, the evolution of the cluster is assumed to continue in an open-ended fashion. Third, according to the traditional view, the oligopolistic firms of a certain country (in effect, the United States) are held to assume dictatorship in utilizing their sources of competitiveness. Our view, however, permits a different picture: Japanese firms may sometimes generate an original product (e.g., the VCR), but U.S. firms might obtain competitiveness in its complementary goods (e.g., video software).

Cross-Border Networks in Global Competition

We shall now turn to a schematization of cross-border networks, putting emphasis on their basic characteristics and information structure (Aoki 1988). Actually, our emphasis on the network view provides an illustration of the evolutionary development of industrial networks crossing national borders

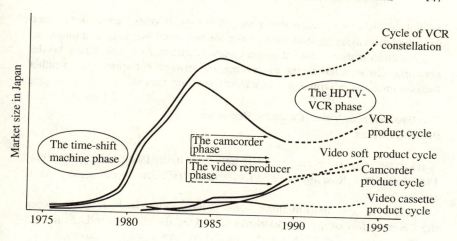

Fig. 1.   The schematic systemic product cycles of the VCR constellation

through self-organizing interactions between quasiautonomous participants. Networks take not only the joint venture form, but also that of long-term collaboration or cooperation. Although this type entails some costs in settling the protocols between networkers with different sociocultural "codes," international networkers are likely to contribute to taking advantage of contingent business opportunities through their active interactions. The cross-border network type of strategy differs from a globalization type like the Porter model in that the latter retains a centralized management system (Porter 1986). If the dominant world markets became more homogenous through dense information interflows, firms could employ the globalization strategy more. However, if markets remained differentiated due to the incorporation of "on-the-spot" information at each location, firms could hardly ignore the strategic value of cross-border networks. This tendency seems to have surfaced, for instance, in segments of the automobile industry.

Acknowledging that the role of cross-border networks is of great importance, then, we shall clarify their unique functions. First of all, the character of the network regulator (the top management in Western terms) seems different from that of its counterpart in the globalization strategy. In the latter, the top tends to adopt top-down management based mainly on the information generated by itself, typified by the strong business knowledge of executives or a sophisticated strategy formulated by an expert group. In contrast, in the cross-border network, the regulator tends to be invisible in the course of detailed strategy formulation—or, rather, having settled the robust future vision of a firm, the regulator permits spontaneous global coordination to form. The distilled knowledge about the worldwide business situation, the *global context,* becomes the basis of coordination. This is in line with the crucial differences between the management styles of the cross-border network and globalization strategies: in the former, emphasis is placed on *global* process coordination rather than on *centrally planned* control. Cross-border networks also emphasize the emergence of network entrepreneurship rather than on encounters with a few outstanding entrepreneurs.

The Evolution of Video Cassette Recorder (VCR) Systems

A review of the rivalry in the VCR field (see Itami 1989; Nakagawa 1984, 1987, and 1989; Rosenbloom and Cusumano 1987) gives a rationalization of our discussion.

Let us review the formation process of the standard in the rivalry between the Betamax format and the VHS format, taking the case of the U.S. market as an example. The VHS family wanted to find a way to hinder Sony's preemption of the U.S. market by signing an OEM contract with RCA. To do so, Matsushita sent a senior engineer, who pointed out that the two-hour limit of the Betamax format would be too short for the U.S. market, since recording a U.S. football game would require a four-hour capacity. The engineer duly offered four hours, since RCA showed great interest in the suggestion and responded with the possible purchase of a half-million sets in the coming five years. Matsushita quickly set up the company-level project team that comprised 700 engineering personnel and cleared the target in six weeks. Soon after the introduction of the four-hour capacity version, the major U.S. manufacturers, which were all close to adopting the Betamax format, decided to adopt the VHS system. The industrial impact of the OEM contract was even greater than this. RCA set the VHS format VCR at $1,000, a price $300 lower than Sony's Betamax. Matsushita thought this price setting somewhat irrational, since their own calculations indicated $1,300 as the fair market price of the innovation, that is, the home VCR. Obviously, RCA's discount price setting foreclosed the possibility of a price range that would be adequate to guarantee innovator's profits.

In our network terms, this description can be summarized as follows. First, networkers formulate cross-border networks quite spontaneously, largely on the basis of their "on-the-spot" information. Second, the process coordination appearing in the network gradually sets out the *global context* of the emerging industry. Although the Betamax side first proposed the combined product attributes of a high-quality picture, smaller cassette, shorter recording limit, and high price (adequate for the innovation) as a candidate market selection criteria, the process coordination actually settled on the criteria proposed by the VHS side, that is, a combination of a larger cassette, longer recording capacity, and lower price. In terms of the technological aspects, the global context suggests that it is the combination of a marketable product concept and the ensuing manufacturing process, rather than the core technologies, that decided the winning VCR system. At this initial stage, the VHS side never actually foresaw the dominant position of VHS in the system rivalry. However, hindsight suggests that the extended recording capacity of the VHS format played a crucial role in deciding the winner in this phase.

Because we see the VCR as a totally systemic innovation, we should widen our focus to include such systemic elements as video camcorders, cassette tapes, and video software. Let us summarize the case by introducing video software into our discussions. Unlike the hardware, the impetus to create a video software market was set in motion in the United States and it was the arrival of U.S. movie software in 1983 that activated the rental business in Japan and changed the sluggish trends in the software market. Not surprisingly, the new availability of video software provides the VCR with a totally new role, that is, as a reproducer of video software. This additional role adds new aspects to the format standardization process: first, software suppliers (e.g., joint ventures or licenses of the U.S. movie software distributors) searching for the scale economies to be had from single-format software production seem to be trying to back the winning horse; and second, customers try to purchase the better selling format software for fear of becoming "angry orphans" (David 1987). In addition, VCR manufacturers obviously pay close commercial attention to the changing market share of their co-specialized assets due to the associated "network externalities." This feedback obviously contributed to setting the evolutionary pattern of the VHS format.

Finally, let us add some comments from our network viewpoint. As we have explained, it was the cross-border networks of the U.S. movie software suppliers that played the major role in introducing the new trend into the Japanese market. On the other hand, the Japanese VCR manufacturers (except, perhaps, Sony) had neglected the strategic importance of video software. Together with the emergence of a single, dominant VHS format, however, they seem to have acknowledged the new *global* context, seeing the VCR as a reproducer of video software and recognizing the importance of the *software aspects* of the systemic innovation in the competition. Admittedly, the firms have started to challenge the newly erected target: internally, they began forming software distribution networks of their own in the mid-1980s, and, internationally, Sony purchased CBS and Columbia Pictures Entertainment, and JVC became the owner of a movie studio in Hollywood.

REFERENCES

Aoki, M. 1988. *Information, Incentive, and Bargaining in the Japanese Economy.* Cambridge: Cambridge University Press.
Arrow, K. J. 1974. *The Limit of Organization.* New York: Norton.

Arthur, W. B. 1985. "Competing Technologies and Lock-in by Historical Small Events: The Dynamics of Allocation under Increasing Returns." Center for Economic Policy Research, Publication no. 43, Stanford University.

Baba, Y. 1986. "Japanese Color TV Firms' Decision Making from the 1950s to the 1980s: Oligopolistic Corporate Strategy in the Age of Microelectronics." Ph.D. diss., University of Sussex.

Baba, Y. 1989. "The Dynamics of Continuous Innovation in Scale-Intensive Industries." *Strategic Management Journal* 10:89–100.

David, P. A. 1987. "Some New Standards for the Economics of Standardization in the Information Age." In *The Economics of Technology Policy,* ed. P. Dasgupta and P. L. Stoneman. Cambridge: Cambridge University Press.

Hayek, F. A. 1945. "The Use of Knowledge in Society." *American Economic Review* 35:519–30.

Hayek, F. A. 1989. "The Pretence of Knowledge: Nobel Memorial Lecture, December 11, 1974." *American Economic Review* 79, no. 6:3–7.

Heertje, A. 1988. "Schumpeter and Technical Change." In *Evolutionary Economics: Applications of Schumpeter's Ideas,* ed. H. Hanusch. Cambridge: Cambridge University Press.

Imai, K. 1988. "Patterns of Innovation and Entrepreneurship in Japan." Paper presented at the 2d Congress of the International Schumpeter Society, Siena, Italy.

Imai, K. 1989. "Evolution of Japan's Corporate and Industrial Networks." In *Industrial Dynamics,* ed. B. Carlsson. Boston: Kluwer Academic Publishers.

Imai, K., I. Nonaka, and H. Takeuchi. 1985. "Managing the New Product Development Process: How Japanese Companies Learn and Unlearn." In *The Uneasy Alliance—Managing the Productivity-Technology Dilemma,* ed. K. B. Clark, R. H. Hayes, and C. Lorenz. Boston: Harvard Business School Press.

Itami, H. 1989. *Nihon no VTR Sangyo: Naze Sekai o Seiha Dekitanoka.* Tokyo: NTT Press.

Katz, M. L., and C. Shapiro. 1985. "Network Externalities, Competition, and Compatibility." *American Economic Review* 75:424–40.

Klein, B. 1977. *Dynamic Economics.* Cambridge, Mass.: Harvard University Press.

Klein, B. 1984. *Prices, Wages, and Business Cycles: A Dynamic Theory.* New York: Pergamon.

Langlois, R. N. 1988. "Economic Change and the Boundaries of the Firm." *Journal of Institutional and Theoretical Economics* 144 (4):635–57.

Nakagawa, Y. 1984. *Nihon no Jikikiroku Kaihatsu.* Tokyo: Diamond Inc.

Nakagawa, Y. 1987. *Jisedai Video Senso.* Tokyo: Diamond Inc.

Nakagawa, Y. 1989. *Sony Shinwa wa Yomigaeruka.* Tokyo: Kodansha.

Nelson, R., and S. Winter. 1982. *An Evolutionary Theory of Economic Change.* Cambridge, Mass.: Belknap Press.

Pavitt, K., M. Robson, and J. Townsend. 1989. "Accumulation, Diversification, and Organization of Technological Activities in U.K. Companies, 1945–83." In *Technology Strategy and the Firm: Management and Public Policy,* ed. M. Dodgson. London: Longman.

Piore, M. J., and C. F. Sabel. 1984. *The Second Industrial Divide.* New York: Basic Books.

Porter, M. E. 1986. "Competition in Global Industries: A Conceptual Framework." In *Competition in Global Industries,* ed. M. E. Porter. Boston, Mass.: Harvard Business School Press.

Rosenbloom, R. S., and M. A. Cusumano. 1987. "Technological Pioneering and Competitive Advantage: The Birth of the VCR Industry." *California Management Review* 24 (4):51–76.

Schumpeter, J. A. 1942. *Capitalism, Socialism, and Democracy.* New York: Harper.

Teece, D. J. 1988. "Technological Change and the Nature of the Firm." In *Technical Change and Economic Theory,* ed. G. Dosi, C. Freeman, R. Nelson, G. Silverberg, and L. Soete. London: Pinter.

Vernon, R. 1966. "International Investment and International Trade in the Product Cycle." *Quarterly Journal of Economics* 80(2):190–207.

Williamson, O. E. 1985. *The Economic Institutions of Capitalism.* New York: Free Press.

Controlling the Market for Corporate Control: The Historical Significance of Managerial Capitalism

William Lazonick

Financial Commitment and Innovation

What mode of corporate governance can best enable U.S. industrial enterprises to create value and contribute to national economic prosperity? During the 1980s, amid dramatic changes in the financial structures of major U.S. industrial corporations, many economists extolled the "value-creating" virtues of "the market for corporate control"—the exercise of control over the disposition of corporate assets and revenues by means of financial claims acquired through the medium of public securities markets.[1] A willingness to rely on the market for corporate control to determine the investment strategies of industrial corporations is consistent with the market-oriented ideology of mainstream economics. But, as I shall argue here, the belief in the efficacy of the market for corporate control is inconsistent with the history of *successful* capitalist development in the United States and abroad over the past century.[2] The history of successful capitalist development, marked by changing international industrial leadership, shows that value-creating investment strategies increasingly require that business organizations exercise control over, rather than be controlled by, the market for corporate control.

My arguments may be counterintuitive to economists trained to believe that superior economic performance is secured by market coordination rather than organizational (or planned) coordination of economic activity. For conventional economists, the "efficient" economy is one in which free markets in labor and capital permit the reallocation of factors of production to their "optimal" uses. From this perspective, any impediments to the "optimal" allocation of scarce resources to alternative uses—at any time and also over time as more efficient uses appear—are deemed to be "market imperfections."

---

1. See Jensen 1988; Jarrell, Brinkley, and Netter 1988.
2. See Lazonick 1991.

The basic problem with this market-oriented perspective is that it contains no theory of *the generation of more efficient uses* of productive resources over time. This criticism is not novel. Joseph A. Schumpeter made it almost a half-century ago (1950).[3] The mainstream of the U.S. economics profession, satisfied perhaps with U.S. international dominance of the world economy in the post–World War II decades, just swept the criticism under an intellectual rug, tightly woven with mathematics, statistical techniques, and general equilibrium theory. Now that U.S. international economic leadership is beginning to unravel, the market-oriented ideology of mainstream economics is wearing thin. Even some economists, despite their training, are seeing through the threadbare patches in the neoclassical fabric to notice why. On the macroeconomic level, conventional economics contains no theory of economic *development* in general and, hence, no theory of changes in international industrial leadership in particular. On the microeconomic level, it contains no theory of the process of *innovation* and, hence, no theory of changes in competitive advantage among business enterprises.

Based on the historical record of twentieth-century capitalist development and shifts in international industrial leadership, my fundamental thesis is that organizational coordination has increasingly replaced market coordination in ensuring the development and utilization of productive resources. The basic evidence to support the thesis is the growing importance of organizational structure—what I have elsewhere called the planned coordination of the specialized division of labor (Lazonick 1991)—for the success of innovative (or developmental) investment strategies.

My focus will be on the historical role of "financial commitment," as distinct from financial mobility, in the rise of U.S. managerial capitalism and on how, in recent decades, the weakening of financial commitment has contributed to U.S. industrial decline. How was financial commitment structured in major U.S. industrial corporations in the first half of this century, when the United States came to dominate the international economy? And what role has the erosion of financial commitment played in the decline of U.S. industrial power over the last few decades? I shall not pretend to offer definitive answers to these questions here. Given the failure of mainstream economics to deal with the business organization as an engine of innovation, my purposes are to raise these questions, to show the relevance of a focus on innovation for addressing them, and to demonstrate the possibility that the historical analysis of the rise and decline of U.S. managerial capitalism can generate plausible answers to them. My basic argument concerns the incentives and abilities of strategic managers of U.S. industrial corporations to use the earnings of the enterprises that they control to finance innovative investment strategies. I

---

3. See also Lazonick 1991, chap. 4.

argue that, given the intensified global competition of recent decades, pressures created by the rise of the market for corporate control have biased many once-dominant U.S. industrial corporations against innovative competitive responses.

Financial Commitment in the Nineteenth Century

The integration of asset ownership and managerial control characterized the finance of industry in the nineteenth-century United States. Owners of firms made strategic investment decisions, relying on their own capital and that of friends, family, and former business associates to launch new ventures. They then relied on retained earnings to transform the new ventures into going concerns.

Despite the lack of developed markets for industrial securities in the nineteenth century, owner-managers of going concerns found ways to raise additional capital without diluting either their ownership shares or managerial control. One method was for a group of industrial capitalists to found a bank from which they could have privileged access to loan capital (Lamoureaux 1986). Such an inherently friendly financial institution would not put the squeeze on its borrowers in downturns. The lending of the bank's invested capital back to the industrialist investors in effect permitted each member of the industrial group to diversify his investments across the group's various businesses while retaining ownership and control over his own. The system also permitted each member to secure a return on funds that were temporarily idle but that might soon be needed by the member's business enterprise. By creating a diversified local capital market, a bank also enticed local insurance companies to invest in its stock, increasing the loanable funds available to the industrialists who had founded the bank.

But the absence of well-developed markets in industrial shares made it difficult for industrialists to break the link between ownership and control if they wanted to retire from active management or realize the monetary value of their accumulated assets. One option for the owner-manager who had built up the firm was to exercise his prerogative of living off the productive assets that he had accumulated, perhaps ultimately running the business into the ground. Alternatively, he could preserve the firm's assets by passing control and ownership along to a family member or by selling the business to another owner-manager (or group of owner-managers), if a buyer with the requisite financial resources and managerial capabilities could be found. In either case, the integration of ownership and control was preserved because owners remained managers.

The separation of asset ownership and managerial control in the United States began with the railroads (Chandler 1954). Local merchants and other businessmen who stood to gain from a railroad connection with another region contributed the share capital that enabled construction on the roadbed to begin. Most of the remaining railroad capital was raised by floating bonds, an activity that led to the rise of the Wall Street investment banks and, as the railroads expanded their investment scale and geometric scope, the creation of hierarchies of salaried managers to run what Alfred Chandler has called the nation's first big business (Chandler 1965).[4]

The permanency of the railroads as going concerns made it possible for the original owners to sell their shares to portfolio investors. These transfers of ownership, in conjunction with the convertability of many railroad bonds into equity shares, resulted in the formation of secondary markets in railroad stocks and the separation of asset ownership from managerial control. The separation was viable precisely because the railroads had invested in organizational capabilities—owners could come and go, but the managerial organizations that ran the railroads stayed intact. Critical to the coherence and continuity of these managerial organizations were the career managers who, prefiguring twentieth-century modes of management development and organizational commitment, began as technical specialists but had opportunities to move up and around the corporate organization to general management positions.

Speculation in railroad stocks, takeovers, and bankruptcies marked the later decades of the nineteenth century. Those railroads that had developed superior organizational capabilities in the middle decades of the nineteenth century found themselves better prepared to respond to this early market for corporate control, whether financiers exercised control through the stock or bond market. For example, in 1869, the Pennsylvania Railroad drew on its already developed organizational capability to expand its system westward in order to counter Jay Gould's attempt to take control of the railroad's connections west of Pittsburgh. Even when, as happened from time to time in the last decades of the nineteenth century, a major railroad went bankrupt, its managerial structure remained intact as the reorganized company resumed building its transcontinental system (Chandler 1977, 135–36, 170).

Until the merger movement that began in the 1890s, a national market for *industrial* securities did not exist in the United States (Navin and Sears 1955). Unlike new railroads, which could count on privileged access to the demand for transportation services over local routes, any particular industrial concern could not, as a new venture, offer investors any certainty of even capturing local markets. Industrial entrepreneurs had to rely on their reputations and connections to raise private capital, and equity investors had to be prepared to lose their capital without any possibility of exit via the (nonexis-

---

4. See also Chandler 1977, 3–5.

tent) stock market. For example, Andrew Carnegie drew on connections that he had made as a railroad executive to finance his venture into steel making, while Alexander Graham Bell secured financial backing from the parents of two deaf children to whom he had been teaching speech.[5] Once the most successful new ventures became going concerns, they were able to finance their continued expansion on the basis of retained earnings. Indeed, Andrew Carnegie used his "ironclad agreement" with his financial partners to plough back earnings into his steel-making business rather than give in to their persistent demands for dividends. Over the long run, shareholder value in the Carnegie Steel Company was in no way diminished by Carnegie's insistence on pursuing a strategy of continuous innovation.

As in the case of Carnegie, by the 1890s, a large number of owner-managed industrial enterprises had, by using earnings to finance continuous innovation, transformed themselves into not only going but dominant concerns. In the process, they ceased to be merely owner-managed, or "entrepreneurial," firms. Central to the success of these firms was the recruitment, training, retention, and motivation of specialized personnel organized into the hierarchical and technical division of labor known as managerial structures (Chandler 1977). Staff personnel developed new products and processes that were the essence of a technologically dynamic firm's investment strategy. Line personnel ensured the high-speed and continuous utilization of the productive resources in which the firm had invested.

The firms that dominated in industrial competition were those that made financial commitments, not only to investments in plant and equipment but, even more fundamentally, to the training and remuneration of key personnel, thereby transforming the individual rationalities of participants in the specialized division of managerial labor into firm-specific, collective rationalities that constituted a powerful productive force. They dominated, moreover, despite the high fixed costs inherent in their investments in organization building. Through the superior development and utilization of productive resources, the managerial organizations that emerged in the last decades of the nineteenth century permitted the transformation of the high fixed costs of innovation into high-quality products at low unit costs.

Managerial Capitalism

In many of the more capital-intensive industries, dominant firms were central actors in the merger movement of the 1890s and early 1900s that sought to eliminate competition and consolidate market shares among the remaining

---

5. See Livesay 1975, chaps. 4 and 5; Reich 1985, 130, 132. See also Doerflinger and Rivkin 1987, chap. 5.

few. Over the long run, the most successful mergers proved to be in those industries in which continued product and process innovation and high-speed utilization of production and distribution facilities were most important for sustaining competitive advantage. Not by accident, competitive advantage in these industries went to those firms that had put in place the superior managerial capabilities for the development and utilization of productive resources.

But the great merger movement did more than merely concentrate market shares. With J. P. Morgan taking the lead, Wall Street financed the mergers by selling to the wealth-holding public the ownership stakes of the entrepreneurs who had built up their companies from new ventures to going concerns during the rapid expansion of the U.S. economy in the decades after the Civil War. The result was to transfer ownership of corporate assets from the original owner-managers to a widely distributed population of the wealth holders. The enhanced dominance of the new combinations plus the backing of Wall Street encouraged private wealth holders to invest in industrial stocks. By the early 1900s, the merger movement had created a highly liquid market in industrial securities, thus making stock ownership all the more attractive; beyond the price of the stock, share holding did not require that the new owners make any further commitment of time, effort, or finance to "their" firms.

In contrast to the owner-managers who had built the new public corporations into going concerns, the new owners were portfolio investors. The purchase of common shares did not finance *new* investments in organization and technology. Rather it financed the *retirement* of the old owners from the industrial scene. The separation of ownership from control that occurred in U.S. industrial enterprises at the turn of the century enhanced the managerial and financial capabilities of dominant firms. These firms already had powerful managerial organizations in place that could take over strategic command from the retiring entrepreneurs. By reducing the possibility of nepotism in top-management succession, the removal of proprietary control opened up new opportunities for upward mobility for career managers, these opportunities cementing their commitments to the long-run fortunes of their particular firms. Over the courses of their careers, these career managers, many of whom held science-based college degrees, developed irreplaceable knowledge of their firms' technologies and organizational structures. During the first decades of this century, it was such managers, their upward mobility unimpeded by family control, who typically rose to top-management positions in major industrial firms. Not coincidentally, the first decades of this century also saw the dramatic transformation of the U.S. system of higher education away from the elite British model (with its aristocratic pretensions) to one that served the growing needs of U.S. industrial corporations for managerial personnel (Noble 1979; Lazonick 1986).

From the perspective of sustained industrial innovation, therefore, the key impact of the separation of ownership from control in the United States was to overcome the *managerial* constraints on the building of organizational capabilities and the growth of the firm. Moreover, the way in which ownership was separated from control enhanced the financial commitment of these firms. Prior to the turn-of-the-century merger movement, most industrial share issues in the United States were, as in Britain, preferred stocks that, unlike common stocks, created fixed claims on the future earnings of the enterprise. The great merger movement, however, created a widespread secondary market in industrial securities that made the higher risk of common stock more acceptable to portfolio investors willing to speculate for the sake of capital gains. Despite after-the-fact complaints of "watered" stock, the asset base for the major common stock issues—those listed on the New York Stock Exchange—was the *existing* revenue-generating organizational capabilities of the industrial enterprises. As I have mentioned, the financial capital raised from these issues was not (contrary to shareholder folklore) used to finance new investments in organization and technology but to permit owner-entrepreneurs to take their leave without disrupting the continuity of the enterprise.

The "Loyal" Shareholder

The new "owners," moreover, were willing to hold common shares in these enterprises despite their lack of power to ensure the distribution of earnings. The track records of these dominant firms, their enhanced positions of market dominance through mergers, the reputations and financial connections of the prominent Wall Street investment banks, and the listing requirements of the New York Stock Exchange all combined to ensure the widespread distribution of share holding (Michie 1987).[6] The result was a national market in industrial securities characterized by the fragmentation of the new owners into a multitude of remote and passive shareholders. The managers of the major industrial corporations were left firmly in *financial* control. A cautious dividend policy not only gave them privileged access to the earnings of the firm but also boosted their bond rating with Standard and Poor's or Moody's. This enhanced financial standing enabled the industrial managers to leverage their financial resources, if need be, for the sake of pursuing innovative investment strategies. After the turn-of-the-century merger movement, the main industry-related business of Wall Street investment bankers was to market the bond issues of those going, and growing, concerns with which they had developed close relations.

---

6. See also Carosso 1970, chaps. 2–4 and Carosso 1987.

The fact is that (again contrary to shareholder folklore), common share issues have never been important in U.S. industry as a means for financing enterprise *expansion*. Robert Taggart has shown that the large volume of new share issues represents only a small proportion of the capital raised by U.S. corporations (Taggart 1986). As a general rule in the United States, the issue of new shares is a one-shot deal that occurs when owner-entrepreneurs (and their venture capitalist partners) take their firms public. The period from the 1890s through the 1920s was one in which the entrepreneurial firms that emerged as dominant in late nineteenth and early twentieth centuries went public, and, as Alfred Chandler and others have shown, these firms have continued to dominate U.S. industry, even though some of them have disappeared through mergers and acquisitions (Chandler 1977, 1990b; Edwards 1975). As I have noted, moreover, the new share issues did not finance investment in new assets; they merely transferred ownership claims on existing assets. In addition, as we shall see, in the boom of the late 1920s (and in sharp contrast to the practice of the 1980s), many industrial corporations issued shares that they knew to be overvalued in order to retire debt.

The structure of U.S. securities markets renders the use of share issues to finance expansion expensive, not because of the transaction costs involved in equity financing, but because of the adverse signals that an attempt at equity financing would send to potential investors. In effect, in choosing equity over debt financing for the expansion of assets, the manager of a going concern would be telling portfolio investors that he or she does not have the confidence that the firm is enough of a going concern to meet the additional debt-service requirements of the new investments had they been financed by a bond issue, and, indeed, that he or she lacks confidence that, over the long run, the new investments will generate a rate of return in excess of the corporate bond rate. The attempt by a going concern that has access to debt financing to finance expansion with equity would therefore be self-defeating.

During the 1910s and 1920s, while the major industrial corporations were establishing their positions as ongoing concerns, there was a further dispersion of ownership of industrial stocks among the wealth-holding public (Means 1930). The dispersion of ownership consolidated managerial control in the dominant corporations. As the secondary security markets developed into veritable national institutions, portfolio investors became increasingly willing to hold common stocks, particularly during periods such as the late 1920s when spectacular capital gains were being made. In 1927, U.S. corporations issued $1,054 million of preferred stock and $684 million of common stock; in 1929, these figures were $1,695 million and $5,062 million. During the Great Depression and World War II, issues of preferred stock were generally greater than issues of common stock, but during the post–World War II decades the reverse was typically the case. In 1946, common issues were $891 million and preferred issues were $1,127 million. But in 1969, at the peak of the conglomerate movement, these figures were $7,714 million and $682 million—a common-preferred ratio of 11:1.[7]

Throughout the twentieth century the small common shareholder has lacked *direct* power to influence the distribution of surplus revenues. Yet evidence on well-managed firms up to the present shows that managers are reluctant to change, and particularly to cut, dividend levels (Lintner 1956; Black 1976; Donaldson 1984, 83–84). In a period of declining profitability, managers are reluctant to cut dividends because of the fear of antagonizing the firm's "loyal" shareholders who, in Gordon Donaldson's words, "are the antithesis of portfolio investors who trade in and out of the company's stock and make alternative investments easily (Donaldson 1984, 49)." In a period of expanding profitability, the same absolute level of dividends results in a falling payout ratio and an increased ability of managers to incur more debt without increasing the firm's debt-equity ratio. Under such circumstances, management may be able to increase dividends without jeopardizing the financing of a projected innovative investment, but may be unwilling to do so to avoid having to cut dividends should these projections prove insufficient to carry the strategy through to success.

Financial Commitment in the Era of Dominance

It is obviously much easier for shareholders to be disloyal when asset ownership has been concentrated in a few hands than when it has been fragmented. If, as I shall argue, shareholders of industrial assets were more loyal before about 1960 than after, it was because, in the earlier period, asset ownership continued to be highly fragmented. During the first half of this century, the most powerful *financial* institutions, which could have potentially concentrated ownership and vied for financial control of the industrial corporations, did not challenge managerial control or undermine financial commitment.

When a firm went public, a Wall Street investment bank, of which J. P. Morgan was by far the most powerful, would use its power to ensure that family members departed as managers of the newly public corporations (DeLong 1989). But (unlike the German Great Banks) J. P. Morgan had little, if anything, to do with developing the individual capabilities of the salaried managers who took over or with building the organizational capabilities that permitted the dominant enterprises with which Morgan maintained connections to continue to undertake and implement innovative investment strat-

---

7. U.S. Bureau of the Census 1976, 1005–6. During the 1970s this ratio fell to less than 3:1, with preferred issues averaging $2805 million per year. In the 1980s, however, the ratio went back up to about 8:1. *Economic Report of the President 1989* 1989, 415.

egies. As institutions that made money marketing corporate bonds to finance enterprise expansion, the primary interest of Wall Street investment banks was that their client industrial enterprises be willing and able to undertake innovative investment strategies. In contrast to the current dominance of financial over industrial interests that I shall document later, Wall Street was, in the first half of this century, at the service of the development of managerial capitalism.

The prime customers for corporate bonds were commercial banks, mutual savings banks, and insurance companies. In 1929, these financial institutions together held over 27 percent of the outstanding U.S. corporate bonds, but only 1 percent of outstanding corporate stocks. By 1952, these institutional investors held over 69 percent of the outstanding U.S. corporate bonds (with life insurance companies alone holding 58 percent), but less than 2 percent of U.S. corporate stocks (Goldsmith 1958, 224–25). In an era when ordinary households had few alternatives for portfolio investment and when the level of interest payable by banks was constrained through regulation, these financial institutions made their money on the differential between their borrowing and lending rates of interest, not by exerting pressure on industrial corporations to increase their dividend levels or the market value of their stock. In the era of U.S. industrial dominance, the markets for bonds and stocks were segmented, with the powerful bondholders largely indifferent to stock yields and the fragmented shareholders unable to make a difference.

Shareholders did not lose out by their lack of financial control. In the 1920s, as the major manufacturing corporations were paying their workers somewhat higher wages and expanding market shares by reducing product prices to consumers, they were paying out well over 60 percent of net income as dividends to shareholders (U.S. Bureau of the Census 1976, 200, 941).[8] During the 1920s, large manufacturing corporations still had enough retained earnings to fund virtually all their fixed capital outlays. The culmination of several decades of industrial innovation had created a positive-sum situation in which it was possible for many different interests simultaneously to experience gains (Lazonick 1990, chap. 7).

As industrial stocks became grossly overvalued during the late 1920s, many firms sold additional shares, not to finance new investment, but to retire outstanding debt. The result was, of course, simply to feed the speculative frenzy. Indeed, the high profits left many manufacturing corporations so awash with cash that, rather than make even more direct investments, they took advantage of the speculative fever to lend some of their surplus funds on the New York call market where gamblers were paying as much as 12 percent for brokers' loans. As the volume of brokers' loans outstanding almost tripled from the end of 1924 to the end of 1928, the proportion of the loans made by

---

8. See also Koch 1943.

nonbank lenders increased from 25 percent to 60 percent. As the stock market began its decline and margins could not be met, the same corporations were the first to call their loans, thereby forcing the market down even further. The nonbank lenders decreased their loans outstanding from $3.9 billion at the end of 1928 to $2.5 billion at the end of 1929 to $610 million at the end of 1930, whereas the brokers' loans of the New York City banks declined from $1.6 billion at the end of 1928 to $1.2 billion at the end of 1929, and actually rose by $80 million over the following year (Galbraith 1980, 19–20; Keehn and Smiley 1988; U.S. Bureau of the Census 1976, 1009).

The phenomenal value-creating capabilities of the major manufacturing corporations had set the stage for the Great Crash. Unlike top industrial managers who were well aware of any slackening of demand for existing products and who were in the best positions to assess the organizational and technological problems of moving into new product lines, portfolio investors simply had no concept of the limits to industrial expansion under existing institutional arrangements. A major limit was the restricted organizational capability of the dominant industrial enterprises to move into new lines of business once the modern plant and equipment to service their traditional product markets had been put in place. The 1920s saw the *emergence,* but not, as yet, the widespread diffusion, of the multidivisional organizational structure that would enable manufacturing corporations to build on their technological and organizational strengths to move into new product lines and market areas in the 1940s and 1950s.[9]

With the accumulation of internal financial reserves outstripping the requirements for new investments, the dominant U.S. industrial enterprises entered the Great Depression unburdened by debt. The widely dispersed shareholders were, moreover, unable to use the crisis of the 1930s to raid the corporate treasury. True, during the 1930s these firms lost control over their shop-floor work forces—a control that management had won during the "positive-sum" decade of the 1920s.[10] Thrown out of work in the 1930s, the blue-collar workers joined independent industrial unions to secure their economic futures. But during the decade, the dominant industrial corporations ensured their long-term continuity by keeping their managerial structures intact. With financial commitments unchallenged, these corporations continued to make developmental investments in technology and organization in preparation for the return of more prosperous macroeconomic conditions.[11]

Indeed, as in the 1920s, so too in the 1930s U.S. manufacturing corpora-

---

9. Chandler 1966. For the slow diffusion of the multidivisional structure in Britain and its relative ineffectiveness even when put in place, see Channon 1973; Hannah 1983; Marginson et al. 1988.

10. See Lazonick 1990, chap. 9.

11. For general evidence, see Bernstein 1987, chap. 4. For a specific case study that spans the 1930s, see Hounshell and Smith 1988.

tions continued to augment their R&D capabilities. In 1921, the research laboratories of U.S. manufacturing enterprises had 2,775 scientific and engineering personnel, or 0.56 research professionals per thousand manufacturing employees. By 1933, the number of research professionals had risen to 10,927, or 1.93 per thousand manufacturing employees. In 1940, the R&D laboratories of manufacturing firms had increased the employment of scientific and engineering personnel to almost 28,000, or about 3.5 per thousand manufacturing employees (Mowery 1986, 191–92; Chandler 1985). At least one corporation—IBM—was able to keep its entire work force fully employed during the 1930s by selling business machines to the New Deal government (Sobel 1981, chap. 4). By virtue of this organizational continuity in the service of innovative investment strategy, the very same corporations that had brought U.S. industry to international dominance by the 1920s extended that dominance during and after World War II.

U.S. Industrial Decline

Just over a hundred years ago, in 1888, with an average 46 percent ad valorem tariff on the 66 percent of all imports that were dutiable, the U.S. economy ran a deficit of $41 million on its merchandise balance of trade (Sheiber, Vatter, and Faulkner 1976, 286; U.S. Bureau of the Census 1976, 864). For the next eighty-two years, with the exception of one (1935), the United States had a positive merchandise trade balance. Fluctuations in the merchandise trade balance in the 1970s (four years of surplus and six years of deficits) gave optimists reason to believe that, once U.S. industry recovered from a variety of "shocks," it would again assume its preeminent position.

    That optimism was unwarranted. The 1980s saw a dramatic decline in the merchandise trade balance from −$31 billion in 1980 to −$170 billion in 1987. Despite a marked improvement in exports at the end of the decade, imports increased fast enough to generate a deficit in the trade balance of −$129 billion in 1988 and −$133 billion in 1989 (*Economic Report of the President* 1989, 428; *New York Times,* Dec. 17, 1989). In 1980, the optimists could still point to a positive manufacturing trade balance of about $19 billion. But since then, and despite the weakening of the U.S. dollar since the mid-1980s, the trade balance in manufactures has been in deficit, increasing to −$145 billion in 1986 and −$154 billion in 1987. Mirroring U.S. industrial woes were the Japanese trade surpluses in manufacturing that averaged over $100 billion per year during the first half of the 1980s (Cohen and Zysman 1987, 63).

    The U.S. economy is in the throes of long-term industrial decline, in part because of the failure of the major U.S. industrial enterprises to pursue innovative investment strategies, and in part because of the rise of foreign competitors with much greater organizational capabilities and financial commitments. The rise of these competitors—and for the United States it is Japanese competition that is most relevant—calls for greater organizational capability and financial commitment on the part of the U.S. business enterprises if the U.S. economy is to generate the higher quality products at lower unit costs that can recapture lost markets and take advantage of new market opportunities (Lazonick 1991, chap. 3).

The rise of a market for the control of corporate assets and revenues may not be the root cause of U.S. industrial decline, but it has become integral to the dynamics of the weakening of U.S. incentives and abilities to innovate. In particular, I shall indicate how the transformation of financial markets in corporate securities over the past few decades has increased the incentive and ability of industrial managers to choose investment strategies that benefit short-term earnings performance while eschewing innovative investment opportunities that are the sine qua non of industrial dominance.

The Way It Used to Be

Drawing on the historical outline of financial commitment in the U.S. rise to industrial dominance that I have already presented, let me briefly recapitulate the way it used to be, when common stocks were in the hands of individual investors and corporate bonds were in the hands of institutional investors. With their power to influence corporate payout policy low and the transaction costs of trading in shares high, most individual shareholders were, perforce, loyal. Just as today an individual can choose a particular type of mutual fund to suit his or her needs and wants, so could (and can) an individual investor choose a particular portfolio of industrial securities that met (or meets) his or her preferences for short-term dividends versus capital gains. For those shareholders who looked to their portfolios for predictable streams of income, corporate managers sought to keep the level of dividends stable or gradually rising as earnings and the needs of enterprise investment strategies permitted. Except in a period of general depression beyond the control of the particular firm, a decrease in dividends represented a managerial admission of inferior performance and could be counted on to create disloyal shareholders.

Save for a macroeconomic catastrophe such as the Great Depression, the dominant industrial corporations could also (precisely because they were dominant) count on a predictable cash flow from retained earnings to provide the financial bases for investments in expansion and innovation. Meanwhile, the institutional investors of that earlier era—insurance companies, commercial banks, and mutual savings banks—continued to channel household savings into long-term industrial investments by absorbing the bond issues of the industrial corporations. In a regulated financial environment, holders of bank deposits and insurance policies got a low but stable return on their savings while the dominant industrial corporations, with their investment-grade ratings from Wall Street, had, again by virtue of their dominance, access to relatively low-cost funds for industrial expansion. During the 1940s, the rate on Moody's Aaa-rated corporate bonds averaged 2.71 percent, varying between a low of 2.53 in 1946 and a high of 2.83 in 1942 (U.S. Bureau of the Census 1976, 1003).

Disloyal shareholders did exist in the first half of the century, and even many shareholders who would have otherwise been counted as "loyal" found it worthwhile to trade rather than hold during the speculative mania of the late 1920s. As we have seen, even corporate management became involved in the pre-Crash boom, as they sold overvalued shares to retire debt and as they made funds available on the call market. It may be that these preoccupations with the stock market distracted industrial CEOs from sustaining the innovative investment processes that could have permitted "fundamental values" to keep pace with soaring market prices and could also have helped forestall the recession in industrial activity that preceded the Great Crash.[12] Nevertheless, despite the speculative stock trading of the late 1920s and, in some ways, because of it, the dominant industrial enterprises emerged from the Great Crash and the Great Depression with sufficient financial commitment to continue to build the organizational capabilities of their managerial structures and sustain the innovative investment strategies that had made them dominant initially.

A New Economic Era

Since the 1950s, the basic economic conditions that influence the investment strategies of U.S. industrial corporations have changed in two fundamental ways, the one having to do with the rise of international competition and the other with the transformation of U.S. financial markets. First, and of greater importance, U.S. industrial enterprises no longer dominate the international economy. The new international competition makes the success of an innovative investment strategy a much more uncertain affair than it was in the era when, in capital-intensive industries, a few domestic oligopolists competed for market share. In any given industry, even those U.S. enterprises that possess the most organizational capability and financial commitment among domestic competitors, many no longer are the enterprises that can take the lead in generating higher quality products at lower unit costs. Increasingly, the investment strategies of once-dominant U.S. firms must *respond* to foreign competitors who have already implemented innovative investment strategies.

---

12. See Gordon 1974, chap. 2; Baran and Sweezy 1966, chap. 8.

Under these circumstances, quite apart from the transformation of U.S. financial markets, it may be rational for a firm in possession of organizational and physical capital accumulated over decades of dominance to live off its past success rather than invest for the future—to turn to what I have elsewhere described as an adaptive as opposed to an innovative investment strategy.

Given the rise of international competition, the relevant question is whether or not the rise of the market for corporate control in the United States has undermined the incentive and ability of strategic managers of going concerns or new ventures to respond to international competitive challenges. I shall argue that it has. I emphasize that I am not arguing that the rise of the market for corporate control is the root cause of U.S. industrial decline. Nor am I arguing that the corporate takeover, the most obvious manifestation of the existence of the market for corporate control, is the only way in which increased shareholder power has influenced, or can influence, the choices of investment strategy that industrial managers make. Rather, as I will show, my argument is that, through the normal operation of U.S. financial markets and as a result of cumulative (although often cyclically sensitive) pressures that have built up in the U.S. economy since the early 1950s, the rise of shareholder power has eroded the organizational capability and financial commitment of the U.S. industrial enterprise. By tracing the process of financial transformation in the United States over the past four decades—and the resultant sources of shareholder power, I shall suggest a number of ways in which the rise of the market for corporate control has weakened the incentive and ability of strategic managers to engage in innovative investment strategies. In the light of these arguments, I shall leave it to proponents of the market for corporate control to inform me of ways in which the transformation of U.S. financial markets over the past four decades has enhanced the innovative capability of U.S. industry.

The High Cost of Financial Capital

Apart from new ventures (which I shall consider toward the end of this essay), the financial basis of innovative investment strategies in the United States has always been, and remains, retained earnings. For strategic managers of going concerns, retained earnings permit new investments in organization and technology to be financed without incurring legal obligations to pay returns. Retained earnings represent low-cost finance, and control over retained earnings is the quintessential mode of securing financial commitment. In addition, a stream of retained earnings can be used to pay the interest charges on investments that are externally financed. Depending on projected sales revenues, earnings retention, and bond rates, strategic managers can choose a debt-equity ratio that leverages retained earnings without jeopardizing financial commitment—the financial ability of the firm to implement its investment strategy.[13]

Because well-managed firms do not normally fund enterprise expansion by the sale of stock but by retained earnings (leveraged if need be), strategic managers have an interest in low price-earnings ratios (P/E ratios) for the common stocks of their own companies. High P/E ratios place upward pressure on dividends as shareholders seek to maintain stock yields. The alternative for the shareholder is to "declare a dividend" by selling the stock (Lowenstein 1991). Insofar as the traded stock falls into the hands of shareholders who are able (and, by virtue of having to pay a high price for the stock, willing) to put pressure on management to raise dividends and hence yields, retained earnings and financial commitment will be eroded. There is a conflict of interest, therefore, between U.S. shareholders, who want a high P/E ratio and high dividends, and U.S. industrial managers, who, insofar as they function as strategic managers and not as shareholders, want low P/E ratios and low dividends.

As the Japanese have shown in recent years, it is possible to have financial markets that permit portfolio investors to trade and speculate in (typically) small floats of company shares that attain astronomic P/E ratios without affecting the payout policies of the underlying companies, most of whose shares are held by other companies who do not trade in them (Ballon and Tomita 1988; Matsumoto 1989).[14] Basically, Japanese portfolio investors and Japanese direct investors are playing two very different games, one largely speculative and the other largely innovative. Thus far at least (and I do not foresee the segmentation breaking down in the near future), the institutional structures of Japanese finance have ensured that the speculators have not been able to interfere with the innovators. With their overwhelming economic successes during the 1970s and 1980s, moreover, many major Japanese industrial companies have used their earnings to reduce their outstanding debt, in much the same way that major U.S. industrial corporations took advantage of their success to restructure their finances in the 1920s. In securing their long-term financing, Japanese industrial corporations have not fallen under the domination of a market for corporate control.

During the period when Japanese corporations relied on bank loans to finance long-term investments, the Japanese savings system (combined with government subsidies) kept the cost of finance capital low. In historical perspective, major U.S. corporations also enjoyed an era of inexpensive finance—an era when the banking system was highly regulated, the portfolio

---

13. For a "financial goals" orientation that is consistent with my approach, see Donaldson (1984); see also Lowenstein (1991).

14. For a competitive perspective, see Ellsworth 1985; Lowenstein et al. 1988.

investment alternatives for households were relatively restricted, and institutional investors were the primary holders of corporate bonds and held very little common stock. During the post–World War II decades, new types of institutional investors arose, the segmentation between the bond and stock market gradually broke down, and the portfolio investment alternatives for households expanded considerably. In the late 1970s, the banking system was deregulated to conform to these new financial realities. The result, as table 1 shows, was an enormous increase in the real cost of finance capital in the 1980s.

During the 1970s and 1980s the yields (the dividend-price ratios) on New York Stock Exchange common stocks did not quite attain the high levels of the early 1950s, but did recover from the lows of the 1960s. A quadrupling of total dividend payments between 1974 and 1988, with dividends increasing by 11 percent between 1987 and 1988 and by 21 percent between 1988 and 1989 (New York Stock Exchange 1989, 78), permitted the recovery of New York Stock Exchange stock yields despite the rapid increase in stock prices (see table 2). From 1978 to 1989, stock prices increased at an average annual compound rate of over 11 percent per year; these increases even permitted portfolio investors to adjust to the high rates of inflation of the late 1970s and early 1980s.

Meanwhile, the meager (and in some years negative) real interest rates on Aaa-rated corporate bonds in the 1970s were replaced by rates averaging well over 6 percent between 1982 and 1989—rates that, in contrast to previous decades, outstripped the high yields on stocks. In the market for corporate control, holders of corporate securities had found more than one way to

TABLE 1. Average Annual Percentage Yields on Corporate Bonds and Common Stocks, 1950–89

	Real Interest on Bonds[a]	Yield on Stocks[b]
1950–54	0.39	5.85
1955–59	2.12	3.94
1960–64	3.29	3.20
1965–69	2.21	3.18
1970–74	1.63	3.47
1975–79	0.67	4.69
1980–84	5.43	5.06
1985–89	6.45	3.58

Source: Data from *Economic Report of the President, 1990* (Washington, D.C.: Government Printing Office, 1990), 364, 376, 401.

[a]Moody's Aaa-rated bonds only.

[b]Dividend-price ratio for all common stocks listed on the New York Stock Exchange.

TABLE 2.   Average Annual Percentage Changes in Prices of New York Stock Exchange Common Stocks, 1950–89

	Change
1950–55	15.28
1955–60	7.37
1960–65	9.90
1965–70	−0.24
1970–75	5.39
1975–80	8.61
1980–85	10.58
1985–89	14.38

Source: Data from *Economic Report of the President, 1990* (Washington, D.C.: Government Printing Office, 1990), 401.

tap the corporate treasury. Since the 1950s, financial commitment in the United States has rested on weak foundations when compared with the secure modes of industrial finance available to foreign competitors. Yet through the 1970s, the major U.S. industrial corporations kept the real cost of capital under control. It was in the 1980s that the low cost of financial capital needed for direct investment gave way to the high yields on finance capital desired by portfolio investors.

The high cost of finance capital was, I would argue, just the most obvious sign of the erosion of the financial commitment to industrial invest-ment in the United States. High-cost finance tends to be mobile finance, always on the move, searching for higher short-term yields. When U.S. industry was less dependent on the financial markets to supply its funding requirements, the cost of financial capital was low and finance was commit-ted. Now that U.S. industry has become more reliant on the financial markets to fund innovative investment strategies, the cost of financial capital is mobile, thus reducing the incentive for U.S. industrial corporations to under-take innovative investment strategies. The rise of the market for corporate control is not the cause of U.S. industrial decline, but the inability—or even (as I shall argue) unwillingness—of strategic managers to control the market for corporate control is helping to ensure that U.S. industrial decline will not be reversed.

Historical Perspective

The historical outline I shall present here is a prelude to the complete histor-ical analysis of the decline of financial commitment in the United States and its relationship to the nation's long-term industrial decline that remains to be done. The complete analysis ultimately requires a combination of case histories of the investment strategies of particular firms over the post–World War II decades and the competitive dynamics among firms in particular global industries as well as statistical analyses using firm-level data that can differentiate between innovative and adaptive investment behavior.[15]

Conceptualizing the distinction between innovative and adaptive investment strategies is a first step toward a complete historical analysis. From the point of view of the wealth of the nation, it makes no sense to credit the market for corporate control with forcing management to be more "efficient," if cutting unit costs on the basis of given productive capabilities makes it impossible for the enterprise to lower unit costs by investing in the development of superior productive capabilities. Some firms may be able to adapt on the basis of existing productive resources and innovate by developing superior productive resources as *complementary* competitive strategies. But if the financial pressures to adapt become too great, the firm will not, and ultimately cannot, also innovate unless a new source of financial commitment is forthcoming.[16]

The historical perspective that I offer here focuses first on the ways in which strategic managers came to identify more with the fortunes and power that they could attain as individuals by securing higher market valuations of their firms in the short run, and how this strategic orientation fostered the conglomerate movement of the 1960s and left major corporations vulnerable to the market for corporate control in the 1980s. I then indicate how, in the mid-1970s, the productive failures of the conglomerate movement laid the basis for the rise of the junk-bond market, a market that subsequently took on a life of its own in the 1980s, as the battle for corporate control became headline news. I go on to view the rise of the junk-bond market as the result of not only the corporate failures of the 1960s but also portfolio investors' search for higher yields on corporate securities, a search that was begun in earnest by the mutual funds of the late 1950s but that reaped its greatest rewards in the

---

15. For a case study approach that seeks to explore the link between organizational capability and financial commitment, see Rosenbloom 1989. For the type of data that might begin to distinguish between adaptive and innovative responses, see Lichtenberg and Siegel 1989. That there is a need for more microeconomic empirical analysis of particular industries and particular firms is evident in Dertouzos, Lester and Solow 1989. In contrast to my argument that strategic managers can, by their investment strategies and payout policies, influence the long-run cost of capital to their firms, the authors of this important work treat the "cost of capital" as a purely exongenous factor in the determination of managerial time horizons and, hence, in the nature and extent of the firm's investments (59–63).

16. This line of analysis, which is suggested in Joseph Schumpeter's (1947) distinction between creative and adaptive responses, is also inherent in William Abernathy's (1978) notion of the "productive dilemma." See also Clark, Hayes, and Lorenz 1985.

1980s. I then argue that, in the 1980s, the innovative strategies of new ventures have also been adversely affected by the search for higher yields, and that the difficulties of the U.S. venture capital industry over the last several years are directly related to the rise of the market for corporate control. Finally, I conclude with a few words on the problems that financial mobility creates for attaining and sustaining competitive advantage in an international economy in which successful innovation requires ever-increasing financial commitment.

Managers Become Owners

The erosion of financial commitment is facilitated if those who occupy strategic management positions have an incentive to accommodate the desire of portfolio investors for high P/E ratios and high dividends. This possibility arose on a large scale in the 1950s with the adoption of stock options as a standard form of top management compensation. As Wilbur Lewellen shows for a sample of fifty Fortune 500 manufacturing companies, over the late 1940s, the top five executives derived less than 3 percent of their total after-tax compensation from stock-based rewards. This figure had climbed to 14 percent by 1953 and, by 1955, had jumped to 28 percent, so that their total after-tax compensation was 58 percent higher in 1955 than in 1950 and rose at a substantially faster rate than the incomes of doctors, lawyers, and dentists (Lewellen 1968, 172–73; 1971, 50). Over the 1955–63 period, stock-based rewards accounted (on average) for one-third of the total after-tax compensation of these executives (Lewellen 1971, 50).

Underlying the attractiveness of stock options as a form of executive compensation were increases in New York Stock Exchange common stock prices at a rate of over 24 percent per year between 1949 and 1956 as well as tax legislation that favored corporate compensation in the form of capital gains (Lewellen 1968, chap. 4; *Economic Report of the President* 1989, 416). The availability of stock options did not necessarily transform strategic managers into adaptive investors. The options could typically be exercised over a period of ten years, so that short-term time-horizons were not generally built into the compensation schemes. In a rising stock market, however, options exercised earlier added to income earlier, and the exercise of existing options could form the basis for the granting of new options. And the fact is that from the late 1940s to the late 1960s the U.S. stock market was generally on the rise.

Indeed, as stock-based rewards came to represent a substantial proportion of executive compensation, the tendency was for the beneficiaries to come to consider them as basic rewards. For example, in his 1968 book, *Executive Compensation in Large Industrial Organizations*, Lewellen argued that "the most appropriate way to measure on a common basis the worth of the numerous supplements to direct current renumeration is simply to calculate the size of the salary increments which, if substituted for those supplements, would leave the individuals involved as well off (4)." Sure enough, when stock prices declined substantially in 1969 and 1970—the first large decline since 1947—stock-based compensation fell to only 12 percent of total compensation but was replaced by other forms of income (Herman 1981, 95–96). The lesson for top managers was to be concerned with short-run stock market performance so that they could exercise their options early, establish a higher level of "base" pay on the basis of past "performance," and get more options.[17]

The ability of top managers to buy stocks at a discount provided the basis for career employees to be transformed into substantial owners. The exercise of stock options meant a stream of dividends if the managers held the stocks or, in a rising market, capital gains if the managers (usually after a restricted period) sold the stocks. During the 1950s, ownership income began to dwarf compensation income for top managers, rising from 76 percent of compensation income for the top five executives in Lewellen's sample in 1950–53 to 434 percent of compensation income in 1960–63 (Lewellen 1971, 90). With capital gains income over twenty times dividend income, and, hence, constituting the bulk of their total income, the lesson for top managers who were motivated by such matters—a lesson that was driven home to them with the decline of stock prices in the early 1970s—was to prevent even short-run declines in the market value of their companies' stocks. Strategic managers joined portfolio investors in focusing on the "bottom line" of their companies' quarterly corporate reports.

Ownership of one's company is generally touted as a great motivator to superior economic performance—hence the widespread notion that the separation of ownership from control is corporate America's original economic sin. Ownership *is* a great motivator for managers of *new ventures* who have to produce superior products at lower costs before they can gain access to superior (or even any) returns on their investments. Ownership ensures new venturers a share in the gains of enterprise *if and when* they occur, and, indeed, it is for this reason that innovative entrepreneurs and their venture-capital patrons keep ownership of the new venture in their own hands and seek to go public when they have created a going concern. Owner-managers of new ventures have *no choice* but to pursue innovative investment strategies if they want to reap returns.

The choice of investment strategy is by no means so constrained for

17. For a recent critique of the use of stock options for management compensation, see Crystal 1989.

those who control dominant going concerns—the types of firms that are listed on the New York Stock Exchange and represent the core of U.S. industry—precisely because the firms occupy dominant positions in their industries. Whether ownership and control is integrated or separated, the strategic managers of dominant going concerns have the ability to *choose* adaptive strategies that live off the returns generated by the innovative investments of the past as an alternative to devoting financial resources to innovative strategies that can generate returns in the future.

As I have already argued, in the first half of the twentieth century the separation of ownership from control enhanced the innovative capabilities of U.S. industrial corporations because it financed the retirement of individualistic empire builders and permitted professional managers to rise through the ranks and take over the direction of corporate strategy. During the first half of this century, most top managers of dominant firms engaged in what Richard Nelson and Sidney Winter have called "Schumpeterian competition"—competition among a few oligopolistic competitors with substantial accumulations of organizational capabilities and financial resources who were able to take market share away from each other (Nelson and Winter 1982; Chandler 1990b). These firms continued to invest in innovation to ensure that they maintained their market shares. Strategic managers had the industry-specific knowledge to understand the problems and possibilities of alternative innovative projects. Moreover, reliant primarily on managerial incomes that were designed to reward managers as they climbed the organizational hierarchy, the long-run success of top managers depended on the success of the organization as a whole, which in turn depended on controlling retained earnings and pursuing innovative investment strategies. Under such circumstances, strategic managers of dominant going concerns were disciplined in undertaking innovative investment strategies by the terms of their membership in the organization that we call the firm.[18]

Yet even in the first half of this century, when most dominant going concerns in the United States remained innovative, some strategic managers chose the adaptive route. A dramatic example, as Thomas McCraw and Forest Reinhardt have argued, was managerial decision making at U.S. Steel after the turn-of-the-century merger gave it a two-thirds market share in the domestic steel industry (McCraw and Reinhardt 1989). U.S. Steel had the organizational capability and financial commitment to engage in further innovation, and if it had done so it may well have totally dominated the domestic steel industry. But its already huge market share threatened it with antitrust action,

---

18. For a formal model of the impact of takeover threats on the ability of managers to undertake innovative investment strategies, see Foley and Lazonick 1990.

and, under these circumstances, it was to U.S. Steel's advantage to create a price umbrella that allowed other firms to compete. Indeed, as was particularly true in the case of Bethlehem Steel, the higher returns that could be reaped under the price umbrella as well as U.S. Steel's reluctance to compete for market share created incentives for competitors to undertake innovative investment strategies. Based on its prior success, U.S. Steel continued to make money even as it gradually lost market share. Over the decades, however, its reliance on this adaptive strategy led to an erosion of its organizational capability that came back to haunt the company in the 1960s and beyond, when new foreign competitors came on the scene.

For those dominant enterprises that remained innovative in the first half of the century with ownership separated from control, the critical question is whether the reintegration of ownership and control weakened or strengthened the innovative response. My view is that the access of top managers to substantial amounts of ownership income weakened the innovative response by providing them with individualistic alternatives to personal success that could best be achieved by choosing adaptive strategies. Like shareholders in general, owner-managers of these going concerns could benefit handsomely from adaptive strategies that reaped the returns of prior innovative investments (which had typically been made when enterprise ownership had been separated from managerial control), and indeed, insofar as high stock prices put upward pressure on dividends, these returns could be at the expense of retained earnings and, hence, investments that could ensure the future success of the enterprises.

Like shareholders in general, moreover, owner-managers of going concerns that are publicly traded can cash in by selling some of their stock if they foresee a decline in the fortunes of the enterprise (a decline that may very well be of their own making). In the 1980s, many top managers of industrial corporations went much further in devising new ways to cash in by exiting their firms. In creating "golden parachutes" in the event of a takeover and accepting bribes to facilitate a change of management, incumbent executives, in effect, assumed the right to sell not only ownership of shares in their companies but also their positions of managerial control.[19] Starting with the reintegration of ownership and control in major going concerns in the 1950s and 1960s and continuing into the takeover mania of the 1980s, top managers began to set themselves apart from the rest of the managerial structure. As good solid U.S. individualists—as owners of shares rather than managers of organizations—their financial commitment was to themselves, not to their organizations. Such behavior is destructive of not only the financial commit-

---

19. For the magnitudes involved, see Phillips 1990.

ment but also the organizational commitment that, over the course of the twentieth century, has become increasingly important for innovative investment strategies to succeed in international competition.

It might also be mentioned that such behavior is totally absent in dominant Japanese corporations. In Japan, strategic managers can benefit from neither the sale of stock nor the sale of offices. Even if they own shares on their own account, their dividend income is minimal because Japanese firms use their financial resources to further the innovative capabilities of the organization, not to fill the pockets of owners. The personal incomes of top managers are tied to the hierarchical structure of compensation within the enterprise, and their strategic behavior is disciplined by their life-long membership in the organization (Abegglen and Stalk 1985, chap. 8; Ballon and Tomita 1988). A recent U.S. view has it that "Japanese managers are increasingly unconstrained and unmonitored" and that "the long-term result will be the growth of bureaucracy and inefficiency and the demise of product quality and organizational responsiveness—until the waste becomes so severe it triggers a market for corporate control to remedy the excesses" (Jensen 1989, 73–74).[20] Don't bet on it. Their career-long memberships in their firms constrain and monitor Japanese managers to ensure the long-run success of their organizations. Their freedom from the market of corporate control, moreover, far from undermining their innovative response, provides them with the financial commitment to pursue innovative investment strategies. And for those interested in the history of changing international industrial leadership, it is worth pondering that it used to be that way in the United States as well.

Conglomeration

Indeed, the emergence of strategic managers as owners in the 1950s may well have been the cause of the conglomeration movement of the 1960s—a movement that further separated top management from participation in or identification with the organizational goals of the dominant going concerns. For those top managers who found that they could make more money by owning shares than by managing production and distribution processes, it made sense to use corporate financial resources to buy more companies, even if the products and processes that these companies produced bore no relation to the organizational capabilities of the acquiring firms. As is well known, the merger mania that peaked with over 6,000 mergers and acquisitions in 1969, but that continued well into the 1970s, was characterized by an unprecedented movement of major corporations into lines of business in which they had no technological expertise (Chandler 1990a).

---

20. These statements are reproduced in more complete context later in this essay.

The top management of the acquiring firms controlled the financial resources required to undertake innovative investment strategies. But, as far as planning and implementing innovative investment strategies were concerned, the *strategic* managers had to be the "middle" managers who headed the conglomerate divisions and who (initially at least) had the requisite understanding of the division's organizational capabilities. Yet middle managers lacked the direct financial control—the financial commitment—that is essential to the management of innovation. With top management lacking both long-standing organizational links with their strategic subordinates as well as the technological and organizational knowledge to assess the duration and extent of the financial commitment needed to carry an innovative strategy through to success, the capital allocation process of the conglomerates had to be managed by the numbers—and all the more so the more divisions (often 40 to 70) (Chandler 1990a) that were incorporated into the conglomerate structure.

For example, in the first half of this century, top management used return on investment (ROI) as a statistical tool to enable them to keep track of divisional performance. But through their firm-specific knowledge of technology and organization, top managers as strategic managers could distinguish subpar ROI caused by inevitable developmental costs and gestation periods from subpar ROI caused by subpar managerial performance. In the conglomerates, however, a statistical tool that had been an *aid* to strategic decision making became a *basis* for strategic decision making, imparting an inevitable short-term bias to the evaluation of divisional performance.[21] Middle managers who pursued innovative strategies under these conditions quickly learned (if they were still around to make use of the knowledge) that adaptive behavior was more often than not better received at the corporate headquarters.[22]

As the conglomerate movement gained steam in the 1960s, moreover, this short-term bias became accentuated by the purposes for which, and ways in which, acquisitions were made. Even when firms were acquired for cash, the conglomerators were always on the lookout for firms with low P/E ratios, which in itself sent a message to the managers of firms that wanted to avoid a hostile takeover that they had better take steps (such as raising dividends) that might convince the stock market to place a higher value on their shares. Alternatively, the potential targets could take on fixed-interest obligations in order to lower earnings or quickly merge with a friendly company. Long-term investment strategy gave way to short-term reactions to the rise of the market for corporate control.

---

21. See Chandler 1977, chap. 14; Johnson and Kaplan 1987.
22. For an excellent case study, see Holland 1989. See also Mass 1991.

Moreover, increasingly in the 1960s, as the stock market reacted favorably to the increased number of conglomerates, takeovers occurred through the exchange of common stock. The movement was no longer constrained by the acquirer's internal sources of cash. High stock prices enabled the conglomerators to make more acquisitions. Through "pooling of interests" (the consolidation of the financial accounts of the parent and the acquired companies), the acquisition of companies with low P/E ratios produced a one-shot increase in earnings per share of the conglomerate, which in turn generated a higher P/E ratio for the conglomerate shares, which in turn permitted the conglomerate to use a given number of shares to make more acquisitions. In 1965, pooling of interests accounted for about 30 percent of all mergers; in 1968, more than 60 percent (The Editors of *Fortune* 1970, 144).

In early 1969, the editors of *Fortune* wrote that "practically every sizable U.S. corporation, whether it realizes it or not, is under scrutiny by some other corporation as a prospective acquisition" (141). For "the nine out of ten prospects [that] for a variety of reasons don't want to be taken over by the people who would like to take them over," the *Fortune* editors advocated taking on debt, but recognized that "such a countermeasure . . . is as yet unpopular" (141, 143). Nevertheless, despite the alleged unpopularity of leverage, the debt-equity ratio in U.S. manufacturing rose from .40 in 1960 to .48 in 1965 to .72 in 1970 (U.S. Bureau of the Census 1989, 928). The next best countermeasure, according to the *Fortune* editors, was to do whatever was required as soon as possible to boost the market price of the company's stock. And one way to boost market price quickly was for the frightened target to become an acquirer of low P/E companies itself (The Editors of *Fortune* 1970, 144).

All other things being equal, the higher earnings per share that resulted when a high P/E conglomerate acquired a low P/E company made it mandatory for the conglomerate to make more low P/E acquisitions if it wanted to show steady earnings growth and keep its P/E ratio high, which in turn often led to debt-financed acquisitions, which made the whole structure more financially vulnerable. Now, if all other things were *not* equal—if, for example, the conglomerates really generated "synergy" that boosted the long-run earning power of the acquired firms—the acquisition game might have generated economically beneficial results. The separation between financial control and organizational capability, however, produced the opposite effect. Because the middle managers in the conglomerate hierarchy were assigned a strategic function but were denied strategic power, the earnings of the massive conglomerates soon became worse, not better.

In February, 1969, as the conglomerate movement was reaching its peak, the editors of *Fortune* debated the pros and cons of the increasing proportions of debt in corporate capitalizations that had become part and parcel of the later stages of the conglomerate movement. On the pro side, they pointed to the tax advantages of debt financing, the security of debt in an economy committed to full employment, and the low expense of debt financing in an inflationary age. They went on to say, however, that debt has its hazards, "particularly for a conglomerate whose year-to-year increases in reported earnings are in part dependent on the chain-letter effect of new acquisitions."

> Times might not have to get very tough or competitive for such a com-
> pany to find itself looking desperately for hard cash or the equivalent
> thereof to satisfy its bondholders and keep its creditors at bay. Hard-
> pressed conglomerates might, for example, be forced to spin off some of
> their divisions. Given plenty of competition, the great conglomeration
> movement of the 1960s might conceivably be the great deconglomera-
> tion movement of the 1970s. (The Editors of *Fortune* 1970, 108)

The research of David Ravenscraft and F. M. Scherer reveals that the editors of *Fortune* were prescient. Indeed, the *Fortune* editors undoubtedly underestimated just how "tough and competitive" the 1970s would be com-pared to the 1960s. Ravenscraft and Scherer estimate that roughly one-third of the acquisitions made in the 1960s and early 1970s were resold, typically under conditions of financial duress (1987, 190).

The longer run legacy of the buying and selling of companies in the 1960s and 1970s was the entrenchment of financiers in positions of strategic management in many U.S. industrial corporations (Hayes and Abernathy 1980). Of more importance than just the professional backgrounds of those at the top, however, were the incentives that the focus on adaptive strategy created for those rising through the ranks. As the middle managers of the conglomerates found out, with top management looking at the bottom line, rewards, including promotion within the managerial hierarchy, went to those who made the bottom line look good. Because of the internal dynamics of the managerial organization, therefore, over the long run the financial orientation of those at the top, and the firm's focus on adaptive investment strategies, tended to be reproduced. The heightened pressures emanating from the exter-nal economic environment—the competitive pressures of foreign competition and the financial pressures of the rise of the market for corporate control—served to reinforce this internal dynamic.

During the 1980s, an even more fundamental problem arose for the development of a cadre of technologists who might implement, and ultimately direct, the innovative strategies of U.S. industrial enterprises in the future. The financial revolution has gone some way in undermining the incentives for capable college graduates to make career-long commitments to gaining exper-tise in technology and providing their services to developing the products and

processes of particular business enterprises. The earlier continuity and stability of the major U.S. industrial corporations meant that an educated entrant
to the labor force could be quite certain that, over a period as long as some
forty years, the company would be able and willing to offer employment
security, new learning experiences, and upward mobility to its best per-
formers.

The dismantling of corporations in the 1970s followed by the hostile
takeovers and forced downsizing in the 1980s have rendered this career path
highly uncertain (Nussbaum, et al. 1986). Even if the entry positions in
technology are still in place, the long-run employment prospects for the
entrant into all but the most committed companies are anything but secure.[23]
At the same time, the very forces that jeopardize the long-run stability of the
industrial corporation have created alternative employment opportunities that
capable new entrants found difficult to ignore in the 1980s. True, Wall Street
has been laying off personnel since October, 1987. Yet, in 1989, the average
compensation (salary and bonus) for the more highly paid stratum of corporate finance and merger and acquisition specialists at the top ten securities
firms was $450,000 if they entered the firm in 1983, $300,000 if they entered
in 1986, just over $200,000 if they entered in 1987, and about $140,000 if
they entered in 1988 (*Wall Street Journal* 1989, C1, C5). The average compensation for the *lower paid* specialists ranged from just under $300,000 if
they entered in 1983 to $100,000 if they joined the firm in 1988. During the
1980s, it was not only with the Japanese that U.S. industries could not
compete.

Junk Bonds, Raiders, and LBOs

In the transition from innovative to adaptive strategies in U.S. industries, the
conglomerate movement of the 1960s was a turning point in other ways as
well. The restructuring of corporate balance sheets that occurred in the process of conglomeration appears to have contributed to the rise of another
phenomenon that would have a great impact on corporate financial structure in
the 1980s. Robert Taggart argues that, "prior to 1977, the public junk-bond
market consisted almost entirely of 'fallen angels,' or bonds whose initial
investment grade ratings were subsequently lower" (1988, 8). Connie Bruck

---

23. During the 1980s, IBM has had to downsize, but it has been able to do so through
attrition and "golden handshakes" so that it is unlikely that new entrants' perceptions of the
prospects of career employment security with the company have been altered. Nevertheless, IBM
has lost important older personnel who have decided to shake the company's golden hand. And,
in the slowness of its attempt to shift out of mainframes as its main product, even IBM has been
accused of being "preoccupied with meeting Wall Street's demands for quarterly results." See
Business Week, December 18, 1989.

contends that some of these original junk bonds were the "Chinese paper" issued by conglomerates in the 1960s to finance acquisitions (1989, 27, 37–38, 44). Although we do not currently know the extent to which the original supply of junk bonds resulted from conglomeration, research into the issue is likely to show that conglomerate debt that had fallen below investment grade made a significant contribution.

It was not until the late 1970s, when the efforts of Michael Milken to convince institutional investors to buy and sell the existing supply of junk bonds had already created a market in low-grade securities, that, in a more hospitable economic climate, the practice of issuing new junk bonds began. Hence, Taggart's data show the value of the junk bonds of U.S. corporations rising from $6.6 billion in 1971 to $8.2 billion in 1973, and then jumping up to $11.1 billion in the recession of 1974. In 1975, defaults and recoveries decreased the value of outstanding junk bonds to $7.5 billion. In the boom of the late 1970s, the value of junk bonds rose quickly to reach $15.1 billion in 1980.

By 1981, with $17.4 billion of outstanding junk bonds, the market had grown large enough for Drexel Burnham to begin using them, first, to finance hostile takeovers and then to finance managers in leveraged buyouts (LBOs). Between 1982 and 1985, the value of outstanding junk bonds rose by well over 200 percent from $18.5 billion to $58.8 billion (Taggart 1988, 9). Although estimates vary concerning the amount of new issues that were used to finance takeovers and LBOs (14–15), it is clear that the growth of the junk-bond market, manifesting as it did the increased willingness of institutional investors to hold the low-grade, high-yield securities, made it possible for the market to absorb the new issues of junk bonds that financed bigger and bigger deals.

The hostile takeovers and leveraged buyouts of the 1980s appear to have been a major force in producing the decade's high yields on corporate stocks and bonds. Even more so than in the late 1960s, virtually any company could conceivably become a takeover target. And, as in the late 1960s, the target could defend itself either by increasing dividends in the hope of bolstering the market valuation of the company's stock or by taking on debt for the purpose of withdrawing stock from the market. Either defense forced the target to reduce its available cash flow. While it diminished its attractiveness as a takeover target, it eroded its financial commitment. Meanwhile, the very presence of the high-yield junk bonds, and the willingness of institutional investors to hold them, exerted an upward influence on interest rates generally and made even high-grade corporate bonds more risky just because of the possibility that junk would be loaded on top of them only to keep the raiders at bay.

The major corporate raids of the first half of the 1980s were attempts to harvest the fruits of past investments without putting anything in their place. Hence, the focus was on corporations endowed with natural resources—oil reserves and timberland in particular—whose products can always command a market (even if at depressed prices) but are very costly to replace. To justify their own greed, the raiders and their proponents made the self-serving arguments that power hungry incumbent managers were making ill-conceived investment decisions that were wasting the shareholder's dollar; for example, that the declining price of oil made oil exploration unprofitable (Johnson 1986; Jarrell, Brickley, and Netter 1988). But the quantity of energy reserves or other natural resources available to a national economy (and the world economy) is too important an issue, both economically and politically, to be left to the raiders and to be driven by short-run fluctuations in market prices. In the absence of coherent national (or international) natural resource policies that transcend the profit motive, there is a strong argument that, whatever the motivations of the incumbent managers, the investments be made while the business organizations that are capable of making them are still intact.

Faced by the unprecedented power of the corporate raider in the market for corporate control from the early 1980s, many incumbent managers learned to use debt financing as a defense. From 1980 through 1987 the majority of LBOs were divisional buyouts in which the middle managers of the troubled conglomerates reintegrated the strategic management function with the power of financial control. As such, these LBOs restored a necessary condition for undertaking and implementing innovative investment strategies that had been largely absent in the conglomerate organizational structure. In 1980, there were 47 divisional LBOs at a real average value (in 1988 U.S. dollars) of $34.5 million; in 1983, 139 at a real average value of $58.2 million; and in 1986, 144—the peak annual number for the 1980s—at a real average value of $180.7 million. From 1980 through 1987, there were a smaller number of more highly valued LBOs of public companies. For example, in 1986 there were 76 public company buyouts at a real average value of $303.3 million. In that year, the ratio of the average value of public company to division buyouts was 1.7:1—its lowest level in the decade. In both 1987 and 1988, however, the average value of public company LBOs in 1988 dollars was around $480 million, about three times the average value of the divisional buyouts in those years. The number of public company buyouts jumped to 125 in 1988 from 47 in 1987 (Jensen 1989, 65).

LBOs *may* be a way for strategic managers to control the market for corporate control as a prelude to the pursuit of innovative investment strategies. LBOs can remove a company from the market for corporate control so that it can get on with its business of producing high-quality products at low unit costs. How well it can get on with its business depends on the costs of going private relative to its cash flow and the extent to which the owner-managers have an interest in building the company up rather than running it down. A recent study of LBOs between 1981 and 1986 that focuses on plant-level economies as well as trends in company R&D expenditures demonstrates that, for the first half of the 1980s at least, LBOs were undertaken for the purpose of getting a company back on track by protecting the organization from the market for corporate control (Lichtenberg and Siegel 1989).

The very need for companies to undertake these defensive LBOs was created by the preceding rise of the market for corporate control. As a result, even when the pursuit of innovation motivates an LBO, the taking on of unrelenting debt service is both expensive and inherently unstable. The problems inherent in using LBOs to restructure U.S. industry might not be so severe if U.S. companies were just competing among themselves. The problem is that, by and large, they are not. They are competing with business organizations abroad that, in general, do not have to appease the portfolio investor in order to do what an industrial enterprise is supposed to do—generate high-quality products at low unit costs.

The purpose of the high-value public company LBOs—particularly those initiated not by career managers but, rather, by what Michael Jensen calls LBO associations such as Forstman-Little or Kohlberg, Kravis, and Roberts—is not to insulate a going concern from the market for corporate control but, as Jensen puts it, "to disgorge the free cash flow" from companies that have allegedly "matured" (Jensen 1989). Financed largely by the issue of new junk bonds, the strategic managers of these offensive LBOs seek to make good on the high cost of purchase that results from the active bidding for, and speculation in, stocks that accompanies buyout attempts. Their gamble is that they can reduce the LBO debt by putting some divisions of the company up for sale and service the remainder of the debt by making the cash flow of the remaining divisions as "free" from other claims as possible. The sold-off divisions could well fall into the hands of innovative managers, but, with the escalation of LBO purchase prices that attended the grabs for corporate control in the later 1980s, the asking prices tended to be at levels that managers who would pursue innovative strategies could not afford. The speculative character of the offensive LBOs that dominated the late 1980s is reflected in a sharp decline of the credit quality of the new issues of junk bonds (Wigmore 1989; *Business Week* 1990, 68–70). Whereas many of the early 1980s LBOs suppressed the market for corporate control to enable a well-managed company to invest for the future, the LBOs of the mid-1980s represent the ultimate triumph of the market for corporate control. What those LBOs did was to give the holders of debt, rather than workers, managers, suppliers, or customers, the right to capture today's returns on yesterday's innovations.

How We Save Our Money

In historical perspective, the corporate raiders of the 1980s were capitalizing on a transformation of the relationship between finance and industry in the United States that had been underway since the 1950s. Paving the way for the financial revolution of the 1980s over the previous three decades was the growing tendency of strategic managers of U.S. industrial corporations to reap their own personal rewards through participation in the market for corporate control rather than through enhancing the value-creating capabilities of the companies that they were entrusted to manage. But even these managers did not themselves create the opportunities for gain through the securities markets. Underlying the financial transformation of the last four decades is an even more profound institutional problem in the nature of U.S. capital markets that will continue to weaken the financial commitment and erode the organizational capability of U.S. industry, even after (as appears to have been the case by the late 1980s) the current wizards of finance have pushed their money magic as far as it will go.

During the 1970s and 1980s it became fashionable for critics of the performance of the U.S. economy to decry the unwillingness of U.S. citizens to save. What they really meant to say (but rarely did) was that, in contrast to the era of U.S. industrial dominance when U.S. Keynesians encouraged us all to spend, in this era of trade deficits we are spending too much money on goods and services produced abroad. What is more, we borrow against the future to buy goods that do not even generate jobs or develop productive resources in the U.S. economy. To understand the "savings" problem in the United States is not, therefore, just a matter of too much consumption. It is also a matter of how Americans *spend* their money. More than that, the "savings" problem is a matter of how they *save* it. Underlying the ability of those U.S. households that do save in one way or another to extract the kinds of yields on corporate securities displayed in table 1 is the buying and selling power of the institutional investor.

In 1960, institutional investors owned 17.2 percent of the value of shares and accounted for 24.3 percent of the volume of trading on the New York Stock Exchange. By 1982, their share of the equity value had doubled to over one-third, while their share of trading had risen by about three and a half times to 83.8 percent of New York Stock Exchange volume (Hayes 1984, 52). As the institutional ownership of U.S. corporate assets became more concentrated, the turnover of shares on the New York Stock Exchange rose from 12.0 percent in 1960 to 54.0 percent in 1985, while trades of over 10,000 shares increased from 3.0 percent in 1965 to 52.0 percent in 1985 (Light and Perold 1987, 108; Lowenstein 1988, chap. 3). This increase in trading reflects a search for higher yields—a search that is driven by increasingly intense competition among the various types of institutional investors (as well as by the money managers within each type) for the savings of the U.S. household.

Leading the search for higher yields were the mutual funds that, from the 1950s, sought to capitalize on the prolonged boom in stock prices (Brooks 1973, chap. 6; Kaplan and Welles 1969). During the 1950s, common stocks accounted for 85.0 percent of the assets of mutual funds, as compared to about 30.0 percent of the assets of pension funds and only 3.0 to 4.0 percent of the assets of life insurance companies. Through rapid trading of large blocks of stock and the locking in of capital gains in advance of expected stock price declines, mutual fund managers sought to generate higher returns than could be secured from a more stable portfolio. During the 1960s, the mutual funds played an important role in the conglomeration movement by buying up blocks of stock that were rumored to be in play and selling them to the raiders at a higher price (The Editors of *Fortune* 1970, 142). Yet in 1970, mutual funds only accounted for 1.3 percent of the total funds supplied to U.S. money and capital markets, compared to 8.7 percent by federal loan agencies and 31.3 percent by commercial banks. By 1986, mutual funds supplied 17.4 percent of all funds to these markets, slightly more than federal loan agencies and just 1.7 percent less than commercial banks. Common stocks made up only 36.0 percent of mutual fund assets in 1986 because the markets in stocks and bonds, which had previously been highly segmented between individual and institutional investors, had become highly integrated (ACLI 1987, 37).

The success of the mutual funds in generating higher yields led pension fund managers to increase their holdings of common stock—from 30 percent in 1955 to 63 percent in 1968 and around 50 percent in 1986. In 1955, pension funds owned 2 percent, and households 91 percent, of all outstanding equities in the United States; by 1985, the pension fund share had risen to 22 percent and the household share had fallen to 60 percent. Insurance companies also gradually increased their holdings of common stocks so that, by the 1970s, they had more than doubled the proportion of their assets held in equities (ACLI 1987, 36).

Share holding is no longer fragmented in the United States; millions of U.S. households have turned to concentrated investing power to maximize their existing wealth and secure their futures. In general, these households know less than they ever did (which was never much) about how or why the companies in which they own securities are able to generate the returns that accrue to their investment portfolios. The financial institutions that serve these households must compete for their funds by showing high returns on a regular basis and will shift their portfolios in and out of securities to do so (Lowenstein 1988, chap. 3). The managers of pension funds can generally take a longer run perspective on the returns to their portfolios than can the mutual fund managers. Nevertheless, even the pension funds (or insurance companies) are loathe to pass up the gains that, in a speculative financial era, can be made by taking quick capital gains, and their managers may feel under personal pressure to match the performance of the more speculative institutional investors. The more the institutional investors focus on the high returns to their financial portfolios that are needed to attract household savings and on the constant restructuring of their portfolios to maximize yields, the more their goals represent the antithesis of financial commitment. Driven by the need to compete for the public's savings by showing superior returns, portfolio managers who invest for the long term may well find themselves looking for new jobs in the short term.

Since the late 1960s, Wall Street has accommodated the rise of the institutional investor by increasingly turning from its traditional investment banking function to trading in securities, both stocks and bonds.[24] The integration of the stock and bond markets in the portfolios of institutional investors meant that high yields achieved through trading in stocks created pressure for bond trading to return similar yields (adjusting for risk), and higher yields achieved in these secondary markets put pressure on the rates of new bond issues. The rise of the junk-bond market in the mid-1970s, itself made possible by the institutional investors' search for higher yields, in turn put pressure on the stock market to generate higher short-term returns. The yields secured by portfolio investors, in turn, made it impossible for commercial banks, mutual banks, and savings and loan companies to raise funds on the basis of the old rules of the financial game. Financial deregulation in the late 1970s led these institutions to join the search for higher short-term yields. By the early 1980s, all these changes in the structure of U.S. financial markets, assisted by (as Connie Bruck has shown) considerable planned coordination by Michael Milken and company (1989), led to the rise of the junk bond–financed corporate raider. The market in corporate control had been unleashed.

For economists who believe in the efficiency of market coordination, both the integration of financial markets and the rise of the market for corporate control represent the coming of age of U.S. capitalism. It is good for the disposable income of the portfolio investor, both U.S. and foreign. But it is not good for industrial innovation. As U.S. industry faced its greatest competitive challenges in the 1970s and 1980s, industrial enterprises required more, not less, financial commitment. Yet, as the institutional investors succeeded in their search for higher yields, less financial commitment is what U.S. industry got.

---

24. See Auletta 1986, Carrington 1987.

New Ventures and Alternative Opportunities

So much for going concerns. What about new ventures? Perhaps what we are seeing is the movement of capital out of old firms and industries into new ones. What else is a highly liquid capital market for except to ensure that economic resources flow to their most productive uses? Doesn't economic theory tell us that capital immobility is bad, that capital mobility is good?

That is what a particular brand of economic theory tells us. But for understanding how business organizations create value and why some national economies are better at value creation than others, it is a brand of theory that obscures more than it illuminates (Lazonick 1991). If we transcend the free-market ideology from which neoclassical economic theory derives its inspiration and look at the reality of mobile versus committed finance in the 1980s, we can see that the resources that are flowing out of the major U.S. going concerns are insufficiently committed to serve the financial needs of new ventures.

In industries in which product and process innovation takes place on the basis of already developed technologies, new entrants do not arise without a concerted developmental effort within a protected economic environment—as was the case, for example, in the rise of the Japanese automobile producers and electronics manufacturers. Indeed, once Britain had experienced the world's first industrial revolution, a period of state-protected or subsidized development in which high fixed costs could be transformed into low unit costs became essential for every major industry in every successful capitalist economy, including the United States.

It is in industries that are developing radically new technologies—microelectronics and biotechnology are the most prominent examples from recent U.S. history—that new ventures stand the greatest chance of success without the benefit of tariff protection or public subsidy. But, precisely because these enterprises are attempting radical innovation, they have a great need for financial commitment. In the post–World War II decades, the United States had a small but vibrant venture-capital industry, funded mostly by already rich individuals, but occasionally by the more financially independent and innovative going concerns that had themselves developed related technology.[25] Private venture capitalists in particular understood that the innovation process required sustained cooperative efforts by a team of people with unique ideas and skills.

The venture capitalist's role was to perceive the uniqueness of these ideas and skills and the commitment to the development process of the people who possessed them, and then to provide financial commitment until the innova-

---

25. See Wilson 1986, chaps. 1–10; Fast 1977; Florida and Kenney 1990.

tion was high quality enough and low cost enough to generate sufficient earnings to sustain the enterprise as a going concern. If the innovative invest-ment strategy made the transition from new venture to going concern, then the venture capitalists (along with any of the new venture's technologists who held ownership stakes in the enterprise) could reap their returns by selling their shares to the public. By this time, the successful enterprise would have built up a managerial structure that could continue to plan and coordinate enterprise strategy. The very emergence of the new venture as a successful going concern would lead stockholders to look for longer term (by the port-folio investor's standards) capital gains. Growth-oriented shareholders would be willing to hold stock with a high P/E ratio without insisting on excessively high dividends to boost short-term yields. Strategic managers would gain financial control, and with the first-mover advantage of its accumulation of organizational capability, the firm would continue to expand its market share and emerge as a dominant force in its industry.

The last major wave of new ventures that emerged as successful going concerns in the United States took place in computer-related fields and bio-technology in the 1970s (Wilson 1985, chap. 1). At first, the process of rewarding the creators of the innovative going concerns by taking the com-pany public was on course. But, by the early 1980s, the involvement of institutional investors in the new venture process was causing the process to break down.

During the 1970s, in their search for higher yields, those institutional investors that could think longer term than the mutual funds—the pension funds, insurance companies, universities, foundations, and industrial corpora-tions with surplus funds—began to take shares in venture capital funds. The involvement of pension funds in the supply of venture capital became possible when a 1978 U.S. Department of Labor interpretation of the Employee Re-tirement Income Security Act (passed in 1974) indicated that pension funds could make investments that were riskier than holding blue-chip stocks and bonds. From 1978 to 1980, about $500,000 were added to the venture capital pool in the United States annually. In 1981, the new funding climbed to about $1.0 billion, in 1982 to about $1.5 billion, and then in 1983 tripled to about $4.5 billion. From 1984 through 1987, the supply of new capital to the venture capital funds ranged from $3.3 billion (1985) to $5.0 billion (in 1987), but fell off sharply to $2.0 billion in 1988 and has since continued to decline (*New York Times* 1989, Sec. 3, 1, 6).

By 1983, the pension funds were the major source of venture capital, supplying 31 percent of the total outstanding. Individuals and families pro-vided 21 percent, foreign investors 16 percent, insurance companies and corporations 12 percent each, and endowments and foundations 8 percent. By 1988, the pension fund share of the total pool had risen to 46 percent, while foreign investors supplied 14 percent, endowments and foundations 12 percent, corporations 11 percent, insurance companies 9 percent, and individuals and families only 8 percent. By 1989, the venture capital pool in the United States had grown to $31 billion, over ten times the $3 billion available in 1979 (and indeed throughout the 1970s [3, 1, 6]).

Looking at these numbers, the rapid growth of the supply of venture capital in the 1980s would seem to demonstrate the power of a free enterprise system based on financial mobility to allocate capital to its best alternative uses. Unfortunately, in large part *because of* the rapid flow of money into venture-capital funds, the venture-capital industry in the United States is in trouble. The *New York Times* article from which the data in the preceding paragraphs are drawn quotes William Sahlman of the Harvard Business School as saying "for the first time in history a large number of venture capitalists will lose money" (1).

The problems began when new ventures such as Genentech in biotechnology and Lotus Development in computer software hit it big in the early 1980s. Just as in the early 1960s some mutual funds had speculated in the "glamour" stocks of growth companies such as Polaroid and Xerox, driving up P/E ratios, so in the early 1980s the institutional investors (and not just mutual funds) began trading—but in a much bigger way than two decades earlier—in the stocks of virtually any new high-tech company that demonstrated some innovative potential (Brooks 1973, chap. 6; Wilson 1985). At the same time, pension funds in particular began not only to buy high-tech stocks but also to supply funds to the new ventures that hoped to eventually reap the rewards of going public. This supply-side role of the institutional investors had no counterpart in earlier periods of radical innovation. The result of the rapidly growing supply of new venture capital combined with the stock market speculation in high-tech public offerings in the early 1980s was a flood of *new* venture capitalists into the venture-capital industry. Soon there were too many venture capitalists trying to start up too many companies.

Into the first half of the 1970s the U.S. venture-capital industry had been mainly in the hands of Laurance Rockefeller, J. H. Whitney, and the disciples of Georges Doriot. In terms of its investment pool, the venture-capital industry stagnated throughout the early 1970s and grew only modestly in the last years of the decade. There were 2 new funds (which raised a total of $20.2 million) in 1977, 5 in 1978, 7 in 1979, and 10 in 1980. In 1981–83, however, 100 new funds came on the scene, and by 1989 there were more than 650 venture-capital firms in the United States (Wilson 1985, 107).

Drawn into the industry by the increasing willingness of portfolio investors to hold shares in companies that had often not even developed, let alone commercialized, a new product, the venture-capital firms vied with one another not so much for funds (which were no longer in scarce supply) but for the technologists and technologies of each other's new ventures. Many venture capitalists became what John Wilson aptly describes as "vulture capitalists" (chap. 13).

From the perspective of the mid-1980s, John Wilson—a *Business Week* editor—summarized how those industrialists and observers who understood that innovation requires organizational continuity viewed the transformation of the industry. The "two sweeping charges against the venture capital community" were

> that by draining a few successful companies of their most productive managers and engineers, by pirating their technology, and by disrupting key departments and projects, venture capitalists damage the ability of those companies to innovate and to compete in international markets; that by funding excessive numbers of similar companies, many with less than outstanding leadership, they are wasting money and talent, adding little to the progress of technology, and artificially creating overcompetitive situations where no participant can make money. (189–90)

As a result, by 1984, "company after company fell short of its targets, disappeared into bankruptcy, or dragged out a miserable existence as 'living dead,' soaking up money and attention but never really succeeding" (196). Yet, after a drop in the supply of new money to the venture-capital industry in 1984 and 1985, the institutional investors, and particularly the pension funds, started pouring money back in. As the supply was cut back in 1988 and 1989 and as the unprofitability of the venture-capital industry continued, it was not even clear how much of the $31 billion of "venture capital" was being used as venture capital. According to the *New York Times* report,

> critics say the huge amount of money and pressure from institutional investors have made venture capitalists less venturesome, and more short-term oriented, much like publicly traded companies that answer to Wall Street every quarter. Rather than invest small chunks of money to start companies, many put large chunks in more mature companies, which are less risky and closer to going public, and in leveraged buyouts, which provide quicker, and often bigger returns.

The article goes on to quote one venture capitalist as saying, "It's getting more like the money management business" (1989, 6).[26]

If the money that the institutional investors have put in the venture-capital industry has been more of a problem than a solution for industrial

---

26. See also Gallese 1990.

innovation in the United States, we should not expect that the high yields on the securities of going concerns that the institutional investors are distributing to their main clients—those U.S. households that save—is being reallocated to any more efficient uses. Judging from U.S. trade statistics for the 1980s, the increases in the disposable income that the higher yields generate are being allocated to Matsushita VCRs, Hitachi televisions, Nintendo entertainment systems, Sony videocameras, a trade-in for an upmarket Toyota—you name it.

Hence we see the leap of faith made by proponents of the market for corporate control who advise that, for the sake of capital mobility (returning value to the shareholders), "mature" firms should "disgorge their free cash flow." Jensen defines "free cash flow" as the "cash flow in excess of that required to fund all investment projects with positive net present values when discounted at the relevant cost of capital" (1989, 66). The problem is not with the definition but with the neoclassical economist's static view of the world. For the proponent of the market for corporate control, to ignore the dynamic, historical *processes* that determine a firm's projected revenues and cost of capital can serve his or her purposes well. From the dynamic, historical perspective that I have presented in this essay, the "relevant cost of capital" of which Jensen speaks is the high rate of interest on corporate debt that the financial revolution has permitted portfolio investors to extract from going concerns. At the same time, strategic managers' revenue projections from new investment projects that enter into "net present values" must take into account the weakening of financial commitment, and the consequent erosion of organizational capability, that the rise of the market for corporate control has wrought.

Jensen goes on to argue that "for a company to operate efficiently and maximize value, free cash flow must be distributed to shareholders rather than retained." As a "vivid example" of the failure to do so, he points to

> the senior management of Ford Motor Company, which sits on nearly $15 billion in cash and marketable securities in an industry with excess capacity. Ford's management has been deliberating about acquiring financial service companies, aerospace companies, or making some other multibillion-dollar diversification move—rather than deliberating about effectively distributing Ford's excess cash to its owners so they can decide how to reinvest it. (66)

Assume that Ford's strategic managers had taken Jensen's advice. If Ford's shareholders had not used all of the $15 billion dividend just to buy more consumer goods, how might we have expected that they would have invested the rest? Undoubtedly they would have put some of it into mutual funds, which would of course have stood ready to lend the money back to Ford, should Ford's senior management have discovered that, in order to maintain market share and contain unit costs, they have to keep investing not only in their own company, but also in suppliers and dealers. For they might have noticed that their Japanese rivals were making such investments, not only in Japan but also in the United States.[27] But, with its equity base depleted by a massive dividend, Ford's managers would have found it impossible to borrow at investment-grade rates. The suppliers of junk bonds (whoever it is that steps into the breach created by the bankruptcy of Drexel Burnham and the jailing of Michael Milken) would find a new potential customer. Over the long run (say by 1995), the Ford Motor Company, the premier U.S.-based automobile producer of the 1980s, would be on the verge of bankruptcy, like Chrysler (the second-best U.S.-based producer in the 1980s) was back in 1978. But, unlike 1978, in 1995 the federal government would find itself swamped by the public and private borrowing spree of the 1980s. Still trying to recover from its role as guarantor of the savings and loans as well as from the growing defaults on its student loan guarantees (which were made to keep the U.S. system of higher education afloat without increasing the federal budget deficit) and besieged by requests for loan guarantees from a host of collapsing junk bond–financed companies that were the present of the 1980s to the 1990s, Congress would be in no position (and certainly in no mood) to provide loan guarantees to aid Ford's recovery.[28]

To come back from the future, the very threat of shareholder power exercised through the market for corporate control may well induce Ford's strategic managers to undertake imprudent diversification that would reduce financial commitment to what the company can do best—make and sell cars. A superior alternative would be for Ford to manage its $15 billion in surplus funds in a way that makes its financial reserves grow. When new major investments in making and selling cars must be made, the company would then have the funds available. The Japanese call such money management of surplus funds *zai-teku*. As a recent book on Japanese corporate finance recognizes, "the greater the funds a corporation controls, the better its potential to benefit from *zai-teku*." The authors go on to relate how "the Toyota Motor

---

27. For example, Toyota has recently begun to invest in dealerships in the Midwest where the U.S. based companies had been most successful in maintaining their market share (*New York Times,* December 15, 1989, D1). *Business Week* reports that "to stay in the race [against the Japanese], Chrysler is planning to spend $15 billion on products and plants within five years" (December 17, 1989, 46).

28. On the role of government loan guarantees in the successful bailout of Chrysler, see Reich and Donahue (1985). On the potential magnitude of student loan defaults, see "The $5 Trillion Schock," *Newsweek,* December 18, 1989, 26–28.

Corp. revised its earnings for the business period ending July, 1987, from ¥350 billion to ¥380 billion." Quoting from the *Japan Times:*

> Toyota officials attributed the upward revision to massive income result-ing from its securities investment of surplus funds totaling ¥1.4 tril-lion. . . . Toyota's sophisticated portfolio management yields about 9 percent of its surplus cash each year. This amounts to about ¥126 billion of annual income. (Ballon and Tomita 1988, 143)

Jensen has argued that Japanese firms are beginning to suffer from the U.S. disease—a failure to "disgorge their free cash flow." Indeed, he specifi-cally cited the case of Toyota as a Japanese company that is

> flooded with free cash flow far in excess of [its] opportunities to invest in profitable internal growth. . . . Toyota, with its cash hoard of $10.4 billion, more than 25 percent of its total assets, is commonly referred to as Toyota Bank. (1989, 73)

"In short," Jensen concluded, "Japanese managers are increasingly uncon-strained and unmonitored." For this avid proponent of the market for corpo-rate control, Japanese competitive advantage is only transitory. The disease of "managerial capitalism" will afflict Japan, just like it has afflicted the United States.

> [Japanese managers] face no effective internal controls, little control from the product markets their companies already dominate, and fewer controls from the banking system because of self-financing, direct access to the capital markets, and lower debt ratios. Unless shareholders and creditors discover ways to prohibit their managers from behaving like U.S. managers, Japanese companies will make uneconomic acquisitions and diversification moves, generate internal waste, and engage in other value-destroying activities. The long-term result will be the growth of bureaucracy and inefficiency and the demise of product quality and or-ganizational responsiveness—until the waste becomes so severe it trig-gers a market for corporate control to remedy the excesses. (73–74)

If a "free-market" economist such as Jensen fails to understand the role that the rise of the market for corporate control has played in the long-term decline of U.S. industry, we should not be surprised that he understands little about the sources and durability of Japan's relatively recent industrial success. As I have already mentioned, the strategic managers of Japan's dominant industrial enterprises are highly disciplined, not by portfolio investors, but by the participants in the enterprise who really contribute to the process of value creation—the organization's employees. Indeed, the Japanese strategic manager is subject to organizational discipline precisely because he is first and foremost a member of the organization; his own career success depends on the success of the organization as a whole. There are no stock options in Japan, and even if the manager owns shares, his membership in the organization means the shares are not for sale (Ballon and Tomita 1988). As a result, his sole interest is in building organizational capability. And there is no market for corporate control to erode the financial commitment that is required for him to do so.

The real irony is that neither the Japanese strategic manager nor the Japanese business organization is wholly new to the history of capitalist development. For the historical significance of managerial capitalism is that there was a time when the strategic managers of U.S. industrial corporations were also disciplined by their membership in their own business organizations and saw their own individual success as dependent on the long-run growth and stability of the organization as a whole. That also happened to be a time when U.S. industry dominated the international economy.

The organizational basis of Japan's rise to industrial leadership over the past few decades has been a more far-reaching elaboration of the institutions of managerial capitalism that provided the basis for U.S. dominance during the first half of this century (Lazonick 1991, chap. 2; 1990, chaps. 9–10). Through Japan's enterprise-group system, the planned coordination of the specialized division of labor extends across legally distinct firms to ensure that the activities of all participating firms coalesce in the pursuit of common strategic goals. Within dominant Japanese firms, membership in the enterprise extends further down the organizational hierarchy than is generally the case in the United States to include blue-collar workers, enabling management to ensure that the skills and efforts of shop-floor workers further rather than impede organizational goals. The formidable productive power of U.S. managerial capitalism earlier in the century rested on a high degree of collective organization—although confined largely to the managerial structure of the particular firm. In building even more powerful and enduring collectivities that we call business organizations, the Japanese have recognized the historical significance of managerial capitalism.

To the detriment of economic analysis, most U.S. economists have not recognized the historical significance of managerial capitalism. Indeed, rather than enhance the productive capabilities inherited from managerial capitalism for the sake of future prosperity, the free-market orientation of the U.S. polity and economy in the 1970s and 1980s has helped to put the historical significance of managerial capitalism out of sight and out of our mind.

BIBLIOGRAPHY

Abegglen, James C., and George Stalk, Jr. 1985. *Kaisha, the Japanese Corporation.* New York: Basic Books.

Abernathy, William. 1978. *The Productivity Dilemma.* Baltimore: Johns Hopkins University Press.

American Council of Life Insurance (A.C.L.I.) 1987. *Life Insurance Fact Book Update 1987.* New York: Institute of Life Insurance.

Auletta, Ken. 1986. *Greed and Glory on Wall Street.* New York: Random House.

Baran, Paul A., and Paul M. Sweezy. 1966. *Monopoly Capital.* New York: Monthly Review Press.

Ballon, Robert J., and Iwao Tomita. 1988. *The Financial Behavior of Japanese Corporations.* Tokyo: Kodansha International.

Bernstein, Michael. 1987. *The Great Depression: Delayed Recovery and Economic Change in America, 1929–1939.* Cambridge: Cambridge University Press.

Black, Fischer. 1976. "The Dividend Puzzle." *Journal of Portfolio Management* 28:1–15.

Brooks, John. 1973. *The Go-Go Years.* New York: Weybright and Talley.

Bruck, Connie. 1989. *The Predators' Ball: The Inside Story of Drexel Burnham and the Rise of the Junk Bond Raiders.* New York: Penguin.

Carosso, Vincent P. 1970. *Investment Banking in America.* Cambridge, Mass.: Harvard University Press.

Carosso, Vincent P. 1987. *The Morgans Private International Bankers, 1854–1913.* Cambridge, Mass.: Harvard University Press.

Carrington, Tim. 1987. *The Year They Sold Wall Street.* New York: Penguin.

Chandler, Alfred D., Jr. 1954. "Patterns of American Railroad Finance, 1830–1850." *Business History Review* 28:248–63.

Chandler, Alfred D., Jr. 1965. *Railroads: The Nation's First Big Business.* New York: Harcourt, Brace and World.

Chandler, Alfred D., Jr. 1966. *Strategy and Structure: Chapters in the History of the Industrial Enterprise.* Garden City, N.Y.: Doubleday.

Chandler, Alfred D., Jr. 1977. *The Visible Hand: The Managerial Revolution in American Business.* Cambridge, Mass.: Belknap Press.

Chandler, Alfred D., Jr. 1985. "From Industrial Laboratories to Departments of Research and Development." In *The Uneasy Alliance: Managing the Productivity-Technology Dilemma,* ed. Kim B. Clark, Robert H. Hayes, and Christopher Lorenz. Boston: Harvard Business School Press.

Chandler, Alfred D., Jr. 1990a. "The Enduring Logic of Industrial Success." *Harvard Business Review* 68:130–40.

Chandler, Alfred D., Jr. 1990b. *Scale and Scope: The Dynamics of Industrial Capitalism.* Cambridge, Mass.: Belknap Press.

Channon, Derek. 1973. *The Strategy and Structure of British Enterprise.* Boston: Division of Research, Graduate School of Business Administration, Harvard University.

Clark, Kim B., et al. 1985. *Uneasy Alliance: Managing the Productivity Technology Dilemma.* Cambridge, Mass.: Harvard Business School Press.

Cohen, Stephen S., and John Zysman. 1987. *Manufacturing Matters: The Myth of the Post-Industrial Economy.* New York: Basic Books.

Crystal, Graef S. 1991. *In Search of Excess,* New York: Norton.

DeLong, Bradford J. 1989. "Did J. P. Morgan's Men Add Value?: An Historical Perspective on Financial Market Innovation." Cambridge, Mass.: Harvard University. Photocopy.

Dertouzos, Michael L., Richard K. Lester, and Robert M. Solow. 1989. *Made in America: Regaining the Productive Edge.* Cambridge, Mass.: MIT Press.

Doerflinger, Thomas, and Jack Rivkin. 1987. *Risk and Reward: Venture Capital and the Making of America's Great Industries.* New York: Random House.

Donaldson, Gordon. 1984. *Managing Corporate Wealth: The Operation of a Comprehensive Financial Goals System.* New York: Praeger.

Economic Report of the President 1989. Washington, D.C.: GPO.

Editors of *Fortune.* 1970. *Conglomerate Commotion.* New York: Viking.

Edwards, Richard C. 1975. "Stages in Corporate Stability and the Risks of Corporate Failure." *Journal of Economic History* 35:428–57.

Ellsworth, Richard R. 1985. "Capital Markets and Competitive Decline." *Harvard Business Review* 63:58–59.

Fast, Norman D. 1977. *The Rise and Fall of Corporate New Venture Divisions.* Ann Arbor: UMI Research Press.

Florida, Richard and Martin Kenney. 1990. *The Breakthrough Illusion: Corporate America's Failure to Move From Mass Production to Innovation.* New York: Basic Books.

Foley, Duncan K., and William Lazonick. 1990. "Corporate Takeovers and the Growth of Productivity." Barnard College. Photocopy.

Galbraith, John Kenneth. 1980. *The Great Crash 1929.* New York: Avon.

Gallese, Liz Roman. 1980. "Venture Capital Strays Far From Its Roots." *The Business World, New York Times Magazine.* April 1, pt. 2.

Goldsmith, Raymond W. 1958. *Financial Intermediaries in the American Economy Since 1900.* Princeton: Princeton University Press.

Gordon, Robert Aaron. 1974. *Economic Instability and Growth: the American Record.* New York: Harper and Row.

Hannah, Leslie. 1983. *The Rise of the Corporate Economy: The British Experience.* 2d ed. London: Methuen.

Hayes, Robert H., and William Abernathy. 1980. "Managing Our Way to Economic Decline." *Harvard Business Review* 58:4.

Hayes, Samuel, III. 1984. "Investment Banking: Commercial Banks' Inroads." *Economic Review* (Federal Reserve Bank of Atlanta), 52:50–59.

Herman, Edward S. 1981. *Corporate Control, Corporate Power.* Cambridge: Cambridge University Press.

Holland, Max. 1989. *When the Machine Stopped: A Cautionary Tale From Industrial America.* Boston: Harvard Business School Press.

Hounshell, David, and John K. Smith. 1988. *Science and Corporate Strategy: Du Pont R&D 1902–1980.* Cambridge: Cambridge University Press.

Jarrell, Gregg, James Brickley, and Jeffrey Netter. 1988. "The Market for Corporate Control: The Empirical Evidence Since 1980." *Journal of Economic Perspectives* 2, no. 1: 49–68.

Jensen, Michael C. 1989. "Eclipse of the Public Corporation." *Harvard Business Review* 67:73–74.

Jensen, Michael C. "Takeover: Their Causes and Consequences." *Journal of Economic Perspectives* 2, no. 1: 21–48.

Johnson, Moira. 1986. *Takeover: The New Wall Street Warriors: the Men, the Money, the Impact.* New York: Arbor House.

Johnson, Thomas H., and Robert Kaplan. 1987. *Relevance Lost: The Rise and Fall of Management Accounting.* Boston: Harvard Business School Press.

Kaplan, Gilbert E., and Chris Wells, eds. 1969. *The Money Managers.* New York: Random House.

Keehn, Richard M., and Gene Smiley. 1988. "Margin Purchases, Brokers' Loans and the Bull Markets of the Twenties." *Business and Economic History* 2d ser., 17.

Koch, Albert R. 1943. *The Financing of Large Corporations, 1920–1939.* New York: National Bureau of Economic Research.

Lamoureaux, Naomi. 1986. "Banks, Kinship, and Economic Development: The New England Case." *Journal of Economic History* 46:647.

Lazonick, William. 1986. "Strategy, Structure, and Management Development in the United States and Britain," in *Development of Managerial Enterprise,* ed. Kesaji Kobayashi and Hidemasa Morikawa. Tokyo: University of Tokyo Press.

Lazonick, William. 1990. *Competitive Advantage on the Shop Floor.* Cambridge, Mass.: Harvard University Press.

Lazonick, William. 1991. *Business Organization and the Myth of the Market Economy.* Cambridge: Cambridge University Press.

Levin, Doron P. 1989. "New Toyota Target: The Midwest." *New York Times,* December 15.

Lewellen, Wilbur G. 1968. *Executive Compensation in Large Industrial Corporations.* New York: National Bureau of Economic Research.

Lewellen, Wilbur G. 1971. *The Ownership Income of Management.* New York: National Bureau of Economic Research.

Lichtenberg, Frank, and Donald Siegel. 1989. "The Effects of Leveraged Buyouts on Productivity and Related Aspects of Firm Behavior." NBER Working Paper no. 3022, December.

Light, Jay O., and Andre F. Perold. 1987. "The Institutionalization of Wealth: Changing Patterns of Investment Decision Making." In *Wall Street and Regulation,* ed. Samuel L. Hayes III. Boston: Harvard Business School Press.

Light, Larry. 1990. "The Junk-Bond Time Bombs Could Go Off." *Business Week* 16:68–70.

Lintner, John. 1956. "The Distribution of Incomes of Corporations Among Dividends, Retailed Earnings, and Taxes." *American Economic Review* 46:97–118.

Livesay, Harold C. 1975. *Andrew Carnegie and the Rise of the Big Business.* New York: Little, Brown.

Lowenstein, Louis, et al. 1988. "The American Corporation and the Institutional Investor: Are There Lessons from Abroad?" *Columbia Business Law Review* 3:739–49.

Lowenstein, Louis. 1988. *What's Wrong With Wall Street.* Reading, Mass: Addison-Wesley.

Lowenstein, Louis. 1991. *Sense and Nonsense in Corporate Finance.* Reading: Addison-Wesley.

Marginson, Paul, et al. 1988. *Beyond the Workplace: Managing Industrial Relations in the Multi-Establishment Enterprise.* New York: Basil Blackwell.

Markoff, John. 1989. "A Prescription for Troubled IBM." *New York Times,* December 10, secs. 3–4.

Mass, William. 1991. "The Decline of a Technological Leader: Capability, Strategy, and Shuttleless Weaving 1945–74." *Business and Economic History.* 19.

Matsumoto, Toru. 1989. *Japanese Stocks: A Basic Guide for the Intelligent Investor.* Tokyo: Kodansha International.

McCraw, Thomas K., and Forest Reinhardt. 1989. "Losing to Win: U.S. Steel's Pricing, Investment Decisions, and Market Share, 1901–1938." *Journal of Economic History* 49:3.

Means, Gardiner C. 1930. "The Diffusion of Stock Ownership in the United States." *Quarterly Journal of Economics* 44:561–600.

Michie, R. C. 1987. *The London and New York Stock Exchanges, 1850–1914.* London: Allen and Unwin.

Mowery, David C. 1986. "Industrial Research, 1900–1950." In *Decline of the British Economy,* ed. Bernard Elbaum and William Lazonick. Oxford: Clarendon.

Navin, Thomas, and Marion Sears. 1955. "The Rise of a Market for Industrial Securities, 1887–1902." *Business History Review* 24, no. 2: 105–38.

Nelson, Richard, and Sidney Winter. 1982. *An Evolutionary Theory of Economic Change.* Cambridge, Mass.: Belknap Press.

New York Stock Exchange Fact Book 1989. 1989. New York: New York Stock Exchange.

Noble, David. 1979. *America by Design: Science, Technology, and the Rise of Corporate Capitalism.* Oxford: Oxford University Press.

Nussbaum, Bruce, et al. 1986. "The End of Corporate Loyalty?" *Business Week,* August 4, 42–48.

Phillips, Kevin. 1990. *The Politics of Rich and Poor.* New York: Random House.

Pollack, Andrew. 1989. "Venture Capital Loses Its Vigor." *New York Times,* August 3.

Ravenscraft, D., and F. M. Scherer. 1987. *Mergers, Sell-offs and Economic Efficiency.* Washington, D.C.: Brookings Institute.

Reich, Leonard S. 1985. *The Making of American Industrial Research.* Cambridge: Cambridge University Press.

Reich, Robert B., and John Donahue. 1986. *New Deals: The Chrysler Revival and the American System.* New York: Penguin.

Rosenbloom, Richard. 1989. "A Comparison of NCR's and Borroughs' Entry into Computing." Paper presented at the Business History Seminar, Harvard Business School, October 2.

Schumpeter, Joseph A. 1947. "The Creative Response in Economic History." *Journal of Economic History* 7:149–59.

Schumpeter, Joseph A. 1950. *Capitalism, Socialism and Democracy.* 3d ed. New York: Harper.

Sheiber, Harry N., Harold G. Vatter, and Harold U. Falkner. 1976. *American Economic History: A Comprehensive Revision of the Earlier Work by Harold Underwood Falkner.* New York: Harper and Row.

Sobel, Robert. 1981. *IBM: Colossus in Transition*. New York: Times Books.

Taggart, Robert A., Jr. 1986. "Have U.S. Corporations Grown Financially Weak?" In *Financing Corporate Capital Formation*, ed. Benjamin M. Friedman. Chicago: University of Chicago Press.

Taggart, Robert A., Jr. 1988. "The Growth of the 'Junk' Bond Market and Its Role in Financing Takeovers." *Mergers and Acquisitions*, ed. J. Auerbach. Chicago: University of Chicago Press.

U.S. Bureau of the Census. 1976. *Historical Statistics of the United States from Colonial Times to 1970*. Washington, D.C.: GPO.

Verity, John. 1989. "A Slimmer IBM May Still be Overweight." *Business Week*, December 18.

Waldman, Steven, et al. 1989. "The $5 Trillion Schock." *Newsweek*, December 18.

Wall Street Journal. 1989. "Wall Street's Year-End Bonuses are Headed for Seven-Year Low." December 8.

Wigmore, Barrie A. 1989. "The Decline of Credit Quality of Junk Bond New Issues, 1980–1988." November 1989. Photocopy.

Wilson, John W. 1985. *The New Venturers: Inside the High-Stakes World of Venture Capital*. Reading: Addison-Wesley.

Zellner, Wendy, et al. "Chrysler Heads Back to Earth." *Business Week*, December 18.

Emulation and Organizational Change

T. C. R. van Someren

A Description of Innovation and Emulation

The subject of this essay is continuous organizational and technical change in the market economy, and I will concentrate on the theoretical implications emanating from such organizational and technical changes. Before beginning the analysis, however, I will make some preliminary remarks about emulation and innovation in order to make my viewpoint clear.

Innovation is the starting point of a new growth cycle (a new product or new organizational concept) or it triggers off a new industry or subindustry. This definition conforms with Schumpeter's shift of the production function, but, at the same time, it replaces Schumpeter's operational definition of innovation ("new firms, new men"; see Schumpeter [1939], 1982, 92–94).

Emulation is the interaction between technical and organizational changes that follow upon an innovation. Therefore, emulation is complementary to Schumpeterian innovation and is a substitute for the several notions of incremental innovation in the literature. Dynamic characteristics lead to the second element of emulation; emulative behavior implies surpassing competitors by means of technical change and/or organizational change. A list of organizational innovations, limited to the most outstanding changes in the past 150 years, might include the following organizational types.

Corporation
Line-staff functional organization
Holding company
Merger
Cartel
Joint venture
Department store

This essay is part of a study for my dissertation. I am grateful for the valuable comments and inspiring discussions of my mentor, Prof. H. W. de Jong.

Mail order
Management consulting
Zaibatsu
Institutionalization of R&D
Unit operation
Moving assembly line
Multidivisional form
Supermarket
Keiretsu
Business franchising
Containerization
Kanban/just-in-time

Emanating from the growth-cycle concept, three-dimensional growth cycles appear because both organizational innovations and technical innovations are not restricted to a single dimension (see fig. 1). This implies that new cycles are the outcome of the interaction between organizational and technical innovations. A convergence of two emulations can create a new growth cycle or subindustry. For example, the *kanban* system is a convergence of the moving assembly line (manufacturing industry) and the supermarket principle (retail industry).

Innovation Theories

A short outline of the relevant innovation theories will highlight the fundamental concepts of innovation and, especially, the role of organizational innovation.

Most analyses begin with statements put forward by Schumpeter, who identified five cases of innovation, among them technical and organizational innovations (Schumpeter [1934] 1968, 66). Such innovations appear in groups or swarms ([1934] 1968, 223) or clusters and bunches ([1939] 1982, 93, 100–101). Each innovation constitutes a cycle, and they occur in the depression phase and are unevenly (discontinuously) spread through time.

Innovation theorists who followed Schumpeter focused on technical developments. Mensch (1975) tried to confirm the discontinuous feature of innovations, thereby concentrating on basic technical innovations. Nontechnical innovations, which in my interpretation represent organizational innovations, are considered not to belong to the hard core of innovational capabilities (1975, 131). Mensch (1975, 141–49, 180) claimed a confirmation of Schumpeterian discontinuous innovations originating in the stagnation phase of the business cycle. This "bandwagon of basic innovations" was criticized by Freeman, Clark, and Soete (1982, 45–56, 66–67, 153) and replaced by the

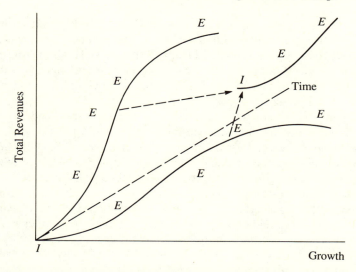

Fig. 1.   Innovation, emulation, and the growth cycle. (*E* = emulation; *I* = Schumpeterian innovation.)

interaction of a cluster of innovations and follow-up innovations located on the steep part of the S-curve of long waves and called "new technology systems" (1982, chap. 4). Freeman, Clark, and Soete also recognized the importance of organizational innovations. However, managerial and organizational innovations follow upon technical change or facilitate technical innovations (1982, 65, 70–71). The contribution of van Duijn (1983, 130–38) further specifies the location of product and process innovations. The former take place in the depression and recovery phase and the latter in the prosperity and recession phase. Organizational innovations are ignored; in his view, organizational changes only influence conditions for technical change.

Besides the theme of long waves, technical trajectories and techno-economic paradigms are major concepts in innovation theories (see Dosi 1984; Freeman and Perez 1988; Freeman and Soete 1987a; Nelson and Winter 1982; Perez 1983). Although differences exist between definitions of these trajectories and paradigms, all are based on the same conceptual footing. First, a taxonomy (see, e.g., Freeman and Soete 1987a, 55–57) is developed that includes incremental, radical, new technological systems and changes in the "technoeconomic paradigm" (Schumpeterian innovations): Rosenberg (1982) stresses the importance of incremental innovations, and some other notions are put forward such as incremental innovations as reinventions (Rogers 1983, 16–17, 173–82). Second, new technoeconomic paradigms are accompanied by new key factors, new sets of inputs, based on technical innovations (e.g., Freeman and Perez 1988, 47–49). The key factors form the core of the new paradigm and these paradigms are supposed to coincide with long waves (see, e.g., Freeman and Perez 1988, table 3.1). It has proven to be difficult to explain shifts in paradigm with technical developments, although socioinstitutional factors have been offered as a solution in addition to technical factors (Freeman and Perez 1988; Perez 1983).

Progressive exploitation of latent economies of scale and increasing mechanization are two common features of trajectories (Dosi 1988, 230; Freeman and Soete 1987a, 38; Nelson and Winter 1982, 259–62). Another frequently stated characteristic is increasing complexity (Dosi 1988, 223; Freeman and Soete 1987a, 38). Perez (1985, 449–51) and Freeman (1987a) refer to economies of scope as a feature of the paradigm based on microelectronics. The trajectories are narrow and are presented as cumulative technical changes (Dosi and Orsenigo 1988, 16–17). Such trajectories represent technical progress that have strong irreversibility features (Dosi 1988, 227).

Furthermore, the technical economic literature considers technical variables to be one of the common "stylized facts" of technical change (Freeman and Soete 1987a, 38). The same point of view is presented by Dosi and Orsenigo: ". . . patterns of interrelation . . . the sources of technical change are not equally distributed across sectors but depend essentially on technology-specific opportunities" (1988, 28). Coombs enunciates this idea as ". . . technological opportunities and trajectories occur in the domain of technology, innovations occur in the domain of products" (1988, 303).

From an organizational perspective, several objections against the mainstream (technical) innovation theories developed after Schumpeter can be formulated. First, organizational innovations are totally neglected or treated as derivatives of technical changes. But technical change cannot be explained without organizational change, and vice versa. In order to cope with these phenomena, the entrepreneurial functions have to be given a prominent place in theory. Second, if organizational innovations are included in the analyses, the technical trajectories become too narrow and cannot consist of cumulative technical change only. Organizational innovations must also have consequences for the definition of key factors because some organizational changes do fulfill the criteria stated by Freeman and Perez (1988, 58) for becoming a key factor.[1] The corporation, merger, moving assembly line, supermarket, and franchising concepts could be identified as "key factors" if necessary for the analysis. However, our concept will not be based on key factors and paradigms because some of these key factors are not specific to a discrete period of time (e.g., mergers, the supermarket pull principle in retailing, and kanban/just-in-time).

---

1. The criteria are falling costs, rapidly increasing supply, and pervasive application.

The economic process is a continuous development of both organizational change and technical change. They cannot exist in a market economy without each other and they also influence each other. Technical changes cannot be implemented without any change in design and/or organizational change and do have consequences for internal and external organization. The reverse is also true: organizational changes create new possibilities for technical changes. The study of technical innovation, therefore, has necessarily to incorporate organizational innovation. The concepts of innovation and long waves have shown that it is difficult to identify which point in time gave rise to the most important innovative activities. In fact, in each period innovations have been developed, and, again, organizational innovations have not been considered on an equal conceptual basis.

This essay develops an alternative in order to cope with these deficiencies of contemporary innovation theories and, at the same time, rehabilitating Schumpeter's notion of organizational innovation. The rest of the essay elaborates the following basic elements of my concept: (*a*) the dynamic relation between organizational change and technical change (emulation); (*b*) the entrepreneurial functions and their relationships to emulation (value conversion); and (*c*) the determinants of the value conversion in the emulation process (economies of scale, economies of scope, and economies of time) and the relationships between these determinants.

The Emulation Process

Three critical remarks in the last section force me to introduce a new concept. This concept has to include (*a*) entrepreneurial functions, (*b*) technical and organizational changes, and (*c*) economic rationality. The next two subsections will elaborate these ideas, which are summarized in figure 2. Exerting the entrepreneurial functions, especially the innovative function, triggers off organizational and technical changes that follow the pattern of the growth cycle. These changes are described with help of the production function from which three determinants (economies of scale, scope, and time) are derived. Ultimately, surplus value is created and the process starts over again.

**The Relation between Organizational
and Technical Change**

Emulation of a product, a process, or an organization is not only an improvement of these categories itself, as the orthodox description of an (incremental) innovation expresses. Emulation also incorporates imitation of a product or process coupled with an organizational change that subsequently creates new possibilities for the product, process, or organization. The perception of emu-

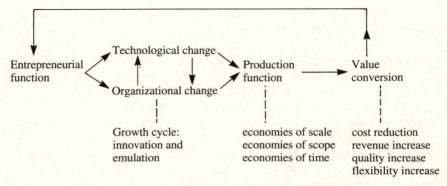

Fig. 2.   The general framework of the emulation process

lation gives substance to the intermingling of organizational and technical change not only according to the organization of R&D activities but also with reference to the interaction between, for example, low-cost distribution channels and the development of a low-cost, high-technology product. It also makes clear why technical developments cannot always be explained by technical changes themselves (e.g., shifts in paradigm). So, why resort to socio-institutional variables when organizational changes have not yet been researched thoroughly?

We reject technological determinism. Williamson confirms this point of view: "In fact, however, technology and organizational modes ought to be treated symmetrically; they are decision variables whose values are determined simultaneously" (1985, 89). On the basis of the previous discussion, four fundamental relations between organizational and technical changes do exist. The first two refer to the trajectory and techno-economic paradigm concept, and numbers three and four form an organizational perspective. Together they converge in emulation.

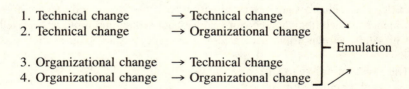

Organizational changes can be followed by other organizational changes.[2] The same holds for technical changes. But not only technical

---

2. For example, traditional point-to-point liner services followed by round-the-world container services, franchising followed by business format franchising, and *kanban*, which is partially based on the supermarket "pull" principle.

changes lead to new technical changes; organizational changes also give direction to new technical possibilities.[3] Now it is possible to outwit a rival without using the best available technology located on the technical frontier. But what is the economic ratio of the interaction between organizational and technical change?

The Entrepreneurial Function

In this essay I take the entrepreneurial function defined by de Jong (1989a, 285–89 and 1989b, 265–74) as the starting point. His argument is that the entrepreneurial functions of organization (Marshall), innovation (Schumpeter), uncertainty reduction, and arbitrage (Kirzner 1973), taken independently, cannot explain economic profit over a long time. Not every entrepreneur is an innovator, and uncertainty reduction does not necessarily lead to economic profit. Therefore, these entrepreneurial functions have to be integrated and, together, they form the necessary conditions for generating economic profit or surplus value. De Jong defines the function of the entrepreneur as "the creation of added value or surplus value" (1989a, 287), which comprises cost reductions, better quality, and higher flexibility. This value conversion concept incorporates the four previously mentioned entrepreneurial functions. For innovations and emulations in time, the emulation process, value conversion has three determinants: economies of scale, economies of scope, and economies of time (for the determinants of market development see de Jong, 1989b, 271–72).

It can now be stated that this concept of the entrepreneurial function links up with both innovation and emulation; it is a value creating process without the necessity of technical innovativeness due to organizational changes.

---

3. Examples are the integration of the R&D laboratories within the boundaries of the firm; unit operations in the chemical industry; and the moving assembly line and the *kanban*/just-in-time organization and the accompanying new layout of the machines created new chances for development of new machines and machine tools (a continuous mutual reinforcing process). Mergers can increase economies of scale and speed up the development process of new products (see, for example, Business Week 2/19/1990); the integration of R&D, manufacturing, design, and marketing with help of new business functions and units (Dean and Susman, 1989; Wheelwright and Sasser, 1989), containerization allowed increasing shipdimensions and implicated new opportunities for shipbuilders, port facilities, computerized logistical systems, etc. Wheelwright and Sasser (1989, 120) mention the design of a new, cost-reduced product based on the needs of their main distribution channel: the competing department stores and discount chains. Another organizational change is the moving assembly line put into operation at Ford in 1913–14. The moving assembly line converges technical and organizational concepts. These had not only been developed at Ford but in several industries in the nineteenth century. Actually, Ford made additional changes on the previous methods. Continuous improvements were made in materials, techniques, accounting, and organization (Nevins 1954).

The Model of the Emulation Process

Both innovation and emulation rehabilitate the importance of organizational change put forward by Schumpeter in contrast to technical innovation theories. The Schumpeterian process is a process of reducing costs. Of course, this is not wrong; on the contrary, it is a very strong concept, but it is incomplete. Starting from the value conversion notion, innovation and emulation are not only dependent on decreased costs, but both technical and organizational changes also add value by increasing quality and flexibility or reducing uncertainty. Therefore, cost reductions do play a significant role within the emulation process, but they are not the only determinant, as the value conversion concept indicates.

According to de Jong (1989a, 289–95), fragmentation of demand breaks up homogeneous demand in segments of higher quality or more advanced products.[4] Heterogeneous demand output is now more efficient than homogeneous large-scale demand due to more flexibility, higher quality, and higher costs offset by higher prices. Thus, given quality and flexibility, small-scale production can be more efficient than large-scale production.

The question now arises, how do these concepts fit into the emulation process? The difficulty to be resolved is that the emulation process not only contains heterogenization but also combinations with homogenization exist (e.g., containerization; *kanban,* which combines mass production with rapid model changes; and franchised speciality shops in department stores). The latter cases combine mass production with better quality and higher flexibility that cannot be explained merely by economies of scale or economies of scope. Another determinant seems to interfere with these two economies. It covers large-scale operation as well as small-scale operation and, therefore, is able to combine these concepts. I will hypothesize that "economies of time" are the key to the combination of flexibility and the potential for economies of scale, economies of scope, and reaction time to rapid market changes. Economies of time are not focused on output per unit of input, but on output per unit of time. This addition of the time factor is a powerful instrument of analysis.

Economies of Time

Two general features of technical trajectories are acknowledged in the technical innovation literature: economies of scale and increasing mechanization. In addition, the paradigm based on microelectronics is coupled with economies of scope.

---

4. Shepherd (1985, 179–81) observes the reversion from large-scale to small-scale technology since the 1930s in the U.S. economy. However, in my view, technology and organizational changes have contributed to this trend.

If the emulation process is taken as the starting point, a different picture appears. For this purpose, three additional remarks have to be made. First, increasing mechanization seems to have a tautological connotation if it is related to technical change. Mechanization can also be the result of organizational changes.[5] Second, economies of scope are not only restricted to the microelectronic paradigm; these economies had appeared in the nineteenth century. In addition, organizational changes can create economies of scope, too.[6] Economies of scope occur throughout time and are not confined to technical changes. Therefore, the bias made clear in these two remarks is due to the technical focus of the technical trajectory. My third comment refers to the static dimension of the definitions. Emanating from emulation, a dynamic determinant is necessary. I advocate the proposition that not only are economies of scale and economies of scope relevant, but economies of time also effect dynamism.

It is known that a production function shifts in time. This refers to time as a historic sequence of time units (T) and has already been integrated into the production function (e.g., Gomulka 1990):

$$Q = F(K; L; T), \tag{1.0}$$

where Q is output, K is capital, L is labor, and T is time. However, this formula boils down to comparative statics, already noted by Schumpeter (1954, 1029) so an extension has to be made. For this purpose, time as a production factor (t) is introduced, which implies that an entrepreneur not only combines labor with capital; additionally, the entrepreneurial task is to make labor and capital combine with the time factor. Principally, an entrepreneur tries to increase the productive time or to reduce nonproductive time or to convert nonproductive time into productive time. Without entrepreneurial action, any theory is static and time as a production factor is meaningless. The moment the entrepreneurial function is exercised, the ubiquitous availability and uniformity of time changes; it becomes scarce. In this way, time becomes an element of innovation and emulation and provides a common basis for

---

5. Cf. the interchangeability concept, which is not identical with mechanization but paved the way for mechanization. But before interchangeability became an important element of the U.S. manufacturing system, the Swiss watch industry in the eighteenth century moved toward increased standardization of some components. This created time advantages, because workers lost no time in checking and fitting; additionally, the quality increased. Thus, nonproductive time was reduced considerably while using the same technology and the same labor division. These economies of time caused improvements of quality as well as cost reductions throughout the whole manufacturing process (Landes 1983, chaps. 16–18).

6. For example, department stores, multidivisional forms, and unit operations. The latter was introduced by Du Pont during the 1920s in the chemical industry. The unit operations initiated chemical engineering and increased the speed of product processing and product development (Clark 1987, 291–92; Hounshell and Smith 1988, chap. 14).

these phenomena. Given this new constellation, what is the contribution of each of the production factors? Land and natural resources provide a material basis, whereas capital goods assist the labor activity. With regard to the time factor, an entrepreneur has to be in time with the unfolded activity: correct timing creates a competitive advantage. In addition, time, combined with labor and capital, has a constructive function. Together with labor, an accumulation takes place expressed by the creation of knowledge, experience, skills, organizational capabilities, and learning curves. Combined with capital, the increasing stock of capital depends on both the time factor and the intensity of capital needed. But the accumulation is not an exogenous process. On the contrary, the entrepreneur can influence the effects of accumulation in various ways, for example, lifetime employment, job rotation, quality circles, or corporation. Now it can also be explained why activities in some industries are not duplicable: due to the accumulation effects, it is very hard for a competitor to attain an equal position (e.g., the oil industry, steel industry, or Swiss watch industry). Therefore, the following production function appears:

$$Q_T = F\ (L,\ K,\ t;\ T),\quad\quad\quad\quad\quad\quad\quad\quad\quad\quad\quad (2.0)$$

where Q_T is output, L is labor, K is capital, t is time as a production factor, and T is the sequence of time units.

Next, the linkage between this production function and value conversion will be made clear. Two main deductions can be made from function 2. First, an additional productivity measure is created: output per unit of time versus output per unit of input. Second, three determinants of value conversion in the emulation process are derived: economies of scale, economies of scope, and economies of time. Emanating from production function 2.0, these derivations are:

—economies of scale,

$$aQ\ =\ F(bK,\ bL,\ t;\ T)\ ,\quad\quad\quad\quad\quad\quad\quad\quad\quad\quad (2.1)$$

where $a > b$ and $t,\ T$ are given;

—economies of scope,

$$Q_A = F(aK,\ cL,\ t;\ T)\quad\quad \text{and}\quad\quad Q_B = F(bK,\ dL,\ t;\ T)\ ,$$

which are separate production functions of Q_A and Q_B;

$$(Q_A + Q_B) = F(eK,\ fL,\ t;\ T)\ ,\quad\quad\quad\quad\quad\quad\quad\quad (2.2)$$

where $e < (a + b)$ and $f < (c + d)$ for a given t and T; and

—economies of time,

$$Q_{A_{t_1}} T_1 = F(K, L, t_1; T_1) \quad \text{and} \quad Q_{A_{t_2}} T_2 = F(K, L, t_2; T_2),$$
$$(2.3)$$

where

$$(K, L, t_2) < (K, L, t_1) \quad \text{and} \quad T_1 = T_2, \quad \text{or}$$

$$(K, L, t_2) = (K, L, t_1) \quad \text{and} \quad T_2 < T_1, \quad \text{or}$$

$$(K, L, t_2) < (K, L, t_1) \quad \text{and} \quad T_2 < T_1.$$

From my emperical findings, it can be concluded that economies of time can be related to the outcome of the emulation process itself (related to competitors) and to the internal development of technical and organizational change itself. Production function (2.0) describes very well both technical and organizational changes. Economies of time in organizational and technical changes (e.g., self-service; pull principle in *kanban*/just-in-time; training and education; railways; or computerized information) are a means to emulate competitors and to gain time. The motivation of the emulator to add something new is to take the lead on competitors. This can be realized through reducing cost measured by a constant input or output (economies of scale and scope) or measured by a constant period of time or simply by saving time (economies of time). Economies of scale and scope are static because they are measured without regard to time. However, in economic reality, changes take place in time and a constant period of time is therefore unrealistic. Moreover, time saving is the only rationale of the value conversion concept. The conclusion can be drawn that economies of time multiply the effects of economies of scale and economies of scope; this is the multiplier effect. Economies of time generate a higher output and create a surplus value that can be used to increase market share or to reap profits. Another implication is that monopoly effects and market power are not only the result of economies of scale but also of economies of time (see Shepherd 1985, chap. 9). Moreover, it means that organizational changes do more than merely increase efficiency or adapt to newly emerged technologies: they can also bring a firm to a dominant position in the market. It is also possible to integrate notions such as X-inefficiency and waste (quality), which can both be expressed as a reduction of the economies of time.[7] These "negative economies of time" reduce the benefits from

---

7. In the *kanban* system, the total quality control concept is used. It strives for a very low level of defects in order to attain maximum economies of speed.

economies of scale and scope. Therefore, economies of time encompass learning effects; X-inefficiency; waste (quality), reaction time to competition (supply), market changes, and product development (demand); information gathering, processing, or presentation; and decision making. Together, these factors converge to increase the speed of the operations at all levels in an organization.

The fundamental relationship between sequential emulations (A, B, C) and the three determinants of economies of time, scale, and scope are demonstrated in figure 3. Figure 3b gives the value conversions of these emulations. The three-dimensional graph (fig. 4) gives additional information; it shows the relative multiplier effect of economies of time.

But first we turn to figures 3a and 3b. If we redefine economies of scale as horizontal economies of scale and economies of scope as vertical economies of scale, it is then possible to relate economies of time to horizontal and vertical economies of scale in a two-dimensional graph (fig. 3a). The total value conversion is dependent on value conversion per measured time unit and the total number of units that the conversion lasts (fig. 3b). It can be stated that both technical and organizational changes try to attain economies of time that are coupled to economies of scale and scope. It is supposed that a continuous increase in the scale of operation in a given method of production will first increase economies of time but, at a given point, will decrease because of congestion in the operations due to insufficient organizational or technical means. At this point, additional emulations (B, C; organizational and/or technical) will have to be introduced that remove the bottlenecks or simply create value conversion.

The economies in the static version add up to $1 \times 4a = 4a$. For the dynamic economies, the calculation is $(2 \times 2a) + (1 \times a) + (0.5 \times a) = 5.5a$.

The downward trend in value conversion in figure 3b represents decreasing marginal revenue and can be related to the decreasing profit rates that accompany a product cycle or growth cycle. Figure 3a does not show the multiplier effect of economies of time in relation to economies of scale and scope. For this purpose we now abstract from our previous redefinition of horizontal and vertical economies of scale and, instead, introduce a three-dimensional graph (fig. 4). As can be seen, the time economies shift the static Marginal Elasticity of Substitution at point B, with maximum static economies of scale, to the optimal dynamic point A. The static economies of scale are traded off against the economies of time. The total emulation advantage is the surface O_1, O_2, t_1; it is the optimum output surface given the input resources (and time as the variable factor). The area O_1, O_2, t_1 is the multiplier advantage. Therefore, emulation has a limit value (the optimal surface) and corresponds to the decreasing marginal value shown in figure 3b.

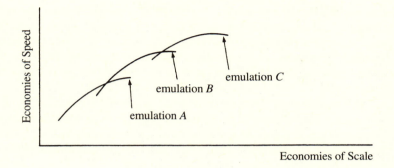

a.   **Speed vs. scale**

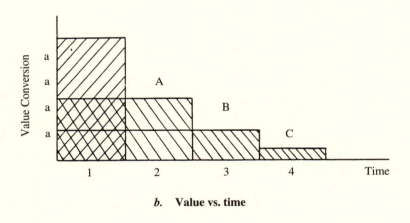

b.   **Value vs. time**

Fig. 3.   Economies of time related to economies of scale and time. ([///] = static economies of scale or scope; [\\\] = dynamic economies of time.)

With the help of this theoretical model, it is now possible to explain some features of Japanese manufacturers compared with European and U.S. manufacturers (see table 1; the model is applicable to all of the innovations mentioned previously).

Despite the smaller scale of Japanese factories, a greater variety of models is offered that are also introduced more frequently. The table also demonstrates the higher quality of the Japanese output combined with a higher

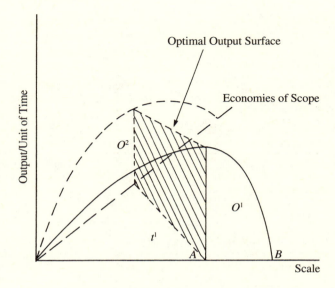

Fig. 4.   The multiplier effect of economies of time

labor productivity. To a large extent, the advantageous position of the Japanese manufacturers is a result of a wide range of organizational changes (e.g., *kanban,* just-in-time, quality circles, lifetime employment, or job rotation).

Conclusion

This essay began with the observation that organizational changes are an underdeveloped area in industrial organization research. Further, innovation theories that followed Schumpeter's insights put a strong emphasis on technical change and determined, in large part, the substantial content of innovation

TABLE 1.   Productivity and Scale in the Automobile Industry 1987/1988

	Japan	United States	Europe
Labor hours needed per standard car	20.0	28.0	39.0
Quality (defects per car)	1.2	1.8	2.6
Average production[a]	500.0	2,200.0	1,800.0
Number of models	72.0	38.0	49.0
Life expectancy of models (in years)	2.1	4.4	3.9

Source: Jones and Womak, *Financial Times,* October 28, 1988.
[a]Production is stated in thousands.

theories. Organizational change is ignored or treated as a derivative of technical change, as the technoeconomic paradigm clearly demonstrates. However, if organizational change is given an equal position to technical change, which is a defensible proposition, and if this notion is combined with the observation of continuous change consisting of both organizational and technical change, then the existing innovation theories are not sufficient for the explanation of continuous change. An alternative, emulation, is proposed that incorporates both organizational and technical change including a dynamic relation between these two categories of change. Moreover, economies of time related to economies of scale as well as economies of scope are general features of emulation. All these concepts are reflected by the optimum output surface that replaces the technical frontier.

REFERENCES

Chandler, A. D. 1977. *The Visible Hand.* Cambridge, Mass.: Belknap Press.
Clark, K. B. 1989. "What Strategy Can Do for Technology." *Harvard Business Review* 6:94–98.
Clark, P. A. 1987. *Anglo-American Innovation.* Berlin: Walter de Gruyter.
Coombs, R. 1988. "Technological Opportunities and Industrial Organisation." In Dosi et al. 1988.
Dean, J. W., and G. I. Susman. 1989. "Organizing for Manufacturable Design." *Harvard Business Review* 6:28–36.
de Jong, H. W. 1989a. *Dynamische Markttheorie.* 4th ed. Leiden: Stenfert Kroese.
de Jong, H. W. 1989b. "Free versus Controlled Competition." In 1989, *Industrial Dynamics,* ed. B. Carlsson, 271–98. Boston: Kluwer Academic Publishers.
Dosi, G. 1984. *Technical Change and Industrial Transformation.* New York: St. Martin's Press.
Dosi, G. 1988. "The Nature of the Innovative Process." In Dosi et al. 1988.
Dosi, G., and L. Orsenigo. 1988. "Coordination and Transformation: An Overview of Structures, Behaviors, and Change in Evolutionary Environments." In Dosi et al. 1988.
Dosi, G., C. Freeman, R. Nelson, G. Silverberg, and L. Soete, eds. 1988. *Technical Change and Economic Theory.* London: Pinter.
Freeman, C. 1987a. "Information Technology and Change in the Technoeconomic Paradigm." In Freeman and Soete 1987b.
Freeman, C. 1987b. *Technology Policy and Economic Performance.* London: Pinter.
Freeman, C., J. Clark, and L. Soete. 1982. *Unemployment and Technical Innovation.* London: Pinter.
Freeman, C., and C. Perez. 1988. "Structural Crisis of Adjustment: Business Cycles and Investment Behaviour." In Dosi et al. 1988.
Freeman, C., and L. Soete. 1987a. "Factor Substitution and Technical Change." In Freeman and Soete 1987b.

Freeman, C., and L. Soete, eds. 1987b. *Technical Change and Full Employment*. London: Basil Blackwell.

Gomulka, S. 1990. *The Theory of Technological Change and Economic Growth*. London: Routledge.

Hassard, J. 1989. "Time and Organization." In *Time, Work, and Organization*, ed. P. Blyton, J. Hassard, S. Hill, and K. Starkey. London: Routledge.

Hounshell, D. A., and J. K. Smith. 1988. *Science and Corporate Strategy: Du Pont R&D, 1902–1980*. Cambridge: Cambridge University Press.

Kirzner, Israel. 1973. *Competition and Entrepreneurship*. Chicago: University of Chicago Press.

Landes, D. S. 1983. *Revolution in Time: Clocks and the Making of the Modern World*. Cambridge, Mass.: Belknap Press.

Mensch, G. 1975. *Das Technologische Patt*. Umschau Verlag.

Nelson, R. R., and S. G. Winter. 1982. *An Evolutionary Theory of Economic Change*. Cambridge, Mass.: Belknap Press.

Nevins, A. 1954. *Ford: The Times, the Man, the Company*. New York: Scribner's Sons.

Perez, C. 1983. "Structural Change and Assimilation of New Technologies in the Economic and Social Systems." *Futures* (October): 357–75.

Perez, C. 1985. "Microelectronics, Long Waves, and World Structural Change: New Perspectives for Developing Countries." *World Development* 13 (3):441–63.

Rogers, E. M. 1983. *Diffusion of Innovations*. 3d ed. New York: Free Press.

Rosenberg, N. 1982. *Inside the Black Box*. Cambridge: Cambridge University Press.

Schumpeter, J. A. [1934] 1968. *The Theory of Economic Development*. Cambridge, Mass.: Harvard University Press.

Schumpeter, J. A. [1939] 1982. *Business Cycles*. Philadelphia: Porcupine Press.

Schumpeter, J. A. 1954. *History of Economic Analyses*. London: George Allen and Unwin.

Shepherd, W. G. 1985. *The Economics of Industrial Organization*. 2d ed. Englewood Cliffs, N. J.: Prentice-Hall.

van Duijn, J. J. 1983. *The Long Wave in Economic Life*. London: George Allen and Unwin.

Wheelwright, S. C., and W. E. Sasser. 1989. "The New Product Development Map." *Harvard Business Review* 3: 112–25.

Williamson, Oliver E. 1985. *The Economic Institutions of Capitalism: Firms, Markets, Relational Contracting*. New York: Free Press.

Appropriation and Profit Incentives in a Leaky System

Anne P. Carter

Introduction

At best, innovators appropriate only a fraction of the total economic benefits that follow technological improvements. To the extent that the benefits of innovation are not fully appropriated by the innovators, they leak out and accrue to other sectors and agents. This essay focuses on the systematic distribution of innovational benefits from the sectors in which they originate to other, intermediate and final sectors of the economy. Mapping the intersectoral transmission of benefits should illuminate several questions of current interest.

1. What are the external effects of a specific innovation? Who gains, who loses?
2. How can these external effects provide incentives for supplier, manufacturer, and user innovation (Von Hippel 1987)?
3. To what extent does incentive to innovate, represented by the profitability of an innovation to a sector, correspond to the innovation's benefit to the economy at large?

This analysis is intended for implementation with input-output tables and other price and national accounts data, but the framework is still at the "design stage." Hypothetical data are used to illustrate how the system works under plausible conditions.

Innovation in an Input-Output Framework

My analysis is rooted in a standard, open static input-output framework. We begin with an input-output coefficient matrix A^0 and a vector of labor coeffi-

The author wishes to thank Andras Brody, Eric Von Hippel, and Goran Ostblom for their encouragement and helpful suggestions.

cients, l^0, measured as wages with a constant wage rate. These are modified by technical change in one or more sectors to become A^1 and l^1. Initial vectors of profit markups, π^0, and of final demands, Y^0, are also specified. For the base period, the real cost and a price system are:

$$X^0 = (l - A^0)^{-1}Y^0; \tag{1a}$$

$$p^0 = (l^0 + \pi^0)(l - A^0)^{-1}. \tag{1b}$$

After innovation, A^0 and l^0 are replaced by A^1 and l^1.

The hypothetical initial system and four coefficient vectors representing alternative structures for the manufacturing sector (M) are specified in tables 1 and 2. Anticipating analysis of the sectoral locus of incentives to innovate, a quasi-triangular structure is assumed. S (supplier) makes inputs to M (manufacturer) which, in turn, provides inputs to U (user). O (other) plays the role of a "general" industry that provides inputs to all sectors (see table 1).

Innovation 1 represents a simple saving of direct labor; innovations 2 and 3 represent direct savings of S and O respectively. Innovation 4 consists of an increase in M's use of S with a simultaneous reduction in labor requirements. All four innovations result in a cost saving of ten percent in terms of initial prices (see table 2).

The assumption of fixed final demand and profit margins, Y^0 and π^0, represents only one very special set of possible consequences of innovation. There are systematic reasons why final demand and profit margins should not remain constant at initial levels. Instead, both are likely to increase with innovation. Depending on macroeconomic conditions, resources released by technological progress may be redeployed to augment final demand. Histor-

TABLE 1. Hypothetical Input-Output System

	S	M	U	O	Final Demand
	Intermediate Coefficients				
S	0.0	0.2	0.0	0.0	10
M	0.0	0.0	0.5	0.0	10
U	0.0	0.0	0.0	0.5	10
O	0.5	0.1	0.2	0.1	10
	Value-added Coefficients				
Labor	0.2	0.4	0.2	0.2	—
Profit	0.3	0.3	0.1	0.2	—
Total	1.0	1.0	1.0	1.0	—

ical trends indicate that this is the norm over the long term. Profit margins are likely to increase to the extent that innovating sectors can appropriate some portion of innovational gains. Profits in other sectors may increase or decrease. The levels of output, X^1, and prices, p^1, that prevail after innovation will depend on the changes in final demand, Y^0, and in profit margins, π^0, that accompany it.

Changes in Final Demand with Innovation

In terms of the real system, technical change will presumably free labor by decreasing the total amount of labor required to deliver the initial final demand, Y^0. The new output vector, X^1, will depend on the extent and pattern of redeployment of the "released" labor through changes in final demand. A wide range of solutions is possible. At one extreme, final deliveries can simply remain at their initial values, Y^0. Then, released labor simply becomes idle. At the other extreme, final deliveries might increase sufficiently to reemploy all of the released labor. A variety of different configurations of final demand would serve to restore full employment. Let Y^{1k} represent one of the new vectors of final demand that would be feasible under the new technological conditions. Then the new vector of outputs, X^{1k}, would be

$$X^{1k} = (I - A^1)^{-1} Y^{1k}. \tag{2}$$

Different assumptions about the levels and configurations of postinnovation final deliveries result, of course, in different output vectors. The following

TABLE 2. Alternative Structures Representing Innovations in Sector *M*

	Innovation			
	1	2	3	4
	Intermediate Coefficients			
S	0.2	0.1	0.2	0.3
M	0.0	0.0	0.0	0.0
U	0.0	0.0	0.0	0.0
O	0.1	0.1	0.0	0.1
	Value-added Coefficients			
Labor	0.3	0.4	0.4	0.2
Profit	0.3	0.3	0.3	0.3
Total	0.9	0.9	0.9	0.9

simulations provide solutions based on three sets of assumptions or "macroeconomic scenarios."

1. Final demand stays constant at initial levels.
2. Final demand is allowed to increase proportionally so as to absorb the initial level of labor. We solve the system by maximizing k, so that

$$(l - A)X \geq kY^0, \tag{3}$$

where $lX \leq L^0$.

3. Additions to final demand over the initial level are maximized. We solve the system by maximizing Y, so that

$$(l - A)X \geq Y, \tag{4}$$

where $Y \geq Y^0$ and $lX \leq L^0$.

Table 3 shows the real output vectors after each innovation, assuming fixed final demand. Since the first innovation consists only of a reduction in the direct labor coefficient, it leaves the vector of sectoral output levels un-

TABLE 3. Sectoral Outputs and Wages after Each of Four Innovations, Fixed Final Demand

			Innovation		
	Initial	1	2	3	4
			Gross Domestic Outputs		
S	14.33	14.33	12.13	14.19	16.61
M	21.67	21.67	21.31	20.97	22.03
U	23.33	23.33	22.62	21.94	24.07
O	26.67	26.67	25.25	23.87	28.14
Total	86.00	86.00	81.31	80.97	90.90
			Wages		
S	2.87	2.87	2.43	2.84	3.32
M	8.67	6.50	8.52	8.39	4.41
U	4.67	4.67	4.52	4.39	4.81
O	5.33	5.33	5.05	4.77	5.63
Total	21.53	19.37	20.52	20.39	18.17

changed. Innovations 2 and 3 reduce sectoral gross outputs, while innovation 4, essentially a substitution of a produced input, S, for labor, tends to increase them.

Table 4 indicates aggregate levels of employment, final demand, and total gross output under the three different macroeconomic scenarios for each of the hypothetical innovations listed in table 1.

Effects of Innovation on Profits and Prices

Changes in Sectoral Profits with Innovation

The portion of innovational savings captured in each sector's profits will vary with circumstances. The increase in profit accruing to sector j in the wake of innovation will be $X_j^1 \pi_j^1 - X_j^0 \pi_j^0$. Alternatively, $X_j^1 \pi_j^1 - X_j^0 \pi_j^0$ can be written

$$(X_j^0 + \Delta X_j)(\pi_j^0 + \Delta \pi_j) - X_j^0 \pi_j^0 = \Delta X_j \pi_j^0 + \Delta \pi_j X_j^0 +$$

$$\Delta X_j \Delta \pi_j \tag{5}$$

Neglecting the (third) interaction term in equation 5, we see that the effect of innovation on sector j's profits has an output component, $\Delta X_j \pi_j^0$ and a margin component, $\Delta \pi_j X_j^0$. The output component reflects changes in the demand for the sector's products as inputs into downstream sectors. In the absence of simultaneous changes in the input structures of downstream sectors, these changes are the indirect effects of changing input requirements in j, including changes in final demand associated with the redeployment of released resources. The margin component depends on changes in j's input structure, on the degree to which upstream sectors pass on their own savings in the form of price reductions for the inputs of j, and on j's ability to appropriate cost savings as profits.

Price Changes Resulting from Innovation

Just as, depending on the composition of final demand, a wide range of changes in outputs might follow innovation, so, depending on possible changes in profit margins, a wide range of price changes might also follow. Two polar sets of prices are of special interest. These are the so-called fix prices, based on holding the initial profit margins, π^0, constant, and flex prices, where initial prices, p^0, are maintained in the face of innovation, and all benefits are appropriated as increased profit margins (see Carter 1990; Leontief 1941; Mathur 1986).

Price Changes with Fix and Flex Pricing

Changes in input-output and labor coefficients can be expected to induce changes in prices in accordance with equation 6. If profit margins remain

TABLE 4. Aggregate Final Demand, Wages, and Output Assuming Alternative Innovations and Macroeconomic Scenarios

Innovation	Final Demand[a]			Wages[b]			Total Gross Output[c]		
	Scenario 1	Scenario 2	Scenario 3	Scenario 1	Scenario 2	Scenario 3	Scenario 1	Scenario 2	Scenario 3
1	40.00	44.48	44.90	19.37	21.53	21.53	86.00	95.62	94.22
2	40.00	41.96	42.17	20.52	21.53	21.53	81.30	85.31	86.00
3	40.00	42.24	42.47	20.39	21.53	21.53	80.97	85.50	86.30
4	40.00	47.40	48.77	18.17	21.53	21.53	90.85	107.67	107.67

[a]Initial level = 40.00.
[b]Initial level = 21.53.
[c]Initial level = 86.00.

constant at π^0, replacement of A^0, l^0 with new input structures A^1, l^1 would result in a new set of prices:

$$p^1 = (l^1 + \pi^0)(l - A^1)^{-1}. \tag{6}$$

With fixed profit margins (fix prices), technical change can still influence sectoral profits to the extent that the outputs of some sectors may rise and those of others may fall.

Each sector may, in principle, face cost reductions as a result of an improvement in its own or in other sectors' technology. With fixed profit margins, innovating sectors must pass their gains along rather than appropriating them as profits. Under these conditions, neither the innovator nor intermediate sectors favored by lower input prices can capture gains through their markups; those gains flow to final consumers as price reductions.

At the other extreme, the innovating sector may appropriate the full cost reduction as increased profit margin, leaving initial prices unchanged (flex prices). Under these conditions, profit margins, π^1, become

$$\pi^1 = p^0 - p^0 A^1 - l^1. \tag{7}$$

Table 5 contains price solutions under various assumptions about which sectors have fix prices and which have flex prices. The first panel of the table shows what prices would be after each innovation if all sectors had fix pricing. The other panels show prices under the assumption that all have fix pricing with the exception of one indicated sector, which has flex prices. The last row in these panels contain the computed profit margin for the flex price sector. Since all innovations involve the same direct cost savings, all have the same effect on postinnovation profit margins.

Note that M, the innovating sector, is the only one that can appropriate the full amount of the cost saving with flex pricing. Others in the flex-price position can, at best, appropriate only those rents that are passed on to them in the form of lower input prices.

Simulations: Distributed Benefits of Innovation with Fix/Flex Pricing

In the next section, a more general price model will be introduced, one that allows for a range of appropriation intermediate between the two extremes of fix and flex pricing. Before this finer grained price system is explained, the results of simulations based on the simpler fix and flex models are summarized. Table 6 shows the systemwide effects of the four hypothetical inno-

TABLE 5. Sectoral Prices after Four Alternative Innovations with Different Assumptions about Fix and Flex Pricing

Sector	Innovation			
	1	2	3	4
	All Prices Fixed			
S	0.98	0.98	0.98	0.98
M	0.89	0.90	0.90	0.89
U	0.94	0.94	0.94	0.94
O	0.97	0.97	0.97	0.97
	Flex Prices in S, Others Fixed			
S	1.00	1.00	1.00	1.00
M	0.90	0.90	0.90	0.90
U	0.94	0.94	0.94	0.94
O	0.97	0.97	0.97	0.97
Margin of S	0.32	0.32	0.32	0.32
	Flex Prices in M, Others Fixed			
S	1.00	1.00	1.00	1.00
M	1.00	1.00	1.00	1.00
U	1.00	1.00	1.00	1.00
O	1.00	1.00	1.00	1.00
Margin of M	0.40	0.40	0.40	0.40
	Flex Prices in U, Others Fixed			
S	1.00	1.00	1.00	1.00
M	0.90	0.90	0.90	0.90
U	1.00	1.00	1.00	1.00
O	1.00	1.00	1.00	1.00
Margin of U	0.15	0.15	0.15	0.15
	Flex Prices in O, Others Fixed			
S	1.00	1.00	1.00	1.00
M	0.90	0.90	0.90	0.90
U	0.95	0.95	0.95	0.95
O	1.00	1.00	1.00	1.00
Margin of O	0.23	0.23	0.23	0.23

vations under various pricing and macroeconomic assumptions. These results are analyzed in greater detail in Carter 1990.

The Distribution of Aggregate Benefits of Innovation between Profits and Price Reductions

The last three rows in each panel of table 6 give an overview of how the benefits of innovation are distributed between increases in aggregate profits and reductions in the prices of final goods. Several general features of this distribution emerge.

1. Since labor is the numéraire in this system, its price is fixed. In accordance with the conventions of national income accounting, total income must equal the total value of products. Hence, the value of labor saved must be balanced by some combination of an increase in profits and a reduction in the prices of final output. Similarly, an increase in final output (in initial prices) must be offset by some combination of price reductions and increases in profits.
2. While the four alternative innovations all bring direct savings of 10 percent of initial costs, economywide benefits, measured by direct plus indirect labor savings, vary significantly.
3. Measured benefits of innovation are, naturally, larger under the assumption of full employment (i.e., if resources freed up by innovation are redeployed to increase final deliveries) than if final demand is fixed. They will also be larger to the extent that proportionality constraints on final demand are relaxed. The numerical results draw attention to the fact that an innovation will save more resources (in an absolute sense) the higher the level of output at which it is evaluated.
4. When the innovating sector, M, has flex pricing, it appropriates the full innovational cost saving into its profit margin. No savings are passed on as price changes. When other sectors have flex pricing, they can capture as profits only those savings that are passed on to them as reductions in the prices of their inputs. Under these circumstances, factor savings due to innovation are balanced by a combination of price reductions and increased profits.
5. Innovations 2 and 3 tend to reduce gross output. With fixed profit margins (fix pricing), lower output implies smaller dollar profits with innovation. Hence, some simulations show revaluations of final products exceeding the total value of labor saved through innovation. Under the more expansive macroeconomic scenarios (2 and 3), innovation leads to larger sectoral gross outputs. Gross profits are more likely to increase with innovation under expansive macroeconomic assumptions.

TABLE 6. Effects of Innovations on Sectoral Profits, Total Profits, and Prices of Final Goods under Various Assumptions about Pricing and Macroeconomic Scenarios

Sector	Labor Saving				Fixed Final Demand Proportions				Variable Final Demand Proportions			
	Innovation 1	Innovation 2	Innovation 3	Innovation 4	Innovation 1	Innovation 2	Innovation 3	Innovation 4	Innovation 1	Innovation 2	Innovation 3	Innovation 4
					All Prices Fixed							
S	0.00	−0.66	−0.04	0.68	0.48	−0.48	0.20	1.61	0.31	0.00	0.72	1.54
M	0.00	−0.11	−0.21	0.11	0.73	0.21	0.14	1.33	1.57	0.00	−0.09	2.96
U	0.00	−0.07	−0.14	0.07	0.26	0.04	−0.02	0.52	0.07	0.00	−0.06	0.22
O	0.00	−0.28	−0.56	0.29	0.60	−0.04	−0.29	1.34	0.26	0.00	−0.24	0.89
Total profit	0.00	−1.12	−0.95	1.15	2.07	−0.27	0.03	4.80	2.21	0.00	0.33	5.61
Reprice final demand	2.17	2.13	2.10	2.20	2.41	2.24	2.21	2.61	2.69	2.17	2.14	3.15
Total benefit	2.17	1.01	1.15	3.36	4.48	1.97	2.24	7.40	4.98	2.17	2.47	8.76
					Flex Prices in S, Others Fixed							
S	0.23	−0.47	0.19	0.95	0.74	−0.28	0.44	1.92	0.56	0.23	0.99	1.85
M	0.00	−0.11	−0.21	0.11	0.73	0.21	0.14	1.33	1.57	0.00	−0.09	2.96
U	0.00	−0.07	−0.14	0.07	0.26	0.04	−0.02	0.52	0.07	0.00	−0.06	0.22
O	0.00	−0.28	−0.56	0.29	0.60	−0.04	−0.29	1.34	0.26	0.00	−0.24	0.89
Total profit	0.23	−0.93	−0.72	1.42	2.32	−0.07	0.27	5.11	2.45	0.23	0.60	5.92
Reprice final demand	1.90	1.94	1.90	1.90	2.15	2.03	1.98	2.29	2.44	1.94	1.88	2.84
Total benefit	2.13	1.01	1.18	3.33	4.47	1.96	2.25	7.40	4.89	2.17	2.48	8.76

Flex Prices in M, Others Fixed

S	0.00	-0.66	-0.04	0.68	0.48	-0.48	0.20	1.61	0.31	0.00	0.72	1.54
M	2.17	2.02	1.89	2.31	3.14	2.44	2.36	3.95	4.25	2.17	2.05	6.12
U	0.00	-0.07	-0.14	0.07	0.26	0.04	-0.02	0.52	0.07	0.00	-0.06	0.22
O	0.00	-0.28	-0.56	0.29	0.60	-0.04	-0.29	1.34	0.26	0.00	-0.24	0.89
Total profit	2.17	1.01	1.15	3.36	4.48	1.97	2.25	7.41	4.89	2.17	2.47	8.77
Reprice final demand	0.00	0.00	0.00	0.00	0.00	0.00	0.00	0.00	0.00	0.00	0.00	0.00
Total benefit	2.17	1.01	1.15	3.36	4.48	1.97	2.25	7.41	4.89	2.17	2.47	8.77

Flex Prices in U, Others Fixed

S	0.00	-0.66	-0.04	0.68	0.48	-0.48	0.20	1.61	0.31	0.00	0.72	1.54
M	0.00	-0.11	-0.21	0.11	0.73	0.21	0.14	1.33	1.57	0.00	-0.09	2.96
U	1.17	1.06	0.96	1.28	1.56	1.23	1.14	1.95	1.26	1.17	1.08	1.50
O	0.00	-0.28	-0.56	0.29	0.60	-0.04	-0.29	1.34	0.26	0.00	-0.24	0.89
Total profit	1.17	0.01	0.15	2.36	3.36	0.92	1.19	6.22	3.41	1.17	1.47	6.89
Reprice final demand	1.00	1.00	1.00	1.00	1.11	1.05	1.06	1.19	1.49	1.00	1.00	1.88
Total benefit	2.17	1.01	1.15	3.36	4.47	1.97	2.25	7.41	4.90	2.17	2.47	8.77

Flex Prices in O, Others Fixed

S	0.00	-0.66	-0.04	0.68	0.48	-0.48	0.20	1.61	0.31	0.00	0.72	1.54
M	0.00	-0.11	-0.21	0.11	0.73	0.21	0.14	1.33	1.57	0.00	-0.09	2.96
U	0.00	-0.07	-0.14	0.07	0.26	0.04	-0.02	0.52	0.07	0.00	-0.06	0.22
O	0.67	0.35	0.04	1.00	1.34	0.63	0.34	2.17	0.96	0.67	0.40	1.67
Total profit	0.67	-0.49	-0.35	1.86	2.81	0.39	0.66	5.63	2.91	0.67	0.97	6.39
Reprice final demand	1.50	1.50	1.50	1.50	1.67	1.57	1.58	1.78	1.99	1.50	1.50	2.38
Total benefit	2.17	1.01	1.15	3.36	4.48	1.96	2.24	7.41	4.90	2.17	2.47	8.77

Changes in Sectoral Profits with Innovation

The first four rows in each panel of table 6 represent the changes in profits of each individual sector resulting from each innovation. The top panel of table 6 represents the effects of each innovation on sectoral profits assuming fix prices in all sectors. Lower panels show computed profits assuming that a single sector (S, M, U, or O) has flex pricing while all the others have fix prices. Implications of innovation for profits vary among innovations, among sectors, and with macroeconomic and pricing regimes assumed. Study of these implications provides some insights into sectoral incentives to innovate.

1. When it has flex pricing, sector M profits by introducing any of the four innovations. Also, other sectors derive substantial profit from innovation in M when they are in the flex price position and M is not. With one exception (innovation 2, with S in the flex position), the sector with flex pricing stands to benefit from any innovation in M. Thus, one very plausible rationale for "supplier innovation," "user inovation," or innovation supported by any "other" sector would be that sector's superior ability to appropriate. This ability might reflect its competitive structure or some technical feature of the innovation that bears on a producer's ability to retain technical secrets.

2. Because innovation in M affects gross outputs of all sectors, other sectors may profit (or lose) from an innovation even if they have fix pricing. S profits from innovation 4 even when it has fix pricing. Supplier innovation would be warranted because innovation 4 expands S's market significantly. Flex pricing in S reinforces this motivation for supplier innovation by allowing S to increase its profit margin as well as its output when innovation 4 is introduced. Similarly, O also profits from the introduction of innovation 4, even when it has fix pricing. Flex pricing in O also reinforces O's incentive to encourage innovation 4 in M.

3. In general, innovation in sector M carries substantial externalities for other sectors. These externalities may be positive or negative; thus, they may either increase or decrease profits in these other sectors. Presumably, innovative behavior will be motivated by profits in the innovating sector without regard to these external effects on others' profits. The ability to capitalize on such externalities provides an important rationale for "supplier" or "user" innovation. It also provides a rationale for vertical consortia.

4. Note that negative externalities are very common in the simulations for macroeconomic scenario 1, but that positive external effects are more often the norm for the more expansive macroeconomic sce-

narios. It stands to reason that innovation will carry more favorable implications for all sectors when it is seen as leading to high economywide output levels.

5. In these simulations, M profits substantially from all of the innovations when it has flex pricing. Under these conditions, M's profits outweigh the negative externalities in other sectors, so that total profits in the economy increase with innovation. When M has fix prices, gains in some sectors are sometimes smaller than losses in others. Thus postinnovation profits may be smaller than preinnovation profits for the economy as a whole, although innovation is definitely profitable to some individual sector(s).

In sum, the simulations suggest a potential for significant external effects of innovation. The size and incidence of these effects will be sensitive to macroeconomic conditions and sectoral pricing practices. External effects on the profits of other sectors provide an economic rationale for supplier and user innovation and for intersectoral consortia. When benefits of innovation tend to be widely distributed there will be little correspondence between the economywide benefits of an innovation and a single sector's profit incentive to introduce it.

Modeling Partial Appropriation

Obviously, the assumption of an "all or nothing" pass through is unrealistic. Presumably some appropriation of innovational rents is required as an incentive to innovation, but full appropriation may be impossible and the appropriation of benefits from any given innovation is likely to diminish over time. Downstream profits resulting from falling input prices may also be temporary and limited by the downstream sector's ability to appropriate the cost advantage.

To model the transmission of benefits more realistically, the degree to which a sector captures cost reductions in the form of increased profits is made explicit. As a first approximation, we specify a single parameter, μ_{jj}, that characterizes the ability of a given sector j to appropriate reductions in its costs over a given period. This parameter will be defined more precisely subsequently.

Actually, of course, appropriation is a very complex phenomenon that reflects a range of factors: competitive conditions within the sector (Harhoff 1990; Schumpeter 1934), measures such as patenting and trade secret policies adopted by firms to guard the secrecy of new technology (Griliches 1987), the degree to which firms control complementary assets (Teece 1986), and the nature of the technology itself (Von Hippel 1987). Some technologies are harder to replicate than others and, thus, support appropriation by their nature. Within the constraints of the technical situation, however, appropriation is an economic variable. Appropriability limits the level of returns from innovation; appropriability gives one new technology an edge over another in the firm's decision process and, in general, firms can be expected to deploy their resources with an eye toward increasing their appropriation of gains. The parameter μ_{jj} will reflect all of these economic influences and can be expected to change over time. In the Schumpeterian tradition, appropriation coefficients should be high when an innovation is introduced and decrease under the pressures of diffusion and competition.

Appropriation Coefficients

For any sector j, cost reduction resulting from a shift from A^0, l^0 to A^1, l^1 will be

$$p^0 A_j{}^0 + l_j{}^0 - p^1 A_j{}^1 - l_j^1 \tag{8}$$

Cost reduction may be direct, the result of a change in input structure of the sector's own column, or indirect, the result of changes in input prices induced by changes in the structure of other sectors as well. In any given period, most sectors will experience both changes in their own input structure, represented by changes in their own intermediate and labor input coefficients and changes in the prices of the inputs they purchase. Given this simultaneity, it would be difficult to disentangle ability to appropriate gains from one kind of change from gains from the other. As a first approximation, therefore, we do not distinguish the appropriation of gains from introducing new input coefficients from the appropriation of the "windfall" benefits of changing input prices.

Appropriation coefficients are measured as the increase in profit margin following innovation divided by total cost savings:

$$\mu_{jj} = p^1 - (p^1 A_j{}^1 + l_j{}^1 + \pi_j{}^0)/(p^0 A_j{}^0 + l_j{}^0) - (p^1 A_j{}^1 - l_j{}^1). \tag{9}$$

After the introduction of the new technical coefficients, A^1, profits of sector j will be

$$\pi_j{}^1 = \pi_j{}^0 + \mu_{jj}(p^0 A_j{}^0 + l_j{}^0 - p^1 A_j{}^1 - l_j{}^1), \tag{10}$$

where π_j^0 represents the initial profit margin of sector j, μ_{jj} represents the appropriation coefficient for j, and the expression in parentheses represents the difference between pre- and postinnovation costs.

A Price System with Partial Appropriation

Given a diagonal matrix of appropriation coefficients μ, postinnovation prices, p^1, are determined by:

$$p^1 = [\pi^0 + p^0 A^0 \mu + l^0 \mu + l^1(l - \mu)][l - A^1(l - \mu)]^{-1} \qquad (11)$$

Essentially, μ determines the weights of old and new technology in the formation of prices. A high value of μ means that, even if old technology is supplanted by new, prices are sets as if the old technology continued to be used.

Assuming that $p^1 \leq p^0$, the elements μ_{jj} will range between zero and one. A value of $\mu_{jj} = 0$ means zero appropriation and corresponds to the situation of fix (competitive) prices (i.e., zero additional profits or fixed profit margins). Where the elements of the appropriation matrix are zero, all of the gains from innovation are passed along in the form of price reductions. A value of $\mu_{jj} = 1$ means full appropriation (flex prices). With flex prices, no benefits are passed on to other stages and prices remain what they were in the absence of structural change. (If $p^1 = p^0$, eqs. 7 and 9 yield a solution of $\mu_{jj} = 1$, while eqs. 6 and 9 yield a solution of $\mu_{jj} = 0$.)

Simulations of the Effects of Diminishing Appropriation

This more flexible model makes it possible to simulate the "leakage" of innovational rents from innovating to customer sectors as the former's ability to appropriate weakens over time. Table 7 shows how the prices and profit margins of all sectors change as μ_{MM} varies from 0 to 1, assuming $\mu_{SS} = 0.75$ and $\mu_{jj} = 0.00$ for the other sectors. All prices tend to decrease as appropriation weakens in M. Since, by assumption, profit margins are fixed in U and O, only S's profit margin varies inversely with μ_{MM}.

Appropriation and Profit Signals in Adaptive Change

The simulations discussed thus far concern the distribution of benefits from single innovations introduced one at a time. In an interdependent system, of course, the benefits of any innovation in a single sector depend on the input structures prevailing in all other sectors. Figure 1 shows a comparison of the measured benefits of the four innovations in M, assuming fixed final demand, with what the benefits would be if each innovation were introduced along with an improvement in sector S. In real terms, direct labor savings in S increase the total (direct plus indirect) labor savings resulting from innovation 4 (which

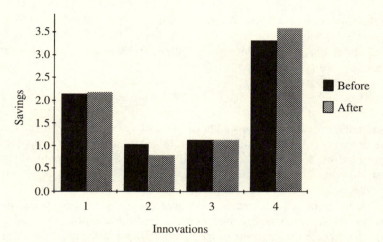

Fig. 1. Economywide labor savings of four innovations in *M* before and after an innovation in *S*

substitutes S for labor) and reduces the relative advantage of innovation 2 (which reduces inputs of S).

Will such changes in the economywide advantages of different innovations be reflected in corresponding changes in their profitability? How innovation in S affects the profit consequences of each innovation in M depends on appropriation in S. If the price of S remains at initial levels ($\mu_{SS} = 1$), then the profitability of any innovation in M to other sectors will be the same as it was in the absence of an innovation in S. Thus, while the real economic benefits of

TABLE 7.   Effects of Decreasing Appropriation in *M* on Sectoral Prices and Profit Margins

μ_{MM}	Sectoral Prices				Sectoral Profit Margins			
	pS	pM	pU	pO	πS	πM	πU	πO
1.00	1.000	1.000	1.000	1.000	0.300	0.400	0.10	0.20
0.90	1.000	0.990	0.994	0.997	0.301	0.390	0.10	0.20
0.80	0.999	0.980	0.989	0.994	0.302	0.381	0.10	0.20
0.70	0.999	0.970	0.983	0.991	0.304	0.371	0.10	0.20
0.60	0.998	0.959	0.977	0.987	0.305	0.361	0.10	0.20
0.50	0.998	0.949	0.971	0.984	0.306	0.351	0.10	0.20
0.40	0.998	0.938	0.965	0.981	0.307	0.341	0.10	0.20
0.30	0.997	0.928	0.959	0.977	0.308	0.331	0.10	0.20
0.20	0.997	0.917	0.953	0.974	0.310	0.321	0.10	0.20
0.10	0.996	0.906	0.947	0.971	0.311	0.310	0.10	0.20
0.00	0.996	0.896	0.941	0.967	0.312	0.300	0.10	0.20

innovation in M change with innovation in S, profit incentives to innovate may or may not change correspondingly, depending on how changes in real costs are filtered through the price system. Table 8 shows how variations in the appropriation coefficient, μ_{SS}, affects sectoral profits following each of the four innovations in M. (Zero appropriation is assumed for U and O.)

Note that a structural improvement in S increases the profit margin of M only when there is less than full appropriation in S ($\mu_{SS} < 1$). Because innovation 4 (in M) increases the use of S while innovation 2 decreases it, improvement in S increases profit margins in M by more for innovation 4 than for innovation 2.

In summary, appropriation coefficients facilitate the analysis of changes over time in the sectoral distribution of profit incentives of innovation. Prices and profits of downstream sectors become better guides for efficient resource allocation as appropriation in the innovating sector diminishes.

Questions for Future Research

Simulations with hypothetical data help to anticipate sensitivities and surprises in a complex model. But the big payoff, if there is one, comes with empirical implementation. Unfortunately, the real-life counterparts of the activity vectors for single technologies used in my simulations are hard to find. Can input-output information support significant research in this area? Perhaps. Input-output tables are very detailed in comparison with macroeconomic data, but even very disaggregated tables combine a mix of plants and technologies in a single sector.

My earlier experience using input-output data to explore questions of innovation provides a basis for some optimism. Carter 1970 documents significant adaptivity among sectoral input structures. Input structures for a later

TABLE 8.   Sectoral Profit Margins after Innovations 4 and 2 with Full Appropriation in *M* and Varying Appropriation in *S*

	After Innovation 4				After Innovation 2			
	πS	πM	πU	πO	πS	πM	πU	πO
Old structure in S								
$\mu_{SS} = 0.0$	0.30	0.40	0.10	0.20	0.30	0.40	0.10	0.20
$\mu_{SS} = 0.5$	0.30	0.40	0.10	0.20	0.30	0.40	0.10	0.20
$\mu_{SS} = 1.0$	0.30	0.40	0.10	0.20	0.30	0.40	0.10	0.20
New structure in S								
$\mu_{SS} = 0.0$	0.30	0.43	0.10	0.20	0.30	0.41	0.10	0.20
$\mu_{SS} = 0.5$	0.35	0.42	0.10	0.20	0.35	0.41	0.10	0.20
$\mu_{SS} = 1.0$	0.40	0.40	0.10	0.20	0.40	0.40	0.10	0.20

period clearly showed less factor-saving advantage when combined with input coefficients of earlier years for other sectors than they did in the context of contemporary structures. This suggests that it should also be possible to sort out at least some of the positive and negative externalities of structural change in specific sectors.

Whether sectoral price information and profit information will be sufficiently robust to yield meaningful measures of appropriation remains to be seen. It may be possible to estimate appropriation indirectly from input-output information for two periods. For each sector j we would estimate μ_{jj} from base and given year input-output structures and labor coefficients, prices, and base-year profit margins:

$$\mu_{jj} = p_j^1 - \Sigma_i p_i^1 A_{ij}^1 - l_j^1 - \pi_j^0/\Sigma_i(p_i^0 A_{ij}^0 + l_j^0 - p_i^1 A_{ij}^1 - l_j^1). \tag{12}$$

A pair of input-output data sets would yield a single set of sectoral appropriation coefficients. Using time-series of input-output tables with corresponding labor coefficients and prices, it should be possible to judge whether appropriation coefficients tend to be stable or how they vary over time.

Ideally, one might also wish to compare estimated appropriation coefficients for the United States with parallel estimates for other countries. Differences in appropriation patterns and practices may be a significant element in explaining differences in patterns of innovation among countries. Beyond input-output data, it is also possible that more direct estimates of appropriation coefficients could be made for industrial networks of limited scope where detailed historical information is available. Models of such networks could be imbedded in a general equilibrium model with more aggregated treatment of the remaining sectors.

These and other empirical paths remain to be explored. I hope this essay has given some indication of why they might be worth exploring.

REFERENCES

Carter, A. P. 1970. *Structural Change in the American Economy.* Cambridge, Mass.: Harvard University Press.
Carter, A. P. 1990. "Upstream and Downstream Benefits of Innovation." *Economic Systems Research.* Forthcoming.
Fontela, E., M. LoCascio, and A. Pulido. 1989."Productivity Surplus Distribution: Spanish and Italian Results." Paper presented at the 9th international conference on input-output techniques, Keszthely. Photocopy.
Griliches, Z., ed. 1987. *R&D, Patents, and Productivity.* Chicago: University of Chicago Press.

Harhoff, D. 1990. "Motivations for Supplier Innovation." Massachusetts Institute of Technology. Photocopy.

Leontief, W. W. 1941. *The Structure of the American Economy.* Oxford: Oxford University Press.

Mathur, P. N. 1986. "Technical Progress, Price Changes in Monopolistic and Competitive Industries, Phillips Curve, and its Shift with High Interest Rates in the United States." Paper presented at the 8th international conference on input-output techniques, Sapporo. Photocopy.

Schumpeter, J. A. 1934. *The Theory of Economic Development.* Cambridge, Mass.: Harvard University Press.

Teece, D. J. 1986. "Profiting from Technological Innovation: Implications for Integration, Collaboration, Licensing, and Public Policy." *Research Policy* 15 (6):285–305.

Von Hippel, E. 1987. *The Sources of Innovation.* Oxford: Oxford University Press.

Productivity, Profitability, and Innovative Behavior in West German Industries

Horst Hanusch and Markus Hierl

Introduction

The present investigation is part of a research project that concerns problems of structural dynamics in the manufacturing sectors of the Federal Republic of Germany. It presents the first results that reveal the connections between technical efficiency and profitability. The distribution of these two aspects of entrepreneurial performance within a sector can give a good picture of the structural characteristics of particular branches. The technical efficiencies of enterprises are found by means of so-called frontier-production functions. We have based our work on the research made in connection with an investigation of communally owned public utilities in the FRG (Hanusch and Jänsch 1988). This approach has become a generally accepted method of measuring efficiencies and has been applied in numerous investigations of measuring the efficiency of the industrial sector in several countries (see, e.g., Forsund and Hjalmarsson 1987). There also exist valuable investigations of profitability by industrial branches and individual enterprises and their differences (for a good survey, see Schmalensee 1985 and 1989). However, as far as we know, little attention has been paid to the connection between technical efficiency and profitability.[1]

We also, for the first time for the FRG, take account of expenditures for R&D by individual firms and compare them with technical efficiency. We assume that innovative activities are an important determinant for the success of an enterprise and for its economic efficiency.

Our calculations are based on annual reports and data on innovative

We thank Dr. Lothar Scholz, Heinz Schmalholz, and Horst Penzkofer for their kind permission to use the Ifo-Innovation data base and for many helpful discussions. Thanks are also due to Manuel Trajtenberg and Helge Majer for their critical comments. Wolfgang Stolper helped with the translation.

1. See, e.g., Lippman and Rumelt 1982; Schohl 1990.

activities in the FRG of two key branches of the economy, machinery construction and electronics. For these two branches there are data for individual
firms for the period from 1960 to 1985.

The results of our study are similar, to some extent, to those from other
investigations. Thus, technical efficiency in the investigated branches is very
high, and there are only minor interfirm differences. This result corresponds
to the general tenor of a study by Caves (1985) of the U.S. economy.

Although only relatively minor differences in the efficiency of individual
enterprises could be observed, a close connection between technical efficiency
and profitability could nevertheless be determined. This connection is not,
however, linear as one might have expected. We observed a nonlinear relationship as follows. On the average, every improvement in technical efficiency leads to an increase in profitability that is greater the closer an enterprise gets to the production frontier. This remarkable result is highly
significant for both investigated sectors. In addition, a greatly reduced sample
of enterprises in the machinery sector allowed us to observe tendencies that
suggest that it is not the most efficient enterprises that have the highest R&D
expenditures.

We will first briefly describe the available data on which our investigation
is based. We next calculate the expected technical efficiency of the individual
firms by means of frontier-production functions. We then derive the relations
between technical efficiency and profitability and we consider to what extent
the two derived magnitudes may depend on the innovative activities of the
individual firms. We finally summarize the most important results and briefly
describe the next steps of our research project to be undertaken.

The Data

The basis of our investigations are annual statements of accounts of German
stock corporations (*Aktiengesellschaften*) that are available (with variations)
for individual firms from 1960 to 1985. The limitation to corporations is
unavoidable because German federal law requires only stock corporations to
publish annual statements of accounts. Since larger enterprises are usually
organized as stock corporations, we are aware that the limitation of our data to
this type of legal organization could result in a bias of the results toward large
enterprises. This is all the more possible because the machinery construction
sector, particularly in the FRG, is traditionally characterized by medium-sized
enterprises.

Our sample of the machinery sector consists of twenty-nine and fifty-four
enterprises, depending on the particular year, and covers between 12 percent
and 21 percent of the total sales of the sector. In the electronics sector, a

maximum of twenty-four enterprises account for 26 to 59 percent of sectoral sales. However, the relationship between the surpluses and sales of individual enterprises of our data set corresponds to the average of the sector.

In order to estimate a frontier-production function we also need the input-output magnitudes of individual enterprises. We have taken the necessary components from the profit-and-loss statements of the corporations and calculated these magnitudes as follows.[2]

1. *Output.* The sum of total sales, capitalized firm-internal services, and inventory changes, deflated by the index of producer prices for the individual sector.

2. *Input.*

   a) *Labor.* The sum of wages, salaries, legal, and voluntary fringe benefits, deflated by an index of wages and salaries. The latter was calculated according to the share of wage and salary earners in the total employment of a sector.

   b) *Capital.* The sum of depreciation of plant and equipment and interest payments deflated by an index of gross investment in plant and equipment. This method of calculation does not, unfortunately, reflect the actual economic and technical capital consumption of an enterprise, because provisions of the tax laws allow discretion in valuation for balance sheet purposes. We believe that this fact is the main reason our estimated parameters for capital in the production frontier do not show the desired significance. For this reason, we will not give an interpretation of our results for individual input factors. We believe, however, that this does not effect the observed deviations of the outputs of individual firms from the production frontier. These deviations can be interpreted even when the inputs are only incompletely determined.

   c) *Materials.* The sum of expenditures on raw material and supplies, deflated by an index of the price increases for intermediate inputs.[3]

For the investigation of innovative activities, we relied on selected data from the Innovation Tests of the Ifo-Institute for Economic Research in Munich. The R&D expenditures were deflated by the R&D price index of the

---

2. The price indices are all taken from different publications of the Statistisches Bundesamt, *Fachserien* 16–18.

3. The calculation of a price index for intermediate inputs turns out to be difficult because there does not exist any such index in the official statistics. Thus, we had to construct our own index: $SM^n/(GSP^n/p_0 - GSVA^r)$, where SM^n = nominal sectoral materials, GSP^n = nominal gross sectoral product, p_0 = producer price index, $GSVA^r$ = real gross sectoral value added.

Statistical Office of the European Communities (EUROSTAT 1987). The Ifo-Innovation Test is very recent; hence, data were available only for a relatively short period. Moreover, firms participate in the Innovation Test on a voluntary basis so that enterprises are not always prepared to give the necessary information. The data set has, therefore, considerable gaps. Thus, we had to limit ourselves to the machinery sector and to reduce the number of observations to thirty-four. The results based on such a limited basis cannot, of course, be considered firm. However, particular tendencies may be recognized because the R&D expenditures of the observed enterprises in relation to employment or total sales correspond to the sectoral average.[4]

Estimation of Technical Inefficiency

The systematic analysis of technical inefficiency goes back to Farrell (1957). It reached its high point in the composed error models of Aigner, Lovell, and Schmidt (1977) and Meeusen and van den Broeck (1977). The analysis is based on a stochastic production frontier (Z) as follows:

$$Z = f(X) \cdot e^{v+u}$$

This formula is based on the estimation of a traditional average production function $Q = f(X) \cdot e^v$, which considers e^v as a statistical noise term. In a second step, this term is corrected by a nonpositive disturbance e^u. This term models technical inefficiency. For this term we have assumed a half-normal distribution, as is usual in most of the literature.

Frequently, there is collinearity in the estimation of production functions between the individual factors. This suggests an additional factor that influences all variables. We could, however, reduce the danger of collinearity by normalizing all variables by the number of employees. We next had to decide upon the type of production function to be employed for our calculations. Estimations of Cobb-Douglas functions, however, yielded poor results compared to translog functions. It was, therefore, not difficult to decide in favor of the latter, assuming, however, linear homogeneity.

The results of our estimations are reproduced in table 1. We again stress, however, that we do not insist that the parameters for the individual factors

---

4. The sectoral average is calculated according to different volumes of the Stifterverband für die Deutsche Wissenschaft's periodical reports of R&D expenditures. However, if it is considered that "Large R&D Expenditures" are more broadly defined by the Ifo-Institute than by the Frascati convention used by the Stifterverband, the R&D expenditures of the investigated enterprises are below the sectoral average.

reflect actual production elasticities. The translog production function can be stated as:

$$\ln(Q) = \beta_0 + \sum_i \beta_i \ln(X_i) + \frac{1}{2} \sum_i \sum_j \beta_{ij} \ln(X_i) \ln(X_j)$$
$$+ \sum_i \beta_{it} t \ln(X_i) + \beta_t t + \beta_{tt} t ,$$

with a time index, t, and three inputs, n (labor), c (capital), and m (materials).

The level for the technical inefficiency of a sector is given by λ. The factor λ is defined as the relationship of the standard deviation of the technical inefficiency of the individual enterprises in our sample to the standard deviation of the statistical noise. This factor is close to 1 for both sectors. This suggests only a small efficiency gradient. This is also confirmed by considering the expected degree of efficiency for the individual firm. This magnitude can be calculated on the basis of the conditional probability for technical

TABLE 1.   Regression of a Three-Factor Frontier-Production Function of the Translog Type

	Electronics	Machinery
β_0	0.552265*	0.899210*
β_c	0.512940E-01	0.812164E-01*
β_n	0.843288*	0.909615*
β_m	0.105418	0.916852E-02
β_t	0.365955E-01*	0.275259E-02
β_{cc}	0.282878E-01	−0.314355E-01*
β_{nc}	0.846448E-01*	0.828226E-01*
β_{cm}	−0.112933*	−0.513870E-01*
β_{ct}	−0.723891E-03	−0.263810E-02*
β_{nn}	−0.110806*	−0.478657E-01*
β_{nm}	0.261611E-01*	−0.349569E-01*
β_{nt}	0.956068E-02*	0.302202E-02*
β_{mm}	0.867715E-01*	0.863440E-02*
β_{mt}	−0.883679E-02*	−0.383924E-03
β_{tt}	−0.719117E-03*	−0.163392E-03*
λ	1.14185*	1.04516*
σ	0.87235E-01*	0.113881*
ϕeff	0.9494	0.9375
R^2	0.9674	0.9587
N	405	954

Notes: t is a time index; $\lambda^2 = \sigma_u^2 / \sigma_v^2$; $\sigma^2 = \sigma_u^2 + \sigma_v^2$.
*$p = .05$.

inefficiency on the assumption that the term for total noise for the estimation of the frontier-production function is $\epsilon = v + u$ (compare Jondrow et al. 1982):

$$E(u|\epsilon) = \sigma_u^2 \sigma_v^2 / \sigma \{ f(\epsilon\lambda/\sigma)/[1 - F(\epsilon\lambda/\sigma)] - (\epsilon\lambda/\sigma) \}, \text{ eff} = e^{-E(u|\epsilon)},$$

where f and F represent the standard normal density and cumulative distribution function, respectively.

The average efficiency in the machinery sector is 0.9375, in electronics it is 0.9494. The overwhelming number of the observed firms show an efficiency of over 90 percent. This result also confirms the known results for the FRG in the literature. The small differences among the enterprises and the high level of technical efficiency are certainly also an expression of the international competitiveness of these enterprises. Both machinery and electronics are sectors that produce internationally on a very high technical level.

Technical Efficiency and Profitability

We have made two hypotheses to empirically investigate the connection between technical efficiency and profitability. The first hypothesis concerns the basic problem of whether the two magnitudes are connected at all.

1. Technical efficiency and profitability of an enterprise are independent of each other.

If our results negate this hypothesis, it would confirm the well-documented insight in business economics that differences in productive efficiency influence the economic results of an enterprise (Peters and Waterman 1982).

We decided to look somewhat more deeply into the basic connection between efficiency and profitability. We started to ask, in addition, how this relationship looks for the group of extremely efficient and the group of extremely inefficient firms. Our hypothesis is:

2. There is a nonlinear connection between technical efficiency and profitability.

If this hypothesis is confirmed, the nonlinear connection may be one of two types: either concave or convex. In the first case, we may suppose that the leading enterprises hit a profitability threshold at a very high level of efficiency. It is likely, moreover, that their efforts to raise efficiency further will, as a rule, yield diminishing returns. In addition, inefficient enterprises must expect a more than proportional loss of profitability if they move yet further away from the production frontier. This, in turn, is likely to exert strong pressure not to let the existing productivity gap increase further. In this case, their best strategy is imitation. The weak enterprises will then always try to adapt themselves to new technologies.

With a convex curve, the economic situation for the enterprises is entirely different. In this case, enterprises can count on increasing returns in their attempts to improve efficiency. They have a more than proportional incentive to maintain an efficiency advantage or to increase it further. Their best strategy is innovation in this case. The enterprises must continuously try to further improve their production processes by new technologies. Even the weaker enterprises will have to concentrate on this strategy because only this will ensure an above average profitability. The structure of a sector will, in such a case, be characterized by relatively small deviations of the technical efficiency of individual enterprises from the production frontier.

To test these hypotheses we have used the following nonlinear model.

$$\ln(\text{prof}) = \alpha_0 + \alpha_e \cdot \ln(\text{eff}) + \alpha_t \cdot t + \alpha_b \cdot \ln(bes) + \alpha_{ee} \cdot \ln(\text{eff})^2$$
$$+ \alpha_{et} \cdot t \cdot \ln(\text{eff}) + \alpha_{eb} \cdot \ln(\text{eff}) \cdot \ln(bes) + \alpha_{tt} \cdot t^2$$
$$+ \alpha_{bt} \cdot t \cdot \ln(bes) + \alpha_{bb} \ln(bes)^2$$

This is a function of the translog type. This type is an approximation to any twice differentiable function, and its variables are:

eff = relative technical efficiency of the enterprises as shown by the estimation of the frontier-production function;

prof = *a*) surpluses in 1,000 DM per employed deflated to the year 1980; or
b) surpluses in 1,000 DM per output;

t = time index; and

bes = total number of employees.

To test the second hypothesis we calculated the first and second derivatives of the estimation function and the efficiency elasticity of profitability. The derivatives are given by:

$$\frac{\delta(\text{prof})}{\delta(\text{eff})} = \frac{\text{prof}}{\text{eff}}[\alpha_e + 2 \cdot \alpha_{ee} \cdot \ln(\text{eff}) + \alpha_{et} \cdot t + \alpha_{eb} \cdot \ln(bes)] ,$$

and

$$\frac{\delta^2(\text{prof})}{\delta(\text{eff})^2} = \frac{\text{prof}}{\text{eff}^2}\{[\alpha_e + 2 \cdot \alpha_{ee} \cdot \ln(\text{eff}) + \alpha_{et} \cdot t + \alpha_{eb} \cdot \ln(bes)]^2$$

$$- \alpha_e + 2 \cdot \alpha_{ee} \cdot [1 - \ln(\text{eff})]$$

$$- \alpha_{et} \cdot t - \alpha_{eb} \cdot \ln(bes)\} .$$

The efficiency elasticity of profitability expresses the percentage increase of surpluses per employee if the relative technical efficiency increases by one percent. This elasticity was calculated with its logarithmic form:

$$\eta = \frac{\delta\ln(\text{prof})}{\delta\ln(\text{eff})} = \frac{\delta(\text{prof})}{\delta(\text{eff})} \cdot \frac{\text{eff}}{\text{prof}} .$$

This results in the following equation for the elasticity:

$$\eta = \frac{\delta(\text{prof})}{\delta(\text{eff})} \cdot \frac{\text{eff}}{\text{prof}} = \alpha_e + 2 \cdot \alpha_{ee} \cdot \ln(\text{eff}) + \alpha_{et} \cdot t + \alpha_{eb} \cdot \ln(bes) .$$

To reduce autocorrelation of the error term in the model, we applied the first differences of the variables. The results of the estimation are found in table 2.

The α_e parameter of the efficiency variable is highly significant for both sectors. The hypothesis of the independence of technical efficiency and profitability may, therefore, be rejected.

Since the second derivative of the estimation function is positive for all four estimated models over the whole efficiency range, the profitability-

TABLE 2.   Regression of Technical Efficiency, Employment, and Time on Profits

	Electronics		Machinery	
	Profits per Employee	Profits per Output	Profits per Employee	Profits per Output
α_e	17.992**	17.258**	13.058**	−160.296**
α_{ee}	31.725*	34.013**	88.219**	−243.078**
α_{et}	0.189*	—[a]	0.846**	2.453**
α_{eb}	−0.217**	−0.035**	2.087**	18.802**
R^2	0.548	0.786	0.551	0.606
N		372[b]		872[b]

[a]Not significantly different from zero.
[b]Due to the calculation of logarithms and first differences, the sample size N was reduced compared to the frontier estimation.
$*p = .10.$ $**p = .05.$

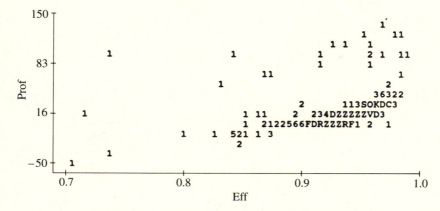

Fig. 1.   Machinery sector empirical profitability-efficiency curve, profits per employee. (Frequencies are shown by 1 = 1 observation, 2 = 2 observations, . . . , 9 = 9 observations, A = 10 observations, B = 11 observations, . . . , Z ≥ 35 observations.)

efficiency curve is strictly convex for both sectors. A negative first derivative that indicates a decreasing slope could occur in our estimated models depending on the regression coefficients and on both parameters t and *bes*. However, this is only the case for five extreme observations in the machinery sector with small values of t and *bes*. Introducing the estimated parameters of table 2 into the elasticity equation, it is immediately apparent that all observations in both sectors (with the exception of the five extreme ones in the machinery sector) fall inside the elastic regions of $\eta > 1$. Thus, the profitability curve is an increasing and convex function of efficiency for both branches (see figs. 1–4).

For the enterprises in both sectors, this result depends on achieving more than proportional increases in profits through the introduction of improved methods of production. Our next task is to investigate whether they have, in fact, fully utilized this possibility.

On the Importance of Innovative Activities

As we have pointed out, our investigation of innovative activities had to rely on a greatly reduced sample. At present, we have reliable data only for enterprises in the machinery sector, but we soon hope to be able to supplement these data with information for the electronics sector. We have thirty-four observations for the machinery sector, which limits, of course, the generality of our results.

Our first interest concerned the question of whether, in our sample, the average R&D expenditures per employee (innov) of efficient and inefficient

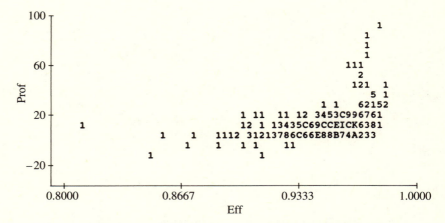

Fig. 2. Electronics sector empirical profitability-efficiency curve, profits per employee. (Frequencies are shown by 1 = 1 observation, 2 = 2 observations, . . . , 9 = 9 observations, A = 10 observations, B = 11 observations, . . . , Z ≥ 35 observations.)

enterprises could be distinguished. To do this, we formed two classes within our sample of the most efficient and the most inefficient enterprises. We then tested the Null hypothesis ("the two classes do not differ in their average R&D expenditures") by means of a two-sample t-test. The results are shown in table 3.

The Null hypothesis can be rejected for the machinery sector even though the sample is relatively small. Enterprises in the efficient group spend, on the average, DM 5,122 per employee for R&D. This is much more than the

TABLE 3. Two-Sample, *T*-test Results for the Response to Innovation (in 1,000 DM)

	RNDX = 0 (below mean)	RNDX = 1 (above mean)
N	10	24
95% confidence level	2.262084	3.7993
Mean	3.1800	5.1223
95% confidence level	4.0979	6.4453
Standard deviation	1.285164	3.133407
Standard error	0.4064	0.6396

Notes: Tests of unequal variances are: T-value = -2.5631 (p = .0150); df = 33.9455; difference = -1.9423 (95% confidence level = -3.4823); standard error = 0.7578 (95% confidence level = -0.4023); F-ratio = 5.9445 (p = .0044).

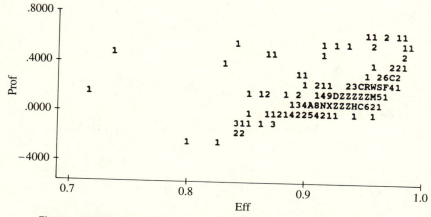

Fig. 3.   Machinery sector empirical profitability-efficiency curve, profits per output. (Frequencies are shown by 1 = 1 observation, 2 = 2 observations, . . . , 9 = 9 observations, A = 10 observations, B = 11 observations, . . . , Z ≥ 35 observations.)

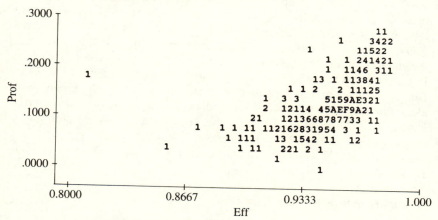

Fig. 4.   Electronics sector empirical profitability-efficiency curve, profits per output. (Frequencies are shown by 1 = 1 observation, 2 = 2 observations, . . . , 9 = 9 observations, A = 10 observations, B = 11 observations, . . . , Z ≥ 35 observations.)

expenditures of inefficient enterprises, which spend only DM 3,180 per employed.

Additional information may be derived from a scatter diagram that gives real R&D expenditures per employee on the one axis and the relative technical efficiency of the individual enterprises on the other. Thus, figure 5 gives a more differentiated picture.

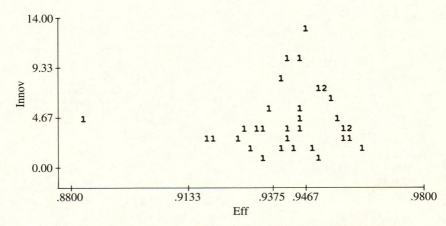

Fig. 5. Scatter diagram of the distribution of R&D expenditures

Neither the most efficient nor the most inefficient enterprises in our sample are in the top group of enterprises with above average R&D expenditures. Rather, the enterprises with the highest R&D expenditures are among the enterprises whose relative technical efficiency is only a little above the average. The interpretation of this result must remain open. It might mean that the enterprises with the highest technical efficiency are not quite aware of the importance of R&D expenditures in the struggle for profits and market share. But the result may also suggest that enterprises in the second group make extra efforts to get to the forefront of production technology by means of R&D expenditures. Our results also show that such a strategy would promise an above average increase of profits. There is, however, a danger for the present leaders that the less-efficient enterprises will catch up with them or even surpass them.

Summary and Open Questions

We have presented the first results of a research project that investigates the structural dynamics of manufacturing industries in the FRG, dealing primarily with the relationship of profitability and technical efficiency. The investigation is based on a data set of annual statements of accounts and R&D expenditures in the machinery and electronics sectors for a period of, at most, twenty-six years. The main results of our study may be summarized as follows.

Our estimations of frontier-production functions show only small differences in efficiency among the enterprises in the two sectors. Neither the machinery nor the electronics sector is characterized by great differences in relative technical efficiency. In addition, there is a significant connection in both sectors between the increase in technical efficiency and increasing marginal profits. This may mean that the leading enterprises of a sector are subject to strong pressures to maintain or even increase their relative technical efficiency to avoid the danger of becoming less profitable than competing enterprises.

Our first results from a reduced sample with additional information about R&D expenditures of enterprises in the machinery sector suggest that this connection may not be sufficiently recognized by the enterprises. This is also suggested by the fact that the enterprises with above average R&D expenditures are to be observed only in the group of enterprises with slightly above average technical efficiency.

Although our analysis is based on a period of twenty-six years, it is nevertheless static because the development of enterprises over time is not followed. First results for this problem are expected soon. We also intend to expand our investigations to other sectors. Our first interest would be directed to sectors whose past development has been less favorable than that of the machinery and electronics sectors. In this expanded analysis we also intend to investigate to what extent intersectoral differences are reflected in the profitability-efficiency curves. Finally, we intend to investigate the influence of market structure, since there is probably a hidden factor influencing the profitability of individual sectors.

REFERENCES

Aigner, D. J., C. A. K. Lovell, and P. Schmidt. 1977. "Foundation and Estimation of Stochastic Frontier Production Function Models." *Journal of Econometrics* 6:21–37.
Caves, R. E. 1985. *Interindustry Differences in Productivity Growth and Technical Inefficiency.* Discussion Paper no. 1130. Cambridge, Mass.: Harvard Institute of Economic Research.
EUROSTAT. 1987. *Öffentliche Aufwendungen für Forschung und Entwicklung 1975–1985.* Luxemburg: EUROSTAT.
Farrell, M. J. 1957. "The Measurement of Productive Efficiency." *Journal of the Royal Statistical Society,* ser. A, 120:253–81.
Forsund, F. R., and L. Hjalmarsson. 1987. *Analysis of Industrial Structure: A Putty Clay Approach.* Stockholm: Almquist and Wicksell.
Hanusch, H., and G. Jänsch. 1988. "Produktivität im öffentlichen Sektor." Research Project financed by the DFG. Augsburg. Typescript.
Jondrow, J., C. A. K. Lovell, I. S. Materov, and P. Schmidt. 1982. "On the Estimation of Technical Efficiency in the Stochastic Frontier Production Function Model." *Journal of Econometrics* 19:233–38.
Lippman, S. A., and R. P. Rumelt. 1982. "Uncertain Imitability: An Analysis of

Interfirm Differences in Efficiency under Competition." *Bell Journal of Economics* 13:418–38.

Meeusen, W., and J. van den Broeck. 1977. "Efficiency Estimation from Cobb-Douglas Production Functions with Composed Error." *International Economic Review* 18:435–44.

Peters, T. J., and R. H. Waterman, Jr. 1982. *In Search of Excellence: Lessons from America's Best Run Companies.* New York: Harper and Row.

Schmalensee, R. 1985. "Do Markets Differ Much?" *American Economic Review* 75:341–51.

Schmalensee, R. 1989. "Interindustry Studies of Structure and Performance." In *Handbook of Industrial Economics,* vol. 2, ed. R. Schmalensee and R. Willig, 951–1009. Amsterdam.

Schohl, F. 1990. "Differential Profit Rates, Growth Differentials, and Efficiency: Searching for the Schumpeterian Corporation." Working Paper. University of Darmstadt, Department of Economics. Mimeo.

Statistisches Bundesamt. Various years. *Fachserie* 16, Reihe 4.3; *Fachserie* 17, Reihe 2; *Fachserie* 18, Reihe S9 and Reihe 1; Wiesbaden: Statistisches Bundesamt.

Stifterverband für die Deutsche Wissenschaft. Various years. *Forschung und Entwicklung in der Wirtschaft.* Essen.

Business Competence, Organizational Learning, and Economic Growth: Establishing the Smith-Schumpeter-Wicksell (SSW) Connection

Gunnar Eliasson

Likewise we found a remarkable difference in the organization of work at our shipyards compared to those in other countries. Here, almost two days of work were needed to accomplish what took only one day in England or Holland. . . . On this and other things I want to say that . . . Swedish hands, when appropriately directed and put to use, lack neither skill nor force.

—Johan Westerman 1768, 6.

The Intellectual Dimension of Economic Activity

The cornerstone of western intellectual thought is the search for a true state of affairs, which is *assumed* to exist, an idea that runs through science and art. This idea of something ultimate that is invariant to our endeavors to uncover it is comforting. As human beings, we need it to feel at ease in a seemingly disorderly world. The notion of an equilibrium, preferably a situation of perfect information, hence, leads our mind to reject on prior grounds evidence against it. Business leaders need this intellectual comfort to dare make the bold decisions required of them, you and I need it to feel at ease, and economists need it to be able to advise politicians. Healthy minds do not ask questions that are too deep to make them skeptical about their prior assumptions. In fact, the important part of business competence is to organize "the mind of the firm" so that decisions can be made.

In the old days, with primitive observational techniques in the social

This essay has been through several stages of revision. Along the way many people have contributed critical remarks, enthusiastic support, and observations. I want to thank Pontus Braunerhjelm, Bo Carlsson, Bill Comanor, Christina Hartler, Jonas Häckner, Thomas Lindh, Erik Mellander, Karl Markus Modén, Pavel Pelikan, and Frank Stafford in particular. Whatever errors remain are, however, entirely my own.

sciences, the minds of economists could wander rather freely along strange roads. Even though economic knowledge could not be measured, nor its existence proven, it was an obvious fact that knowledge, and hence learning, mattered. Early texts in economics were very open to this unobservable entity. John Stuart Mill (1848) made knowledge a critical factor in economics. The Swedish economist, Westerman, who traveled to England to learn about "the new machines" was very clear in his assessment (1768). What mattered was not the machines, but the human competence to organize machines and men, to know what products to produce and how to make customers happy with them.[1] The absence of data, however, allowed social scientists to speculate rather freely about the nature of economic competence.

This situation changed with the improvement of economic measurement techniques, beginning with the development of consistent cost accounting systems for firms and continuing with the establishment of elaborate national accounts systems. The minds of economists were forced to conform to measurement. Economics became a "hardware science," and knowledge was forgotten for more than a century (Eliasson 1989a; Stigler 1961). The problem is that the intellectual dimension of economic activity is still there. The intellectual veil of the economy is not neutral; it imposes its mind on the hardware performance of the real economy and it draws considerable resources (Eliasson 1990b and 1990d). So it is outright wrong to neglect it.

General equilibrium has to include capital market equilibrium, meaning a situation where rates of return of all agents equal the interest rate. Since a rate of return independent of the stock of capital cannot be defined—except as a statistical artifact—this is a nonexistent situation ex post.[2] Both ex-ante and ex-post individual firm rates of return differ from the market interest rate by a measure that I will call $\bar{\epsilon}_j$ (for the firm j). There is a distribution of $\bar{\epsilon}$ that separates the rates of return from the market interest rate (see fig. 1). Before modern, general equilibrium–based finance theory reinterpreted these epsila as a (stochastic) distribution of insurable risks around the exogenous equilibrium interest rate, McKenzie observed that (perhaps) these deviations could be interpreted as returns (negative or positive) to firm-specific assets, or as competence that did not appear explicitly in the accounts of the firm (1959). In Eliasson 1985a (chap. 6), I have followed up on this and made $\bar{\epsilon}$ corrected for

---

1. Westerman's little book, in fact, contains an early formulation of the economic efficiency of national work specialization and the benefits of trade. Westerman suggested to the King of Sweden that more of that be promoted.

2. This also means that an equilibrium point—if it exists—cannot be *computed;* it has to be approached through search (experimentation). Since search is costly, the existence of equilibrium will depend on whether search costs are *computable*. The answer to that question is part of the story of this essay.

inflation the underpinning of total factor productivity growth, or the shift factor in the production function. I will return to the mathematics of this derivation at the end of this essay.

I make the firm, existing on a unique or specific knowledge asset ("top level organizational competence"; Eliasson 1990b), the main agent behind economic growth. The firm is defined by its *financial objectives* and its capacity to steadily upgrade its competence through organizational learning. The competence endowment of the firm confers economies of scale to all other factors of production. Organizational learning draws considerable resources, not in the least in the form of mistakes, causing learning to be subjected to rapidly diminishing returns. Organizational learning includes the capacities to create new competence internally (innovation) and to acquire knowledge in external markets. It also includes methods of efficiently *diffusing* new knowledge through the organization, while keeping the knowledge *within* the organization. Apparently, the acquisition of knowledge in external markets requires *receiver competence,* a competence that also has to be learned. Since competence is human, or team embodied, it is to some extent tradable in the labor or in the stock markets (Eliasson 1990a and 1990b).

While Romer (1986) saw knowledge as an externality that conferred economies of scale to all other factors of production, I reinterpret that idea (Eliasson 1989a and 1990b) in terms of a general organizational knowledge, learned or acquired by the firm as it carries out production and participates in market competition. The accumulated knowledge earns a rent ($\bar{\epsilon}$) that is the rationale for the existence of the firm. In order to exist, however, this knowledge has to be embodied in the organization. If it diffuses too easily, so does the rent and, hence, the firm itself. It has to have the character of property, that is, either to be protected (ownership, patent, copyright) or be proprietary through "tacitness." Since competence is, to a large extent, tacit and acquired through experimental learning, it has no well-defined reproduction value. The difficulties associated with measuring tacit organizational knowledge directly illustrate this and establish the imperfect nature of markets that trade in such assets.

Entrepreneurial competence is defined by Schumpeter [1912] 1934 as the competence to create new combinations that enter the capital market as temporary monopolies ("firms"; 1934). This is the function assigned to the entrepreneur by Schumpeter. The other side of this competence is to spot market imperfections and exploit them. This is the innovative trader of Kirzner (1973). Hence, entrepreneurial activity manifests itself as competition based on the competence to create new organizational knowledge (innovation), thereby reducing the economic value of existing structures of knowledge. The term that I use is *organizational learning,* on which the firm bases its *rent* ($\bar{\epsilon}$)

and, hence, its existence. Competence capital acquired by organizational learning is defined by its rent ($\bar{\epsilon}$). Organizational learning is the essence of the dynamic competition that drives economic growth in Smith (1776); Clark (1887); and Schumpeter [1912] 1934. It explains the divergence between the ex-ante rate of return and the interest rate, and can be interpreted as the force behind the disequilibrium, cumulative process of Wicksell (1898).[3] I call this alternative to the classical Walras-Arrow-Debreu (WAD) model, the Smith-Schumpeter-Wicksell (SSW) model. It is fairly straightforward to demonstrate that the ex-ante difference ($\bar{\epsilon}$) of the SSW economy, based on a belief in a superior competitive situation on the part of the individual, the entrepreneur, or the firm is a powerful economic force that shapes future industrial structures.

This disequilibrium variable $\bar{\epsilon}$ can even be measured. To measure the capital that generates the rent—the content of the knowledge—is, however, impossible, since it embodies the capacity to generate new, previously unknown knowledge. There is, nevertheless, a way to observe the nature of $\bar{\epsilon}$. You need knowledge to organize knowledge creation or acquisition. Hence, one can study *how* organizational learning is organized in firms or acquired in external markets. This has been done in a separate paper (Eliasson 1990a).

This long introduction was needed to orient the rest of the essay. I have introduced the firm, the supply agent as based on tacit organizational knowledge, that is constantly updated and accumulated, using up resources, including the costs of failure. This accumulation process that is fundamental for economic growth, I have called *organizational learning*. The next section introduces the experimentally organized economy (Eliasson 1987 and 1988b) by changing a few assumptions in the classical model. I then present the firm as an organizational learner in that environment. It is established that learning costs are large, being partially incurred through failing business experiments, implying that, at each point in time, organizational learning is subjected to strongly diminishing returns. I also demonstrate how a few modifications of the static, classical model (e.g., entry and exit, and a Salter-type state representation of the economy) are sufficient to create path dependence and nonstationary behavior and to restrict the organizational learning capacity of the individual firm (bounded rationality). Finally, I demonstrate that returns to tacit firm competence ($\bar{\epsilon}$) relate directly to measured total factor productivity growth.

---

3. Note, however, that Wicksell was mostly concerned with (cumulative) inflation. His proposition about the source of inflation can, however, be extended to cover economic growth (see Åkerman 1952; Dahmén and Eliasson 1980).

Experimental Organizational Learning as the Source of Economic Growth

Agents compete by learning to be better. The technology of learning determines agents' competence to figure out what all other agents will do and how markets work. While standard learning literature restricts this competence or knowledge to the choice of optimal forecasting methods to decode the signals emitted by the economic system, the economy I am studying requires a definition of learning that goes beyond the interpretation (by statistical estimation) of codable and tradable information. The accumulation of tacit, human-embodied knowledge makes it necessary to distinguish between the creation and the diffusion of knowledge, i.e., between innovation and learning, each of which possess particular efficiency characteristics and each of which is discussed in different sets of literature.

Once we distinguish between the creation and the diffusion of knowledge, the higher order of learning about the best way to create new economic knowledge (to innovate) enters. The competence to acquire efficient learning techniques is, in turn, subjected to learning, and so on. It is, as Pelikan argues, odd that economics has (for so long) assumed that the most important capital item behind the wealth of a nation, namely economic competence, has always been assumed to be abundant and that its allocation draws no resources (1989). The accumulation and use of economic competence is a dynamic process concerned with the creation and diffusion of new knowledge rather than with the allocation of existing knowledge. The economic value of existing knowledge is constantly destroyed by the creation and diffusion of new knowledge. You can, however, learn to do this better and better, a *learning technology* that you can in turn learn to improve upon. And so on. This is sufficient to preclude predictability at the microdecision level. It introduces trial and error as the normal mode of behavior.

From the Classical Model to the Experimentally Organized Economy

As a decision maker in the market, however, you have to put a halt to this infinite regress in your search for higher orders of learning and awareness in order to be able to reach a decision. To competently realize this "approximation," or choice of decision model, defines the competence of the firm. The social scientist or economist, on the other hand, is not allowed to do the same, because he or she then closes his or her eyes to an entirely new dimension of economic behavior, about which the economists of the Austrian and the Schumpeterian tradition were aware, a dimension that was washed away by the Walras-Arrow-Debreu (WAD) tradition.

My story is most clearly understood if I first relate it to the classical (WAD) model, as it appears in stochastic form in modern learning literature (Blume and Easley 1982; Bray 1982; Frydman 1982; Lindh 1989) or subsets thereof, such as rational expectation or efficient market theory. The following assumptions define the classical model.

1. Agents maximize expected utility—MAX(U).
2. Expectations are formed from subjective probability distributions conditioned by "all available information" (Ω), that is, historic realizations of all stochastic variables—EXP(X) $= P(X|\Omega)$.
3. Agents form (from points 1 and 2) actual, ex-post probability distributions that are identical with the subjective probability distributions under point 2—EX POST $P(X) \equiv P(X|\Omega)$.
4. EX POST $P(X)$ are stationary.[4]

This is the classical model, formulated on a rational expectations mode, as it appears in modern finance (efficient market) and modern learning theory.

Point 4 is needed for economic ("econometric") learning, something made clear by Haavelmo (1944). A steady stream of observations from the realization of $P(X)$ will eventually, and with the precision desired, allow an unbiased estimate of the parameters of $P(X)$.

Point 3 hides the fundamental equilibrium conditions of the classical model that should be given up in any essay on Schumpeterian economics. In no way—says point 3—will the search for information (read: attempts to estimate the parameters of $P[X]$) change the distribution function $P(X)$. Ex ante is always identical to ex post, barring a randomly distributed difference term.

Ex-ante and ex-post distribution functions define the *state space* of the classical model. Changes in state space are occasioned by *events* (Fama et al. 1969), defined as changes in the set of available information or shifts in the conditional probability distribution ($P[X|\Omega]$ to $P[X|\Omega']$), and agents quickly learn the parameters of the new probability distribution $P(X|\Omega')$. Efficient markets immediately return the ex-ante, ex-post distributions to a stationary distribution. This leaves no room for the Schumpeterian innovator or entrepreneur, who changes the parameters of the system, only for the Kirznerian trader or entrepreneur, who equilibrates the system after it has been perturbed.

---

4. Most analyses assume stationarity. There are, however, attempts to break through this restrictive assumption (see Wallis 1980). To avoid a "technical misunderstanding," please note that both points 3 and 4 are stochastic equilibrium conditions. During a learning phase, nonstationarity is possible. To avoid having learning itself affect the stationary equilibrium, learning costs have normally been assumed to be zero. See, however, Fourgeaud, Gouriecroux, and Pradel 1986, where the equilibrium is made dependent on the learning process.

A couple of innocent assumptions, however, prevent you from reverting to the classical model. The capacity to learn about the heterogeneous business opportunities by analytical methods depends on the size of state space. If made sufficiently large, nonstationarity will eventually prevent classical or rational expectations–type learning (Eliasson 1990b). The decision of the firm thereby dramatically changes. Each agent now has to evaluate, at each point in time, not only all future path choices he or she can make, but also how to react to the corresponding choices of all other agents. This requires learning capabilities of higher orders, and establishes *experimental exploration,* into state space as the only viable learnng method, and thereby path dependence.

Now each actor realizes that he or she has to take on business risks that cannot be assessed on the basis of a historic flow of realized economic activity. "Regime shifts" prevent that. History cannot be assumed to have been generated by a "learnable" stationary process.[5] Hence, there will be no insurer willing to pick up the risk on the basis of past risk experience. Pure uncertainty prevails as distinct from computable risks (Knight 1921), and the firm, or the entrepreneur, establishes itself in the market by absorbing this uncertainty on the basis of his or her self-perceived ability to convert uncertainty into computable risks (Eliasson 1990b).[6] (How the firm acquires the organizational competence to do this is the rest of my story, after I have made a few observations from the history of economic thought.)

The Realization Function, or the Stockholm School Connection

You may believe that you understand the mechanisms that determine your economic environment except for random disturbances. You then face a lottery, the expected value of which you can learn by playing repeated games. Computable risk taking is your business. Posit, however, that this assumption about stationarity is wrong. Suppose the parameters of the casino are changed now and then to prevent your learning. The nature of your business risks should now be looked for in the transition from ex-ante plans to ex-post

---

5. Standard, rational expectations–based learning within the WAD framework may even be theoretically impossible. First, the specification of the "boundedly rational" decision models may be both different and misspecified. If this is the case, the parameters of the underlying distributions of fundamentals cannot be estimated by the agents. This becomes obvious if we remember that these distributions themselves represent, at each point in time, the combined behavior of all biased decisions in the economy. Second, to be able to make a decision or operate a "seemingly estimable" decision system, the information-decision model has to be reasonably simple, and, hence, as a rule misspecified. However, if you formulate a realistic interpretation and decision model, it will soon take you outside the domain of estimation techniques that give unbiased parameter estimates.

6. In fact, as an "insurer" on the basis of subjective probability; cf. Keynes 1921.

realizations. The *realization function* is a notion that originated in the thinking of the Stockholm school economists (Wicksell, Myrdal, Lindahl, Svennilson, Lundberg, etc.; see Eliasson 1967 and 1969; Modigliani and Cohen 1961; Palander 1941). In dynamic markets, innovative competitors change the parameters of the game constantly and make the realization function a nonstationary process, thus violating assumptions 3 and 4 in the classical model. The businessman now faces uncertainty and will rush around looking for transformations that allow him or her to compute and predict.[7] By making Schumpeter's unpredictable innovator/entrepreneur the agent that changes the parameters of the economic system and the moving force behind the systematic discrepancies arising out of the realization process, I have established a nice connection between Wicksell and the Stockholm school economists on the one hand, and Adam Smith and the Austrian school and the early Schumpeter on the other—the SSW model. But this unpredictability originating in the path dependence and nonstationarity of the realization process removes the possibility of full information.

The Literary Trail

It is commonly assumed (Romer 1986; von Weizsäcker 1986) that knowledge—in contrast to machine capital—does not depreciate. True, knowledge does not wear down physically from use as machines do. But its value to one firm as a capital input in production depreciates due to its diffusion to other firms. True, this diffusion also speeds up the growth of the economy. Knowledge, however, also depreciates in value to its user from the creation of superior, competing knowledge. Technological competition (by my definition, see Eliasson 1987) destroys the economic value of the knowledge bases on which firms operate. And modern knowledge (technology) from the past has no economic value in today's production, except as an early state by way of which current knowledge has been learned (path dependence; see Eliasson 1989a).[8]

---

7. Rothschild (1974) gives a very simple example of how path dependence can arise in a classical search market setting, even though he does not use the term. A gambler faces the problem of deciding which of two one-armed bandits to play, about one of which (the first) he or she believes he or she knows the probabilities of gain and loss. Whenever trying the second machine, about which he or she knows nothing, he or she compares the random drawing with what he or she believes about the first machine and, accordingly, revises his or her expectations about which machine is the best. As a consequence, his or her choice of machine will depend on the sequence of random drawings he or she happens to pick. This is a typical example of path dependence. In the micro-macro model, similar path dependence arises out of—among other things—the differential entry and exit patterns that depend on the market regime parameter settings, which correspond to the probability parameters of the one-armed bandits.

8. It is instructive to compare this dynamic view of the experimentally organized economy with Hirschleifer's view of overinvestment in R&D (1971) and a number of recent R&D race

Following Menger (1872) and Böhm-Bawerk (1881), von Weizsäcker (1986) distinguishes between three levels of economic activity: (1) *consumption*, (2) *production*, and (3) *innovation*. He establishes the important externality of innovation as the increased potential for new innovations that creates path dependence and concludes that competition policy "must foster competition by innovation and must discourage competition by imitation." This, however, means halting even before Schumpeter (1934) and losing the Wicksellian (1898) and Stockholm school connection altogether. This conclusion makes von Weizsäcker add that "the following generation of economists are called upon to undertake further research with the sagacity of a Böhm-Bawerk and the imagination of a Schumpeter, before we can speak of a definite theory of economic progress." Let me make a try. But such statements make me wonder what the generation between Schumpeter and us did.

First of all, the ex-ante perception of a superior commercial solution (the entrepreneurial idea) is what defines the subjective competence needed to (dare to) set up a business experiment. The hypothesis of this essay is that such entrepreneurial experiments drive the dynamics of the economy and, hence, macroeconomic growth. This was the idea of Smith (1776), Schumpeter (1934), and—broadly interpreted (see Åkerman 1952; Dahmén and Eliasson 1980)—also of Wicksell (1898). This growth process of the SSW model—as we have concluded—is necessarily experimental, since the entrepreneur is frequently wrong. Mistakes have to be counted as part of the learning cost for firms and the economy at large. There is no way of distinguishing clearly between innovation and imitation, only that both destroy (as Schumpeter contended) existing economic values. The essence of growth, hence, is the creation and depreciation (destruction) of economically useful knowledge. That is the same as saying that a large number of business experiments have to be carried out for some, or a few, successful outcomes to occur. The net outcome of the many ensuing capital gains and losses are the costs of growth. The few successes dominate the long-run movement of the entire economy. This establishes the nature of knowledge, as reflected in positive ex-ante $\bar{\epsilon}$, as the competence to create new knowledge that makes other innovations obsolescent, that also compete through the creation of new

---

models (for an overview, see Reinganum 1989) that are based on the classical model. The overinvestment argument has to be based on the assumption that there is only one optimal solution that you can either identify analytically or recognize (as the best) when you find it. Suppose, on the other hand, that "best" is not well defined, and that you will have to compare what is offered with other solutions in order to determine what is best. Then, overinvestment in R&D is a necessary condition for finding the best solution, and a standard information cost of creating successful innovations. Worse still is that however many search investments you make, you can never be sure that you have found the best solution, provided you have made state space (the "urn") sufficiently large or irregular. If you have only *one* mountain in state space, there are efficient algorithms for going to the top; if you are in a mountain range, it is quite another matter to find the highest peak.

knowledge. This *experimentally organized economy* emerges out of the classical WAD model (Eliasson 1987, 1988b, 1990b) as state space (or the opportunity set) is made sufficiently large to make behavior boundedly rational. Tacit organizational competence arises, and free innovative entry in competition with incumbent producers is what sets the dynamics of markets on the move (Eliasson 1991). In the SSW world, Say's law is contradicted and money made nonneutral, as pointed out by Morishima and Catephores (1988). The WAD model becomes useless for a wide variety of applications related to the allocation of resources. But this change of assumptions is what it takes to formulate the competitive process that moves total factor productivity growth. The reader should be aware that this is no small statement to make, even though Schumpeter said it in 1912. In the WAD model economy, populated by an infinite number of infinitely small actors that engage in atomistic competition, such events cannot occur.

New IO theory allows economies of scale and, hence, gives a size dimension to the actors. The game of competition among the few takes place in contestable market theory, the new theory of international trade, and so on, but the analytical problem is still to establish static equilibrium conditions even if the wording conveys a flair of dynamics. No destruction of values occurs. The dynamic market process of Adam Smith (1776), John Bates Clark (1887), and Joseph Schumpeter (1934) cannot be derived from such mathematical structures.

The Firm as an Experimental, Organizational Learner

In the experimentally organized economy, the idea of full information has only one meaning, namely your personalized, subjective conceptualization (hypothesis) of your external environment. This hypothesis of yours requires the implicit assumption by you that most actors (competitors) do not see what you see. This is the rationale for your existence on the basis of your competence or "firm-specific knowledge." The option that your (perceived) competence might make you a winner is what makes you act.[9] This also means that many of you will frequently be fundamentally wrong, a fact that must be part of the learned knowledge base of all rational, surviving firms.

Your Personal View

In the experimentally organized economy, everyone views the world through his or her personal information or interpretation filter. This "personalized

---

9. If all agents perceived your opportunity to earn a rent, the opportunity would be competed away ex ante, and the classical model would require that you also recognized that fact. There would be no ex-ante reason to act. Hence, no one would act; hence, there *would* be a reason to act; hence, if everyone . . . Perfect information diffusion gives rise to paradoxes.

theory" determines success or failure in the market and the heterogeneity of the opportunity set. The way individuals, or teams of individuals in firms, upgrade their economic interpretation filters—through trying it in the market—becomes a decisive part of the performance characteristics of the economy. In turn, this upgrading depends on the compensation or incentives that come with experimental action.[10]

The individual actor looks at the world through his or her ex-ante interpretation model that makes it possible for him or her to calculate and take deliberate steps. This makes firm managers take (for them) rational and deliberate steps that to outsiders may look very daring. This is obvious from the way business firm information systems are designed (Eliasson 1990c). The ways each agent assesses the environment and revises his or her theory about the environment set the parameters of the model economy and determine the experimental path the entire economy takes. (The competence of each agent is partly composed of its *ability to choose the right theory* to act upon, but also on its ability to *identify and correct mistakes*. The first task is a matter of tacit knowledge [intuition]. Analysis enters at the second control step [Eliasson 1990b].)

Joseph Schumpeter was aware of these matters when he made double-entry bookkeeping one of the great discoveries of man (1942, 123). This device made it possible for firms to carry out rational cost and profit calculations. The financial control system of the firm became a device through which an unstructured (uncertain) business situation was converted into a situation of subjectively computable risks, an operationally meaningful proposition that may be interpreted as the foundation of the firm and be attributed to Knight (1921).[11] Coase's (1937) proposition that relative transaction cost differences in coordinating economic activities in hierarchies and in the market were the foundation of the firm, on the other hand, cannot be refuted. Coase failed to define transactions costs empirically. This is a slippery concept, and Dahlman (1979) and later Wärneryd (1990), going through the implications of Coase's proposition, conclude that the only transaction costs left to compare are resource losses due to imperfect information or uncertainty. In my terminology of the experimentally organized economy, such "Coasian" transaction costs then must be due to mistaken business decisions. This is the same as saying that the transaction costs that hold a business together (as a team) are the costs for organizational (experimental) learning. If the firm "fails to learn more than rivals" it breaks up. This notion of the firm, based on its perceived (by the top team) competence to create intellectual order (computability) of an uncertain business situation, also clarifies the largely tacit, nontradable nature of that

---

10. It also depends on the perceived risks.

11. Even though it is somewhat unclear whether Knight really intended this interpretation; see Eliasson 1990b.

competence. The "boundedly rational" vision of the top competent team sets the direction of the firm and defines its "competence" (Eliasson 1990b). The outsider cannot understand it.

The experimentally organized economy also makes life difficult for agents themselves. With a sufficiently large number of actors (including potential entrants), each agent knows he or she will have to act even though he or she does not feel ready to act, because otherwise one or more of the competitors will come up with a better solution. Hence, mistakes will be frequent and a cost will be incurred to keep the growth process in motion.

This suggests that four intellectual processes must be at work simultaneously at different levels within a business organization, namely: one *creative* process aimed at creating the business idea or hypothesis that will ultimately determine the business rent, one *analytical* process to monitor (test) the business experiment, one *operations management* process controlling physical activities, and, finally, one *learning* process that feeds experience back to improve the (creative) business hypothesis. Table 1 summarizes this intellectual structure of the firm as it has to look in the experimentally organized economy. The link between innovation and learning is the concern of this paper. The innovative process cannot be directly observed, only the outcome can. The other three processes are, however, intellectually well structured, since they constitute different forms of communication and, hence, require a code for communication (Eliasson 1976, 1984a, 1990c). Similarly, even though learning is mostly a "tacit" process within the top competent team of the firm, understanding it means looking for an organizational design for the process of recruiting that talent for the team.

One should note, in passing, that the idea of the firm as a principal-agent relationship becomes natural in the experimentally organized economy. Principals have difficulties understanding what downstream agents do in their organizations. Hence, they organize information systems to efficiently monitor and push agents' performance in terms of a well-defined objective vari-

TABLE 1.   The Intellectual Structure of the Firm

Process	Activity
Innovation	Creating the business hypothesis (setting up the experiment)
Analysis	Monitoring performance against the hypothesis; *identification* of mistakes and *correction* of mistakes
Operations	Managing physical production, once business viability has been established through analysis
Learning	Experience feedback to innovation

Source: Eliasson 1990b.

able. I have called this internal learning game MIP (maintain or improve profits) targeting (Eliasson 1976, 236 ff, 258 ff). There is, however, one type of activity that is not as easily monitored, namely the *selection* of innovative talent within the organization.[12] This selection at the top competent team level is much more sophisticated because it also selects those who set the objectives that control talent selection itself. Selection then becomes an integrated part of organizational learning. This is much more fundamental than a traditional allocation problem. It includes the "joint production" (Rosen 1972) of generating both added product value and added firm-specific competence, including the competence to select additional competence. How to prevent inbreeding of old competence (Meyerson 1991; Smith and White 1987) to make way for new, unknown competence without creating chaotic internal organizational problems is no small competence demand on the top competent team.[13]

Measured learning costs are substantial and growing as a share of total costs (Eliasson 1990d). Adding failing business experiments to the cost accounts makes learning costs very large and—in the experimentally organized economy—largely unpredictable. Some additional insight follows from these observations. The more innovative a business activity is, the larger the propensity to fail and the larger the (expected) proportion of learning costs incurred through mistaken decisions. Hence, the larger the ambition to aim for the small probability of a very large success, the stronger (in the aggregate) diminishing returns to learning. And the smaller the incentives to aim for them is, the more difficult it is to appropriate the competence acquired, that is, to prevent imitation. The more pronounced the innovation strategy, in addition, the more important it is for the firm to develop a competence to

---

12. Some partial aspects of this have been analytically studied as an allocation problem in the management hiring and compensation literature (e.g., Harris and Holmström 1982; Holmström 1982a, and 1982b; Ricart i Costa 1987).

13. The notion of learning and competence accumulation as the source of competitive performance in the experimentally organized economy also makes it natural to reinterpret Lazear's (1981) lifetime employment compensation idea in terms of learning. This yields a view of the firm as a habitat of risk-averse but competent employees who buy insurance for future variations in their income streams from the risk-willing owner/entrepreneur by accepting a lower wage than their marginal productivity contributions with an upward tilting of their compensation schedule in the form of unemployment insurance or retirement plans with late payouts. Organizational competence, however, not only includes the task of organizing profitable internal insurance for talented but risk-averse labor, but also the short-term exploitation of internal scale economies by executive "superstars" (Rosen 1981 and 1982). The experimentally organized economy requires risk-willing agents capable of converting an uncertain situation onto an insurable footing and/or agents that act to protect their wealth. Most human beings lack the capacity to act independently in this environment and are in the market trading work input for income and protection. The employment and compensation contract gives this protection but also serves the purpose of locking in both the humans and their talent in a team for a considerable time (Eliasson 1990b).

identify and correct mistakes quickly, that is, to minimize costs of mistakes. These observations point in one direction, namely the growing importance of large-scale organizational technique in creating, protecting, and rapidly commercializing innovations in advanced industrial nations, while at the same time effectively minimizing the incurred experimental costs. Insofar as it is true that creative, innovative activity cannot be efficiently organized within large firms, this suggests that advanced industrial nations will have to develop the particular organizational structure needed to both effectively promote innovative work (perhaps in small firms) and effectively carry innovations to a large industrial scale. This requires the parallel development of sophisticated markets for both small-scale venture activities and daring venture financing needed for a viable experimental organization of the economy (Eliasson 1988a, 1990a, 1990c).

A Generalized Salter-Curve Analysis of Innovative Learning and Enforced Competition

The preceding principal argument for the experimentally organized economy is, of course, the strongest. The realization process may, however (erroneously), be thought of as stochastic, making economic growth appear to be completely stochastic. In this section, I use the Swedish micro-macro (M-M) model (Eliasson 1985a and 1989c) and its selection mechanisms to show that, in this nonlinear, Salter-curve framework, the stationarity assumption has to be eliminated. In another paper (Eliasson 1990a), I have reinforced this conclusion by showing how real firms organize their learning activities and how rapidly diminishing returns (through the costs of failure) are associated with innovative learning. The experimental organization of the economy, hence, is revealed through observing the ways its actors organize their learning.

A market, or the entire economy, can be represented at each point in time by a distribution of potential performance characteristics, such as the rates of return over the interest rate ($\bar{\epsilon}$) shown in fig. 1. These types of distributions—especially if presented as productivity rankings of establishments (see fig. 2)—are often referred to as Salter curves (1960). Each firm is represented in this curve by a ranking on the vertical axis (the columns in figs. 1 and 2), with the width of the column measuring the size of the firm as a percentage of the size of all other firms. Figure 1 shows that, even though the firm indicated increased its rate of return between 1982 and 1992, its ranking declined. Figure 2 shows the same firm's labor productivity and wage cost positions. Finally, each firm has its own potential productivity frontier, under which it operates to position itself on the productivity and rate of return rankings. This is still actual, ex-post performance 1982 and (simulated) 1992. The dynamics of markets, on the other hand, are controlled by the *potential ex-ante set* of

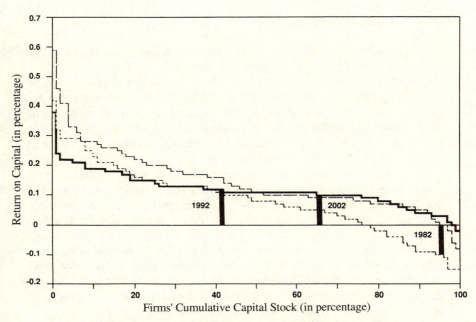

Fig. 1.   Rate of return over the interest rate (ϵ) distributions, 1982, 1992, and 2002. (From experiments in Swedish micro-to-macro model.)

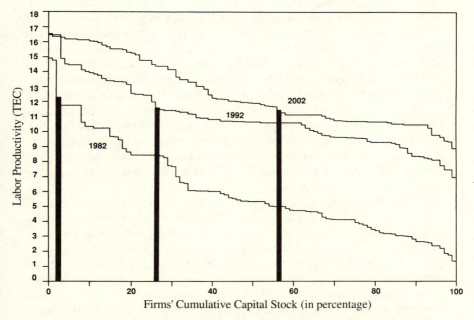

Fig. 2.   Labor productivity distributions, 1982, 1992, and 2002. (From experiments in Swedish micro-to-macro model.)

distributions that capture the planned action of all other firms, including reductions in unused capacity, new entry, and exit.

There is a third set of Salter curves that tell how each firm sees itself positioned relative to other firms. The real world of the experimentally organized economy and its model approximation, the Swedish micro-to-macro model, show large differences between *actual* and *perceived* positions. These ex-ante distributions show the potential for the firm to outbid other firms in wages or in paying higher interest rates.

Learning about one's competitive situation—in reality or in theory—occurs in different dimensions. Prices offered in the market tell how other firms—notably the best firms—view their competitive situation. Competition, production, hiring, and so forth, can also be directly observed. When entering the market, the firm learns directly, for instance, that competitors can do better. Firm management then knows that this can be done and that it had better improve in order not to be pushed down along the Salter distribution and, perhaps, out. Similarly, if the firm finds itself close to the top, it knows that several "closely inferior" firms feel threatened and are taking steps to better their positions through innovation or imitation.

If potential Salter distributions are sufficiently steep and if firms know it, firms—and especially the top, left-hand group—will feel threatened and actively aim to improve their positions on the Salter curve. If such innovative activity, notably through entry, is freely allowed, necessary conditions have been established for maintaining Salter distributions sufficiently steep to move the entire economy through a self-perpetuated competitive process (Eliasson 1985a and 1989c). These conditions become both necessary and sufficient if state space—which I prefer to call the opportunity set (Eliasson 1987 and 1990b)—is sufficiently large. This establishes the link between dynamic competition through entrepreneurship and innovative entry, argued by Smith (1776) to be the critical function behind economic growth, that perpetuates a disequilibrium economic process of the Wicksell (1898) type. The Swedish micro-to-macro (M-M) model exhibits these features. As I have described it, dynamic competition determines entry and exit and, hence, the selective process that creates a path-dependent evolution and nonstationary behavior that prevents classical learning.

The M-M model is deterministic because it "predicts" through deterministic simulation. The question about learning was whether you would be able to learn the structure of the model (to perform that prediction) from observing the output from a large number of such simulations with such precision that it would predict over a chosen future period, barring a stochastic error. This question reduces to three problems: (1) finding an acceptable, estimable approximation of the M-M model, (2) estimating the parameters of that approximate model, and (3) if the error terms between the M-M simulation ("reality") and the corresponding computed model values pass a test for randomness over any chosen simulation period, classical learning is feasible. This is a major experiment to carry out, even on the model, and thus far I have not found the time to do it. The following is, however, sufficient for my argument. The M-M model includes a large number of strong nonlinearities that generate expansions and contractions of the kind that would suggest locally chaotic behavior. Endogenous entry and exit are conditioned by the market parameter settings and irreversibly move the economy along an experimental path that cannot be determined from external observations of the economy, only through knowing its full parameter setting in advance. Thus, the major macroeconomic collapses that can be simulated (Eliasson 1984b) originate endogenously in changing Salter distributions and cannot be predicted on the basis of external observations using known estimable modeling techniques (classical learning). The same collapses can be removed, for instance if entry is allowed (Eliasson 1991), a typical nonlinearity that generates a path-dependent macroevolution of the macroeconomy. This is sufficient to rule out classical learning in the experimental setting of the M-M model.

Organizational Competence, Competition, and Economic Growth

Competence being the ultimate, dominant capital input of a firm, its incentive system should be organized such that returns to the competence to coordinate inputs to the benefit of the owners of the firm are satisfactory. At the firm level, however, such competence has to be more broadly defined than technological competence and "being informed." The top competent team of the firm earns a profit from integrating supply, demand, and financing. Exploiting market imperfections is an important business activity and part of the value that is created. Competence is, however, human or team embodied and not subject to the same contractual property rights as physical goods. It is acquired through experimental learning in the market. It is not easily tradable and difficult to learn or imitate by outsiders if they lack the requisite receiver competence. Failures are frequent. "Obsolete" competence can rarely be replaced by crash learning or innovation programs, especially on a broad, industrywide basis. Strongly diminishing returns to learning rapidly set in due to frequent failures.

Competence coordination and monitoring is a matter of managing people with competence. It involves not only incentives to contribute but also to stay with the team. In this final section, I link innovative competence to firm objectives (profits) and the creation of economic value over and above resources put in (total factor productivity growth, DTFP). I will do this mathematically in terms of the information and monitoring system of a firm as it appears in the Swedish micro-to-macro model. The task is to establish a relationship between the competence rents ($\bar{\epsilon}$), firm total productivity change (DTFP), and growth in output (DQ).

I restrict (for simplicity) measured inputs that produce output (Q) to labor (L) and capital ($\bar{K}$). Variable DX stands for the rate of change in X. Define:

$$\epsilon = PQ - TC , \tag{1}$$

$$TC = wL + (r + \rho - \frac{\Delta p^K}{p^K})K , \tag{2}$$

$$R^{NE} = R^N + (R^N - r)\phi , \tag{3}$$

$$R^N = M\alpha - \rho + \frac{\Delta p^K}{p^K} , \tag{4}$$

$$M = 1 - \frac{w}{p}\frac{1}{\beta} . \tag{5}$$

It follows immediately that:

$$\bar{\epsilon} = R^N - r, \quad \text{and} \tag{6}$$

$$pQ = TC + \bar{\epsilon}K. \tag{7}$$

In equations 1–7, the variables are defined as follows.

R^N = nominal rate of return to total assets K

R^{NE} = nominal rate of return to net worth ($E = K - D$)

ρ = rate of depreciation

M = operating surplus per unit value

D = nominal debt

w = cost per unit of labor input (L)

r = interest rate

p^K = capital goods deflator

p = value-added (Q) deflator

ϕ = D/E

α = pQ/K, capital productivity uncorrected for relative (p, p^K) price change

β = Q/L (labor productivity)

The quantity $\bar{\epsilon}$ is the difference between the rate of return on total assets (R^N) and the interest rate (r) paid by the firm. Figure 2 shows $\bar{\epsilon}$ to be positive or negative. But a firm cannot survive with a negative $\bar{\epsilon}$. Equations 2 and 7 make ($r + \bar{\epsilon}$) the equilibrium price for capital services that exhausts total product value (PQ) when $R^N = r$ and $\bar{\epsilon} = 0$. The condition of $\bar{\epsilon} > 0$ arises—as suggested by McKenzie (1959)—as a consequence of unmeasured capital that is not included in K. This asset has a time dimension in the sense that returns come in with a delay. Even with a negative $\bar{\epsilon}$, the corresponding asset might have a large positive present value. Part of this time dimension can be interpreted as a risk factor that demands a reward (a risk premium). A positive $\bar{\epsilon}$ might also arise out of the competence of firms in exploiting imperfections in other markets. This "trading competence" is an asset in itself. If convergence prevails, firms perform a socially useful service when speculating in imperfect markets by pushing prices toward equilibrium values. The cost for such Kirznerian (1973) "trading" is the speculative return to traders.

There is a lot to say about the present value of future $\bar{\epsilon}$. I have gone through those elaborations in Eliasson 1990b. To the extent that $\bar{\epsilon}$ measures value created by unmeasured capital, it must have something to do with economic growth. Therefore, I prove the following theorem (see the Appendix):

$$DQ = s_1 DL + s_2 D\bar{K} + \frac{\Delta\epsilon}{pQ} \qquad (8)$$

Equation 8 tells that the rate of change in Q ($DQ = \Delta Q/Q$) is identical to a weighted average of the rates of change in labor input (DL) and capital input ($D\bar{K}$) plus the money change in excess profits ($\Delta\epsilon$) as a share of value added. The weights are the shares of wages and capital costs respectively of value added.

Equation 8 is an identity that expresses a profit variable in terms of a weighted average of volume inputs and outputs. To go on, we need assumptions about production technology that restricts the economy that generates these data. Many technologies are compatible with constant income shares s_1

and s_2, the most well known being the power function (the so-called Cobb-Douglas) specification.

After differentiation, the entire class of functions

$$Q = CL^{s_1}K^{s_2}T \tag{9}$$

becomes equation 8, where shift factor T represents exogenous disembodied technical change. From equations 8 and 9, total factor productivity change becomes

$$DTFP = DT = \Delta\epsilon/pQ \tag{10}$$

under Cobb-Douglas technology. This is enough for my purpose. I have demonstrated—for one particular production technology—that the estimated (on specification 8) shift factor (DTFP) picks up a host of economic influences related to the allocation of resources and the exercising of competence within the firm. As a consequence, the return on that unmeasured capital—which I have labeled $\bar{\epsilon}$—also shows up in the "technical shift factor." This competence input—by definition—also includes the ability to deal with uncertainty (successfully taking business risks).

This technology factor, however, also picks up the competence of the entrepreneur or trader exploiting market imperfections, for example, successfully hiring talented people at lower wages or salaries than their marginal productivities. Capital gains will also appear in ϵ. Since capital gains also result from trading in imperfect markets, they reflect the competence of the entrepreneur to trade and should not be deflated away in productivity measurements. This competence can be exercised through the formation of synergistic teams, in which individual contributions are magnified through the exercising of top entrepreneurial competence. Scale effects originating in top entrepreneurial knowledge make markets imperfect by definition. Positive value additions to output are created, whether the firm operates as a Kirznerian equilibrator or trader or imitator, making money from moving the economy closer to equilibrium, or as a Schumpeterian entrepreneur, enhancing productivity by changing the parameters of the system. It is not, however, universally accepted that such improvements in allocational efficiency should appear as technical changes in macroeconomic production-function analysis, and much work has been devoted to correcting price indexes for the effects of market imperfections. (For a discussion, see Färe and Grosskopf 1990; Morrison 1990).[14] This analysis, hence, merges a theory of organizational change

---

14. Assume equilibrium prices. A new competitive situation is reflected in a new set of equilibrium prices, and all quantities adjust to this new price configuration along the production

and macroeconomic growth. Organizational learning endogenizes macroeconomic growth.

The preceding discussion raises a profound question. If imperfections in markets are not fundamentally due to asymmetrically distributed information or slow learning or adjustment behavior, but rather to fundamental inconsistencies in beliefs, competence endowments, or the formation of business judgments, actions taken on the basis of such inconsistent opinions will constantly reshape the structures that, any time, represent the productivity characteristics of the firm or the economic system, which, in turn, shape future ex-ante perceptions of what is to come, and so on. The path the economy takes will generate ex-ante/ex-post realizations that will be reflected in the shift factor DTFP in equation 10 as positive or negative contributions to output. This essay has been devoted to showing that the use of economic knowledge embodied in the organization of the firm or the economy, notably the organization of human competence, determines the character of these value contributions. The ultimate organizational technology of a nation then becomes the art of organizing itself, such that these value-added contributions are steadily positive. Then economic growth occurs.

APPENDIX: PROOF OF EQUATION 8

From equations 1 and 2,

$$PQ = wL + (r + \rho - \frac{\Delta p^K}{p^K})K + \epsilon ,$$

take differences, assuming p, w, r, p^K are fixed,

$$P \cdot \Delta Q \equiv w\Delta L + [r + \rho - \frac{\Delta p^K}{p^K}]p^K\Delta\bar{K} + \Delta\epsilon .$$

Thus,

$$\frac{\Delta Q}{Q} = DQ \equiv \frac{wL}{pQ}DL + \frac{[r + \rho - \frac{\Delta p^K}{p^K}]\Delta p^K\bar{K}}{pQ} \cdot D\bar{K} + \frac{\Delta\epsilon}{pQ} ;$$

---

frontiers. This is the method of computable equilibrium modeling. The a priori restriction on production technology usually demands a particular price index to leave the shift factor (DTFP) invariant to such adjustments.

$$DQ = s_1 DL + s_2 D\bar{K} + \frac{\Delta \epsilon}{pQ} \; ;$$

$$s_1 = \frac{wL}{pQ} \; ;$$

$$s_2 = \frac{(r + \rho - \frac{\Delta p^K}{p^K})p^K \bar{K}}{pQ} \; .$$

Q.E.D.

REFERENCES

Åkerman, J. 1952. "Innovationer och kumulativa förlopp" (Innovations and Cumulative Economic Developments). *Ekonomisk Tidskrift* 54:185–202.

Anderson, G. M., and R. D. Tollison. 1982. "Adam Smith's Analysis of Joint-Stock Companies." *Journal of Political Economy* 90:1237–56.

Arrow, K. J. 1959. "Toward a Theory of Price Adjustment." In *The Allocation of Economic Resources*, ed. M. Abramowitz et al. Stanford, Calif.

Arrow, K. J. 1962. "The Economic Implications of Learning by Doing." *Review of Economic Studies* 29:155–73.

Blume, L. E., and D. Easley. 1982. "Learning to Be Rational." *Journal of Economic Theory* 26:340–51.

Bray, M. 1982. "Learning, Estimation, and the Stability of Rational Expectations." *Journal of Economic Theory* 26:318–39.

Böhm-Bawerk, E. von. 1881. *Rechte und Verhältnisse vom Standpunkte der Volkswirtschaftlichen Güterlehre*. Innsbruck.

Clark, J. B. 1887. "The Limits of Competition." *Political Science* 2 (1): 45–61.

Coase, R. H. 1937. "The Nature of the Firm." *Economica* 4:386–405.

Dahlman, C. J. 1979. "The Problem of Eternality." *Journal of Law and Economics* 2:141–62.

Dahmén, E., and G. Eliasson. 1980. "Företagaren i det ekonomiska skeendet" (The Entrepreneur in the Market Environment). In *Industriell utveckling i Sverige: Teori och verklighet under ett sekel* (Industrial Development in Sweden: Theory and Practice during a Century), ed. E. Dahmén and G. Eliasson. Stockholm: IUI.

Day, R. H., and G. Eliasson, eds. 1986. *The Dynamics of Market Economies*. Stockholm: IUI; Amsterdam: North-Holland.

Eliasson, G. 1967. *Kreditmarknaden och industrins investeringar*. Stockholm: IUI.

Eliasson, G. 1969. *The Credit Market, Investment, Planning, and Monetary Policy— An Econometric Study of Manufacturing Industries*. Stockholm: IUI.

Eliasson, G. 1976. *Business Economic Planning—Theory, Practice, and Comparison*. New York: Wiley.

Eliasson, G. 1984a. "Informations- och styrsystem i stora företag" (Information and Control Systems in Large Business Organizations). In Eliasson-Fries-Jagrén-Oxelheim, *Hur styrs storföretag? En studie av informationshantering och organisation* (How Are Large Business Groups Managed? A Study of Information Handling and Organization), ed. G. Eliasson, et al. IUI—Liber, Kristianstad: IUI-Liber.

Eliasson, G. 1984b. "Micro Heterogeneity of Firms and the Stability of Industrial Growth." *Journal of Economic Behavior and Organization* 5.

Eliasson, G. 1985a. *The Firm and Financial Markets in the Swedish Micro-to-Macro Model—Theory, Model, and Verification.* Stockholm: IUI.

Eliasson, G. 1985b. "De svenska storföretagen—en studie av internationaliseringens konsekvenser för den svenska ekonomin." In *De svenska storföretagen* (The Giant Swedish Multinationals). Stockholm: IUI.

Eliasson, G. 1986. "Kompetens, kommunikation och kunskapsuppbyggnad" (Competence, Communication, and Knowledge Accumulation). In *Kunskap, information och tjänster,* ed. G. Eliasson et al. Stockholm: IUI.

Eliasson, G. 1987. *Technological Competition and Trade in the Experimentally Organized Economy.* IUI Research Report no. 32. Stockholm: IUI.

Eliasson, G. 1988a. *The International Firm: A Vehicle for Overcoming Barriers to Trade and a Global Intelligence Organization Diffusing the Notion of a Nation.* IUI Working Paper no. 201. Stockholm: IUI.

Eliasson, G. 1988b. "Schumpeterian Innovation, Market Structure, and the Stability of Industrial Development." In Hanusch 1988.

Eliasson, G. 1989a. "The Dynamics of Supply and Economic Growth—How Industrial Knowledge Accumulation Drives a Path-dependent Economic Process." In *Industrial Dynamics,* ed. R. Carlsson. Boston: Kluwer Academic Publishers.

Eliasson, G. 1989b. *The Economics of Coordination, Innovation, Selection, and Learning—A Theoretical Framework for Research in Industrial Economics.* IUI Working Paper no. 235. Stockholm: IUI.

Eliasson, G. 1989c. *Modeling Long-Term Macroeconomic Growth as a Micro-based, Path-dependent, Experimentally Organized Economic Process.* IUI Working Paper no. 220. Stockholm: IUI.

Eliasson, G. 1990a. "A European Market for Managerial Competence." Paper presented at the conference on "Financial Regulation and Monetary Arrangements after 1992," Marstrand, Sweden.

Eliasson, G. 1990b. "The Firm as a Competent Team." *Journal of Economic Behavior and Organization* 13(3).

Eliasson, G. 1990c. "The Firm, Its Objectives, Its Controls, and Its Organization." IUI Working Paper no. 266; IUI, Stockholm.

Eliasson, G. 1990d. "The Knowledge-based Information Economy." In Eliasson et al. 1990.

Eliasson, G. 1991. "Deregulation, Innovative Entry, and Structural Diversity as a Source of Stable and Rapid Economic Growth." *Journal of Evolutionary Economics,* no. 1: 49–63.

Eliasson, G., S. Fölster, T. Lindberg, T. Pousette, and E. Taymaz. 1990. *The Knowledge-based Information Economy.* Stockholm: IUI.

Fama, E. F., et al. 1969. "The Adjustment of Stock Prices to New Information." *International Economic Review* 10:1–21.

Fourgeaud, C., C. Gourieroux, and J. Pradel. 1986. "Learning Procedures and Convergence to Rationality." *Econometrica* (4): 845–68.

Frydman, R. 1982. "Toward an Understanding of Market Processes: Individual Expectations, Learning, and Convergence to Rational Expectations Equilibrium." *American Economic Review* 72 (4): 652–68.

Färe, R., and S. Grosskopf. 1990. "Theory and Calculation of Productivity Indexes Revisited." Department of Economics, University of Illinois. Mimeo.

Haavelmo, T. 1944. "The Probability Approach in Econometrics." *Econometrica* 12, suppl.: 1–115.

Hanusch, H., ed. 1988. *Evolutionary Economics—Applications of Schumpeter's Ideas*. Cambridge: Cambridge University Press.

Harris, M., and B. Holmström. 1982. "A Theory of Wage Dynamics." *Review of Economic Studies* 49:315–33.

Hirschleifer, J. 1971. "The Private and Social Value of Information and the Reward of Inventive Activity." *American Economic Review* 61(4): 561–74.

Holmström, B. 1982a. "Managerial Incentives—A Dynamic Perspective." In *Essays in Honor of Lars Wahlbeck*. Helsinki: Swedish School of Economics.

Holmström, B. 1982b. "Moral Hazard in Teams." *Bell Journal of Economics* 13 (2): 324–40.

Keynes, J. M. 1921. *A Treatise on Probability*. London: Macmillan.

Kirzner, I. 1973. *Competition and Entrepreneurship*. Chicago: University of Chicago Press.

Knight, F. 1921. *Risk, Uncertainty, and Profit*. Boston: Houghton Mifflin.

Lazear, E. P. 1981. "Agency, Earnings Profiles, Productivity, and Hours Restrictions." *American Economic Review* 71 (4): 606–20.

Lindh, T. 1989. "Lessons from Learning about Rational Expectations." IUI Working Paper no. 238. IUI, Stockholm.

McKenzie, L. N. 1959. "On the Existence of General Equilibrium for a Competitive Market." *Econometrica* 27 (1): 54–71.

Menger, C. 1872. *Grundsätze der Volkswirtschaftslehre*. Vienna.

Meyerson, E. 1991. "The Recruitment Processes for Leadership—Internal Dynamics and External Control." (Ph.D. diss., University of Stockholm).

Mill, J. S. 1848. *Principles of Political Economy with Some of Their Applications to Social Philosophy*. London: Little Brown.

Modigliani, F., and K. Cohen. 1961. *The Role of Anticipation and Plans in Economic Behavior*. Urbana: University of Illinois Press.

Morishima, M., and G. Catephores. 1988. "Anti–Say's Law versus Say's Law: A Change in Paradigm." In Hanusch 1988.

Morrison, C. J. 1990. "*Market Power, Economic Profitability and Production Growth Measurement; An Integrated Structural Approach*." NBER Working Paper no. 3355, National Bureau of Economic Research.

Palander, T. 1941. "Om 'Stockholmsskolans' begrepp och metoder." *Ekonomisk Tidskrift*, Årgång 43: 88–143.

Pelikan, P. 1989. "Evolution, Economic Competence, and the Market for Corporate Control." *Journal of Economic Behavior and Organization* 12:279–303.

Reinganum, J. 1989. "The Timing of Innovation, Research, Development, and Diffusion." In *Handbook of Industrial Organization,* ed. R. Schmalensee and R. Willig. Amsterdam: North-Holland.

Ricart i Costa, J. E. 1987. "On Managerial Contracting with Asymmetric Information." Paper presented to the EARIE Conference, Madrid.

Romer, P. M. 1986. "Increasing Returns and Long-term Growth." *Journal of Political Economy* 94 (4): 1002–37.

Rosen, S. 1972. "Learning by Experience as Joint Production." *Quarterly Journal of Economics* 86 (3): 366–82.

Rosen, S. 1981. "The Economics of Super Stars." *American Economic Review* 71 (5): 845–58.

Rosen, S. 1982. "Authority, Control, and the Distribution of Earnings." *Bell Journal of Economics* 13 (3): 311–23.

Rothschild, M. 1974. "A Two-Armed Bandit Theory of Pricing." *Journal of Economic Theory* 9:185–202.

Ruist, E. 1950. "Vad är produktivitet?" (What is Productivity?). In *Industriproblem 1950.* Stockholm: IUI.

Ruist, E. 1960. *Industriföretagets produktionseffektivitet: Några mätningsmetoder* (Production Efficiency of the Industrial Firm: Some Methods of Measurements). Stockholm: IUI.

Salter, W. E. G. 1960. *Productivity and Technical Change.* Cambridge: Cambridge University Press.

Schumpeter, J. A. 1934. *The Theory of Economic Development.* Cambridge, Mass.: Harvard University Press.

Schumpeter, J. A. 1942. *Capitalism, Socialism, and Democracy.* New York: Harper and Row.

Smith, A. 1776. *An Inquiry into the Nature and Causes of the Wealth of Nations.* Reprint. New York: Modern Library, 1937.

Smith, M., and M. C. White. 1987. "Strategy, CEO, Specialization, and Success." *Administration Science Quarterly* 32:263–80.

Stigler, G. J. 1961. "The Economics of Information." *Journal of Political Economy* 69 (3): 213–25.

von Weizsäcker, Ch. 1986. "Rights and Relations in Modern Economic Theory." In Day and Eliasson 1986.

Wallis, K. F. 1980. "Econometric Implications of the Rational Expectations Hypothesis." *Econometrica* 48 (1): 49–73.

Wärneryd, K. 1990. *Economic Conventions: Essence in Institutional Evolution.* Stockholm: EFI and Stockholm School of Economics.

Westerman, J. 1768. *Om de svenske näringarnes undervigt gentemot de utländske dymedelst en trögare arbetsdrift* (On the Inferiority of the Swedish Compared to Foreign Manufacturers because of a Slower Work Organization). Stockholm.

Wicksell, K. [1898]. 1965. *Geldzins und Güterpreise* (Interest and Prices).

Commentary

William S. Comanor

In his essay, "Business Competence, Organizational Learning, and Economic Growth," Eliasson suggests that the general equilibrium tradition of Walras, Arrow, and Debreu [WAD] has led us astray. Particularly in matters that determine the wealth of nations, he argues that it has little to offer. That tradition ignores various concerns that, according to Eliasson, are critical to determining international distributions of income and wealth, so we should look in other directions for insights in this area. He implies (but does not state) that WAD's focus on optimizing consumer welfare for settled technologies and fixed levels of resources is a second-order concern of much less importance.

The critical assumption that Eliasson questions is that "economic competence has always been assumed to be abundant and that its allocation draws no resources." To Eliasson, economic competence is the most important item that determines national well-being; yet related allocation issues are typically ignored. He suggests that economic competence is the most essential resource from which maximum consumer welfare is achieved. To consider it fixed and outside the realm of economic concern is to ignore this most essential item.

The question of economic competence raises issues that do not often arise within the dominant general equilibrium tradition. Perhaps that is because equilibrium conditions are set at the margin, while questions of relative economic competence typically concern inframarginal units of output. Economic competence, which is translated into effectiveness or efficiency, can only be appraised relative to some standard, so we are inevitably concerned with the relative performance of different individuals and firms. This question deals with the relative costs and relative quality levels of different firms in the same industry, although these differences may extend across firms from different countries. So what is at issue here is the distribution of rents that arise from different levels of competence across firms and, often, across nations.

What Eliasson's focus directs us to is Ricardian economics. The essential results of that branch of economics are well known: prices and quantities are set by the least productive or least competent producer. Moreover, such producers define the marginal conditions in an industry so that prices are set in terms of their costs, while other, more productive firms achieve additional profits or rents according to their differential efficiency.

Recall another result from Ricardian economics. It is that prices paid by consumers for any particular good or service depend on the marginal or least productive producer. On the other hand, profits for productive or competent firms depend on inframarginal results; of course, no profits are earned by producers at the margin. While these results are well known, they have considerable bearing for the importance of the question of economic competence that Eliasson raises. What these results suggest is that there can be substantial returns to economic competence, to be earned by more productive producers, even while the prices paid by all consumers depend on the production costs of the least productive or least competent suppliers. Thus, consumer prices, like all final equilibrium positions, do not depend on the achievements of the more competent firms in an industry unless the productive capacity of these firms permits them to expand output so greatly as to absorb the entire industry.

These results, standard in Ricardian economics, indicate that, for products exchanged in world markets, relative business competence and relative efficiency do not affect consumer prices and quantities as much as they determine the international distribution of Ricardian rents. While consumer prices can be the same in all countries, and regardless of whether the product is produced by a more or less efficient producer, more effective firms will achieve a substantial return that is associated with their relative economic competence.

While these results were defined originally for homogeneous products produced at different costs, they also apply to products with different levels of embodied quality. The price for a quality-adjusted product is set by the least effective producer, who may be the seller of a poor-quality item. So long as we are dealing with a competitive industry, this type of producer is the marginal supplier on whose basis the market price is set.

These results are implicit in Eliasson's discussion of economic competence. As in the world of Ricardo, they are exogenous to the supplying firm at any time. But where Ricardian economics stops with a discussion of how these rents are generated, Eliasson is equally concerned with how they are used. He is interested not only in the international distribution of such rents, but also in how different countries use these rents once acquired. The response that they contribute to the consumption standards of the owners of the firm is not sufficient to Eliasson. Indeed, he raises the largely political question of how a society employs these rents and suggests that the answer to this question has critical importance for a country's further development. First, these rents can simply be used for consumption purposes by the owners of the firm, who may be the wealthier class in a given society. On the other hand, they can be employed directly by the achieving firm or firms to develop new technology and to contribute to additional economic competence. Or, if this is not done by a particular firm, the rents can be taxed away and employed elsewhere. This is a major distributive factor for the wealth positions of different nations, but it is one, as Eliasson points out, that is not captured or examined in the dominant general equilibrium tradition.

A second issue that Eliasson considers is how economic competence is acquired, and notes that such issues have long been ignored. One reason for this meager attention is the assumption, implicit in various discussions, that the relevant elements of economic competence could all be purchased in the marketplace, so there was little reason to believe that substantial differences would persist in long-run equilibrium. The argument went as follows. There was a market for management within which competence was embodied so that it would be quickly diffused across firms and countries. As this diffusion process occurred, differences in economic competence or effectiveness would disappear and so would the Ricardian rents that followed from these differences.

While this conclusion followed from the assumption that a competitive market existed for management services, to Eliasson it was not quite so simple. He argues that firms have to be organized in specific ways to search for improved learning and economic competence. To this end, he considers what he calls the intellectual structure of the firm—its receptivity to new ideas, new products, and new production techniques. While Eliasson's discussion is useful, there are still large gaps in our understanding of why some firms and countries are much more effective in these areas than others. After all, a large-scale market for management exists, so we still must ask why some firms take effective advantage of this market but not others.

These are all issues that call for further exploration. While Eliasson suggests some factors that have a bearing on these issues, his discussion leaves many unanswered questions. For example, one sees an increasing number of joint ventures across international boundaries. How important are such ventures as a vehicle for diffusing business competence across nations? Recent joint ventures in the automobile industry between U.S. and Japanese firms were justified in this regard, so there is much to be learned from their results. Such matters relate to the effectiveness or performance of the market for management and economic competence. Essentially, Eliasson points out that it cannot simply be assumed that an efficient market in this area solves all such problems. And, in this regard, he is surely correct.

In his essay, Eliasson has raised some important issues that have a bearing on the relative standing of firms and nations. What is unfortunately apparent is that there still remain a vast number of unanswered questions. There is much work to be done.

The Role of Positive-Sum Games in Economic Growth

Burton H. Klein

Competitiveness in international markets depends on the relative rate of improvement in a country's market basket of goods measured in terms of better quality products and reductions in relative prices. For example, inasmuch as Japanese automobile manufacturers have gained an impressive export advantage by providing, at lower prices, the technical characteristics commonly associated with European automobiles, Japanese luxury cars will soon be passing Mercedes Benzes and BMWs on German autobahns. When, in international competition, the price of a product produced in one country declines relative to the price of similar products manufactured elsewhere, this indicates that firms in that country obtained an advantage by exploiting previously undisclosed opportunities.

Changes in relative prices depend on the relationship between average wage rates and productivity increases. Today, wage-rate differences among major industrial countries are less than 5 percent. Therefore, to achieve a relative price advantage, a country's increases in wage rates must be kept in line with its productivity increases (Bureau of Labor Statistics 1989a). As described by the U.S. Bureau of Labor Statistics, the more rapidly wage rates increase in relation to productivity rates, the more rapidly unit-wage costs will increase.

As table 1 shows, during the past ten years, average unit-wage costs in Japanese manufacturing increased at a slower rate than in the other industrial countries, partially because annual increases in wage rates slowed from 15 percent to 8 percent and partially because the Japanese productivity rate was almost 50 percent higher. Although, as countries, they experienced smaller increases in productivity, by their firms exercising a high degree of wage constraint West Germany, the Netherlands, and Belgium were able to feature relatively small increases in unit-wage costs. In contrast, in France, Italy, Sweden, and the United Kingdom, increases in unit-wage costs were twice as rapid.

TABLE 1. Percentage Changes in the Economic Performance of Nine Industrialized Countries, 1973–88

	Unit-Labor Cost	Wage Rate	Employment	Productivity Growth	Output Growth
United States	4.5	7.1	−0.2	2.5	2.4
Japan	2.1	7.9	0.1	5.7	5.8
Belgium	3.8	9.7	−2.9	5.7	1.8
France	8.5	12.2	−1.8	3.7	1.0
West Germany	3.6	7.0	−1.2	3.3	1.3
Italy	11.4	16.7	−0.9	4.7	3.8
Netherlands	2.8	7.2	−1.6	4.3	1.7
Sweden	7.9	11.1	−0.7	2.9	1.4
United Kingdom	9.9	13.5	−2.7	3.3	0.2

Source: U.S. Bureau of Labor Statistics, "Output, Employment, Hours, and Compensation in Manufacturing" (August, 1989).

Relative changes in unit-wage costs obviously have a bearing on changes in relative prices; for example, it is no accident that, unlike any other industrial country, the average relative prices of Japanese manufactured products, as measured by the price deflator, have declined about 0.5 percent annually during the past ten years (Bureau of Labor Statistics 1989). However, because quality is not taken into account, relative changes in unit-wage costs can only be used to make rough predictions of balance of payments differences.

The following data were obtained from publications of the International Monetary Fund. In terms of the IMF measure (SDRs), during the period from 1981 to 1987, the countries with the largest export surpluses were Japan (about 45 billion), West Germany (about 33 billion), the Netherlands (about 6 billion), and Belgium (about 3 billion). In contrast, during the same period, the U.S. trade deficit averaged almost 85 billion, France's was about 7 billion, and the United Kingdom's trade deficit rose from 1.5 billion in 1982 to 12 billion in 1988 (International Monetary Fund 1989). Though I understand that its balance of payments deficit is quite large, Sweden is not an IMF member. The important exception was Italy, which, although featuring the highest increases in unit-wage costs, somehow managed to reduce its balance of payments deficit to zero. However, this was accompanied by more than twice the decline in the value of the lira than occurred with respect to the value of the dollar (Economic Report of the President 1990, 418).

The preceding discussion implies that opportunity-seeking competition provides a constraint on wage-rate increases and acts as a stimulus to productivity performance. However, inasmuch as both depend on key differences between zero- and positive-sum games, some important theoretical points will be taken up first.

Open- versus Closed-System Paradigms

In the preface to *Risk, Uncertainty, and Profit* (written in 1915), Frank Knight observed:

> I must regard it as one of the major errors in the classical tradition that it failed, and still largely fails to make a sharp and correct theoretical distinction between the working of a system under given conditions, including movement towards equilibrium, and changes in the given conditions or content of the system itself. (1921, 19)

To resolve the dilemma posed by Knight, it is necessary to distinguish between closed- and open-system paradigms. Classical economics is based on a closed-system paradigm. Within such a system, household utility functions are assumed to be independently determined, and firms' production functions (i.e., technological recipes) are assumed to remain unchanged. Indeed, according to the classical theory of competition, in a static equilibrium, firms will employ identical production functions. To be sure, new ideas may alter the balance in the form of shifting demand or supply curves; but, once such exogenous events are taken into account, the economy is always seen as returning to a safe, static equilibrium. Hence, except for such events when an entire economic system is brought into equilibrium via the law of supply and demand, it is closed.

In contrast, by engaging in rivalry, members of an open system interact to change their ideas. In Knight's terms, the "content" of an open system will change; in my terms, "initial conditions" will change. As an illustration, assume that, initially, common market competition took the form of designing, say, German automobiles in terms of German tastes, Swedish cars in terms of Swedish tastes, and so forth. It can be safely assumed that when, on the basis of negligible tariff barriers, such products were sold in various European countries, firms were required to interact. No doubt, during the "auctions" involved in keeping inventories of unsold products to a minimum, some firms fared better than others. Consequently, if a firm hoped to be more successful in future auctions, opportunities had to be discovered for either more rapidly improving the quality of its products or reducing its prices—which, in either event, required a greater degree of risk taking. The Japanese challenge originated from discovering a concept to lower costs and bring about impressive improvements in quality simultaneously.

Escaping an Unwelcome Tax Collector

Suppose that a firm in one or another industry takes a significant technological risk to develop a new opportunity for improving its competitive position.

When successful it will, of course, impose competitive risks on its rivals. As a consequence, when highly successful in one round of the game, a firm will benefit from a "negative tax" in the form of increased profits and sales while its rivals will have to pay a "positive tax" in the form of reduced profits and sales. Accordingly, firms will have an incentive to innovate to escape a tax that might be imposed by rivals. When the difference between winning big and losing big is large in one or another industry, the average propensity to engage in risk taking (PERK) will be high, as will be the rate of progress. At the other extreme, when the tax difference approaches zero, firms will neither take risks nor impose them on rivals. This is the special and limiting case of a closed system.

However, risk taking per se (e.g., gambling in lotteries) does not result in economic progress. Rather, the competitive search for opportunities by which to escape the positive tax is the impetus. Risk taking enters the picture because the more ambitious the advance (e.g., an automobile engine without spark plugs as compared with a slightly better spark plug), the more risk and uncertainty will be involved.

Following the distinction made in the physical sciences, a static phenomenon is described as one in which initial conditions remain unchanged and a dynamic phenomenon is one in which initial conditions change. From this point of view, a closed-system paradigm is to be associated with unchanging production functions (i.e., technological recipes), hence, with static phenomena, and an open-system paradigm with changes in initial conditions, hence with dynamic phenomena, that is, economic evolution.

The Concept of a Dynamic Equilibrium

The executives of firms do not, of course, have any way to predict how much risk their rivals are taking in their R&D portfolios. Hence, they must base their decisions on the release of newly developed products into the marketplace. If, on the basis of such information, it is ascertained that a firm has been too cautious, there will be an incentive to increase its degree of risk taking during the next round of the game. On the other hand, firms can, and do, go out of business by betting on highly risky projects that are not likely to materialize within five years while their rivals are betting on projects likely to pay off in two years or so. Consequently, there is a tendency for firms to engage in a mutual readjustment process in which the value of PERK is held within rather narrow limits. When this happens, then, based on my measure of competition, the rate of progress measured in terms of the productivity rate will remain approximately constant: such steady state evolution is described as a "dynamic equilibrium."

In the German edition (1912) of *Theory of Economic Development*, Schumpeter wrote:

a dynamic equilibrium does not exist. Development in its ultimate nature consists of the disturbances of an existing static equilibrium and does not have a tendency to return to a previous or any other equilibrium. Development alters the data of a static economy. . . . Development and equilibrium are opposite phenomena excluding each other. Not that a static economy is characterized by a static equilibrium and a dynamic economy by a dynamic equilibrium; on the contrary, equilibrium exists only in a static economy. Economic equilibrium is essentially a static equilibrium. (1934)

When Schumpeter wrote this passage shortly after the turn of the century there may have been only one meaning attached to an equilibrium. To show that is not true today, however, consider the *Random House Dictionary*'s description of an equilibrium: "A state of rest or balance due to the actions of balancing forces." In the field of economics, a static equilibrium can be described as a condition that, when disturbed, will return to a state of rest. On the other hand, a state of *balance* need not imply a return to a previous equilibrium. The example provided in the same dictionary is that of a chemical equilibrium "in which chemical action and its reverse reaction proceed at identical rates." However, in a chemical equilibrium, there is no return to a point of rest; initial conditions constantly change.

In the field of economics, a dynamic equilibrium has the same flavor as a chemical equilibrium. First, a dynamic equilibrium involves opposing forces, that is, as in any other game, in each round there are winners and losers. Second, in the economic game, there is likely to be a balance of opposing forces because, as I have pointed out, in industries in which firms compete against well-known rivals, the best strategy for any player consists of not taking significantly greater nor lesser risks than opponents. Though a Nash equilibrium is usually described as being static, in which one firm will not change its pricing decisions if another does not, it also can be used to describe a dynamic equilibrium. If other firms do not change their propensity to engage in risk taking, a particular firm will have no incentive to change its PERK. In such an equilibrium, technological recipes change at more or less constant rates.

Positive-Sum Games

A static equilibrium situation is one in which demand is elastic with respect to a one-time price reduction, as, for example, households that substitute tea for coffee when the relative price of the former declines. In contrast, a dynamic positive-sum game is one in which a wider and wider number of consumers respond to a series of price reductions and quality improvements, as, for example, more people will enter the market when the price of television sets, computers, or high-grade cameras declines and their quality improves. Thus, whereas static equilibrium analyses are based on a closed-system paradigm and the associated concept of a zero-sum game, dynamic equilibrium analyses are based on an open-system paradigm and, because changes in initial conditions are involved, they are described as dynamic games.

Neither in zero-sum nor positive-sum games is the market response known in advance. Suppose that a firm in one or another industry acts on the assumption that the elasticity of demand for the industry as a whole is known in probabilistic terms and it undertakes a series of experiments (commonly described as Bayesian experiments) to determine the actual market response. After reducing its prices by 10 percent (with other firms in the industry following suit), output in the industry may or may not increase. In either event, once the experiment has run its course, the industry will return to a static equilibrium situation.

Of course, all this assumes that, once reached, the new static equilibrium will be stable. However, because a clever entrepreneurial team that is able to imagine and deduce can outperform an entrepreneurial team that can only deduce, no static equilibrium is stable, that is, a firm that has no ability whatsoever to innovate is in grave danger. True, before the avalanche of foreign imports, the high costs of entering an industry often served to minimize this danger. Today, however, only under two circumstances is the value of PERK likely to sink to zero. The first is when industries are shielded from foreign competition by high transportation costs (e.g., the cement and burial industries). The second is when propagandistic advertising is more appealing to consumers than genuinely improved products (e.g., the cosmetics and high-fashion industries). At the other extreme, in positive-sum games, PERK has a relatively high value. For survival, firms must be able to compete in two dimensions (price and quality) simultaneously. A firm that competes in only one or the other dimension can be successfully challenged by a rival that performs as well in the same dimension but better in the other. In such games, firms not only take their competitors into active consideration—to survive, they must.

Technically speaking, a positive-sum game can be described as any in which an industry's total output grows more rapidly than the sum of the weighted capital and labor inputs; a zero-sum game can be described as one in which the outputs can be precisely accounted for in terms of inputs. However, many industries involved in playing close to zero-sum games receive windfall benefits in the form of technological advances brought about in other industries that show up in the form of highly irregular productivity rates and are not accompanied by declines in relative prices. In contrast, in positive-sum-game industries, productivity gains occur at remarkably steady rates. Moreover, rapid growth in output and productivity terms tend to go hand in hand. Thus, during the 1960s and 1970s the following U.S. industries, which reduced their relative prices one standard deviation or more more rapidly than the average, achieved output growth rates of about 9 percent and productivity growth rates of about 7 percent annually—more than double the rates achieved in manufacturing as a whole: electronic computing equipment, semiconductors, television, hosiery, pharmaceutical preparations, electric housewares and fans, tufted carpets, rugs, organic fibers, flat glass, phonograph records, optical instruments, and dolls (Klein n.d.).

The degree of dynamic competition will be measured in two ways. According to the first, the higher the degree of opportunity-seeking competition, the more rapidly relative prices will decline. According to the second measure, the degree of competition depends on the variance in profit rates applying to particular products: the larger the spread, the greater the degree of dynamic competition will be. Though it can be shown that the measures will provide essentially the same results when an industry is in a dynamic equilibrium, the same is not necessarily true when additional competitive pressures require that firms achieve higher valued dynamic equilibria.

Positive-sum games are accompanied by high and steady productivity rates because they provide the needed insurance to stay in the game. To be sure, if a firm has close to a 100 percent batting average by being first in the development of new products, it need not have a high productivity rate. While several firms, including Hewlett-Packard, Sony, and IBM, were in such a position during the 1960s, the same is not true today as a result of rapid imitation of their products. To reduce their prices and costs, they had to double or triple their productivity rates (Klein n.d., chap. 6). In a more evenly matched contest, generating high productivity rates is a necessity because those whose products are less successful in any round of the game must quickly reduce prices to prevent inventories from accumulating. Indeed, even if the contest starts as a way to improve product quality, price competition, too, will be featured: during the auction days, the less successful firms must reduce their prices. The wider the disparities between more and less successful products, the greater will be the insurance required to stay in the game. When firms take more or less the same degree of risk in each time period, a continuing decline in relative prices is the result.

There are three principal sources of productivity gain. One consists of more cost-effective product innovations. For example, like radio tubes, semiconductors were initially individually produced until a member of one of the newly founded firms got the idea of producing them on sheets like postage stamps and, then, separating them; this planar process resulted in the first semiconductors used in computers. Then, someone else on the same development team later asked, "Why go to the trouble of separating each one? Why not, instead, print the circuit board on top?" This idea resulted in integrated circuits. Following these developments, a series of subsidiary innovations made possible 40 percent annual increases in the amount of information contained on a chip without a significant increase in the prices of computer chips. As a result, 10 percent annual productivity increases occurred in both the semiconductor and computer industries (Klein n.d., chap. 5).

A second source of productivity gain is, of course, investment in improved machines. The big payoff has come from substituting, wherever possible, machines for people in the most menial tasks—those which are most boring and commonly result in quality problems—and using workers not as machines but, rather, as troubleshooters, an approach that raises the value of both human and physical capital. For example, welders and welding robots may work as a team with each member engaging in those operations in which it has a relative advantage.

Finally, under appropriate circumstances, improvements of existing assembly lines can be a very important source of productivity gain. A manager of the Sony Manufacturing Corporation of America showed me data that indicated a 5 percent productivity rate has been achieved on the basis of worker improvements of existing production lines plus relatively minor expenditures for new equipment (about double the rate in U.S. manufacturing). This achievement was confirmed when I visited Deere, Hewlett-Parkard, and IBM—firms that have also adopted the Japanese approach to manufacturing (Klein n.d., chap. 6).

When, as during positive-sum games, firms impose substantial risks on each other, like football teams, they must possess *both* good offensive and defensive capabilities.

Offensive Capabilities

Ask an informed insider what particular person brought about a significant innovation—for example, integrated circuits or a trival production-line innovation—and in nine out of ten cases you will be told that the exact developer of the innovation was in question. More often than not, the hints for new innovations as well as the insights needed to disclose the possibility of new competitive opportunities result from chance conversations. A synergism consists of a cooperative action in which the total effect is greater than the sum of the effects considered independently. Hence, synergistic behavior plays an all-important role in the generation of innovations.

Bruce A. Langager and Julianne H. Prager, who work in Corporate Technical Planning and Coordination at 3M, have collaborated on an interesting essay that criticizes the conventional method of management.

First, the individual misses out on the stimulation that accompanies exposure to interdisciplinary groups. Secondly, the company misses out on the synergism that occurs when receptive technical minds come together. This synergism frequently results in clues to solve one's own problems as well as sparking new ideas which can lead to major new technology and product developments.

To exploit this synergism (and thereby increase the likelihood of good luck), firms in highly competitive industries employ a variety of measures designed to result in a wide diversity of interactions; from day to day it cannot be predicted who will be telephoning whom or who will be visiting whom. For example, U.S. computer firms not only transfer scientists and engineers from one laboratory to another every few years, but, from time to time, the missions of the various laboratories are changed. One of the measures employed by 3M to increase the diversity of interactions is an annual technology fair. Under Corning's director of research there is an office comprising both chemists and marketing people; their entire mission consists of reestablishing "informal networks."

Operating in a very challenging environment, as measured by the competitive tax difference, will involve dealing with very strong uncertainties (i.e., good and bad surprises). On the other hand, when the tax difference is small, firms will be more tightly structured and the internal pattern of communications will be far more predictable. To make the point in another way, in firms that innovate regularly, "strategy" is determined by the outcome of the interactions, and in those that innovate only occasionally, strategy is imposed from above.

How well each of the major sources of productivity gain will be exploited depends, in turn, on the diversity of interactions. In the United States, firms that exploit this synergism in their R&D operations also tend to have a highly questioning environment in their manufacturing operations. That, in turn, is the reason why, from a statistical point of view, high productivity rates correspond with steady productivity rates.

But assume that the management of a firm chooses to closely relate its manufacturing and product development activities by requiring workers to remedy production line problems when possible and, when not able to do so, those in product development are promptly informed (typically located in the same or an adjacent building). The essential idea behind having semifinished products arrive at the next station just in time to be used is not to minimize inventory costs but, rather, to quickly expose problems by making every worker on a production line a quality inspector for the previous person. Remedying problems on existing production lines is not only an important source of productivity gain, but feedback from workers about problems they cannot solve calls attention to design problems that need to be dealt with in the development of the next generation of products. Thus, after adopting the just-in-time inventory approach, Deere, Hewlett-Packard, and IBM reduced their product malfunction rates by more than a factor of two. Reliability of their products was improved by cutting the number of their components from 20 to 40 percent; as a consequence, by being less costly to produce, those better quality products provided another important source of productivity gain (Klein n.d., chap. 6).

To more fully exploit the benefits of this approach, firms either have their own internal machine development activities (e.g., as in the cases of Sony, Honda, and IBM) or, more commonly, work closely with machine tool firms (as in the cases of Deere and Hewlett-Packard). Because they have an important voice in determining both the characteristics of IBM-produced machines and which machines should be purchased from outside sources IBM's workers are now described as "capital owners." At Honda, the close linkage between manufacturing and machine development activities is regarded as so important that it was decided to provide its Ohio operation with its own capability for developing new machines.

As a result of greatly increasing the diversity of interactions in Deere, Hewlett-Packard, and IBM, these firms have either doubled or tripled their productivity rates while cutting their production malfunction rates by half or more. And the productivity rates of Sony and Honda plants in the United States are within 5 percent of the rates achieved by those firms in Japan.

Dynamic Flexibility

By making it possible to shift a production line from the manufacture of one to another already *existing* product with only minor penalties, static flexibility provides a hedge against short-run demand uncertainties. In contrast, a dynamically flexible plant is designed to produce an entire family of related products—including those not yet on drawing boards. In other words, technological recipes can be changed with minor penalties. With a dynamically flexible production process, the cost of making a typical number of changes in a computer after market testing is likely to be only about one-fifth as great as it would have been with specialized tooling (Klein n.d., chap. 6). In response to dealer complaints, Honda makes changes in both its automobiles and production lines before the next model year. Firms that receive bad news during the auctioning process can, if their production and product development activities are closely coupled, develop a new product in half the time that otherwise would be required.

True, dynamically flexible plants are not only more costly, but require an investment in training employees to detect and deal with production line problems as they arise. As in the case of Keynes's stockholder, the possibility of higher present earnings is deliberately sacrificed to provide a hedge against a more uncertain future. Dynamic flexibility provides a hedge against bad luck and should be regarded as a defensive capability.

A production process designed to produce an entire package of products can also be readily changed in response to the discovery of new opportunities to reduce costs or improve quality. In contrast, a highly dedicated machine specialized to produce a particular product (for example, a transfer machine in which raw material is fed in at one end and, via a series of highly specialized operations, a finished product emerges from the other end) is very difficult to change—so much so that, unless it possesses a capability to develop such machines, a firm must return it to the original tool manufacturer for reworking.

In U.S. firms, dynamic flexibility is commonly achieved by computer assisted design and manufacturing processes (CAD/CAM). Firms such as Hewlett-Packard, Honda, IBM, and Sony use such technology extensively. Consequently, they are able to achieve productivity gains of about 5 percent annually, mainly by correcting problems on existing production lines.

This is not to say, however, that the dynamic flexibility of a firm—its ability to bring about quick changes in technological recipes—is limited by its machines. Japanese firms take CAD/CAM as their model of the factory of the future and have taken the lead in extending its role. Deere is also working in this direction; for example, Deere workers have developed simple computer-controlled machines using scrap materials. When it is not possible to use computerized machines, by virtue of possessing internal machine tool organizations or by working closely with machine tool firms, manufacturers can quickly and inexpensively change the characteristics of their dedicated machines—if not in a few hours, as in the case of CAD/CAM, in a matter of a week or two. At the other extreme, even though no firm relies more on CAD/CAM than IBM, it must rely on an internal capability to quickly rework its electric motors.

The Nature of Economic Progress

Firms may, of course, exploit synergism to multiply the likelihood of good luck only in the R&D laboratories, engaging in Tinkertoy experiments that cost only about one-fourth as much as full-scale development projects to limit the consequences of bad luck. Or, in a highly competitive environment, firms may feature a highly interactive environment in their factories and engage in production line experiments. However, when engaged in such practices, firms are not making the best use of their resources at every moment. As Schumpeter made the point,

> a system—any system, economic or other—that at every given point in time fully utilizes its possibilities to the best advantage may yet in the longer run be inferior to a system that does so at no given point of time, because the latter's failure to do so may be a condition for the level of speed of long-run performance. (1942, 83)

My statistical results show that the U.S. industries that were involved in robust positive-sum games made impressive savings in labor and capital inputs and a variety of inputs purchased from other industries. How, then, can the so-called gap between the inputs and outputs be explained? As a consequence of having been provided with only the ability to deduce, classical economic man can only make choices among existing alternatives. Fortunately, however, real-world entrepreneurs can both imagine and deduce; if this were not so we would still be living in the Stone Age. It is *imagination* in the context of synergistic interactions that explains how economic progress comes about. If resources were used to the best advantage at every moment in time, dynamic capitalism could not exist. Inputs growing at smaller rates than outputs is an indication that capitalism is operating at a profit—the greater the competitive tax differences, the greater the profit. During the past ten years, productivity in Japanese manufacturing, taking into account both labor and capital inputs, has been increasing at about three times the U.S. rate (Harberger 1990). From this it can be inferred that the average value of PERK is higher in Japan, and that, because both synergistic interactions and dynamic flexibility play more important roles than in the United States, Japanese capitalism is operating at a higher profit.

The Relationship between PERK and the Rate of Progress

In an essay published in a previous Schumpeter Society volume (1988), I showed that, during the 1960–80 period, with the exception of 7 of 387 industries, it was possible to predict that necessity (measured in terms of the rate that relative prices were declining) and luck (measured in terms of productivity rates and their degree of steadiness) went hand in hand at the 5 percent confidence level (Klein n.d., chap 5). As in modern biology, for the 5 percent of the species that have survived, the stochastic and deterministic forces work jointly (chap. 3). The logic of the argument can be best understood in terms of relating the width of two distributions to the rate of progress.

Case A: Relative prices are declining slightly. In an industry, say, one in which firms manufacture electric toasters, the value of PERK is close to zero. Firms operate on the basis of the rule that 70 percent of R&D projects must pay off within a year or less. Now, suppose we take a series of snapshots of the differences between toasters in various years and are able to plot those differences on a chart. It can be safely assumed that the snapshots would reveal very small differences between toasters, that is, the differences would lie close to the center of a distribution.

When competition is measured in terms of the profits earned on toasters, it is safe to assume that, though not all firms would earn the same profits year after year, this distribution also would be tightly clustered: if all ten attempts of firm A to bring about significant advances succeed in one year, only five attempts might succeed in another year.

We can infer that the rate of progress made in improving toasters will be very small—to obtain a significantly better toaster one might have to wait ten years or so. On the other hand, assume that toaster manufacturers stopped engaging in dynamic competition and, instead, manufactured unchanged toasters only slightly different than each other (i.e., as in a spatial equilibrium). In that event, the two clustered industry distributions would entirely collapse and the rate of progress would decline to zero. It can reasoned, therefore, that the rate of progress made in developing new toasters is a function of the widths of the two distributions. However, when the tax difference is small, it can be reasoned that a minimal amount of insurance in the form of productivity gains will be required.

Case B: Relative prices are declining at 10 percent annually. This is equivalent to assuming a modest increase in the value of PERK: only five or six projects are required to pay off within a year, with the result that the product and profit distributions will be slightly wider. In principle, this should result in a slightly more rapid rate of progress. However, because there is no way to calculate the probability of an innovation being successful (which is to say that the uncertainties are strong), it is also impossible to make fine-grained distinctions between low- or high-risk projects. To be sure, firms do make rough distinctions between low-risk, high-risk, and especially risky R&D projects, but that is a quite different matter.

Case C: Relative prices are declining but not by as much as one standard deviation below the average. The distributions spread out substantially. Think of firms as engaging in experiments for our benefit. We can predict that, at some point, luck and necessity will begin to work hand in hand. But we do not know just how wide the distributions need be for this to occur. So, imagine that we observe firms' experiments until the two distributions become wide enough to come almost—but not quite—within the acceptance region of Wilcoxon's signed rank test, which is to say, we peek at the data. As a consequence, we discover that, when industries' relative prices are declining at an appreciable rate, the average output and productivity growth rates shoot up by about 50 percent—while at the same time productivity gains become far steadier on a year-to-year basis. Consequently, we can infer that a discontinuous change has occurred with respect to the behavior of firms. It can be safely assumed that, at least in their R&D laboratories, they rely on the basic synergism required to multiply the possibilities of good luck and on Tinkertoy experiments to limit the consequences of bad luck.

In short, it can be assumed that with a large enough competitive tax difference to result in good and bad luck entering the picture, the experiments to develop new products will widen sufficiently to result in a discontinuous change in the rate of progress at some point.

Case D: Relative prices decline by one standard deviation or more. For the basic hypothesis not to be falsified, these industries must come fully within the acceptance region of the test, which, of course, they do. When we again peek at the data, we will find that output and productivity rates have shot up from about 4 to 7 percent annually on the average, and that productivity gains have increased at steady exponential rates in the average industry in this category. Thus, we infer that the basic synergism is more fully exploited and dynamic flexibility plays a greater role than in case 3.

Thus, as is shown in figures 1 and 2, the relation between PERK and the rate of progress is highly nonlinear. The reason for the nonlinearity is shown in figure 1 of the diagram: as the value of PERK increases at some point, luck begins to play a prominent role. Because firms are not likely to be equally favored by good luck, the distribution of the outcome of the R&D experiment will widen and the rate of progress will shoot up rapidly, after certain thresholds are reached—the vertical lines shown in figure 2. It is assumed that the curve finally flattens out because, no matter how many innovations are generated in a particular time period, there is some upper limit on the number that can be assimilated into an ongoing production process.

An Experiment

During the period from 1973 to 1988, both output and productivity growth in Japanese manufacturing averaged almost 6 percent annually, suggesting that, in U.S. terms, the *average* Japanese industry was involved in something more than a marginal positive-sum game. Reasoning from these data we can infer that, on the average, Japanese manufacturing firms tax each other to a greater degree than U.S. firms.

How can we check this conclusion? First, assume that, with relatively few exceptions, U.S. workers and managements are in a Prisoner's Dilemma situation: if they were to cooperate to generate more rapid productivity gains and quality improvements, firms would be able to compete better internationally and workers would be assured longer lasting jobs plus somewhat more rapid increases in real wages (during the period from 1973 to 1988, the standard of living of the average U.S. worker actually declined [Economic Report of the President, 1990, 344]). The experiment consists of the U.S. government levying a tax on manufacturing corporations designed to have the effect of widening the competitive tax difference.

It can be safely assumed that the management-worker dilemma has been

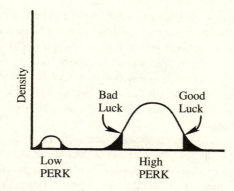

Fig. 1. Density versus high and low PERK

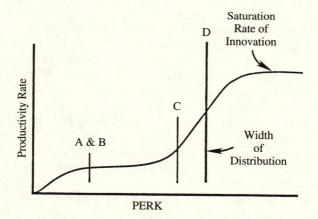

Fig. 2. Productivity rate versus PERK. Vertical lines correspond to cases A, B, C, D representing the extent of distribution as determined by the spread of R&D.

resolved in the case of Japan. If it can also be shown that in other important respects the tax would, in fact, result in the adoption of practices typically associated with Japan, it can be inferred that the average value of PERK in Japan is substantially greater.

One feature of the proposed tax on manufacturing corporations consists of taxing increases in sales attributable to price increases at progressive positive rates so high that it will be unprofitable to raise prices; such taxes will be added to firms' usual corporate taxes. A second feature involves taxing price reductions at highly progressive *negative* rates, to the point that, if a firm's average relative prices were declining at 5 percent annually, 50 percent of the savings to consumers would be subsidized by the public at large. Corporations that chose this route could subtract the price savings to consumers from their regular corporate income taxes and, if the sum turned out to be negative, they would then receive a rebate from the government. A third feature of the tax proposal is that any further cost savings resulting from contracting abroad would, for tax purposes, be disallowed. Finally, the "experiment" would expire when the trade deficit had been eliminated, but no later than seven years after its inception.

There is no way to predict to what degree firms would subscribe to the second feature of the tax. For the purpose of the present argument, however, it is not necessary to predict the response. Surely some combination of rates would result in the management and workers in one or another firm recognizing that a cooperative effort to improve productivity and quality at more rapid rates would be in their mutual interest. If a 50 percent maximum price savings to consumers did not suffice, surely a 90 percent figure would be quite enticing. To be sure, if a firm were to adopt the equivalent of the just-in-time-inventory concept, important benefits could not be reaped before two years had passed; about that amount of time would be required to train workers to detect and deal with unsolved production line problems. From this point of view, the larger the tax savings, the greater the willingness of firms to forego immediate profits in order to obtain longer term benefits would be. Moreover, keep in mind that firms not willing to make the latter choice would risk being subjected to double taxes, once in the form of the tax savings they would forego and once in the form of lost sales and profits if a firm in the same industry opted to reduce its taxes and succeeded in introducing a more competitive product.

Though there is no way of predicting how soon a bandwagon effect would begin, surely, faced with such a prospect, more and more firms would cross the threshold where luck and necessity begin to enter the picture (i.e., the vertical lines shown in fig. 2). As a result of matching BLS data with foreign trade statistics on a sampling basis, I discovered, with very few exceptions, those industries that had been reducing their relative prices by more than the average, but less than one standard deviation—industries involved in playing marginal positive-sum games—were able to dramatically boost their productivity rates in the face of pressures to engage in a greater degree of price constraint. As a matter of fact, 75 percent of the industries in that category became involved in more robust positive-sum games (Klein n.d., chap. 5). Consequently, with more and more industries achieving productivity increases of no more than 4.5 percent annually (which would require that they feature relative price declines of 2 to 3 percent annually) and with wage-rate increases no more rapid than those of West Germany, U.S. firms would be in a far better position to compete internationally. Note that firms such as Sony and Deere, which have fully adopted the just-in-time inventory approach, are achieving productivity gains at a 6 to 8 percent annual rate and simultaneously achieving commensurate improvements in the quality of their products.

Consider the other effects of such a tax.

1. As in Japan, central labor unions would no longer play an important role. Industrywide bargaining can play a role only when there is virtually no competition within an industry. But strong penalties are involved when increasing unit-wage costs more rapidly than those of rival firms; that is, there is a real risk that workers will become unemployed. For this reason, unit-wage costs in those industries in which relative prices had been declining increased by only half as much as those in the average U.S. industry. (Klein n.d., chap 5)

2. As in Japan, central unions would no longer be able to impose work rules. Generally speaking, whether or not so intended, such rules have the effect of jeopardizing improvements in both productivity and quality. For this reason, unionized firms that have adopted the Japanese approach to manufacturing have either worked out formal arrangements with the central unions or have been able to reach an agreement whereby central unions "winked" at locally established work rules.

3. It often has been said, and not without reason, that Japanese firms do not press for immediate profits to the degree that U.S. firms do. There can be no doubt that the shorter a firm's time-horizon, the poorer its ability to compete will be. Match two sets of firms against each other, one insisting on a payoff from R&D in a year or less and another willing to gamble on bets not likely to materialize within three years. Even assuming that a far smaller proportion of the latter's gambles are successful, it is easy to show that the second group would overtake the first in a relatively short time.

   As I have indicated, the tax plan would almost automatically lengthen the time-horizon of U.S. firms. Those firms that opted for substantial tax benefits would have to lengthen their time-horizons, and those that refused would be subject to strong penalties.

4. Consider two sets of industries, manufacturing and supplier industries —any supplier industry. If one or another manufacturing industry, such as our hypothetical toaster industry, is operating at a low value of PERK, it will have no incentive to demand a high rate of progress on the part of a supplier industry. Quite the contrary, making good use of innovations brought about in supplier industries presupposes changes in the methods of operation of a manufacturing industry. For example, it can be safely assumed that, if the development of battery-powered

watches had entirely depended on the acceptance of this new technology by traditional watchmaking firms, only motion-driven watches would be in existence today—if the development of transistors had entirely depended on the long-established vacuum tube manufacturers, transistors would now be used only as a substitute for radio and television tubes. Conversely, if firms in a manufacturing industry operate at a high value of PERK, we can be quite certain that a supplying industry will respond. Again, response on the part of one firm in such an industry can inflict sharp penalties on its rivals; for example, those semiconductor firms that did not respond to the high degree of competition in the computer industry simply went out of business.

Japanese machine tool firms come under the second heading, and this is an important part of the reason why, after their invention in the United States, U.S. imports of computer-controlled machines from Japan have risen so sharply. As of 1955, German firms were responsible for 35 percent of the export of all machine tools, U.S. firms for 30 percent, U.K. firms for 12 percent, and Japan had not entered the race. As of 1987, the German share of the total market had declined to 23 percent, the U.S. share was 4 percent, the U.K. share was 3 percent, and the Japanese share had become 20 percent (Carlsson n.d.).

In sharp contrast with Japanese automobile firms, firms in the U.S. automobile industry—the principal customer of the machine tool industry—for many years refused to buy significantly better tools because such action would add to the risks of bringing about the annual model changes. And, while one machine tool manufacturer located in Keene, New Hampshire, was unable to sell an idea for an improved transfer machine in the United States, it was lucky to engage in a collaborative development with a Japanese automobile manufacturer that has resulted in a 25 percent reduction in downtime and sales of the improved product to European auto firms.

The impact of the proposed tax? If, by virtue of a steady stream of improvements in its machines a manufacturing firm could go from a 2 to a 3 percent price-reduction path by cooperating with one or several machine tool firms, it obviously would be in their mutual interest. For example, after adopting the just-in-time approach, Deere did engage in a cooperative development project with a U.S. robot manufacturer aimed at "teaching its robots how to weld." As it turned out, the new concept that emerged—one in which welders and welding robots operated as a team, and with each member engaging in those tasks in which it had a relative advantage—not only provided important benefits for Deere by raising the value of both human and physical capital, but also is reported to have resulted in a more salable product from the robot manufacturer's point of view.

Adoption of the proposed tax plan would make the U.S. manufacturing economy more like that of Japan. However, the probability of U.S. politicians being willing to sanction such a bold experiment is quite another matter.

REFERENCES

Carlsson, Bo. N.d. "Small-Scale Industry at a Crossroads: U.S. Machine Tools in Global Perspective." Booklet 259. Industriens Utrednings-Institut. Stockholm, Sweden.

Economic Report of the President. 1990. Washington, D.C.: GPO.

Harberger, Arnold C. 1990. "The Sources of Growth Revised." Presidential Address. The Western Economic Association. San Diego, California.

International Monetary Fund. 1989. *Annual Report of the Executive Board.* June.

Klein, Burton H. 1988. "Luck, Necessity, and Dynamic Flexibility." In *Evolutionary Economics Application of Schumpeter's Ideas,* ed. H. Hanusch. Cambridge: Cambridge University Press.

Klein, B. N.d. *Opportunity-Seeking Competition: Making Luck and Necessity Work Hand in Hand.* Forthcoming.

Knight, Frank M. 1921. *Risk, Uncertainty, and Profit.* Boston: Houghton Mifflin.

Schumpeter, Joseph A. 1942. *Capitalism, Socialism and Democracy.* New York: Harper and Row.

Schumpeter, Joseph A. 1934. *The Theory of Economic Development.* Trans R. Opic. Cambridge, Mass.: Harvard University Press.

Shionoya, Yuichi. 1990. "The Origin of the Schumpeterian Research Program." *Journal of Institutional and Theoretical Economics* 146:314–27.

U.S. Bureau of Labor Statistics. 1989a. *International Comparisons of Hourly Compensation Costs.* Washington, D.C.: GPO.

U.S. Bureau of Labor Statistics. 1989b. *Output, Employment, Hours and Compensation in Manufacturing.* Washington, D.C.: GPO.

Commentary

Joseph A. Weissmahr

Burton Klein has presented a wide-ranging panorama of the relationship between positive-sum games and economic growth. It is an extremely important, but so far neglected subject. Positive-sum games are extremely important, not only for economic growth, but also for evolutionary economics in general because profits, productivity increases, and all forms of evolution are the result of positive-sum games.

I will discuss one central question: What are the necessary and sufficient conditions for achieving a positive-sum game in the economy? Burton Klein states that the necessary and sufficient condition for achieving a positive-sum game is economic competition far from equilibrium.

I agree with the second part of this statement, that the evolutionary process of a positive-sum game is feasible only in an economy operating far from equilibrium. Klein is to be commended for recognizing that Schumpeter made a big mistake when he tried to graft his evolutionary ideas onto the body of equilibrium economics. Schumpeter's ideas were sidetracked because novelty disturbs the equilibrium. Klein recognizes that the economy is an open system that can grow and evolve because it operates far from equilibrium.

Now I come to the first part of Klein's conditions for a positive-sum game. Here I have some doubts about his concept of competition as the cause for the achievement of a positive-sum game. A closer analysis shows that competition is really the result of a chain of knowledge applications. It is true that all new or improved products have to compete in the marketplace, but the key step in the positive-sum process of increasing productivity is innovation. I would, therefore, suggest that it is not competition, but innovative knowledge application by creative individuals that is one of the necessary ingredients of a positive-sum game, while competition is the selection process of the evolutionary economy.

Concentration on competition as the sole cause also indicates that Klein believes the interaction of human actors is not only a necessary but also sufficient cause for achieving a positive-sum game. Here, Klein follows the anthropocentric tradition of conventional economic theory.

301

I would like to suggest that, in order to understand how a positive-sum game is achieved in an evolving economy, two steps have to be taken. The first step is to abandon the notion that the ideal economic state is equilibrium. Klein has accomplished this first step, but this is not enough. The second step consists in the insight that economic evolution cannot be explained by the action of human actors alone.

The first step is easier to accept. It is quite clear that evolution and equilibrium are incompatible because equilibrium can be reached only if nothing new happens, whereas the essence of evolution is change. The second step is more difficult, because we have to overcome very deep-seated preconceptions about the importance of human agents in the economy. The logic of the situation, however, is inescapable. Either we believe that humans are the only important actors in the economy, which means that we have to believe in the labor theory of value and regard the economy as a zero-sum game, or we must find an additional active agent operating in the economy.

The necessity of these steps follows from the characteristics of evolutionary processes. Economic evolution manifests itself in the appearance of qualitative novelty and quantitative gain for all human actors. As you remember, a positive-sum game is defined as a game in which all human players finish the game with a quantitative plus. This quantitative gain must come from outside the circle of human actors, otherwise there would not be a positive-sum gain.

Fortunately this mystery was analyzed in a little-known section of the famous book by Von Neumann and Morgenstern, *Theory of Games and Economic Behavior,* first published in 1944. They extended their analysis of zero-sum games to positive-sum games by the simple and ingenious device of introducing a "fictitious" additional player—the so-called $(n + 1)$ player— who supplies what the totality of real players (1 to n) are winning. They also specify that the $(n + 1)$ player must have no direct influence on the course of the game in the sense hat he or she does not ask anything in return and does not enter into coalitions. Von Neumann and Morgenstern introduced the fictitious $(n + 1)$ player as a mathematical device in order to make the sum of the winnings of the real human players (1 to n) and the losses of the $(n + 1)$ player equal to zero. However, their mathematical analysis confirms that human actors alone cannot achieve a positive-sum game. An essential requirement is an external $(n + 1)$ player who supplies, without asking anything in return, what the totality of real human players are winning.

It is surprising that it did not occur to Von Neumann and Morgenstern that if their analysis is correct and if the economy is a positive-sum game, then their "fictitious" $(n + 1)$ player *must* exist in our universe. And, indeed, the altruistic $(n + 1)$ player does exist: it is the sun, which supplies solar radiation without asking anything in return and without entering into coalitions. It is the existence of solar energy flow that makes a positive-sum game among human players possible. Humans use converted solar energy in the form of food, coal, oil, and renewable energy for their survival, growth, and multiplication, and for building up their economy.

The important point is that energy is more than a commodity. It is an independent driving force and profit factor in the evolutionary economy. Now, what are the conclusions from these considerations? First, Burton Klein is right in his analysis that a positive-sum game is incompatible with equilibrium. This means that the evolutionary economy must be modeled as an open system operating far from equilibrium, because only open systems can evolve by taking up energy for maintaining and building up their structure.

The second conclusion is that there are *two* driving forces behind the evolutionary economy: the first is creativity supplied by human players, and the second is energy flow, from the $(n + 1)$ player. Human creativity is the source of knowledge, which enables humans to use increasing amounts of energy flow and thereby to improve the use of human time.

The "gift of nature," as the Physiocrats called it, will have to be reincorporated into economic theory in order to explain how quantitative gain is achieved by the totality of human players during the process of economic evolution. Another indication of the importance of energy flow for the economy is that human actors doing physical work can be substituted by energy flow applied through machines. This substitution results in cost savings, which are an important source of profit in the economy. If energy flow is a source of profit, it surely must be incorporated into economic theory as an active force.

Based on these considerations, the central question posed in the beginning, what are the necessary and sufficient conditions for achieving a positive-sum game in the economy, can be answered in the following way. New knowledge application and energy application are the two necessary and, in combination, sufficient ingredients for achieving a quantitative positive-sum result, which manifests itself in the economy in productivity increases, economic growth, and the improvement of human time.

The third conclusion is that competition is not the cause of the positive-sum game achieved in the process of evolution. Competition serves as the evolutionary selection mechanism in nature and in the economy. The selective pressure of competition, however, has a secondary motivating influence on human actors in the economy. Competition between economic units in the better utilization of energy and human time leads to change and places a premium on the adaptability of organizations and the learning ability of individuals. Competitive selection assures that, from the large number of experimental knowledge application trials, only the most productive will survive, and that, by the elimination of routine subhuman work, the creative human potential will be continually developed.

REFERENCE

von Neumann, John, and Oskar Morgenstern. 1953. *Theory of Games and Economic Behavior*. 3d ed. Princeton: Princeton University Press.

Technological Regimes, Learning, and Industry Turbulence

David B. Audretsch and Zoltan J. Acs

Introduction

The increase in the number of U.S. manufacturing establishments by 32,000—from 448,000 in 1980 to 480,000 in 1986—does not suggest a particularly important role for the entry of new establishments.[1] On average, there was an increase of just slightly more than 1 percent in the number of establishments each year. However, when the *gross* rather than *net* amount is examined, a considerably different picture emerges. In fact, 205,000 new manufacturing establishments entered between 1980 and 1986, representing a gross entry rate of 45.8 percent.[2] At the same time, 173,000 manufacturing establishments exited, resulting in an exit rate of 38.6 percent. Thus, the entry of new establishments is a fundamental force shaping U.S. manufacturing.[3]

Why does such a high degree of entry take place in U.S. industries? The conventional wisdom in industrial economics is that new firms are induced to enter an industry by the existence of economic rents. Entry is, therefore, an interesting economic phenomenon because it erodes these excess profits, thereby restoring equilibrium to a market.[4] In Audretsch and Acs 1990, we propose an alternative function of entry that is essentially Schumpeterian in nature.[5] That is, new firms in an industry do not always produce the same goods using the same inputs and production methods. Rather, in doing some-

We wish to thank Alan Hughes, Steven Klepper, Robert McGuckin, Richard R. Nelson, F. M. Scherer, Sidney G. Winter, and the participants at the 1990 Schumpeter Society meeting for their helpful suggestions, and Jianping Yang for his computational assistance. All errors and omissions remain our responsibility.

1. Data from Acs and Audretsch 1990, table 5.1.
2. The gross entry rate is defined as the number of new establishments in manufacturing between 1980 and 1986 divided by the number of establishments in 1980.
3. For an analysis of entrepreneurship in the United States, see Evans and Leighton 1990.
4. See, for example, many of the studies contained in Geroski and Schwalbach 1990.
5. See also Scherer 1991.

thing different, such as engaging in innovative activity, an entrant frequently serves as an *agent of change*.

To what extent are new firms in an industry able to serve as agents of change? The answer to this question is implied (to some extent) by two quite different literatures. Winter (1984) and Gort and Klepper (1982) argue that technological conditions determine the relative ease with which firms outside an industry are able to innovate and, therefore, enter. The models of learning by doing introduced by Jovanovic (1982) and Pakes and Ericson (1987) suggest that firms may enter an industry at suboptimal scale in order to obtain the opportunity to learn and subsequently expand if they are successful.

In fact, the technological regime characterizing the industry and the role that learning by doing plays may explain a considerable amount of industry turbulence, or the extent of firm movements into, within, and out of an industry. In this essay, we explore the roles of the technological regime and learning in determining industry turbulence and examine whether the determinants of industry turbulence vary for large and small firms.

By combining two new sources of data we are able to construct novel measures of both the technological regime as well as the extent of industry turbulence. In the second section of this paper we introduce the concept of turbulence and intraindustry dynamics. In the third section we develop a model relating the technological regime to industry dynamics. The manner in which the concepts of turbulence and the technological regime are measured is explained in the fourth section, and the hypothesis is tested in the fifth section.

Finally, in the last section, a summary and conclusions are presented. We find that when the knowledge obtained from actual experience in the industry is a crucial input in producing innovative activity, fewer firms will attempt to enter the industry and, subsequently, fewer will fail, leading to relatively low rates of turbulence. However, when knowledge from outside the industry is a key input into innovative production functions, entry is more likely to occur. Of course, those firms that are unable to successfully learn and adopt will subsequently fail; thus, the turbulence rate will be relatively high. Consistent with this is the finding that small-firm turbulence is actually greater in capital-intensive industries. Small firms that successfully innovate will become viable, but many of the remaining firms will recede and ultimately fail. Thus, small-firm turbulence is particularly high in capital-intensive industries, where firms must quickly learn or face extinction.

Intraindustry Dynamics

Alfred Marshall described the process of industry evolution by analogy, where one can observe ". . . the young trees of the forest as they struggle upwards through the benumbing shade of their older rivals" (1920, 263). Marshall's view of industry dynamics is not so different than the prevalent view held by most economists in industrial organization today, although this process has gone under the guise of various terms. Roughly speaking, the extent to which firms enter, grow, decline, and exit an industry has been called mobility, turnover, dynamic evolution, or turbulence, depending upon the author. We adopt the term *turbulence* here to avoid confusion with the European meaning of turnover, which is widely used to mean sales, and mobility, which has most recently come to refer to movement of firms between strategic groups within an industry (see, for example, Oster 1982). Instead, we draw upon the concept of turbulence (Beesley and Hamilton 1984; Gudgin 1978), which we define as the extent of movements of firms within as well as into and out of an industry.

The extent of intraindustry firm movement is important for several reasons. For example, Simon and Bonini argued that, "As a matter of fact, a measure of mobility . . . would appear to provide a better index of what we mean by 'equality of opportunity' than do the usual measures of concentration" (1958, 616). Grossack (1965) similarly argued that a measure of intraindustry firm movements may provide important dynamic information than can supplement the strictly static measure of market concentration.

In 1971, the Bolton Committee in the United Kingdom argued that new firms in an industry would promote new products and ultimately shape the evolutionary path of an industry, as well as constrain any market power exercised by entrenched firms.

> We believe that the health of the economy requires the birth of new enterprises in substantial number and the growth of some to a position from which they are able to challenge and supplement the existing leaders of industry. . . . This "seedbed" function, therefore, appears to be a vital contribution of the small-firm sector to the long-run health of the economy. We cannot assume that the ordinary working of market forces will necessarily preserve a small-firm sector large enough to perform this function in the future. (Bolton Report 1971, 85)

Caves and Porter argued that the theory of entry be extended to a more ". . . general theory of mobility of firms among segments of an industry, thus encompassing exit and intergroup shifts as well as entry" (1977, 241). While the traditional analyses suffer from neglecting structural restraints on the ability of firms to change their market share, the ease with which market share can be altered should be constrained by the ". . . same type of structural forces that deter the firm from increasing its output from zero to positive (entry) as from small share to large share (mobility)" (Caves and Porter 1977, 250).

Despite the recognition that the process by which firms enter, grow, recede, and exit plays a crucial role in the evolution of industrial markets, there have been only a few empirical studies to actually attempt to measure the extent of intraindustry firm movements. Most of these (Bond 1975; Collins and Preston 1961; Kaplan 1954; Mermelstein 1969) have been oriented toward making intertemporal comparisons of the largest U.S. corporations. The conclusion of these studies was unequivocal: the rate of turnover, at least among the largest corporations, has been declining over a long time. For example, Collins and Preston found that, ". . . in spite of the stability of the usual concentration measure there has been a significant decline in equality of opportunity in the upper reaches of the U.S. economy since the turn of the century" (1961, 100).

While there are no unambiguous criteria for judging the extent of turbulence (Scherer 1980, 55), there have been at least three important issues raised concerning the empirical methodology.[6] First, measures of intraindustry firm movements over a period as long as a decade obscure changes for shorter periods. For example, Boyle (1971) found that the coefficients for measures for paired years differ significantly from the ones for decades. Second, the preoccupation with changes among the 100 largest corporations has no unique economic significance. The relevant measure should include a wide spectrum of firm sizes (Boyle and Sorenson 1971; Porter 1976). According to Boyle, virtually no studies ". . . have paid sufficient attention to the admonition in recent years" (1971, 165). Third, and perhaps most significant, is the criticism that the appropriate unit of observation for examining turbulence should be the industry and not the aggregation of the largest firms (Kamerschen 1971; Stigler 1956). For example, Stigler warns,

> the statistical universe of the 100 or 200 largest corporations is inappropriate to studies of monopoly and competition and we may hope that Kaplan will be the last study to fall prey to its dramatic irrelevance. For Kaplan's central ideal—that the extent of instability in the relative fortunes of the leading firms is an informative symptom of competition—is important and deserves to be applied on a correct industry basis. (1956, 35)

A Model of Industry Turbulence

Like Gort and Klepper (1982), Winter (1984), and Helmstädter (1986), our model is evolutionary in nature. The driving force of the dynamic evolution of the model is what Winter called the "technological regime." According to

---

6. Most of the theoretical criticisms of attempts to measure industry turnover or mobility are discussed in Boyle 1971; Kamerschen 1971; Mermelstein 1969 and 1971; Stigler 1956.

Winter, "an entrepreneurial regime is one that is favorable to innovative entry and unfavorable to innovative activity by established firms; a routinized regime is one in which the conditions are the other way around" (1984, 297). Thus, the probability of making an innovation for any given firm, i, can be viewed as being influenced from the extent to which an industry can be characterized by an entrepreneurial regime, α, or a routinized regime, β:

$$i = \frac{K}{1 + \beta e^{-\alpha t}},$$ (1)

where K is a constant determining the asymptotic conditions and t represents the time period.

Based on Gort and Klepper (1982), α and β can be viewed as being determined by the underlying sources of information about new product technology. These two sources of information are from firms already in the market and from firms outside the set, or on the fringe, of the major incumbent producers. The first information source, which determines β, is the product of experience and contains both transferable and nontransferable components. Gort and Klepper emphasize that the accumulated stock of nontransferable information is the product of learning by doing, which firms outside the industry, by definition, cannot possess. The greater the role that the accumulated stock of nontransferable information plays, the higher the value of β and the greater the extent to which innovative activity emanates from the major incumbents.

When β is relatively small and α is large, new firms will tend to have the innovative advantage. In contrast, incumbents will tend to be more innovative when β is large and α is small. In fact, we have found that there is considerable empirical evidence supporting the existence of these distinct technological regimes (see Acs and Audretsch 1987 and 1988).

In Gort and Klepper's (1982) model, entry behavior is derived directly from these technological regimes, such that the probability of any given firm entering, $P(E)$, is given by

$$P(E_t) = f(\alpha_t, \beta_t, \pi_t),$$ (2)

where π_t is defined as the profit of incumbent producers at time t. The variables α_t and β_t represent the influence of the technological regime on the probability of entry. Gort and Klepper essentially assume that $\partial f / \partial \alpha_t > 0$ and $\partial f / \partial \beta_t < 0$. When β_t is relatively high and α_t is relatively low, innovation as a vehicle for entry is less of a viable alternative for firms either outside of or on the fringe of the market. However, entry by outside firms is encouraged when the second source of innovation-producing information is relatively more important. Arrow (1962), Mueller (1967), and Williamson (1975) have all pointed out that when such information created outside of the industry cannot be easily transferred to those firms existing within the industry (perhaps due to organizational factors), the holder of such knowledge has no choice other than to enter the industry in order to exploit the market value of his or her knowledge.[7]

Subsequent to entering an industry, a firm must decide whether to maintain output at the same level, expand, contract, or exit. The probability of a firm remaining in the industry in period t, or $P(Q_{it} > 0)$, is essentially determined by the extent to which a firm is burdened with an inherent size disadvantage, the profitability of the incumbents (π), and the probability of innovative activity:

$$P(Q_{it} > 0) = g[i_t, \pi_t, c(Q_i) - c(Q^*)], \tag{3}$$

where $c(Q_i)$ is the average cost of producing at a scale of output Q_i, and $c(Q^*)$ is the average cost of producing at the minimum efficient scale of output (MES), or the minimum level of production required to exhaust scale economies, Q^*.

The firm's actual level of output in period t is determined by its actual innovative activity, I_t,[8] plus some factor of its output in the previous period, $\bar{Q}_t$,

$$Q_{it} = \bar{Q}_t + Q(I_t), \tag{4}$$

where

$$\bar{Q}_t = \lambda(Q_o + Q_{it-1}), \tag{5}$$

Q_o is an autonomous level of output, and λ represents the portion of the previous period's output that can be maintained in the market. Factors such as market growth influence the value of λ.

Thus, equations 3–5 essentially represent the learning process by entrepreneurs that has been described by Jovanovic (1982) among others. In particular, Jovanovic assumes that individuals are unsure about their ability to manage a business and its prospects for success. While they may enter a market based on a vague sense of expected profitability, they discover their ability to manage in the given environment once their business is established. With the passage of time, they alter their behavior as they learn to disentangle

---

7. For further explanations see Mueller and Tilton 1969; Tilton 1971.
8. It should be noted that $E(i_t) = I_t + \mu_t$, where μ is stochastic.

their inherent ability from random business fluctuations. Those entrepreneurs who discover that their ability exceeds their expectations expand the scale of their business, while those discovering they have less inherent talent than expected contract the scale of output or possibly even exit the industry. An implication of the model is that firms begin at a small scale and then, if merited by subsequent performance, expand. Pakes and Ericson (1987) and Cohen and Klepper (1991) build on Jovanovic's model by arguing that firms can actively accelerate the learning process by investing in R&D, thereby endogenously raising the value of I_t. Those firms that are successful grow, while those that are not successful either remain small or exit the industry.

An important implication of the preceding model is that firms are more likely to enter an industry, even at a suboptimal scale, if the technology is such that there is a greater chance of new products coming from firms other than incumbents. If firms successfully learn and adopt, they grow into viably sized enterprises. If not, they stagnate and may ultimately exit. An implication is that the amount of industry turbulence should be positively related to the potential for new and fringe firms to become successful and, at the same time, the extent to which those less successful firms are forced to decline and/or exit the market.

Measurement

We use the dynamic measures from the USELM file of the U.S. Small Business Data Base (SBDB), introduced in Acs and Audretsch 1989a, to construct turbulence measures that most closely resemble the measure used in Beesley and Hamilton 1984. Specifically, we define turbulence as the absolute value of all employment and contractions within an industry (or firm-size class) between 1976 and 1980. That is, a given amount of market growth will dictate a corresponding amount of additional employment, presumably from both existing firms as well as from new entrants. However, to the extent that existing firms experience employment reductions as well as exit the industry, the overall amount of expansion and entry and, subsequently, the overall amount of turbulence will be larger.

In order to standardize turbulence for industry size, the turbulence rate for firm-size class j, TR_j, is defined as:

$$TR_j = (EXP_j + CONTR_j + BIRTH_j + DEATH_j)/(EMPL76_j), \quad (6)$$

where EXP_j is the amount of employment expansion in firm-size class j between 1976 and 1980, $CONTR_j$ is the amount of employment contraction in firm-size class j between 1976 and 1980, $DEATH_j$ is the amount of employment lost due to firm exits, $BIRTH_j$ is the amount of employment in new firms entering the industry, and EMPL76$_j$ is the amount of employment in firm-size class j in 1976.

More precisely, expansion is defined as the number of jobs in a specific firm-size class that emanate from new positions generated by firms *in existence* during the initial period. By definition, expansion is bounded by zero, which would indicate that the firms in that size class that were in existence during the first year did not create any employment beyond that amount already in effect in the initial period. Contraction is defined as the number of jobs in a specific firm-size class that were eliminated by firms that were in existence during the entire period. Contraction is also bounded by zero, which would indicate that none of the firms in that size class that were in existence during the initial year decreased the number of jobs over the relevant period. Of course, if a firm exits the industry, the loss of employment will not be included in the contraction measure. However, a separate variable, DEATH, measures the amount of employment in the firm-size class that is lost due to firm exits.

It should be emphasized that boundary crossings over time do not create a problem when the USELM file of the SBDB is used. That is, a firm's expansion or contraction is classified according to the size-class based on the firm's employment in 1976, regardless of any subsequent upward or downward movements of the firm into adjoining size classes.

As Beesley and Hamilton (1984) note, factors that have a symmetrical effect on entry and exit or expansion and contraction will have little impact on TR. There is also reason to suspect that the determinants of small-firm turbulence are considerably different than those for all firms. In fact, for the 247 four-digit standard industrial classification (SIC) industries included in the sample, the small-firm (fewer than 500 employees) turbulence rate exceeds the large-firm (at least 500 employees) turbulence rate by 35.10 percent.

Winter's (1984) concept of distinct technological regimes and Gort and Klepper's (1982) notions of the accumulated stock of nontransferable information acquired from learning by doing and innovative knowledge from firms outside the industry do not lend themselves to exact measurement. However, it is perhaps not unreasonable to consider the measures of small- and large-firm innovation, which we introduced in Acs and Audretsch 1987 and 1988, as proxy measures indicating the extent to which firms outside the major producers are able to innovate. The small-firm innovation rate (SIE) is defined as the number of innovations contributed by firms with fewer than 500 employees divided by small-firm employment. The large-firm innovation rate is defined as the number of innovations contributed by firms with at least 500 employees divided by large-firm employment. When SIE is high relative to the overall innovation rate (TIE), the technological and knowledge conditions may dictate a market that is more conducive to entry by innovation. Under such an entrepreneurial regime, α would be expected to be relatively high and β relatively low. However, when SIE is small relative to TIE, technology and knowledge are better characterized by a routinized regime, whereas presumably α is low and β is high.

Of course, those new firms entering but not able to innovate or otherwise learn and adopt may be forced to contract and ultimately exit. Thus, TR should be positively related to SIE and negatively related to TIE.

The extent of skilled labor comprising the labor force (SKILL) may also reflect the degree to which knowledge particular to the existing firms in the industry is crucial to innovative activity and would, therefore, be expected to be negatively related to TR. Gort and Klepper (1982) also argued, and found evidence suggesting, that markets are most accessible to outside firms in the early stage of the life cycle, when the growth rate is high. Therefore, the mean annual real growth rate between 1972 and 1977 (GR) is expected to be positively related to turbulence.

One of the implications of the passive and active learning models by Jovanovic (1982) and Pakes and Ericson (1987) is not only that those firms that do not learn and adopt must exit the industry, but that the greater the cost disadvantage incurred by firms not able to successfully learn and adopt, the more rapid will be their decline and departure. This implies that industries that are capital intensive and where scale economies play an important role may be particularly subject to high rates of turbulence, at least among small firms.

The technology and knowledge conditions inherent in α and β may provide outside firms with the opportunity for entry and growth through successful innovation. However, the typical entrant in a high MES (minimum efficient scale) industry is at a suboptimal scale and, therefore, must either successfully innovate or else depart the industry. Thus, high MES industries may be particularly subject to a high degree of turbulence among small firms that hope to discover the successful innovative strategy, many of which will be forced to exit the industry. This suggests that TR, at least for small firms, is expected to be positively influenced by the minimum efficient level of output as a share of total industry sales (MES/S), capital intensity, or 1977 gross assets divided by employment (K/L), and the amount of capital required for a firm to produce the MES level of output (KREQ).

Recent studies (Acs and Audretsch 1989a and 1989b) have identified advertising intensity to serve as a greater impediment to small-firm entry than capital intensity. Therefore, the advertising-sales ratio (AD/S) may promote industry stability more than turbulence and is expected to be negatively related to TR.

Industry profitability, measured by the 1977 price-cost margin (PCM), is expected to be negatively related to TR, since firms are more likely to survive in highly profitable industries. As Beesley and Hamilton (1984) point out, industry profitability may promote entry without a concomitant positive effect on exits and in fact, may reduce the number of industry exits, thereby reflecting less and not more turbulence.

Berry (1974) and Beesley and Hamilton (1984) argue that turbulence for large firms, but not for small firms, may be higher in concentrated than in nonconcentrated markets, because ". . . only large firms are able to encroach—via the setting up of dependent units—into areas already dominated by other large firms" (Beesley and Hamilton 1984, 227). Thus, TR is hypothesized to be positively related to CON, except in the case of small firms. All variables are explained in more detail and data sources are provided in the Appendix.

Empirical Results

Table 1 shows the regression results for estimating the turbulence rates of all firms (col. 1), small firms (col. 2), as well as the small-firm turbulence rate divided by the turbulence rate for all firms (col. 3) and the small-firm turbulence rate divided by the large-firm turbulence rate (col. 4). The regressions were estimated using 247 four-digit SIC industries, and a small firm is defined as having fewer than 500 employees.[9]

There are four important results in table 1. First, as the positive coefficient of SIE in the first two columns indicates, there is substantial evidence supporting the hypothesis that there is relatively more turbulence in markets where small firms are able to implement a strategy of product innovation, but relatively less turbulence in markets where they are not able to innovate. Further, as the negative coefficient of TIE suggests, holding the small-firm innovation rate constant, increases in the overall innovative activity of the industry lead to less and not more turbulence. This is consistent with Gort and Klepper's (1982) notion that markets in which the knowledge accumulated from experience plays a crucial role in innovative activity will tend not to be accessible to new firms, while markets in which such knowledge is relatively less important in producing innovations will generate much more activity from outside and fringe firms. These results apply for small firms as well as all firms.

Second, as the positive coefficient of KREQ in column 2 indicates, there is at least some evidence that the extent of turbulence within smaller firm-size classes is positively related to capital intensity. However, the negative (and

---

9. It should be noted that the coefficient of GR, SIE, TIE, and the intercept have been divided by 100, the coefficients of AD/S have been divided by 10,000, and the coefficients of KREQ have been multiplied by 10,000 for presentation purposes in cols. 1 and 2 of table 1. Similarly, in cols. 3 and 4, the coefficients of K/L and CON have been multiplied by 100, the coefficients of PCM have been multiplied by 10,000, and the coefficient of KAPR by 10,000.

statistically insignificant) coefficient of *K*REQ in column 1 implies that capital intensity does not stimulate turbulence in general. The positive coefficients of *K*REQ, MES/*S*, and *K*/*L* in columns 3 and 4 substantiate the hypothesis that while capital intensity may promote higher rates of turbulence among small firms, it does not among larger ones. This is consistent with the previously discussed notion that, at least under certain technological conditions, smaller firms may still enter markets with substantial scale economies and capital requirements, but those firms not able to successfully learn and adopt are quickly forced to decline and exit. The larger firms, which Evans (1987a and 1987b) found to be older and more experienced, have already survived some of this learning process and, thus, experience lower rates of turbulence. The negative and statistically significant coefficient of AD/*S* in column 1 and the positive and statistically significant coefficients of AD/*S* in columns 3 and 4

TABLE 1. **Regression Results for Turbulence Rates**

	All Firms (1)	Small Firms (2)	Small Firms/ All Firms (3)	Small Firms/ Large Firms (4)
PCM	−0.0028	−0.0726	−3.8776	−4.1381
	(0.0073)	(2.0714)**	(0.4809)	(−0.3887)
GR	7.3606	1.6066	−0.3450	−1.4332
	(1.3533)	(3.2922)**	(−0.3074)	(−0.9498)
SIE	1.2997	0.1379	−0.0847	−0.0708
	(2.8471)**	(3.3672)**	(−0.8990)	(−0.5590)
TIE	−2.6193	−0.1277	0.2535	0.2677
	(−2.3489)**	(−1.2767)	(1.1020)	(0.8651)
SKILL	−2.2735	0.3114	1.6117	2.0173
	(−0.3365)	(0.5137)	(1.1563)	(1.0763)
AD/*S*	−4.0130	−0.3234	1.6307	2.3437
	(−1.7626)*	(−1.5830)	(3.4716)**	(3.7105)**
CON	8.7681	−0.1719	−1.8887	−2.8133
	(4.2011)**	(−0.9177)	(−0.4386)	(−0.4859)
K/*L*	−1.2750	−0.2700	2.7775	2.4669
	(−0.6229)	(−1.4703)	(0.6577)	(0.4344)
MES/*S*	−6.9018	−1.2359	0.0418	0.0547
	(−0.6766)	(−1.3503)	(1.9881)**	(1.9334)*
*K*REQ	−7.7122	4.6689	1.1294	1.2954
	(−0.5074)	(3.4235)**	(3.6014)**	(3.0719)**
Intercept	0.4847	1.7395	0.9071	0.8477
	(0.3441)	(13.7640)**	(3.1214)**	(2.1693)**
R^2	0.148	0.217	0.186	0.167
F	4.091**	6.546**	5.406**	4.727**

Notes: Small firms are defined as having fewer than 500 employees. Figures in parentheses are *t*-statistics. Statistical significance is measured with two-tailed tests.
*$p = .10$.   **$p = .05$.

also imply that advertising intensity is negatively related to the extent of turbulence, although its impact is stronger for large firms.

Third, as the positive coefficient of CON in column 1 suggests, there is actually more, not less, turbulence in concentrated markets. Further, as the negative (and nonsignificant) coefficient of CON in column 2 implies, the turbulence rate among smaller firms may not be as strongly affected by market concentration as that of their larger counterparts. Finally, the negative coefficients of PCM and positive coefficients of GR in the first two columns are consistent with the hypothesis that turbulence rates are diminished in highly profitable industries, but they are stimulated in growing markets. As the statistically nonsignificant coefficients of PCM and GR in the last two columns suggest, PCM and GR apparently have similar effects on the turbulence rates of large and small firms.

Conclusions

While a heated debate has been raging over the last decade about what exactly constitutes a barrier to entry (see Stiglitz 1987), empirical studies have consistently compiled rather startling results—entry by new firms into an industry is apparently not substantially deterred in capital-intensive industries.[10] In Acs and Audretsch 1989a and 1989b, we said that even small firms are not significantly deterred from entering industries that are relatively capital intensive. This raises several questions at the heart of intraindustry dynamics. How is it that small firms are able to enter an industry at a suboptimal scale? How are they able to survive subsequent to entry? By examining the extent of market turbulence, or firm movements into, within, and out of an industry, we are able to shed some light on these questions.

We find evidence supporting the hypothesis of Gort and Klepper (1982) that the source of knowledge that produces innovations plays a key role in intraindustry dynamics. If innovative activity is particularly dependent upon knowledge that can be accumulated only through experience in the industry, the existing producers will have the innovative advantage and new and fringe firms will not find the industry to be especially accessible. Because relatively few firms will attempt entry into such an industry, there will also be a correspondingly low number of exits, resulting in a low rate of turbulence. On the other hand, if the knowledge required to produce innovations emanates largely from outside the industry or outside of the main producers in the industry, the market will be accessible to new and fringe firms.

However, just because the structure of knowledge and technology creates a market that is accessible, this does not imply that entrants and expanding

---

10. For a review of these studies, see Acs and Audretsch 1990, chap. 5.

fringe firms will automatically survive. Rather, the learning-by-doing theory suggests that only those firms that are able to successfully learn and adopt will grow and/or survive. Not only do our empirical results support the hypothesis that there will be a greater extent of turbulence in industries in which small firms are able to implement a strategy of innovation, but that, unless the small firms are able to participate in the ongoing innovative activity, the turbulence rate will be relatively low. In addition, we find that the turbulence rate for small firms, but not for large firms, tends to be greater in capital-intensive industries. This is consistent with the hypothesis that in such industries the small firms that successfully innovate and otherwise adopt (or are just plain lucky) grow to become viable entities, while the less fortunate small firms quickly decline and exit the market. Because the larger firms tend to have accumulated more experience, the extent of turbulence among large firms is considerably less in capital-intensive industries.

One of the most striking findings of our study is that the small-firm turbulence rate is more than one-third greater under the entrepreneurial regime than under the routinized regime. While much attention has been directed in the popular press and by policymakers on both sides of the Atlantic about the desirability of fostering a vital sector of highly innovative small firms in new, high-technology industries, our results strongly suggest that a high rate of turbulence is associated with such markets. That is, any policymaker advocating programs designed to encourage small entrepreneurial firms in new, high-technology industries should also recognize the accompanying firm failures and (at least temporary) job displacement and unemployment. The experience of the United States suggests that while such industries may be the engines for generating innovative activity and perhaps ultimately employment growth, extensive turbulence is apparently intricately entwined with industries under the entrepreneurial regime.

APPENDIX: DATA SOURCES AND FURTHER EXPLANATIONS

The innovation data for the number of small-firm innovations and total innovations that are used to construct the innovation rates, SIE and TIE, come from the U.S. Small Business Administration Innovation Data Base. This data base is described in detail in Acs and Audretsch 1988.

Industry Profiles (Bureau of the Census, 1981, Annual Survey of Manufactures, 1977. Washington, D.C.: GPO, 1981) is the source of the capital-labor ratio (K/L), four-firm concentration ratio (CR), annual growth rate (GR; the 1972 survey was also used to calculate GR), value of shipments (S), and minimum efficient scale (MES). The MES is measured as the mean size of the largest plants accounting for one-half of the industry value of shipments.

*K*REQ is measured as the amount of capital required to produce the MES level of output, defined as total industry assets divided by value of shipments multiplied by MES.

The employment data by firm size, births (BIRTH), deaths (DEATH), expansion (EXP), and contraction (CONTR) are from the U.S. Small Business Administration Office of Advocacy Small Business Data Base. More detailed description of the data can be found in Boden and Phillips 1985.

The advertising-sales ratio (AD/*S*) was derived by using the 1977 value of shipments data and advertising data from the U.S. input-output table. The measure of skilled labor (SKILL) is from 1972 Bureau of the Census of Manufactures, *Occupation by Industry.* SKILL is measured as the percentage of employment consisting of professional and kindred workers plus managers and administrators plus craftsmen and kindred workers.

REFERENCES

Acs, Zoltan J., and David B. Audretsch. 1987. "Innovation, Market Structure, and Firm Size." *Review of Economics and Statistics* 69:567–75.

Acs, Zoltan J., and David B. Audretsch. 1988. "Innovation in Large and Small Firms: An Empirical Analysis." *American Economic Review* 78:678–90.

Acs, Zoltan J., and David B. Audretsch. 1989a. "Births and Firm Size." *Southern Economic Journal* 55:467–75.

Acs, Zoltan J., and David B. Audretsch. 1989b. "Small-Firm Entry in U.S. Manufacturing." *Economica* 56 (2): 255–65.

Acs, Zoltan J., and David B. Audretsch. 1990. *Innovation and Small Firms.* Cambridge, Mass.: MIT Press.

Audretsch, David B., and Zoltan J. Acs. 1990. "Innovation as a Means of Entry: An Overview." In *Entry and Market Contestability: An International Comparison,* ed. Paul Geroski and Joachim Schwalbach. London: Basil Blackwell.

Arrow, Kenneth J. 1962. "Economic Welfare and the Allocation of Resources for Invention." In *The Rate and Direction of Inventive Activity,* ed. R. R. Nelson. Princeton, N.J.: Princeton University Press.

Beesley, M. E., and R. T. Hamilton. 1984. "Small Firms' Seedbed Role and the Concept of Turbulence." *Journal of Industrial Economics* 33:217–32.

Berry, C. H. 1974. "Corporate Diversification and Market Structure." *Bell Journal of Economics* 5 (1): 196–204.

Boden, Richard, and Bruce D. Phillips. 1985. "Uses and Limitations of USEEM/USELM Data." U.S. Small Business Administration Office of Advocacy, Washington, D.C.

Bolton Report. 1971. *Committee of Inquiry on Small Firms.* London: HMSO.

Bond, Ronald S. 1975. "Mergers and Mobility among the Largest Manufacturing Corporations." *Antitrust Bulletin* 20:505–19.

Boyle, Stanley E. 1971. "Large Industrial Corporations and Asset Shares: Comment." *American Economic Review* 61:163–67.

Boyle, Stanley E., and Robert L. Sorenson. 1971. "Concentration and Mobility: Alternative Measures of Industrial Structure." *Journal of Industrial Economics* 19:118–32.

Caves, Richard E., and Michael Porter. 1977. "From Entry to Mobility Barriers." *Quarterly Journal of Economics* 91:241–61.

Cohen, Wesley M., and Steven Klepper. 1991. "Firm Size versus Diversity in the Achievement of Technological Advance." In *Innovation and Technological Change: An International Comparison,* ed. Zoltan J. Acs and David B. Audretsch. Ann Arbor: University of Michigan Press.

Collins, Norman R., and Lee E. Preston. 1961. "The Size Structure of the Largest Industrial Firms 1909–1958." *American Economic Review* 51:986–1011.

Evans, David S. 1987a. "The Relationship Between Firm Growth, Size, and Age: Estimates for 100 Manufacturing Industries." *Journal of Industrial Economics* 35:567–81.

Evans, David S. 1987b. "Tests of Alternative Theories of Firm Growth." *Journal of Political Economy* 95:657–74.

Evans, David S., and Linda Leighton. 1990. "Some Empirical Aspects of Entrepreneurship." In *The Economics of Small Firms: A European Challenge,* ed. Zoltan J. Acs and David B. Audretsch. Boston, Mass.: Kluwer Academic Publishers.

Geroski, Paul, and Joachim Schwalbach, eds. 1990. *Entry and Market Contestability: An International Comparison.* London: Basil Blackwell.

Gort, Michael, and Steven Klepper. 1982. "Time Paths in the Diffusion of Product Innovations." *Economic Journal* 92:630–53.

Grossack, I. M. 1965. "Toward an Integration of Static and Dynamic Measures of Industry Concentration." *Review of Economics and Statistics* 47:301–8.

Gudgin, G. 1978. "Industrial Location Processes and Regional Employment Growth. Farnborough: Saxon House.

Helmstädter, E. 1986. "Dynamischer Wettbewerb, Wachstum, und Beschäftigung." In *Technologischer Wandel—Analyse und Fakten,* ed. Gottfried Bombach, Bernhard Gahlen, and Alfred E. Ott. Tübingen: Schriftenreihe des Wirtschaftswissenschaftlichen Seminars Ottobeuren.

Jovanovic, Boyan. 1982. "Selection and Evolution of Industry." *Econometrica* 50:649–70.

Kamerschen, David R. 1971. "Large Industrial Corporations and Asset Shares: Comment." *American Economic Review* 61:160–62.

Kaplan, A. D. H. 1954. *Big Enterprise in a Competitive System.* Washington, D.C.: Brookings Institution.

Marshall, Alfred. 1920. *Principles of Economics.* 8th ed. London: Macmillan.

Mermelstein, David. 1969. "Large Industrial Corporations and Asset Shares." *American Economic Review* 59:531–41.

Mermelstein, David. 1971. "Large Industrial Corporations and Asset Shares: Reply." *American Economic Review* 61:168–74.

Mueller, Dennis C. 1967. "The Firm Decision Process: An Econometric Investigation." *Journal of Political Economy* 81:58–87.

Mueller, Dennis C., and J. Tilton. 1969. "Research and Development Costs as a Barrier to Entry." *Canadian Journal of Economics* 2:570–79.

Oster, Sharon. 1982. "Intraindustry Structure and the Ease of Strategic Change." *Review of Economics and Statistics* 64:376–83.

Pakes, A., and R. Ericson. 1987. "Empirical Implications of Alternative Models of Firm Dynamics." Department of Economics, University of Wisconsin at Madison. Typescript.

Porter, Michael E. 1976. *Interbrand Choice, Strategy, and Bilateral Market Power*. Cambridge, Mass.: Harvard University Press.

Scherer, F. M. 1980. *Industrial Market Structure and Economic Performance*. 2d ed. Chicago: Rand McNally.

Scherer, F. M. 1991. "Changing Perspectives on the Firm Size Problem." In *Innovation and Technological Change: An International Comparison*, ed. Zoltan J. Acs and David B. Audretsch. Ann Arbor: University of Michigan Press.

Simon, Herbert A., and Charles P. Bonini. 1958. "The Size Distribution of Business Firms." *American Economic Review* 48:607–17.

Stigler, George J. 1956. "The Statistics of Monopoly and Mergers." *Journal of Political Economy* 64:33–40.

Stiglitz, Joseph E. 1987. "Technological Change, Sunk Costs, and Competition." *Brookings Papers on Economic Activity* 3:883–937.

Storey, David. 1989. "Firm Performance and Size: Explanation from the Small Firm Sectors." *Small Business Economics* 1 (3): 175–80.

Tilton, J. 1971. *International Diffusion of Technology: The Case of Semiconductors*. Washington, D.C.: Brookings Institution.

U.S. Bureau of the Census. 1972. Census Population 1970 Subject Report PC(2)-7c. *Occupation by Industry*. Washington, D.C.: U.S. Government Printing Office.

U.S. Bureau of the Census. 1981. Annual Survey of Manufactures, 1977. *Industry Profiles*. Washington, D.C.: U.S. Government Printing Office.

Williamson, Oliver E. 1975. *Markets and Hierarchies*. New York: Macmillan.

Winter, Sidney G. 1984. "Schumpeterian Competition in Alternative Technological Regimes." *Journal of Economic Behavior and Organization* 5:287–320.

Modularity, Innovation, and the Firm: The Case of Audio Components

Paul L. Robertson and Richard N. Langlois

Introduction

The degree of vertical integration in an industry depends on both supply and demand conditions. The effects of such supply factors as the division of labor, economies of scale, and the presence or absence of external economies have been thoroughly explored over a period of more than two hundred years.

Demand factors have received less attention. In particular, the tendency of economists to assume product homogeneity has obscured the fact that the structure of an "industry" and the characteristics of the firms it comprises can vary greatly depending on how consumers define its "product." Over time, the nature of what consumers believe is the essence of a given product often changes. Consumers may add certain attributes,[1] drop others, or they may combine the product with another product that had been generally regarded as distinct. Alternately, a product that consumers had treated as an entity may be divided into a group of subproducts that consumers can arrange into various combinations according to their personal preferences.

In this essay, we tentatively explore the relationship between supply and demand conditions in shaping the nature of an industry and the scope of activities of specific firms. On the supply side, we consider the importance of technical and organizational factors in influencing the production cost and, therefore, the price to consumers of employing various degrees of vertical integration. We also recognize the vital role of suppliers as innovators who can bring new components and new arrangements of existing components to the notice of consumers.

On the demand side, we look at how autonomous changes in consumer

---

1. In the sense of Lancaster 1971; we discuss this approach in greater detail subsequently. Note that, although we couch our discussion in terms of a final consumer, the analysis also applies *a fortiori* to intermediate products, since, we believe, consumers of such products are even more sophisticated and well informed about product attributes than typical final consumers.

321

tastes and the reaction of consumers to changes introduced by suppliers help to shape the definition of a product. In choosing what to purchase, consumers seek out a variety of attributes. Depending on the attributes they desire and their perceptions of which possibilities are presented by suppliers, consumers may choose to combine components (or sources of attributes) in various ways consistent with their budget constraints. These range over a spectrum from an entity—a product that brings together in a single, standardized package components that provide all of the desired attributes—to a modular system that is acquired bit by bit, allowing consumers to construct for themselves the packages that meet their individual preferences for attributes.

Therefore, the nature of an industry and the extent of vertical integration depend not only on what patterns of production minimize production and transaction costs, but also on which attributes consumers may wish. As a result of "bundling," "unbundling," and "rebundling" various attributes, the definition of a product and the structure of the industry that manufactures it may change dramatically.

We begin by outlining the theoretical underpinnings of the relationship between vertical integration and desired product attributes. The second half of our essay confronts these concepts with a case study of the audio component industry.

Vertical Integration and Product Attributes

The Boundaries of the Firm

One of the central insights of the economics of vertical integration since Coase (1937) is that the boundaries of the firm are influenced not only by the production costs of the various stages of production but also by the costs of transactions between stages.

In his well-known 1951 article, George Stigler stressed the role of production costs. Building on Smith's theory of the division of labor, he cast the making of a product in terms of successive stages of production, each of which has its own cost characteristics. Not all of these stages operate at constant returns to scale, which affects the response of the process to an increase in final output (what Smith called the extent of the market). Some stages may experience decreasing returns, posing a kind of bottleneck to the process. Nathan Rosenberg has suggested that such bottleneck stages may be focal points for innovation (1976, 125);[2] this is an idea to which we will return. It may also happen, however, that some stages are not bottlenecks but

---

2. For an extended example, see Hughes 1983 and 1989. Hughes refers to bottlenecks as "reverse salients."

"antibottlenecks," that is, they experience increasing returns to scale. Stigler argues that such stages will spin off to become what Smith would have called "peculiar trades" of their own. Vertical integration thus decreases with the extent of the market.

As writers in the Coasean tradition have pointed out, however, one cannot, in fact, draw any conclusions about the boundaries of the firm from production costs alone. By itself, the division of labor suggests how production will be organized. But it says nothing about how the various stages will be owned and coordinated. Even stages that are closely linked technologically may, in principle, be separately owned if the costs of transactions across that ownership boundary are low. Only when transaction costs are high may joint ownership of stages be necessary.

What are the sources of these transaction costs? One important school stresses the cost of measuring the output of successive stages (Barzel 1982), while another stresses the specificity of assets (Klein, Crawford, and Alchian 1978; Williamson 1985). But there are arguably other kinds of transaction costs—or other ways of looking at transaction costs. This is especially true when we consider the phenomenon of change in the process of production. Indeed, change itself may provide a source of transaction costs. For example, the costs of informing outside suppliers of a process innovation and persuading them of its value may be high relative to the costs of internalizing those stages of production (Langlois 1988; Langlois and Robertson 1989; Silver 1984). This is especially important when the innovation is systemic (Teece 1986), that is, when change in one stage of production must be coordinated with many other stages.

Innovation may also foster vertical disintegration. This may happen when there is a high level of relevant Marshallian external economies (Langlois 1990). For example, there may be a rich network of vertical suppliers ready to supply parts at low cost. A more interesting example, however, would be the existence of a *horizontal* network of competitors.

In general, whether the innovator chooses to use outside contractors or to produce components internally may depend on whether the benefits of the innovation can be appropriated by an external supplier. If the innovator can easily appropriate the rents of innovation—as through a patent—there is little need to integrate. But if appropriation is difficult, suppliers may garner some of the rents, and the innovator might be motivated to take an equity position in suppliers or even to integrate operations if the transaction costs involved are high (Teece 1986). Nevertheless, even when there is no patent or other protection, horizontal networking can allow an innovator to earn higher profits than if it attempted to appropriate all of the benefits itself. This can occur when the innovation is a form of "software" that requires the user to obtain dedicated hardware. For example, the profitability of producing prerecorded video cassettes for the home market is dependent on widespread ownership of video cassette recorders (VCRs). Because of the longstanding fragmentation of the motion picture industry, which provides the primary input, it is improbable that any single supplier of prerecorded cassettes could itself offer enough variety to induce large numbers of domestic users to invest in the hardware. Therefore, the ability of prerecorded cassette firms to appropriate profits is, in part, a function of their membership in a *network of competitors*.

The benefits arising from networks of competitors will work against vertical integration. As Graham points out, one reason for the failure of RCA's VideoDisc alternative was that the firm attempted to appropriate all of the rents arising from its new hardware, the recorder, by controlling the output of software, the VideoDiscs (Graham 1986, 214–16). As RCA was the only source of the discs, the range available to the public was tiny in comparison to the selection of VCR cassettes. If there had been more producers of discs, there would have been a chance that both they and RCA would have prospered; but RCA failed as a hardware supplier because it made its product unattractive by narrowing access to the software.

Another—and perhaps related—case in which change may lead to disintegration is when the change is in the nature of a product innovation or when modularity makes innovation autonomous rather than systemic. It is this possibility to which we now turn.

Product Innovation and Consumer Transaction Costs

All the theories examined so far treat innovation and the boundaries of the firm in terms of an unchanging product. Process innovation provides the engine of change that leads to increased division of labor or external economies. Moreover, the product is treated as an ultimate entity rather than as part of a system of products that final customers may purchase to satisfy their needs. Hence, the possibility of transaction costs on the part of consumers is also ignored.

In reality, as we all know, products change frequently. As they become either simpler or more complicated, the extent of the division of labor in the production process may also change: fewer components may require fewer stages of differentiation, while more components may require more stages. These changes, in turn, may alter the scope for spin-offs.

In addition, changes in product technology may well arise exogenously as the industry under consideration adopts improvements generated in other fields. For example, there may be five stages in the production of a particular good, the famous widget (fig 1a).[3] Through a form of technological con-

---

3. Note that we must now change the metaphor of "stages of production" slightly. In the standard analysis of vertical integration, we think of stages of production as a linear production

a.   **Stages of production of the original widget.**

b.   **Stages of production of the improved widget.**

Fig. 1.   Producing the improved widget

vergence,[4] two new components developed in other industries may turn out to be desirable adjuncts to the original good (fig 1*b*). The question is, will these new components be supplied by outside firms, perhaps their original manufacturers, or will they be internalized through vertical integration by the widget makers? The answer, as usual, will depend on the extent of economies of scale and the transaction costs involved. If the minimum efficient scale (MES) of production of the new components exceeds the needs of any individual widget maker, then the component manufacturers are likely to remain independent as long as the transaction costs of dealing with outside suppliers are smaller than the additional production costs the widget firms would incur by producing at less than MES (Williamson 1985, chap. 4).[5]

---

technology, as in the processing of steel from ore to milled bars. In fact, the process is seldom so linear. This is even more the case when we begin talking—as we are now—of the technology of production of utility in a Lancasterian sense. Now our "stages of production" are no longer sequential—or even a *process* technology strictly speaking. In our terms, the stages of production would be the various components of a stereo system or a microcomputer, which can be combined in various ways to produce the intangible output the consumer seeks.

4. See Rosenberg 1976, chap. 1.

5. Neoclassical economics has taught us to think of MES as a matter of technology that is independent of the firm using the technology. In fact, of course, production cost is an extremely firm-specific matter. As Nelson and Winter (1982, chaps. 4 and 5) suggest, production is a matter of the skills a firm possesses; such skills are often inarticulate and learned gradually over time. The firm's cost of internalizing a given activity will depend on how appropriate to the task the firm's skills are, which often means how similar the activity is to the activities the firm already engages in (Richardson 1972). One force for vertical disintegration, then, is the dissimilarity among stages of production. The skills necessary to make turntables may be very dissimilar from those needed to make amplifiers; the skills applicable to making disk drives may be quite dissimilar from those needed to fabricate semiconductor memories. One might, indeed, go so far as to wonder whether such dissimilarity does not increase with the complexity and technical sophistication of the final product.

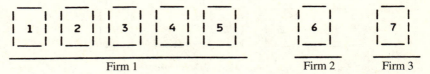

Fig. 2.   **Firms involved in the production of components of the improved widget**

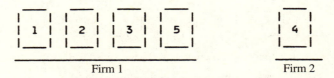

Fig. 3.   **Production of widgets with a changing component 4**

Suppose, however, that the new components are not necessary—that they may in fact be superfluous or even repugnant to many widget users. In this case, the decision to purchase them could be delegated to the users rather than to the widget manufacturers. Users would buy the same type of widgets that they had traditionally purchased and then, if they wished, buy one or both of the additional components, perhaps from a different shop. The production of new widgets would then come to resemble figure 2. Alternately, the rate of technological change of the various components that make up the widget may vary. Component 4, for example, might enter a new phase of rapid development while the remaining inputs do not vary. Furthermore, customers might have reason to believe that this component would continue to improve dramatically for some years. They would then wish to purchase a widget that embodies the traditional components 1, 2, 3, and 5, but that offers the opportunity to upgrade component 4 as improved variations come on the market.

Again, whether component 4 would be manufactured by the widget maker or by someone else would depend on the relationship between production costs and transaction costs. If the widget firm decides internalization is impractical, the situation shown in figure 3 would arise. Customers would purchase component 4 separately and the remainder as a package. This assumes, of course, that the new variant is compatible with existing components. The established widget firms will have an interest in trying to avoid compatibility to continue selling existing models that embody all five components. But the developers of the new variant of component 4 will want to achieve compatibility to allow consumers to adopt their product without fuss. As we will show in the case study, the outcome will depend on the relative power of the two groups in the marketplace.

In the situations portrayed in figures 2 and 3, customers are no longer purchasing a single appliance (as depicted in fig. 1). Instead, they have moved to a modular system in which they can take advantage of interchangeable components rather than having to accept an entire package that is prechosen by the manufacturer.

For most kinds of products—toasters or automobiles, say—manufacturers offer preset packages. One can choose from a multiplicity of packages, but one cannot choose the engine from one kind of car, the hood ornament from another, and the front suspension from a third. Not only are there transaction costs of such picking and choosing (Cheung 1983, 6–7), there are also economies of scale in assembling the parts into a finished package. Indeed, it is these economies of scale more than transaction costs that explains the tendency of assemblers to offer preset packages. If there were only transaction costs of discovering which parts are available and what their prices are, we would expect to see not preset packages but a proliferation of middlemen who specialize in packaging components tailored to buyers' specific tastes. For most appliancelike products, however, the economies of scale of assembly lead to integration of the packaging and assembly functions.

Attributes and Product Differentiation

One way to think about this is in terms of the modern theory of product differentiation.[6] Instead of seeing a product as an ultimate entity, view it instead as an input (or set of inputs) to the production of utility through the consumer's "consumption technology" (Lancaster 1971). In technical terms, the consumer chooses among available bundles (or combinations of bundles) to reach the highest indifference surface possible. Each bundle represents a location (technically speaking: a vector) in "product space," and each consumer has a preferred place in that space—a bundle with his or her favorite combination of attributes. If there are scale economies, some producers can gain advantage by choosing the locations in this space where they think the density of demand will be highest. An example of this is Ford's Model T. The undifferentiated, no-frills product may not have suited everyone's tastes exactly. But the progressive reductions in price that long production runs made possible brought the Model T within the budget constraints of a growing number of people who were willing to accept a relatively narrow provision of attributes rather than do without.[7]

---

6. For a straightforward introduction, see Waterson 1984, chap. 6.

7. Although price factors can be important, we must be careful not to place too much emphasis on them. Poor or unsophisticated consumers will be much more susceptible to low-cost products (have lower budget constraints); but, as incomes and sophistication increase, a higher proportion of buyers will seek a better selection of attributes. A sufficient number of people were

In the extreme case of no economies of scale, the entire space can be filled with products, and each consumer can have a product tailored exactly to his or her requirements. The type of product we have called a modular system approximates this extreme: both the transaction costs of knowing the available parts and the scale economies of assembling the package are low for a wide segment of the user population. By picking and choosing among an array of compatible components, the consumer can move freely around a large area of the product space.

In the case of sound reproduction, for example, the list of attributes can be extensive and the trade-offs among them complex. The product technology the consumer chooses is a function of the attributes sought. As the range of the voice is limited, high fidelity can be achieved more easily for voice than for music: in contrast to lovers of piano sonatas, consumers who confine their listening to news broadcasts can get by easily with small radios and have no practical use for a sophisticated combination of components. When immediacy is needed, a radio or telephone will provide better service than a phonograph. The ability to store sound, on the other hand, can be accomplished using a record, tape, or compact disk, but not directly by a telephone or radio. When reciprocal communication is wanted, a telephone will suit the purpose while a radio receiver will not.

When the bundle of overlapping attributes for different consumption technologies is small or they conflict in some way, consumers will use different appliances or systems. Although there are considerable technical similarities between the telephone and radio voice transmission, the differences have been more significant, ensuring that two distinct networks and sets of reception appliances have remained in use.[8] Where attributes do not conflict, however, the presence of a high degree of technological convergence will open the way for the development of multipurpose appliances or modular systems, as in the case of a stereo set featuring several sound media that share amplification and reproduction equipment. Again, compatibility is crucial. Producers may have an incentive to create proprietary products in an attempt to capture sales of most or all potential subcomponents. But, as we will suggest, such a strategy often backfires, and the high demand that unbundling allows can often force a compatible modularity on the industry.

Thus, innovation can affect consumption technology in two major ways.

---

able to afford better bundles of attributes that, even at the peak of its popularity, the Model T did not force Cadillac, Lincoln, or Packard from the market. And, as incomes rose generally in the 1920s, the Model T itself succumbed as a higher proportion of consumers had the means to purchase superior selections of nonprice features.

8. In this case, the conflict arises primarily from the incompatibility of a high degree of reciprocal communication with a need for orderly programming of radio broadcasts. The two types of voice transmission are beginning to converge in the realm of cellular telephones, where computer technology comes into play to control broadcast and reception.

First, new products can satisfy a desire for attributes that had not yet been satisfied or, indeed, even noticed. Second, through technological convergence, new ways of packaging or bundling consumption technology, and therefore providing attributes, become feasible.

Autonomous versus Systemic Innovation

The benefits of modularity appear on the producer's side as well as on the consumer's side. A modular system is open to innovation of certain kinds in a way that a closed system—an appliance—is not. A decentralized and fragmented system can have advantages in innovation to the extent that it involves attempting many alternate approaches simultaneously, leading to rapid trial-and-error learning. This kind of innovation is especially important when technology is changing rapidly and there is a high degree of both technological and market uncertainty (Nelson and Winter 1977). In a modular system, there are many more entry points for new firms, and thus for new ideas, than in an industry producing functionally similar appliances. To this extent, then, a modular system may progress faster technologically, especially during periods of uncertainty and fluidity.

Another reason that innovation may be spurred by modularity lies in the division of labor. A network with a standard of compatibility promotes autonomous innovation, that is, innovation requiring little coordination among stages. By allowing specialist producers (and sometimes specialist users) to concentrate their attention on particular components, a modular system thus enlists the division of labor in the service of innovation. We would expect innovation to proceed in the manner Rosenberg and Hughes suggest: with bottleneck components—those components standing most in the way of increased consumer satisfaction—as the focal points for change.

Systemic innovation requires coordination across stages. This would be more difficult in a modular system, and even undesirable to the extent that it destroyed compatibility. We would expect, however, to see systemic innovation *within* the externally compatible components. The internal "stages of production" within a modem or a tape deck can vary greatly from manufacturer to manufacturer as long as the component continues to connect easily to the network. The components may, in other words, be appliances. To the extent that the coordination this internal systemic innovation requires is costly across markets, we would expect to see greater vertical integration by makers of components than by purveyors of the larger systems.

The Development of High Fidelity and Stereo Systems

The evolution of modular high fidelity and stereo component systems in the post–World War II period resulted from two separate but related developments, both of which originated before 1939. The first, the spread of an underground movement for greater fidelity in sound reproduction, involved better recording techniques and superior reproduction equipment. The second was the introduction of 33- and 45-RPM records and the associated use of vinyl, which greatly enhanced the usefulness of recordings, particularly for lovers of classical music. Thus, the connection between changes in hardware (the components) and software (records and later tapes and compact disks) was established from the beginning.

Early Developments

Before the 1930s, the phonograph was an appliance.[9] Even then, conservatism was strong in the industry and change was propelled largely by external forces, including the drastic sales decline that followed the spread of the radio in the 1920s. Record sales in the United States dropped from $52 million in 1920 to $21 million in 1925. At that time, records were still recorded and played back acoustically, using mechanical vibrations to cut grooves into wax originals and to transmit sound from records to listeners via a horn. Although various instruments operate over a range of approximately 20 Hz to 20,000 Hz (20–16,000 cycles per second), from the lowest note on the organ to the highest overtones of the oboe, acoustic records generally reproduced a range of 350 to 3,000 Hz (*Fortune*, September, 1939, 74–75, 92; Inglis 1990, 29; Read and Welch 1976, 237).

When the research department of Western Electric (which later became Bell Telephone Laboratories) developed electric recording techniques and, later, a superior phonograph in the 1920s, the improvements were initially turned down by Victor (the largest record and record player manufacturer), which indicated that the sounds produced would be unpleasant to listeners, who were used to the "true or miniature" sound of the acoustic Victrola. Nevertheless, under the impact of falling sales, electric recording methods were soon adopted, and Brunswick shortly thereafter introduced the first electric phonograph, which it called the Panatrope. Sales of records rebounded quickly, reaching around 65 million units in 1929 (*Fortune*, September, 1939, 92, 94; Read and Welch 1976, chap. 17).

Early Stages of Modular Systems

The origins of modularity in subsequent decades can be traced to the development of the Brunswick Panatrope. Although there had been earlier radio-

---

9. A phonograph included all the equipment necessary for reproduction. With the advent of electric models in the late 1920s, this meant a speaker and an amplifier as well as the turntable. A record player was only a turntable and had to be plugged into a radio. Finally, a "combination" included both a radio and a phonograph in a single unit.

phonograph combinations, they were essentially two appliances encased in a common cabinet because radio signals could not be reproduced acoustically (Read and Welch 1976, 268–69). The Panatrope, which had a vacuum tube amplifier and a speaker, therefore permitted technological convergence, since both radio signals and signals transmitted from the phonograph pickup were now reproduced identically. This soon led to a degree of modularity. For example, in 1933 RCA began to offer a record player for $9.95 that could be plugged into a radio (Wallerstein 1976, 58).

Although various enthusiasts attempted to achieve higher fidelity before 1939, significant improvements in both recordings and broadcasts did not come until the postwar period.[10] Hardware and software requirements went together, because high-fidelity components were of no particular value without high-quality recordings. At the end of World War II, most records had an upper limit of 8,000 Hz because of distortion in the higher ranges. Even this limited span was further truncated by contemporary phonographs, which seldom reproduced sounds above 4,000 Hz. While this captured most of the fundamentals, the overtones were lost. One major firm, English Decca, introduced Full Frequency Range Recordings (FFRR).[11] At the same time, the company began to sell an inexpensive portable phonograph in Britain with a range from 50 to 14,000 Hz. However, for reasons that are obscure but that Read and Welch imply involve a conspiracy among other manufacturers, the set was never introduced in the United States (*Fortune,* October, 1946, 161; Read and Welch 1976, 338).

Record and phonograph manufacturers in the United States had long resisted attempts to improve the range of their products on the grounds that their customers preferred a diluted sound. One survey, conducted by the Columbia Broadcasting System, indicated that, by a margin of more than two to one, listeners liked standard broadcasts of up to 5,000 Hz better than wide-range programs that went up to 10,000 Hz. Owners of FM radios, who would have had greater exposure to wide-range reproduction, nevertheless preferred the narrow range by more than four to one. And, even more astonishingly,

---

10. In practice, fidelity has turned out to be a concept with several meanings. When pioneers such as Edison sought fidelity, they wanted their recordings to sound exactly like the original performances. This warts-and-all approach has subsequently been adopted by some acoustic puritans including Read and Welch and also Maxfield, one of the pioneers of electrical recording techniques at Western Electric. Among other things, these observers decry the ability of recording engineers to produce musical painted ladies by using techniques developed since the 1920s to alter the nature of the product by compensating for expected distortion, splicing together portions of different performances, etc. (Read and Welch 1976, chap. 17). With the growing sophistication of recording equipment, this tendency to meddle with performances has increased in recent years. In the absence of any "real" standard of how a recording should sound, the quality of recordings has become a subjective matter to be decided by recording engineers and consumers who can choose from a range of sound mixtures according to personal preferences.

11. English Decca markets its records on the London label in the United States.

professional musicians voted by fifteen to one in favor of the standard range.[12] If, as it appeared, the most discerning of listeners were content with a limit of 5,000 Hz, there seemed to be no reason to improve recordings or equipment (*Fortune*, October, 1946, 161; Read and Welch 1976, 346–47).

Even before the war, however, there was a move for greater fidelity among some enthusiasts. The most famous of these was Avery Fisher, who had majored in English and Biology at New York University and later worked as an advertising manager and book designer for Dodd Mead. In 1937, he formed Philharmonic Radio to produce high-quality sets. He sold the company during the war, and in 1945 started Fisher Radio, the firm that would eventually make him a multimillionaire (Eisenberg 1976, 76–77).

The Move Toward Systems in the Postwar Period

The high-fidelity movement gained impetus during World War II when U.S. troops stationed in Europe became aware of the extent to which the United States lagged in both record and phonograph technology. In addition, many of the people stationed in Europe were trained in radio or electronic technologies that were transferable to high-fidelity uses, and some brought back equipment (Mullin 1976, 62–64; Read and Welch 1976, 333, 347–48). When their suggestions for improvement were rebuffed by the established firms, a number of them went into business as components manufacturers.

While a few manufacturers like Fisher, Capehart, and Scott did produce high-quality phonographs and combinations in the immediate postwar years (*Fortune*, October, 1946, 190, 193, 195), there was a movement from integrated appliances to components that resulted from both supply and demand conditions. Many of the new firms were run by specialists who could not afford to manufacture across a broad scale even if they had had the expertise. On the demand side, interest in modularity was fueled by rapid but uneven rates of improvement across components that encouraged buyers to maintain the flexibility to update. The individualistic and subjective nature of "fidelity" also encouraged a proliferation of components, as buyers sought to build systems to suit their idiosyncratic tastes.

One famous example was T. R. Kennedy, Jr., whom *Fortune* billed as "a 'golden ear' of the richest sheen."[13] The magazine described the set that Kennedy, a radio engineer, put together for his own use.

---

12. The problem was apparently caused by phase distortion, which leads to "listener fatigue." It can be eliminated by using amplifiers with frequency ranges that greatly exceed the actual hearing range.

13. According to *Fortune*, a "golden ear" such as Kennedy is "a purist [who] insists that the tones be noise-free and undistorted, sharp, clear, and full from treble to bass." Their opponents

His receiver is well designed and, of course, has an FM circuit. His main amplifier was built at the Bell Telephone Laboratories. His speaker has three units. To forestall phonograph vibration, the motor is mounted separately, while a dental-machine belt carries the rotary motion to a turntable anchored in 600 pounds of sand. The pickup arm sports a feather-light sapphire needle, kept at an even temperature and humidity in an airtight container until just before it is used. Kennedy makes his own superior recordings of broadcast music. As a result, his parlor concerts are unsurpassed for fidelity. He has been accused of making a fetish of it, of listening to tone rather than to music. "Listen!" he says. "Compare music from my equipment with what the average combination gives. You'll throw rocks at your set." (*Fortune*, October, 1946, 161)

Such an outfit did not come cheaply, especially in 1946. The total cost of around $1,400 comprised an AM-FM chassis costing $600; an amplifier, which had both bass and treble equalizers, at $150; a turntable at $175; a pickup at $180; and a custom-built speaker system for $250. (The cost of the sand was not given.)

As we have seen, components in the sense of add-on equipment had been available for many years. The Duo Jr. record player that RCA began to offer in 1933 was one example. In general, the "war of the speeds" between Columbia and RCA, who introduced 33- and 45-RPM records, respectively, opened the field to component makers by disturbing consumer perceptions of the existing paradigm.[14] This was reinforced in the early 1950s by even more options, such as tape recorders (Read and Welch 1976, 350). Listeners who took fidelity seriously now had a wide choice of equipment.

The Importance of Compatibility

Compatibility among the range of options was developed through the market as component manufacturers were forced to cooperate, at least up to a point, in order to be able to sell their products at all.

Another strong influence . . . was the competition for business on the part of the smaller manufacturers who specialized in such parts as pickups, amplifiers, and speakers; or even in such smaller components as

---

were "tin ears," who, like the listeners surveyed by CBS, were so accustomed to distortion that they preferred it to high fidelity. "Some people don't even like what they hear in a concert hall. The real thing, they say, is too bright and loud" (*Fortune*, October, 1946, 160–61).

14. Columbia offered a 33-RPM attachment in 1948, and RCA placed its 45-RPM, rapid-drop changer on the market in the following year.

resistors, volume controls, etc. In their zeal, they were often forced to demonstrate the superiorities of equipment by assembling complete sound reproducing systems incorporating in them the requisite high-quality apparatus made by others. When the larger manufacturers refused to buy superior parts as a result of such demonstrations . . . which became frequent after the war, the answers were obvious. Consequently, many smaller manufacturers of improved components either went into the manufacture of more complete units, by acquiring licenses to manufacture other parts from other patent holders, or went into the business of selling directly to the public. (Read and Welch 1976, 347)

Packaged systems, of course, remained available. With the exception of Fisher and later Magnavox, which was originally a manufacturer of speakers, it was, however, rare before the 1970s for firms to produce both components and packages. Separate stores for high-fidelity and later stereo equipment developed in which customers could hear various combinations before deciding (Read and Welch 1976, 351–52). Only components that were compatible could be demonstrated. Similarly, the growth of the kit industry relied on interchangeability. Finally, because many of the best components were developed in Britain or Europe, international standards became common.[15]

The Origins of 33-RPM Records

Although Decca's original FFRR recordings were on 78-RPM disks, a major impetus behind the development of high-fidelity reproduction was the introduction of long-playing 33-RPM records and 45-RPM singles. The history of the long-playing record illustrates the distinction between autonomous and systemic change: because RCA tried to treat a systemic change as autonomous, the first introduction of 33-RPM records failed.

By the 1920s, the format of 10-inch and 12-inch 78-RPM records had been established. This was entirely adequate for the vast bulk of records sold, which were "singles," frequently popular tunes but also arias sung by well-known operatic soloists.[16] But, as the maximum playing time per side for a 12-inch 78 was barely five minutes, longer classical works required several disks and were frequently disrupted, sometimes in midmovement. Moreover, as a result of the Depression and inept management in the industry itself, sales of records and phonographs slumped again in the early 1930s. Only 10 mil-

---

15. Garrard, for instance, used different-sized flywheels for the U.S. and European markets, allowing for local differences in electricity transmission. Otherwise, the same record changers were compatible with other components everywhere.

16. The first great recording star was Enrico Caruso, who earned royalties of more than $3 million (*Fortune*, September, 1939, 73).

lion records were sold in 1932, and total retail sales of both records and equipment in the United States fell from a peak of $250 million to around $5 million (*Fortune,* September, 1939, 94). It was in this climate that RCA made the first attempt to market 33-RPM vinyl disks.

In 1932, RCA introduced 33-RPM records that, to reduce surface noise, were made from a vinyl compound rather than the shellac mixture used for the 78s. The RCA records featured grooves that were only a little narrower than standard 78 grooves, however, which limited 33-RPM playing times to only around twice that of 12-inch 78s. More importantly, the wide grooves required wide styli and heavy pickups, which cut through the soft vinyl after the records had been played a few times. RCA did not address these hardware problems. Because of the scarcity of suitable turntables and the fragility of the records, RCA terminated the experiment the following year (Read and Welch 1976, 339–40; Wallerstein 1976, 57).

The Early Stages of LP Records at Columbia

The man who made the decision to withdraw the 33-RPM records from the market in 1933 was Edward Wallerstein, the general manager of the Victor Division of RCA. He subsequently moved to Columbia, and, despite the Victor experience, he commissioned a team at Columbia to develop the process further.[17] From the beginning, Columbia seems to have taken a systemic approach. As early as 1939, Wallerstein ordered that everything recorded at 78-RPM also be recorded on 16-inch 33-RPM blanks. These were then stored and available for reissue as LPs in the late 1940s (Wallerstein 1976, 57).

In order to increase playing time and (literally) reduce the wear and tear on vinyl, Columbia engineers concentrated on 1-mil microgrooves that could be used with a lighter stylus and pickup. Narrower grooves provided only part of the solution, however, as long as they were spaced as far apart as 78-RPM grooves on shellac-based records. As late as 1946, Columbia could provide only 11 to 12 minutes per side. To determine the desired length, Wallerstein surveyed the classical repertoire and found out that, with 17 minutes per side, 99 percent of classical pieces would fit on a single, two-sided disk. By approximately doubling the number of grooves to between 190 and 225 per inch, Columbia engineers were soon able to exceed the 17-minute standard, and the firm decided to market 33-RPM long-playing records in the fall of 1948 (Read and Welch 1976, 340; Wallerstein 1976, 57–58).

---

17. There was considerable rivalry between Wallerstein and Peter Goldmark over the respective roles that each had played in the commercial development of LP records (Goldmark 1973). Our concern here, however, is with the general path of development and not with precedence within the Columbia organization.

Networks in Hardware and Software

Columbia recognized, of course, that simply offering the records would not be sufficient. Easy availability of 33-RPM record players would also be required. As Columbia, in contrast to RCA Victor, did not manufacture electrical equipment itself, the success of the LP (a Columbia trademark) depended on convincing one or more outside firms to manufacture players. Wallerstein recalled a promotional technique that he had used at RCA in 1933. In order to revive sales of records then, he established a record club that offered an inexpensive record player, the Duo Jr., that could be plugged into a radio set. RCA sold the player at cost, $9.95 (Wallerstein 1976, 58). Therefore, when Columbia discovered that it did not have the skills or time to develop its own record players, it approached several manufacturers. The company chose Philco as the initial supplier, with Columbia providing much (according to Wallerstein, all) of the basic technology. Wallerstein's recognition of the importance of networks was shown by his initial disappointment that only a single player manufacturer was chosen. "I was a little unhappy about this, because I felt that all of the manufacturers should be making a player of some sort—the more players that go on the market, the more records could be sold" (Wallerstein 1976, 61).

In any event, the price of the Philco "attachments" was soon reduced from $29.95 to $9.95, the cost at which Philco supplied them to Columbia. Columbia was able to leave the attachment business within a year as other manufacturers followed Philco's lead (Wallerstein 1976, 61).

Columbia also recognized the importance of networks of competitors. Recognizing that it would prosper if other recording companies adopted the 33-RPM microgroove standard, it offered to license the process, a proposition that was quickly taken up by other, smaller companies. Buyers of classical records responded to the convenience of the LP, the alleged unbreakability of vinyl disks (which RCA had begun to market as 78s in 1946), and the sharp reduction in price. In 1939, for instance, Toscanini's recording of Beethoven's Fifth Symphony, a work of moderate length that could easily be accommodated on a single LP, required an album of four 78-RPM records that cost $2 apiece. As long as a work like Schönberg's Gurrelieder, which required 14 records at $2 each, could be expected to sell only 400 to 500 copies, few companies would be willing to take the risk of recording it (*Fortune*, September, 1939, 100; Read and Welch 1976, 339–430; Wallerstein 1976, 58, 60). Given the high price elasticity of records, the lower price of LPs permitted an important broadening of the repertoire, which reinforced the density of the network and further encouraged consumers to switch to the new standard.

Thus, although there were no basic patents covering the LP process,

Columbia was able to appropriate a large share of the profits by positioning itself as the leading firm in the network of competitors. Other firms that joined the network, such as English Decca, also prospered. But those that initially held out, including EMI and RCA, lost heavily and were eventually forced to conform. RCA, for example, lost $4.5 million on records between June, 1948, and January, 1950, when it began to issue its own LPs. Its classical sales were decimated, and a number of its most important artists, including Pinza, Rubinstein, and Heifitz, either deserted or threatened to do so. Over the same period, Columbia cleared $3 million (Wallerstein 1976, 60–61).

RCA's Response

RCA's first approach to the threat of the LP was to try to block the network by establishing its own incompatible system. Columbia had considered issuing 6- or 7-inch 33-RPM records for the large singles market, but abandoned the idea. This left an opening for RCA, which introduced 45-RPM singles and produced its own record players and phonographs. In order to forestall competition, RCA chose to use a larger spindle that could not accommodate 33 (or 78) records (Read and Welch 1976, 340–42; Wallerstein 1976, 60–61). Although other companies followed RCA with large-hole 45s, however, the incompatibility turned out to be in one direction only, since 45-RPM records could easily be fitted in the center with a metal or plastic disk that permitted use with a standard spindle. Moreover, the 45-RPM microgrooves could be played with a stylus designed for 33-RPM records. In the end, RCA was unable to develop a proprietary hardware system fed by its own software variation. Even though the 7-inch 45-RPM format became the standard for singles, 12-inch 33-RPM LPs captured the market for longer works and collections. RCA eventually joined independent manufacturers in producing phonographs and turntables that operated at all of the major speeds (including 78 RPM) and provided two styli (one for 78 RPM and one for 33- and 45-RPM microgrooves).

The Development of FM Broadcasting

The rapid spread of 33- and 45-RPM record formats contrasts sharply with the long delays required for FM receivers to become a vital part of high-fidelity systems.[18] In practice, FM broadcasts incorporate two important improvements: the use of wideband frequency modulation, in which the frequency rather than the amplitude of the radio signal varies with the audio signal being

---

18. Much of the material on FM reception is derived from Inglis 1990.

transmitted, and the use of very high frequency (VHF) waves for propagation, in contrast with the medium wave frequencies used for AM broadcasts.[19] Together, these two characteristics result in greater reductions in man-made and atmospheric interference, relative immunity from other stations operating on the same frequency, and better fidelity of reproduction, especially in regard to dynamic volume range and frequency response.

Commercial FM broadcasts began in 1940, but on the range from 42 to 50 MHz. On this basis, the industry quickly grew in the United States. By the end of 1941, 58 stations had received construction permits and nearly 400,000 sets had been sold. When the United States entered the war, no further sets were built, although construction of stations did proceed. Nevertheless, the war accelerated technical developments in FM broadcasting as a result of government-sponsored research.

The real barrier to the spread of FM came at the end of the war, when the government decided, on technical grounds, to change the standard broadcast frequencies to 88 to 108 MHz. Although this led to improvements in reception and greatly enlarged the number of channels theoretically available in any locality from 40 to 100, it had the disadvantage of immediately rendering obsolete all existing broadcasting equipment and receivers. In effect, the existing network simply disappeared.

The result was a decade-long decline in the popularity of FM. The number of on-air stations fell from 733 in 1951 to 530 in 1957. The fate of stations such as WTMJ-FM in Milwaukee exemplifies the problems that FM broadcasters encountered. The station, which was owned by the *Milwaukee Journal,* was the fifth-oldest FM broadcaster in the United States. It began experimental transmission in February, 1949, concentrating on music in order to take advantage of the superior fidelity characteristics of FM. Through a systematic publicity campaign, the station was quickly able to build up a substantial audience, with 21,000 FM receivers in its listening area in early 1942. With the exception of occasional NBC war coverage, no programs were broadcast in common with the *Milwaukee Journal*'s AM station (Sterling 1968). At the end of 1945, however, the station was forced to change from 45.5 MHz to 92.3 MHz, in the process losing all listeners who had not purchased new receivers. Because of the expense of building new transmitters to accommodate the frequency change, WTMJ-FM also abandoned its own broadcasts in mid-1946 and shifted entirely to simulcasts, presenting the same program as its AM affiliate. Under the circumstances, it is not surprising that the FM audience dwindled, and, in April, 1950, the station left the air (Sterling 1968).

---

19. At present, the AM (medium wave) band extends from 550 to 1600 kHz and the FM band from 88 to 108 MHz.

The Resurgence of FM Broadcasting

By the time that WTMJ-FM resumed broadcasts in 1959, a series of technical changes had begun to give FM new leverage with listeners. Initially, most popular recordings had a limited dynamic range and therefore did not require the increased fidelity that FM could provide.[20] Especially when most commercial stations concentrated on simulcasts, only the small proportion of classical music listeners benefited from using an FM receiver, which meant that advertising revenues were also constrained. The increased dynamic range of popular music from the late 1950s, however, made FM reception valuable to a wider range of consumers. Second, FM stereo multiplex broadcasts began in 1961, which gave FM stations a distinct advantage that AM stations could not match. From that point, FM stations began to gain ground steadily. By 1975, the FM share of the total listening audience in the United States was slightly more than 30 percent. In 1979, AM and FM reached parity, and in 1988 the FM share was 75 percent (Inglis 1990, 141–45; Sterling 1968).

The Importance of Networks to the Adoption
of the LP and FM

The principal reason that purchasers of high-fidelity components were converted to LP turntables so quickly but resisted the charms of FM tuners for almost two decades was that LPs offered such important advantages when compared to 78-RPM records that a software network was created almost immediately, which consumers were then able to take advantage of through a series of individual purchases of relatively inexpensive record players and phonographs. The great majority of radio listeners, however, could see no immediate technical advantage in investing in FM equipment because the network of high-fidelity popular music software did not exist. Moreover, radio listeners had less control because they were dependent on a network with two stages: the records and the stations that transmitted them. When, as a result of an exogenous change, the dynamic range of popular music was widened and then multiplex became available, the interests of popular and classical music listeners merged. Only at this point did the market become dense enough to justify greater investment by broadcasters in FM programming. The interests of FM consumers and producers, therefore, both evolved, but in a series of fits and starts, as each faced its own bottlenecks that had to be overcome before further progress was possible.

---

20. The fidelity advantages of FM were largely ignored in Britain. When the British Broadcasting Corporation began VHS/FM transmissions in 1955, it was for local stations rather than the Third Programme (Briggs 1979, 562).

Products versus Components

More recent developments, including cassette recorders and CD players, have strengthened the old principle of attaching new options to existing systems. Dedicated audiophiles continue to prefer separate components. In a recent discussion of integrated amplifiers and receivers,[21] *Stereo Review* recommended that listeners buy their preamplifiers, amplifiers, and tuners individually. As the product manager for one of the major component manufacturers explained, "the manufacturer of separate components is under fewer cost restraints. Higher quality parts can be used. Construction is better, too, because components have more room to breathe on a circuit board. And separates offer greater control flexibility as you grow into a more complex system with video, surround sound, and subwoofers" (Gillett 1988, 74, 77).

Because of the uneven pace of development among the various components since the 1940s, it is unlikely that consumers have regarded a high-fidelity or stereo component system as a single "product." Instead, they have perceived a separate set of attributes for each component. Thus, there has been a series of life cycles for a succession of types of software and their associated hardware requirements (78-RPM records, 33- and 45-RPM microgroove records, audio cassettes, and compact disks), amplifiers (monaural and stereophonic), and tuners (AM, FM, and AM-FM). Other components, principally speaker systems, have had similar development patterns. Modular systems in this case exist only insofar as they comprise components that supply the attributes users seek.

From Modular Systems to Appliances?

After more than four decades of development, however, it is questionable if high sophistication is any longer of much value to the consumer. According to one estimate, 80 percent of listeners are "rather deaf" at ranges above 10,000 Hz. Casual empiricism also suggests that many listeners prefer extra volume to better tone when playing music.

In contrast to, say, microcomputers (Langlois 1990), stereo equipment serves only one basic use: the reproduction of sound. New components represent variations on a theme rather than departures into new realms. Except for the most golden of ears or snobs, the point has probably been reached at which packaged systems by such firms as Pioneer and Sony meet all reason-

---

21. An integrated amplifier includes both a preamplifier, which "takes an audio signal from a phono cartridge, tuner, tape deck, or CD player, boosts the gain, or volume, and sends the signal to a power amplifier for further amplification," and the power amplifier that drives the speakers. Receivers add a tuner to the integrated amplifier (Gillett 1988, 74).

able technical specifications.[22] At this mature stage of the product life cycle, the transaction costs of choice for most consumers may outweigh the benefits arising from picking and choosing. Preset packages cover almost the entire product space, not because consumers demand an undifferentiated, no-frills product analogous to the Model T, but because, with maturity, a standardized product has become so well developed that it now meets the needs of almost all users. It remains to be seen when, or if, the microcomputer requirements of business and personal users will become similarly standardized.

REFERENCES

Barzel, Yoram. 1982. "Measurement Costs and the Organization of Markets." *Journal of Law and Economics* 25:27–48.

Briggs, Asa. 1979. *Sound and Vision.* Vol. 4 of *The History of Broadcasting in the United Kingdom.* Oxford: Oxford University Press.

Briggs, G. A. 1953. *Sound Reproduction.* Bradford: Wharfedale Wireless Works.

Cheung, Steven N. S. 1983. "The Contractual Nature of the Firm." *Journal of Law and Economics* 26:1–22.

Coase, Ronald H. 1937. "The Nature of the Firm." *Economica,* n.s. 4:386–405.

Cooper, Arnold C., and Dan Schendel. 1988. "Strategic Responses to Technological Threats." *Readings in the Management of Innovation,* 2d ed., ed. Michael L. Tushman and William L. Moore. Cambridge, Mass.: Ballinger.

Eisenberg, Norman. 1976. "High Fidelity Pathfinders: The Men Who Made an Industry." *High Fidelity Magazine,* April.

Foster, Richard N. 1986. "Timing Technological Transitions." In *Technology in the Modern Corporation: A Strategic Perspective,* ed. Mel Horwitch. New York: Pergamon.

Gillett, Thomas R. 1988. "Separates." *Stereo Review,* November.

Goldmark, Peter. 1973. *Maverick Inventor.* New York: Saturday Review Press.

Graham, Margaret B. W. 1986. *The Business of Research: RCA and the VideoDisk.* New York: Cambridge University Press.

Hughes, Thomas P. 1983. *Networks of Power: Electrification in Western Society, 1880–1930.* Baltimore: Johns Hopkins University Press.

Hughes, Thomas P. 1989. *American Genesis: A Century of Invention and Technological Enthusiasm.* New York: Penguin.

Inglis, Andrew F. 1990. *Behind the Tube: A History of Broadcasting Technology and Business.* Boston: Focal Press.

Klein, Benjamin, Robert G. Crawford, and Armen A. Alchian. 1978. "Vertical Inte-

---

22. Although these systems are sold as entities, most are, in fact, composed of separate components manufactured by a single firm. When they do not include the full range of options such as CD players, they usually offer provisions for plug-in sets for buyers who wish to diversify later.

gration, Appropriable Rents, and the Competitive Contracting Process." *Journal of Law Economics* 21:297–326.

Lancaster, Kelvin. 1971. *Consumer Demand: A New Approach.* New York: Columbia University Press.

Langlois, Richard N. 1988. "Economic Change and the Boundaries of the Firm." *Journal of Institutional and Theoretical Economics* 144 (4): 635–57.

Langlois, Richard N. 1990. "External Economies and Economic Progress: The Case of the Microcomputer Industry." Working Paper 91-1502, University of Connecticut. Photocopy.

Langlois, Richard N., and Paul L. Robertson. 1989. "Explaining Vertical Integration: Lessons from the American Automobile Industry." *Journal of Economic History* 49 (2): 361–75.

Mullin, John. 1976. "Creating the Craft of Tape Recording." *High Fidelity Magazine,* April.

Nelson, Richard R., and Sidney G. Winter. 1977. "In Search of a More Useful Theory of Innovation." *Research Policy* 5:36–76.

Nelson, Richard R., and Sidney G. Winter. 1982. *An Evolutionary Theory of Economic Change.* Cambridge, Mass.: Harvard University Press.

Read, Oliver, and Walter L. Welch. 1976. *From Tin Foil to Stereo: Evolution of the Phonograph.* Indianapolis: Howard W. Sams and Bobbs-Merrill.

Richardson, G. B. 1972. "The Organization of Industry." *Economic Journal* 82 (327): 883–96.

Rosenberg, Nathan. 1976. *Perspectives on Technology.* New York: Cambridge University Press.

Silver, Morris. 1984. *Enterprise and the Scope of the Firm.* London: Martin Robertson.

Sterling, Christopher H. 1968. "WTMJ-FM: A Case Study in the Development of Broadcasting." *Journal of Broadcasting* 12(4): 341–52.

Stigler, George. 1951. "The Division of Labor Is Limited by the Extent of the Market." *Journal of Political Economy* 59 (3): 185–93.

Teece, David J. 1986. "Profiting from Technological Innovation: Implications for Integration, Collaboration, Licensing, and Public Policy." *Research Policy* 15:285–305.

Wallerstein, Edward. 1976. "Creating the LP Record" (as told to Ward Botsford). *High Fidelity Magazine,* April.

Waterson, Michael. 1984. *Economic Theory of the Industry.* Cambridge: Cambridge University Press.

Williamson, Oliver E. 1985. *The Economic Institutions of Capitalism.* New York: Free Press.

Taking Schumpeter's Methodology Seriously

Yuichi Shionoya

Schumpeter once wrote: "Not the first, but the last chapter of a scientific system should deal with its methodology" (Schumpeter 1908, xv). This means that one cannot discuss methodology independently of concrete problems and actual practice in science. Now that all of Schumpeter's work is available, it is both possible and indispensable to discuss their methodology in order to understand his view of economics.

Schumpeter was interested in pairs of grand problems such as statics and dynamics, development and cycles, economic development and sociocultural development, theory and history, science and ideology, economic systems and political systems, and economy and civilization. Thus, he was invariably conscious of wide perspectives on problems and attempted an overall approach to give the total picture. While stressing the need for restricting the scope of problems, he never refrained from considering problems in a much wider context. He was not dogmatic about the use of method or technique of economics; he was generous in admitting different methods for different problems and advocated methodological tolerance. He mastered past scholarly achievements in many fields and, at the same time, went beyond the scope and methods of existing scientific knowledge. His problems were global as well as multifaceted, and his methods were synthetic as well as analytic. In order to understand the structure of the world that Schumpeter described so characteristically, it is necessary to pay serious attention to the methodological principles that, in his mind, justified the particular scope and methods of his work.

Schumpeter's work, extending over many fields, contains ideas that appear so inconsistent with each other that it might lead to impressions of cynicism and even misleading interpretations. This is so because his work has not received an appropriate evaluation from an overall point of view.

The characteristics of Schumpeter's works seem to lie not so much in his separate scientific treatment of the component parts of the total picture as in his comprehensive design, ideas, or insights, which give each component its proper place in the total picture. One cannot adequately evaluate the significance of Schumpeter's separate scientific achievements without an appreciation of his comprehensive vision of economy and society. I propose carrying out such an appreciation through methodological investigation.

There is no need to argue methodology for those scholars who tend to work within an existing paradigm to solve a regular set of problems with some standard technique. But, for Schumpeter, it is essential to discover the context of his thinking by a methodological inquiry and to reconstruct a scientific world by recognizing his hidden habit of thought. The fact that he deliberately avoided arguing about his own scientific system will also necessitate a methodological interpretation of his procedures. Schumpeter's scientific system, if properly interpreted and reconstructed methodologically, might be regarded as based on a scientific research program for a universal social science.

The methodological interpretation of Schumpeter's work, however, has been an almost completely neglected subject. He has been regarded as quite unfamiliar with, and even hostile to, methodology and philosophy. On the contrary, his first book, *Das Wesen und der Hauptinhalt der theoretischen Nationalökonomie* (1908), was a book of methodology. He was brought up in the *Methodenstreit* between Menger and Schmoller. His interest in methodology was maintained throughout his academic life, although he pretended indifference or sometimes hostility to it. This essay will present a methodological framework and principles by which to coherently interpret Schumpeter's substantive scientific system.

Conceptual Framework

I have used the word *methodology* without defining it. I shall now offer a sketch of the conceptual framework in which the methodological interpretation of Schumpeter's work will be developed in accordance with recent developments in the philosophy of science after logical positivism was rejected.

First, we must distinguish between method and methodology. Whereas they are closely related, they are separate. Confusion between them was a source of constant worry for Fritz Machlup. To describe methods does not amount to methodology. A specific field of science is characterized by reference to its scope and methods. A description of scope and methods is not methodology, although methodology papers sometimes carry such titles as "scope and methods" in science. Methods relate to the rules or principles of scientific procedure, including those for forming concepts, making assumptions, building models, formulating hypotheses, observing facts, and testing theories. Following Machlup (1978, 54), I understand methodology to be the philosophical study of reasons behind a prescribed use of methods. Methodology is a branch of the philosophy of science.

Second, science does not stand by methods alone but needs, in the first place, a vision of its subject of research. Vision, a prescientific act, is a

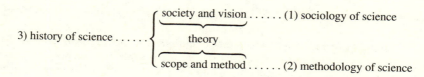

Fig. 1.   Conceptual framework

preliminary image of problems and gives rise to a scope or subject of scientific research. Since this prescientific activity takes place in a society, it is ideologically conditioned by social circumstances. This is the subject of the sociology of knowledge.

Third, history of science observes not only the historical development of scope and method of science, but also the historical evolution of a relationship between society and vision at the prescientific stage. In other words, the history of science is concerned with science as actually practiced in a society yet, at the same time, doing philosophy: it is the historical inquiry of the same materials dealt with in the methodology and sociology of science.

My conceptual framework can be indicated in terms of (1) sociology of science, (2) methodology of science, and (3) history of science (fig. 1). This framework covers all of Schumpeter's metascientific work about economic and social science, except his substantive work on the economy and society. To mention each of his representative works in these fields, sociology is presented in his article, "Science and Ideology" (1949); methodology is in his first book, *Wesen* (1908); and history is presented in his posthumous book, *History of Economic Analysis* (1954).

In discussing the structure and procedures of science, the traditional philosophy of science, especially logical positivism, assumed an ideal theory that is complete. On the contrary, contemporary philosophy of science has increasingly come to realize that there are patterns of reasoning in the context of *discovery* as well as in the context of *justification* of scientific hypotheses and theories, and that a great deal of illumination of the scientific activity can be attained by examining them.

Standard accounts explain the contrast between discovery and justification in the following way (Kordig 1978). Discovery concerns the origin and invention of scientific hypotheses and theories. Justification concerns their evaluation, testing, and confirmation. Problems in the context of discovery are the concern of psychology, sociology, and the history of science. The context of justification is the subject matter of the philosophy of science. Discovery is subjective, but it is only descriptive. Justification is objective, but it is normative because a theory must abide by its rules. Discovery deals with the initial selection of facts for study. Justification evaluates the process of give and take between hypotheses and facts.

In light of this, it can be said that Schumpeter's concern with the sociology of science and the history of science, as well as the methodology of science, anticipated subsequent developments in the philosophy of science. He showed deep interests in the history of economics and introduced a conceptual framework for dealing with ideology that had belonged to the context of discovery, thus providing a basis for the analysis of the context of justification from the viewpoint of the historical growth of theories. His position differed from the positivistic view, which neglected the problems originating in the context of discovery, and also from the sociological view, which dealt with these problems only as the concern of the sociology of science.

Scope and Methods

The best way to identify the scope of Schumpeter's work is to look at a chapter omitted from his *Theory of Economic Development;* that is, the final chapter (chap. 7) of the first German edition of that book published in 1912 (Shionoya 1990b). In the 1926 and subsequent German editions he omitted this chapter for a trivial reason. Accordingly, the 1934 English translation does not contain it. This chapter, entitled "The Overall Configuration of an Economy," presents what might be called an approach to a universal social science. It attempts to outline an approach to a comprehensive explanation of the development of society as a whole, which Schumpeter called "sociocultural development" (Schumpeter 1912, 545). Areas such as the economy, politics, social relations, arts, sciences, and morals are considered. The chapter comprises 86 pages out of 548 pages in the whole book.

Schumpeter's approach to areas outside of economics is clearly based on analogy, assuming comparisons or similarities between economic and noneconomic areas. Metaphors are used step by step to show similarities between the two. The most important subject of analogy is the dichotomy of statics and dynamics that, as far as the social sciences are concerned, he believed had been satisfactorily established only in economics. Schumpeter's view of the statics-dynamics dichotomy for an economy is conceived as a special case of the general hypotheses, with static and dynamic phenomena perceptibly distinguished in every sphere of social life.

In his preface to the second German edition, Schumpeter explained the reason he omitted chapter 7 of the first edition. He observed that it included a "fragment of the sociology of culture" (Schumpeter 1926b, xi), and had unexpectedly attracted much attention, mostly adverse. He thus feared that the reader's attention would be diverted from his major contribution to economic theory. In that chapter, Schumpeter went so far as to present a broad view of the development of society as a whole, including economic development as one element in that process. But it was more important for him to receive recognition for his theory of economic development than for his broad vision of sociocultural development. He eliminated chapter 7 not because he found it false, but because of the special circumstance in which, as he noted, "a fragment of the sociology of culture" was preferred by the German readers to "the problems of dull economic theory" (1926b, xi) and became an obstacle to a discussion of the latter problems.

In fact, chapter 7 is not a "fragment of the sociology of culture"; it is a unique vision of a universal social science, and for this reason it is most unfortunate that it has not become the subject of scholarly investigation. I shall reconstruct Schumpeter's research program in terms of three kinds of scope and four kinds of methods; this discussion will be followed by an interpretation of his methodology.

Schumpeter's fundamental idea is that any research area, such as economy, politics, or morals, should be identified so that it can itself exhibit order; in other words, science should put the identified object in some order by means of the rules of scientific procedure. Schumpeter resorted to the dichotomy of statics and dynamics on the basis of models of man. On the one hand, he asserts that different types of man, such as economic man in economics, should characterize the state of affairs in different areas of social inquiry. On the other hand, he presumes in each area of a society both a static equilibrium state and dynamic development. A static state is linked to the behavior of average people and dynamic development to the behavior of an innovator or leader.

Schumpeter then distinguishes three stages in the social sciences. The scope of science broadens according to stages. The *first* stage is statics; it describes a state of affairs in a specified area as a static, orderly state derived from the adaptive behavior of a majority of individuals. It is well known that the order in the static state of an economy is represented by the concept of equilibrium that is attained through the play of individual self-interest and the workings of a competitive market mechanism, given the quantity of available resources, consumer tastes, the techniques of production, and the social structure. Schumpeter observes that if in a certain area of social life a state of equilibrium can be uniquely determined corresponding to exogenous data, the area in question is logically so self-sufficient that one can legitimately assume an autonomous and independent science for that area. In this sense, equilibrium theory in economics is the magna charta attesting to the autonomy of science (Schumpeter 1939, 1:41). The thrust of Schumpeter's approach to a universal social science in this stage is that the concept of the static state as the routine activity within a fixed framework can be applied to noneconomic areas as well.

The *second* stage is concerned with dynamic development. In every branch of social life, forces are working that will change the static state from within; they destroy the framework of those activities that are only adaptive to given conditions. Development is characterized by innovation. In each area of social life, the individual defined as a "leader" carries out innovation and destroys the existing order. Schumpeter's theory of economic development is a special case of social development, and his concept of the entrepreneur is a special case of "leader" in the economic sphere.

Therefore, each area of social science should have statics and dynamics. We find here his important view of the relationship between statics and dynamics, that whereas static phenomena have an equilibrium, dynamic ones do not.

It follows from our entire thought that *a dynamic equilibrium does not exist*. Development in its ultimate nature consists of the disturbances of an existing static equilibrium and does not have a tendency to return to a previous or any other equilibrium. Development alters the data of a static economy. . . . Development and equilibrium are opposite phenomena excluding each other. Not that a static economy is characterized by a static equilibrium and a dynamic economy by a dynamic equilibrium; on the contrary, equilibrium exists only in a static economy. *Economic equilibrium is essentially a static equilibrium.* (Schumpeter 1912, 489; italics added)

This remark reflects Schumpeter's epistemological view that, because a scientific explanation is incomplete without the reduction of phenomena to an equilibrium state, dynamic theory cannot stand without the support of static theory.

The *third* stage, the most ambitious one, is concerned with the interaction between all areas of social life; the task is to integrate them, giving a picture of "sociocultural development." The question he raises at this stage is:

In spite of the relative independence of all areas, how is it taken as an important truth—indeed, the truth which we cannot so much prove exactly as perceive—that every element in every area at any time is connected with every element in every other area, that all situations of all areas determine each other and depend on each other? If we call the aggregate of these areas the *social culture* of a nation and the totality of its development *sociocultural development,* we can ask: how is it explained by our approach that the social culture of a nation at any time is a unity and the sociocultural development of a nation has always a unified tendency? (Schumpeter 1912, 545–46)

There are two approaches to the integration, static and dynamic. When we look at an area from the viewpoint of statics, static theory provides us with a causal explanation in the sense that the state of affairs in the area is explained by reference to the conditions given from other areas, and that, conversely, the state of affairs in the former area is seen as conditioning the data given to other areas. But when we look at all the areas of social life as a whole, the walls separating the areas must now be removed and every factor in every area must be simultaneously regarded as endogenous. Thus, we have a situation where all the equilibrium states of all areas should be compatible with each other. Schumpeter calls this situation "the static unity of cultural level" (Schumpeter 1912, 546). But this does not take us very far.

When we take the viewpoint of dynamics, on the other hand, the inter-relations between the areas involve reciprocal effects on other areas of innovation emerging in each area: economic development influences the non-economic areas and brings about social change. Analogously, it is supposed that dynamic performance in any area more or less influences other areas. The interrelations between the areas in dynamic processes are different from the static interrelations and provide us with new insights into the development of society as a whole.

Schumpeter describes how such interrelations work: innovation in any area raises the social rank of successful leaders and influences social organizations; it affects the social values concerning what is important, valuable, and desirable; and it ultimately changes the presumptions and conditions of human action in all areas. Whereas various developments in all areas of social life at first appear to be independent of each other because they are carried out by different leaders in different areas, it is Schumpeter's recognition that social classes make developments in all areas an interrelated unity. His theory of social classes plays a pivotal role in integrating all social areas. If the integration could be adequately formulated, we would have a universal or all-encompassing social science addressed to "sociocultural development." Some seemingly paradoxical statements Schumpeter put forward on several occasions can be explained by whether he looked at a part or the total picture of society.

Schumpeter's *Capitalism, Socialism, and Democracy* (1950) was an attempt to carry out, on a large scale, the program of a universal social science that he had indicated thirty years before. Specifically, it deals with the interrelations between the economic and political systems, that is, between capitalism and democracy. The reasoning in that book depends on the concept of the reciprocal interactions of dynamic forces in different areas, economic, political, social, and cultural. It is not in that book that he launched into this theme for the first time. The seminal idea of that book was clearly stated in his *Die Krise des Steuerstaats* (1918) and "Sozialistische Möglichkeiten von heute"

(1920). That book should not be taken as a product of casual effort, but as a development of an idea incubated long in his mind. It is more important that *Capitalism, Socialism, and Democracy* should not be judged by its success or failure in predicting the future of capitalism, but by its methodological contribution to the understanding of economic and social process as a whole and to the practice of a universal social science. This assessment will be derived from the interpretation of Schumpeter's methodology as instrumentalist, which I shall present subsequently.

So much for the scope of Schumpeter's work. I shall now discuss the methods that he applied to the analysis of problems in different scopes. As is well known, Schumpeter enumerated four basic methods of economics: (1) theory, (2) statistics, (3) history, and (4) economic sociology (Schumpeter 1954, 12). According to him, economic sociology, in contrast to the other three methods, goes beyond mere economic analysis. It is defined as a theoretical analysis of institutions that are exogenously given to economic theory.

In discussing these four methods in economics, I propose to combine them with the three scopes discussed previously, as indicated in figure 2, and to view the relationship between theory and history as the key factor fundamentally characterizing the paradigmatic nature of economic research. Statics as a scope of research is a world that is derived from the abstraction of historical and factual conditions in order to clarify economic logic. Theory alone holds in this world. Theory is also applicable to dynamics, which is concerned with economic development; Schumpeter's *Theory of Economic Development* was devoted to such a theory. But since economic development is a phenomenon in the real world, it is susceptible of historical description.

In economics, statistics is a tool for theory and history (in fig. 2, a shaded circle for statistics indicates its status as a supplementary tool), but they play a very important role in cooperation. Insofar as theory contains quantitative variables, it is possible to bring theory into contact with history through the medium of statistics. This contact will involve a feedback process consisting of testing an existing theory in light of historical observation and of inventing a new theory in light of fact finding, as we see in econometrics and econometric history (cliometrics). Schumpeter's *Business Cycles* (1939), subtitled "a theoretical, historical, and statistical analysis of the capitalist process," was a grand effort along this line. In that book, he describes the relationship between history, theory, and statistics as follows.

> Since what we are trying to understand is economic change in historic time, there is little exageration in saying that the ultimate goal is simply a *reasoned* (= conceptually clarified) *history,* not of crises only, nor of cycles or waves, but of the economic process in all its aspects and

Scope \ Method	(1) Theory	(2) Statistics	(3) History	(4) Economic sociology
1. Statics	○			
2. Dynamics	○	●	○	
3. Sociocultural development	○		○	●

Fig. 2.   Relationships of scope and method

bearings to which *theory* merely supplies some tools and schemata, and *statistics* merely part of the material. It is obvious that only detailed historic knowledge can definitively answer most of the questions of individual causation and mechanism and that without it the study of time-series must remain inconclusive, and theoretical analysis empty. (Schumpeter 1939, 1:220; italics added)

But the cooperation between theoretical method and historical method in economics through the medium of statistics is only effective for the study of development in the economic area. The fourth method, economic sociology, is conceived as dealing with the complicated interaction of social and economic forces, which he called sociocultural development. Economic sociology does not incorporate all factors excluded from the scope of economic statics and dynamics; it confines itself to a theoretical analysis of institutions. Therefore, economic sociology is one of the approaches to sociocultural development, with an emphasis on institutions as the determinants of actions, motives, and dispositions of economic agents.

Since institutions provide a set of rules in observance of which certain individual acts recur, they have their own modus operandi and, thus, can be conceptualized in general terms. This makes a theoretical analysis of institutions abstracted from history possible. But the concept of institutions is limited in generality because it is only relative to a historically specified institution; therefore, it can be understood as a compromise between the generality meant by theory and the individuality meant by history. In this broader perspective of sociocultural development, statistics can no longer mediate between theory and history. It is now an analysis of institutions that should mediate between theory and history. In a sense of analogy, the concept of institutions parallels that of statistics with regard to the status of a supplementary tool to both theory and history. (In fig. 2, the circle for economic sociology is also shaded.) Just as statistical records provide abstract theory with historical and specific magnitudes, the concept of institutions provides abstract theory with historical and specific rules and systems. The difference only lies in the difference in the scope of theory.

Instrumentalist Methodology

Schumpeter's first book, *Das Wesen* (1908), shows the precocity and vitality of the young genius. It is one of the earliest attempts to give a methodological foundation to neoclassical economics. The fact that his first book was about methodology is of interest in that it testifies to the nature of his academic interest and capacity.

There were two reasons for his writing a methodology book. First, he found deplorable confusion in economics around the turn of the century, as reflected in the conflicts between schools, disputes over methods, and futile controversies. He believed that the confusion was due to the lack of a clear understanding regarding the foundation, nature, and significance of economics. Second, the German-speaking world was under the influence of the historical school and theoretical economics was depressed. Schumpeter tried to acquaint German economists with economic theory through a methodological orientation rather than through its direct presentation in a mathematical form.

The uniqueness of *Das Wesen* is manifested in the title, "The Nature and Substance of Theoretical Economics." The book is a synthesis of the epistemological "nature" and the theoretical "substance" of economics; it discusses the former in the actual context of the latter. Schumpeter wanted to resolve useless controversies and to attain the circumstance where substantive progress in economics could be made. While methodology was required for the basic elucidation, he did not maintain, a priori, a certain methodological standpoint, but developed it within the context of economic theory.

It is hardly possible that a young man, at the age of twenty-five, hits on a perfectly novel idea. My interpretation is that Schumpeter borrowed the methodology of natural science developed by the fin-de-siècle positivists such as Mach, Poincaré, and Duhem (Shionoya 1990a). His standpoint can be best interpreted as instrumentalism, that is, the view that theories are not descriptions but instruments for deriving useful results and are neither true nor false. Although Milton Friedman (1953) is known as a proponent of instrumentalism in economic methodology, Schumpeter advocated it forty-five years before Friedman. Moreover, Schumpeter's instrumentalism has a clear philosophical source and is explicitly and completely stated along with its methodological terms.

Schumpeter wanted to improve the level of economics by modeling it after exact natural sciences. Therefore, it was quite natural for him to follow the newest methodology of natural science. In spite of differences between natural and social science, he concentrated on the aspects of economic phenomena that are susceptible of exact theorizing so as to detect the universal mechanism of economy. This is the world of statics, for which he developed economic methodology. As we have seen, economic dynamics and economic sociology, with which he was concerned later, were built on the basis of economic statics.

Schumpeter's admiration of Walras is widely known; it was from the methodological viewpoint that he believed in Walras's general equilibrium theory as the framework of exact science. Schumpeter's belief was strongly influenced by Mach's phenomenological physics. Mach rejected the assumption of essence and causal relations behind phenomena and confined the task of physics to a description of functional relations between elements known to us through sense experience. Because Walras's theory describes the economic world in terms of the general interdependence among objective quantities and prices of goods and factors of production, Schumpeter found in Walras an ideal application of Mach's phenomenalism to economics.

Walras and the Lausanne school, however, had less interest in methodology. Schumpeter's *Das Wesen* can be interpreted, in this context, as the first epistemological work that was devoted to a clarification of general equilibrium theory on the basis of Mach' phenomenalist view of science. Moreover, we must note that Schumpeter's most characteristic methodological position in *Das Wesen* is Mach's instrumentalism.

Instrumentalism is currently defined in terms of two aspects of theories: (1) the roles of theories (they are merely tools for generating prediction), and (2) the cognitive status of theories (they are regarded as neither true nor false). In the original view of instrumentalism, the role of theories was considered less rigidly, including explanation, prediction, and description. Schumpeter accepted this broader version of instrumentalism.

Schumpeter's methodological view can be reconstructed through seven propositions.

S1. Hypotheses, rather than being ontologically real, are artificial creations of the human mind.
S2. Theories are not descriptive statements of the real world, and therefore they cannot be judged for truth and falsity.
S3. Theories are merely instruments for the purpose of description.
S4. Theories are to describe facts as simply and as completely as possible.

S5. It is not necessary to seek to justify hypotheses as such in order to establish their truth.

S6. The purpose of hypotheses is to produce a theory fit to facts, and thus they are evaluated by their practical success.

S7. Observational facts exist independently of theories, but for any set of observed facts there might be several different theories.

S1, S2, S3, and S7 are methodological principles, whereas S4, S5, and S6 are practical rules of procedure for the formulation and evaluation of hypotheses and theories. Discussions of rules of procedure in science are not methodology.

The instrumentalist view has practical merits. First, instrumentalism claims that the basic assumptions from which theories are derived are allowed to be artificial and unrealistic. Their only purpose is to derive theories that fit facts. Hence, it is of no use justifying the truth of assumptions or hypotheses. Second, whereas inductivism asserts that knowledge must be judged on the basis of observations, it is impossible to argue inductively from the truth of particulars to a general truth. Moreover, any given set of empirical phenomena can be explained by any infinite number of mutually incompatible hypotheses, so that it is impossible to find a true theory by observational methods. Instrumentalism dismisses the problem of induction by directing sole attention to the usefulness of theories, not to their truth.

Thus, from the instrumentalist standpoint, it is not necessary to argue whether assumptions are realistic or not and which theories are true or not. With regard to the problem of theory choice, Schumpeter applies Mach's principle of economy of thought, the view that the aim of scientific theories is to describe the world as economically as possible. Based on the principle of economy or efficiency of thought, Schumpeter chooses among the theories that, starting from different arbitrary hypotheses, equally fit the facts.

Schumpeter resorted to the instrumentalist methodology in order to overcome the practical difficulties that surrounded the economics of the time. For him, the difficulties were the results of three kinds of useless controversies about methods in economics: (1) the conflict between theoretical and historical methods (Menger versus Schmoller), (2) the controversy over value theory (classical versus neoclassical versus Marxist theories), and (3) the conflict between causal and functional approaches in neoclassical economics (Menger versus Walras). He gave a clear evaluation of these issues from the instrumentalist standpoint. Schumpeter believed that disputes over methods are sterile because they are relative to the problems to which they are addressed and that hypotheses are to be evaluated in light of their efficiency for attaining explanation, description, and understanding of the addressed problems.

Schumpeter on Schmoller and Weber

The relevance of Schumpeter's idea to current scientific research is not limited to the ideas of innovation and entrepreneurship in economic development. For Schumpeter, as we have seen, they are the core ideas applicable to every area of social life. His concept of economic sociology as the institutional approach to sociocultural development plays an essential part in integrating the social sciences. His methodology, the philosophical study of the principles that rationalize certain rules of procedure in science, should hold in all aspects of a universal social science. In order to elaborate on my view of his methodological position, it is worthwhile to examine what methodology he had in mind for economic sociology. This examination involves reviewing his critique of the German historical school with special reference to Schmoller and Weber (Shionoya 1991).

Schumpeter paid the highest tribute to Leon Walras, who recognized the economic order in the general interdependence of economic quantities. At the same time, he appraised Marx and Schmoller, who were concerned with the evolution of economic systems. Schumpeter's admiration of Walras, on the one hand, and of Marx and Schmoller, on the other, seems inconsistent at first sight. But his economic and social theory was based on a combination of the Walrasian vision of economic equilibrium and the Marxist vision of historical evolution. Schumpeter's vision, which lies at the basis of his analysis of the evolution of a capitalist society, was influenced partly by Walras's ideology that the capitalist market system is essentially stable, and partly by Marx's ideology that capitalism will break down through its endogenous development (Shionoya 1986). The apparent contradiction of these two ideologies is saved by the idea, from economic sociology, that the very success of the capitalist economy will produce the noneconomic factors that are inconsistent with it; these factors, in turn, will worsen the innovative performance of capitalism. This is a typical example of Schumpeter's thinking in economic sociology.

In order to cope with these issues of historical evolution, Schumpeter went beyond the analysis of economic development. In this regard, he especially appraised the research program of Schmoller, the leader of the younger German historical school, as a prototype of economic sociology. Schumpeter inherited the wide perspective of historical inquiry from Schmoller and attempted a critical reconstruction of his research program from a methodological standpoint.

Seen from the instrumentalist standpoint, the *Methodenstreit* between Menger and Schmoller over the relative importance of historical and theoretical methods is useless because theory and history are concerned with different research interests, different subject matters, and categorically different hypotheses. Thus, a specific method can claim validity only for a separate problem. Schumpeter strongly advocated, in *Das Wesen*, the separation of history and theory on the basis of the instrumentalist methodology and engaged in the clarification of the methodological foundation of theoretical economics when historical economics was rampant in Germany.

Later, when he himself launched into not only a study of economic development but also economic sociology, Schumpeter advocated the cooperation of history and theory, instead of their separation, in order to deal with dynamic problems of economy. In his essay on Schmoller (Schumpeter 1926a), he attempted a methodological appraisal of Schmoller's historical and ethical economics and characterized his approach as an economic sociology in which history and theory could be integrated. But Schumpeter did not accept Schmoller's research program as it was. Schumpeter's idea of economic sociology demanded a rather radical change in scope, method, and methodology in order to develop the strengths, and restrain the weakness, of Schmoller's research program. I shall now discuss what Schumpeter adopted and discarded from Schmoller.

In his early work on the history of economic doctrines and methods, Schumpeter summarized six basic viewpoints of the German historical school that were particularly pertinent to Schmoller: (1) the belief in the unity of social life and the inseparable relation among its component elements, (2) the concern for development, (3) the organic and holistic point of view, (4) plurality of human motives, (5) an interest in concrete, individual relations rather than the general nature of events, and (6) historical relativity (Schumpeter 1914, 110–13).

The most important significance of the historical method for Schumpeter was the recognition that historical materials reflect the development phenomenon and indicate the relationship between economic and noneconomic facts, thus suggesting how the disciplines of social science should interact. The recognition of development and the unity of social life is a combination of points 1 and 2, the essential view of the historical school as Schumpeter understood it. It is for this reason that Schumpeter found in Schmoller's research program a "prospect of universal social science" (Schumpeter 1926b, 176), where the conventional line of demarcation between separate disciplines should disappear in historical research. Thus, Schumpeter describes the reason historical research should lead to a universal or all-encompassing social science.

[T]he historical report cannot be purely economic but must inevitably reflect also "institutional" facts that are not purely economic: therefore it affords the best method for understanding how economic and non-economic facts are related to one another and how the various social sciences should be related to one another. (Schumpeter 1954, 13)

While points 1 and 2 relate to the scope of the subject matter in the historical school, points 3, 4, 5, and 6 relate to their methods. Schumpeter recognized a purely scientific value in the claims of the historical school concerning points 3 and 4 because they are the proper claims of the sociological or institutional approach distinct from the mainstream neoclassical economics that is based on the assumptions of methodological individualism and the utility maximizer.

Schumpeter did not show much interest in the issue of individuality versus generality of economic phenomena (point 5) and that of relativity versus universality of economic laws (point 6). He did not agree with the narrow-minded view of the historical school, which rejected general formulation and universal laws; he was critical of neo-Kantian philosophy, which went too far into these issues. Instead of being a relentless critic, Schumpeter rather found that Schmoller stuck neither to the individuality nor relativity of historical phenomena, and asserted that Schmoller was interested in history not for the sake of its individuality or relativity but simply because it was the source of knowledge for the establishment of a universal social science. But Schumpeter's methodology meant a refutation of Schmoller's methodological standpoint because, in fact, the latter's methodology precluded carrying out substantive theoretical work.

Since Schmoller depended on naive realism, he was liable to fall into a trap of the never-ending scenario of data collection in pursuit of more realistic assumptions. When he considered the nature of concept formation, he advocated nominalism over realism and argued that concepts are auxiliary means to organize thought, not a perfect copy of reality (Schmoller 1911, 467–68). Since abstraction meant, to him, a deviation from reality, he could not naturally confer any real status to concepts. From this position, one only needs a step forward to get to instrumentalism. But he could not proceed to instrumentalist methodology from the nominalist view of concepts by allowing an instrumentalist role for assumptions and hypotheses; in spite of his nominalist position, his ultimate goal was still scientific realism.

Schumpeter urged engaging in theory construction by putting the brakes on the never-ending process of historical research and following a feedback process between theory and history. According to instrumentalism, assumptions and hypotheses are arbitrary creations of human minds and need not be justified by facts. A theory is neither true nor false; it proves useful if it can cover a large number of facts. While fully accepting the importance of historical research, Schumpeter believed that instrumentalism facilitates deductive attempts even when empirical data are insufficient by Schmoller's standard.

It is interesting to note that the basic issues in the *Methodenstreit* were given philosophical reflection by the neo-Kantian philosophers at the turn of the century in Germany; they especially evaluated the standpoint of the German historical school philosophically. They contrasted the historical sciences with the natural sciences and showed how knowledge of historical individuality is possible. The upshot of neo-Kantian philosophy was that, although the natural sciences are nomothetic, the historical or cultural sciences are idiographic in accordance with the difference of cognitive interest in generality or individuality of reality between the two sciences. The famous methodology of Max Weber was also an attempt to resolve the *Methodenstreit* and depended on the epistemology of neo-Kantianism, in particular that of Heinrich Rickert. What, then, is the relation between the methodology of Mach-Schumpeter, on the one hand, and that of Rickert-Weber, on the other, both of which were addressed to the resolution of the *Methodenstreit?* This is a question that has been discussed neither by Schumpeterian nor by Weberian commentators. Although Schumpeter strongly opposed Weber's methodology in a number of crucial areas, his methodology of economic sociology is very close to that of Weber despite their different origins.

Neo-Kantians introduced the principle of "value relevance" in order to justify the idiographic or individualizing approach in contrast to the nomothetic or generalizing approach. In light of generally valid cultural values, specific elements in social phenomena are regarded as relevant and models are constructed for these elements. Weber's concept of "ideal type" and theory of "understanding" were the formulation of the claims of neo-Kantians. Schumpeter was critical of this approach. With regard to the principle of value relevance, he argued that no justification is needed for assumptions. Values and interests are useful devices for constructing theories, but they are nothing but arbitrary hypotheses. He emphasized that ideal type should not refer to a real entity and, therefore, could not be used as historical description. Specifically, he criticized Weber for searching for the origin of capitalism in protestant ethics. The religious hypothesis is nothing but a fiction.

It is easy to see that Schumpeter's remarks are based on the instrumentalist methodology. As a proponent of an "ideal type" methodology, Weber agrees that theory is a heuristic device for the analysis of empirical diversity. But as a successor to the neo-Kantian axiological theory of knowledge, he adheres to an analysis of the cultural significance of phenomena at the base of concept formation. When compared with Schmoller's naive realism, Weber's position is closer to instrumentalism.

Comparisons of Schumpeter and Weber in the area of economic sociology are not unknown, but comparisons in the area of methodology are also illuminating because their economic sociology was a product of cooperation between theory and history and such a cooperation demanded serious methodological inquiry.

An important implication that we can derive today from Schumpeter's methodology is its relevance to the current debates over institutional economics. The current issues in institutional economics, including the methodological disparities between the old institutional economists (such as Veblen and Commons) and the new institutional economists (based on neoclassical economics), can be more effectively examined in light of the Schmoller-Schumpeter-Weber nexus. Thus, the conflict between the old and the new institutionalism can be seen, in a sense, as a reproduction of the dispute between Schmoller and Menger. The lesson we have learned from Schumpeter's methodology is that the realism of assumptions does not matter, even in institutional economics, which, as the descendant of Schmoller, has often maintained the opposite.

Conclusion

In discussing Schumpeter's system of metascience, I have been concerned with the methodology of science, not with its sociology or history. I cannot enter into the latter fields in detail; it must suffice to make only two comments about them.

First, in a discussion of the sociology of science, Schumpeter emphasized the role of vision in theory construction (Schumpeter 1949). Vision is an idea or preconception with which one grasps the essential feature of reality in a prescientific stage. In terms of instrumentalist methodology, it can be argued that while the choice of assumptions is made arbitrarily by vision, the result of assumptions must explain reality according to the rules of scientific procedure. In other words, vision belongs to the context of discovery. It is important to note that the part of vision that is not successfully formulated in the stage of model building survives and exerts an influence on science. Such a vision might sometimes disappear from science as a mere illusion, but sometimes becomes political judgments or social beliefs and continues to exist in disguise in science, as if it were science. Schumpeter's view that vision as such plays a key role when it is concerned with the process of long-term economic change is quite important in this respect (Schumpeter 1954, 570). As for the long-term economic process where a large number of factors are likely to change, there are many alternatives in regard to assuming a causal relationship and drawing a historical scenario. Moreover, a verification or falsification of a theory of economic development requires an accumulation of long-term experiences, without which any theory of the long-term process would not be more than a vision. Schumpeter admits that, in this case, vision might survive without a crucial check.

Second, in writing a history of economics, Schumpeter declares that he writes the history of the analytic or scientific aspects of economic thought (Schumpeter 1954, 3). His *History of Economic Analysis*, however, is not confined to the history of theories, that is, the "internal history" that regards the history of science as the history of rational thought, evolving according to its own inner logic. Rather, he starts from the discussion of Greco-Roman thought and extensively describes various schools, biographies, the zeitgeist, social and political background, and neighboring fields; it might be thought that these are external factors that should be put aside from the internal history. Schumpeter is actually engaged in the "external history" of economics, which is the view of economics as a social and cultural phenomenon, subject to both rational and irrational influences. If one takes Schumpeter's declaration literally, his actual work appears paradoxical and puzzling. But this is not so in my framework. Doing economic science constitutes a specific area of social activity; it has statics where a certain paradigm is accepted, and dynamics where a scientific revolution is carried out by an innovator and then by his or her followers. For Schumpeter, as we have seen, writing a history of some social area must elucidate the interactions between the specified area and other areas, because the recognition of historical development and the unity of social life is what he learned from the German historical school. Thus, the history of analytical economics cannot be written on the assumption of other things being equal. The historical inheritance of not only preceding theories but also vision emanating from nonscientific areas molds continuity in the history of science or what he calls the "filiation of scientific ideas" (Schumpeter 1954, 6).

Finally, returning to methodology, I venture to propose the central theme of Schumpeter's methodology from the viewpoint of the sociology of knowledge. The relationship between historical facts and theoretical models has remained a perennial question in social science. Various schools of thought have emphasized either standpoint. While Schumpeter was brought up in German historicism, he worked in the world of Anglo-Saxon positivism; his mind was divided between history and theory, but he could not choose between them. As a result, the horizon of his ideas was often too wide to be susceptible to analysis. When he had to argue macroeconomics of money in rivalry with Keynes, he could not help digressing into the sociology of money. Despite a sense of failure in the 1930s as seen in his two unsuccessful books, *Business Cycle* and *Das Wesen des Geldes* (1970), instrumentalism provided Schumpeter with a reliable basis for launching boldly into the coordination of history and theory. When the scale and nature of problems fitted his capacity perfectly, as was the case in the 1940s, he could produce successful, unique achievements such as *Capitalism, Socialism, and Democracy* and *History of Economic Analysis.*

REFERENCES

Friedman, M. 1953. "The Methodology of Positive Economics." In *Essays in Positive Economics,* 3–43. Chicago: University of Chicago Press.

Kordig, C. R. 1978. "Discovery and Justification." *Philosophy of Science* 45:110–17.

Machlup, F. 1978. *Methodology of Economics and Other Social Sciences.* New York: Academic Press.

Schmoller, G. von. 1911. "Volkswirtschaft, Volkswirtschaftslehre, und-methode." In *Handwörterbuch der Staatswissenschaften,* 3 Aufl., Band 8:426–501.

Schumpeter, J. A. 1908. *Das Wesen und der Hauptinhalt der theoretischen Nationalökonomie.* Munich and Leipzig: Duncker and Humblot.

Schumpeter, J. A. 1912. *Theorie der wirtschaftlichen Entwicklung.* Leipzig: Duncker and Humblot.

Schumpeter, J. A. 1914. *Epochen der Dogmen-und Methodengeschichte.* Tübingen: J. C. B. Mohr. Translated by R. Aris, under the title *Economic Doctrine and Method.* London: George Allen and Unwin, 1954.

Schumpeter, J. A. 1918. *Die Krise des Steuerstaats.* Graz and Leipzig: Leuschner and Lubensky. Translated by W. F. Stolper and R. A. Musgrave, under the title "The Crisis of the Tax State." *International Economic Papers* 4(1954): 5–38.

Schumpeter, J. A. 1920. "Sozialistische Möglichkeiten von heute." *Archiv für Sozialwissenschaft und Sozialpolitik* 48:305–60.

Schumpeter, J. A. 1926a. "Gustav v. Schmoller und die Probleme von heute." *Schmollers Jahrbuch* 50:337–88.

Schumpeter, J. A. 1926b. *Theorie der wirtschaftlichen Entwicklung.* 2d ed. Leipzig: Duncker and Humblot. Translated by R. Opie, under the title *Theory of Economic Development.* Cambridge, Mass.: Harvard University Press, 1934.

Schumpeter, J. A. 1939. *Business Cycles.* 2 vols. New York: McGraw-Hill.

Schumpeter, J. A. 1949. "Science and Ideology." *American Economic Review* 39:345–59.

Schumpeter, J. A. 1950. *Capitalism, Socialism, and Democracy.* New York: Harper and Row.

Schumpeter, J. A. 1954. *History of Economic Analysis.* New York: Oxford University Press.

Schumpeter, J. A. 1970. *Das Wesen des Geldes.* Göttingen: Vandenhoeck and Ruprecht.

Shionoya, Y. 1986. "The Science and Ideology of Schumpeter." *Rivista Internazionale di Scienze Economiche e Commerciali* 33:729–62.

Shionoya, Y. 1990a. "Instrumentalism in Schumpeter's Economic Methodology." *History of Political Economy* 22:187–222.

Shionoya, Y. 1990b. "The Origin of the Schumpeterian Research Programme: A

Chapter Omitted from Schumpeter's *Theory of Economic Development*." *Journal of Institutional and Theoretical Economics* 146:314–27.

Shionoya, Y. 1991. "Schumpeter on Schmoller and Weber: A Methodology of Economic Sociology." *History of Political Economy* 23:193–211.

Commentary

Hyman P. Minsky

Professor Shionoya's essay demonstrates a breath of scholarship that is literally breathtaking. Shionoya knows what Schumpeter wrote, when he wrote it, and offers reasons for the various textual changes and omissions. He has done a wonderful job of integrating Schumpeter's thought with the intellectual environment within which it first blossomed. He emphasizes that Schumpeter's ". . . economic and social theory was based upon a combination of the Walrasian vision of economic equilibrium and the Marxist vision of historical evolution," and these visions were contradictory. In what follows I point out that the resolution to what Shionoya identifies as a conflict of visions in Schumpeter follows from the mature Schumpeter's distinction between vision and technique and the relegation of the Walrasian component of the early Schumpeter enthusiasms to technique.

I am not a scholar in Prof. Shionoya's class. The comments that follow are based upon two sources other than his essay. The first is the essays in *Ten Great Economists* that deal with Mitchell and Keynes,[1] two economists (along with others) upon whose shoulders I stood while laboring in the vineyards of money, financial institution, and business cycle theory. The second source is my recollections of Schumpeter's views, derived from the hours I spent in Schumpeter's office on the mezzanine of Littauer in 1942–43 and after 1946.[2]

---

1. Joseph A. Schumpeter, *Ten Great Economists* (Oxford: Oxford University Press, 1951). Page citations are from the Galaxy Press paperback edition of 1965.

2. Prof. Shionoya's title, "Taking Schumpeter's Methodology Seriously," brings to my mind that, in the Harvard of 1946–49, the graduate students, largely but not exclusively veterans of either the service or of Washington, did not take Schumpeter seriously. This was not because the students were in the forefront of the emerging mathematical economics and therefore had surpassed Schumpeter. It was because the main thrust in economics at Harvard was applied: the simplified Keynesian economics of Prof. Alvin Hansen and the quite mechanical application of monopolistic competition theory to problems of industrial organization as set out by Prof. Edward Mason ruled the roost. The representative student was not intellectually engaged with the big issues of the scope and nature of economics and the lessons for a vision of society that were to be extracted from the dismal history of the previous two decades. The prevailing ethos was careerist. The working postulate among the graduate students was not only that big thinking was in the past,

363

A main thesis of Prof. Shionoya is that Schumpeter's view of the appropriate methodology for economics reflected the works of Ernst Mach. Mach, who died in 1916, was at the frontier of the discussion of scientific methodology when Schumpeter was young. The Machian view can best be characterized as instrumentalism. (I believe Mach is a precursor, if not a founding father, of logical positivism.)

Instrumentalism holds that theories are not to be viewed as more or less true representations of reality but as creations of "the scientist." In this view, theories not only do not need to reflect the actual processes of the system, they never can. Theories are created by scientists, they are not discovered. Theories are subject to revision and rejection as evidence accumulates. Scientists think, therefore they doubt, they accept but do not believe, and they assert that what they accept "ain't necessarily so."

Furthermore, aside from being consistent with observations that are deemed important by the collective mind of the scientific community, a theory will be accepted or rejected as it passes or fails some test of usefulness: a theory has weight if it is useful as a guide to policy that can, in some sense, improve matters. However, usefulness and improvement are not unambiguous concepts in economics, as the question "for whom" always needs to be addressed. An economic theory can be judged to be useful and socially enhancing because it offers support for the special privileges of patrons. An implication of instrumentalism is that the social setting, including the benefit and reward system for practitioners of a discipline, affect the substance of a science.

Instrumentalism therefore leads to the proposition that a theory is only conditionally valid. Wesley Mitchell, who Schumpeter admired, characterized the dominant economic theory of his day as apologetics.[3] Schumpeter made much of the *treason of the clerics* to explain the support that intellectuals gave to both Marxism and Keynesianism. Economic thinking can pass a test of usefulness when it lends support to a view of the economy and economic policy favorable to those to whom the economists of the time are beholden.

Developments in philosophy since Schumpeter's day have carried the conditionality of the validity of a corpus of thinking, as emphasized by the

---

but, in truth, it was not worth doing. Their task was to get the Ph.D. and go forth to teach or to serve a government bureau. In the prevailing view, economics was now a normal science, not a grand adventure, and therefore Schumpeter was irrelevant.

3. See Schumpeter's obituary essay on Mitchell in *Ten Great Economists*. The essay, published in 1950, ". . . was completed by Professor Schumpeter only two weeks before his death, which occurred on January 8, 1950" (239). In this essay, Schumpeter comments favorably upon Mitchell's view that the alliance between economic theory and laissez-faire, which characterized the economic theory of Mitchell's formative years, was unwarranted by the substance of economic theory.

instrumentalists, forward to the view that there is never a true reading of a text. The reader is not a mere passive recipient, but an active creator of interpretation. The reader brings priors to the text, priors that can be more or less restricting or binding. In economics, there is another difficulty: history unfolds and institutions evolve. As the world moves through time, each reader has to interpret (extract meaning from) events and institutional changes and integrate the reading of what happened and what is into an interpretation of texts, into a maintained theory. This means that, to a serious scholar, the lessons learned from a text are subject to change.

The essays on Keynes and Mitchell in *Ten Great Economists* are important in understanding the mature Schumpeter's views on how one does economics. In his late essays, Schumpeter divided the doing of economics into vision and technique. In his obituary of Keynes, he wrote ". . . every comprehensive 'theory' of an economic state of society consists of two complementary but essentially distinct elements. There is, first, the theorist's view about the basic features of that state of society, about what is and what is not important in order to understand its life at a given time. Let us call this his vision. And there is, second, the theorist's technique, and apparatus by which he conceptualizes his vision and which turns the latter into concrete propositions or 'theories'" [1951] 1965, 268.

To Schumpeter, Keynes's vision was set early. Schumpeter paraphrased Keynes's sketch of the economic and social background of the political events detailed in *The Economic Consequences of the Peace* to develop a statement of Keynes's vision. To Schumpeter, this vision remained the driving or unifying force through *The Tract, The Treatise,* and *The General Theory.* According to Schumpeter, Keynes's vision was that

> . . . laissez-faire capitalism, that extraordinary episode had come to an end in August 1914. The conditions were rapidly passing in which entrepreneurial leadership was able to secure success after success, propelled as it had been by rapid growth of populations and by abundant opportunities to invest that were incessantly recreated by technological improvements and by a series of conquests of new sources of food and raw materials. Under these conditions there had been no difficulty about absorbing the savings of a *bourgeoisie* that kept on baking cakes "in order not to eat them." But now [1920] these impulses were giving out, the spirit of private enterprise was flagging, investment opportunities were vanishing, and bourgeois saving habits had, therefore, lost their social function; their persistence actually made things worse than they need have been.[4]

---

4. Schumpeter [1951] 1965. According to Schumpeter, Keynes's vision was not far removed from Schumpeter's views.

Keynes reported that *The General Theory* was the result of ". . . a long struggle of escape . . . from habitual modes of thought and expression."[5] In Schumpeter's view, Keynes's struggle had been to find a formalization of what went on in a capitalist economy that was supportive of his vision. As Schumpeter put it, "in those pages of the *Economic Consequences of the Peace* we find nothing of the theoretical apparatus of *The General Theory*. But we find the whole of the vision of things social and economic of which the apparatus is the technical complement. *The General Theory* is the final result of a long struggle *to make that vision of our age analytically operative*" ([1951] 1965, 268; Schumpeter's emphasis).

Keynes's and Schumpeter's visions were similar: both saw the economy as an evolving entrepreneurial system that in no sense could be considered as equilibrium seeking and sustaining. To both, the profit-seeking manager and the financing banker were central to the growth and cyclical characteristics of the economy. To fulfill their vision, both Keynes and Schumpeter needed to integrate the money and financial facets of the economy with the production and consumption facets so that money in no sense can be considered neutral. Keynes achieved this by linking money not only with the financing of investment, which Schumpeter had accomplished in *The Theory of Economic Development*, but also with the price level of capital and financial assets. The liquidity preference theory of money, and the portfolio perspective on asset prices to which it led, was the "technical" breakthrough that was needed to achieve an analytical economics that supported the common dynamic vision of Schumpeter and Keynes.[6]

One reason Schumpeter gives for Keynes's success in developing a technique compatible with his vision was ". . . the mathematical quality of mind that underlies the purely scientific part of Keynes's work. . . ." ([1951] 1965, 261). He believed that the scientific content of economics was measured by the use of mathematics. "The higher range of mathematical economics are in the nature of what is in all fields referred to as 'pure science.'" Keynes, who eschewed mathematics in his exposition, ". . . was not a progressive in analytic method" ([1951] 1965, 261).

Schumpeter lacked the mathematical quality of mind he admired in others. He was psychologically incapable of making the simplifying assumptions necessary to develop a technique compatible with his vision. The cast of his own mind was enveloping, history, institutions, and ideology are all relevant:

---

5. John Maynard Keynes, *The General Theory of Employment, Interest, and Money* (New York: Harcourt Brace, 1936); reprinted as vol. 7 of *The Collected Writings of John Maynard Keynes*.

6. See Hyman P. Minsky (1975, chap. 4) for an exposition of the capital asset pricing model of Keynes that would also serve to complete the monetary part of Schumpeter's *Theory of Economic Development*.

they cannot be eliminated by assumption. In spite of this cast of mind, Schumpeter was an admirer and advocate of mathematics in economics and in particular of Walras's general equilibrium approach to economic interdependency. In Schumpeter's time, today's abstract form of general equilibrium theory, where all of economics is reduced to utility functions, production functions, and maximizing behavior, had not been developed.

Schumpeter's fundamental approach to economics as a discipline, although not perhaps to economics as a science as he thought of science, is caught in the distinction he made between vision and technique. Vision was central to achievement, to the breakthroughs that mark fundamental advances in science. Vision is derived from perceptions of the beast (the data), readings of history, and your forefathers in the discipline, and yes ideology. Although in the 1940s Schumpeter may have portrayed himself as a hide bound conservative, I venture to say that for the young he believed, as the epigram often attributed to Oscar Wilde has it, "a map of the world without a place for Utopia is not worth drawing."

Professor Shionoya points out that Schumpeter's strong admiration and support of Walras is to be found in his first book, *Das Wesen* (1908). This admiration for Walras may well have been a critical element in the deterioration of Schumpeter's performance in later years.

To use a phrasing drawn from Schumpeter's work, the vision he maintained and the technique he viewed as appropriate were inconsistent, as Shionoya recognizes. Schumpeter's vision was essentially holistic, he viewed the economy as an entity, whereas Walras's was essentially reductionist, viewing the economy as the outcome of the behavior of atomistic individuals and firms.

Schumpeter's enthusiasm for Walras is at variance with his division of scientific achievement into vision and technique. The vision underlying Walras, that the behavior of independent units led to an interdependent equilibrium which was best, was not original, it was that of Smith's invisible hand. In the literature that reached fruition soon after Schumpeter's death, the proof of the existence theorem to the effect that a competitive equilibrium is a Pareto optimum provided the technical result that validated Smith's vision.[7]

---

7. B. Ingrau and G. Israel (N.d., 6:1–45, 89–125) argue that general economic equilibrium theory has emulated the methodology of the physical scientists and the technique and ambition of general equilibrium theorists have changed as the methodology of the physical scientists changed. Today's general equilibrium theory, although it is labeled Walrasian, is much more formal and reductionist than the general equilibrium theory of Walras. Walras was not very sophisticated mathematically: he apparently believed that the existence of equilibrium followed from the number of equations being equal to the number of unknowns.

Ingrau and Israel point out that the general equilibrium research program set out to prove the existence, uniqueness, and stability of the economy as they model the economy. Over the

In Schumpeter's formulation of economics, the essential vision is that interdependent markets lead to a cyclical process of resource creation that, over time, leads to economic development. The vision is not that decentralized markets lead to the efficient allocation of predetermined resources. This formulation ran counter to the research program that gave rise to Walras and motivated those who formulated the modern extensions of Walras.

The incompatibility of Schumpeter with the Walrasian approach is further illustrated in a comment he makes in the essay on Mitchell. Writing of Mitchell's work in *Business Cycles*, Schumpeter says

> . . . it formulates one of the two—and there are only two—fundamentally different groups of Business Cycle theories. There is the "theory" that the economic process is essentially nonoscillatory and that the explanation of cyclical as well as other fluctuations must therefore be sought in particular circumstances (monetary or other) which disturb the even flow. . . . And there is the "theory" that the economic process itself is essentially wavelike—that cycles are the form of capitalist evolution— the theory to which Mitchell [and Schumpeter] was to lend the weight of his authority. ([1951] 1965, 252)

The visions of Schumpeter, Mitchell, and Keynes were alike in that they saw the economy as a dynamic system in which endogenously generated "stresses and strains" led to the business cycles of experience. All three saw the need for integrating money and financial forces into the determination of both the dynamic process and the causal mechanism for cycles. In this they were inconsistent with the pure theory that was emerging as their careers wound down. Only Mitchell seems to have fully realized the inconsistency between the vision and orthodox economic theory, although Keynes was the author of the monetary construct that provided the way to integrate money into the dynamic process and that made money and finance nonneutral.

In modern theory, the view that the economic process is essentially nonoscillatory and that cycles depend upon disturbances is typically associated with the view that economic theory shows that the economy can be considered to be an equilibrium-seeking and -sustaining process. This view is

---

more than forty years since Schumpeter's death, it has been shown that a general economic equilibrium exists under very heroic assumptions about what takes place in an economy; this equilibrium is not unique and its stability cannot be demonstrated.

It does not take much imagination to visualize Schumpeter commending the developments in nonlinear dynamics in which exotic, even chaotic, time-series emerge out of some straightforward deterministic set ups. See W. J. Baumol and J. Benhabib "Chaos: Significance, Mechanism, and Economic Applications," *Journal of Economic Perspectives* 3 (1989): 77–105.

exemplified in the business cycle writings of Milton Friedman and Robert Lucas.[8]

The dominance of vision and the role of technique as the support of vision in Schumpeter's mature view of how one does economics is a logical extension of the instrumentalist approach to theory that Shionoya finds in the young Schumpeter. If theory is something that theorists invent to support a vision, then theory serves merely in an instrumental role. Theory is necessary to support a vision, but a particular theory can be discarded when the vision changes either because history, institutions, or the map of Utopia forces a new reading of the complex text that the economy presents. Furthermore, even though the vision may be unchanged, the dynamics of doing theory may lead to new ways of showing the force of the vision. Creative destruction is an intellectual as well as an economic phenomenon: new visions and new theories keep entering the arena.

On the mezzanine of Littauer, Schumpeter instructed about the primacy of vision: in particular that we—the young who engaged him in conversation—should develop our vision, we should have a view that in a sense is prescientific of what the game is about, about the way the beast functions, about the way the various parts of economics and social science are related and, yes, about our own map of Utopia. Once we have a vision, then our control of theory, our command of institutional detail, and our knowledge of history are to be marshaled to support the vision.

This makes economics much like law, in that the rule is "these are the conclusions (visions) from which we derive our premises (theory)."

Schumpeter's methodology of vision and theory, with theory a servant of vision, may seem cynical, but, in truth, it is honest. It is a way of systemizing thought so that dialogue could take place. The division between vision and technique leads to a recognition that we are marshaling evidence when we do theory, when we analyze data, and when we read history. Schumpeter's methodology undercuts much of the pretentious nonsense about economics as a science and elevates the importance of discourse, of dialogue, and of just plain good talk for a serious study of society.

REFERENCES

Baumol, W. J., and J. Benhabib. 1989. "Chaos: Significance Mechanism and Economic Applications." *The Journal of Economic Perspectives* 3:77–105.
Friedman, Milton. 1968. "The Role of Monetary Policy." *American Economic Review* 58:1–17.

8. See Milton Friedman, 1968, 1–17; Robert Lucas, Jr., 1981.

Ingrau, B., and G. Israel. N.d. "General Economic Equilibrium Theory: A History of Ineffectual Paradigmatic Shifts I, II." *Fundamenta Sciential* 6:1–45, 89–125.

Keynes, J. M. 1936. *The General Theory of Employment, Interest and Money.* New York: Harcourt Brace.

Lucas, Robert, Jr. 1981. *Studies in Business Cycles Theory.* Cambridge, Mass.: MIT Press.

Minsky, Hyman P. 1975. *John Maynard Keynes.* New York: Columbia University Press.

Schumpeter, Joseph A. [1951] 1965. *Ten Great Economists.* New York: Galaxy Press.

Contributors

Zoltan J. Acs, Merrick School of Business, University of Baltimore

Daniele Archibugi, CNR-ISRDS, Rome

David B. Audretsch, Wissenschaftszentrum Berlin

Yasunori Baba, National Institute of Science and Technology Policy, Tokyo

Bo Carlsson, Department of Economics, Case Western Reserve University

Anne P. Carter, Department of Economics, Brandeis University

William S. Comanor, Department of Economics, University of California, Santa Barbara

Gunnar Eliasson, Industrial Institute for Economic and Social Research, Stockholm

Kenneth G. Elzinga, Department of Economics, University of Virginia

Horst Hanusch, University of Augsburg, Lehrestuhl für Wirtschaftslehre V

Markus Hierl, University of Augsburg, Lehrestuhl für Wirtschaftslehre V

Ken-ichi Imai, Stanford Japan Center, Kyoto

Burton H. Klein, California Institute of Technology, Emeritus

Alfred Kleinknecht, SEO, Foundation for Economic Research of the University of Amsterdam

Rudi Kurz, Institute für Angewandte Wirtschaftsforschung, Tübingen

Richard N. Langlois, Department of Economics, University of Connecticut

William Lazonick, Department of Economics, Barnard College, Columbia University

Hyman P. Minsky, The Jerome Levy Economics Institute of Bard College and Washington University

Richard R. Nelson, School of International and Public Affairs, Columbia University

Cornelius W. A. M. van Paridon, Scientific Council for Government Policy, The Hague

Mark Perlman, Department of Economics, University of Pittsburgh

Mario Pianta, CNR-ISRDS, Rome

Paul L. Robertson, Department of Economics and Management, University College, University of New South Wales

Frederic M. Scherer, The John F. Kennedy School of Government, Harvard University

Yuichi Shionoya, Hitotsubashi University, Tokyo

T. C. R. van Someren, Tinbergen Institute, University of Amsterdam

Paolo Sylos-Labini, Department of Economics, University of Rome

Joseph A. Weissmähr, Zurich, Switzerland

Paul J. J. Welfens, Department of Economics, University of Muenster

Index

Abegglen, James C., 176
Abernathy, William, 171, 179
Abramowitz, M., 44, 90
Acham, Karl, 15, 20
Acs, Zoltan, 8, 305, 309, 311–12, 316–17
Adams, W., 61
Agriculture, 19, 26, 27, 58, 60, 107
Aigner, D. J., 240
Aircraft industry, 39, 44n., 125
Åkerman, J., 254, 259
Alchian, Armen A., 323
Alexanderson, Ernst Frederik Werner, 29
Ambrosius, G., 126
American and British Technology in the Nineteenth Century (Habakkuk), 26
American Challenge, The (Servan Schreiber), 41
American Council of Life Insurance (ACLI), 185
American Economic Association, 14
American Philosophical Society, 14
Annual Survey of Manufactures, 317
Aoki, Masahiko, 146
Appropriation, 6, 67–71, 229–33, 323
Araskog, Rand V., 175
Archibugi, Daniele, 4, 65, 72, 87–88
Arrow, Kenneth J., 144, 277, 310
Arthur, W. Brian, 2, 141
Atomic Energy Commission (U.S.), 33
Aubert, J. E., 89
Audio components, 321–41
Audretsch, David B., 8, 305, 309, 311–12, 316–17
Auletta, Ken, 186

Austin, Benjamin, 19
Austrian tradition, 8, 9, 255, 258
Automobile industry, 30, 39, 125, 147, 279, 298, 327; productivity and scale, table of, 214
Ayres, Robert, 25

Baba, Yasunori, 5–6, 142
Ballon, Robert J., 168, 176, 192–94
Bank of International Settlements (BIS), 123
Bar, F., 122
Baran, Paul A., 166
Barzel, Yoram, 323
Basberg, Bjorn, 71, 88
Bauer, Otto, 12
Baumol, William J., 44, 97, 136, 368
Baxter, J., 32
Becher, G., 89
Beer, J., 28
Beesley, M. E., 307, 311–14
Belgium, 68, 69, 70, 74, 78, 281
Benhabib, J., 368
Berardi, Gianfranco, 61
Berle, Adolf A., 6
Bernstein, Michael, 163
Berry, C. H., 314
Black, Fischer, 161
Blume, L. E., 256
Böhm-Bawerk, Eugen von, 259
Bolton Report, 307
Bond, Ronald S., 308
Bonini, Charles P., 307
Boorstein, Daniel J., 15
Borcherding, T. E., 126
Bounded rationality, 52, 254